**Advances
in COMPUTERS
VOLUME 20**

Contributors to This Volume

Gary W. Dickson
W. R. Franta
Kai Hwang
E. Douglas Jensen
R. Y. Kain
George D. Marshall
Lionel M. Ni
Jean E. Sammet
Shun-Piao Su
K. J. Thurber

Advances in
COMPUTERS

EDITED BY

MARSHALL C. YOVITS

Purdue School of Science
Indiana University–Purdue University at Indianapolis
Indianapolis, Indiana

VOLUME 20

ACADEMIC PRESS

A Subsidiary of Harcourt Brace Jovanovich, Publishers

New York ■ London ■ Toronto ■ Sydney ■ San Francisco—1981

COPYRIGHT © 1981, BY ACADEMIC PRESS, INC.
ALL RIGHTS RESERVED.
NO PART OF THIS PUBLICATION MAY BE REPRODUCED OR
TRANSMITTED IN ANY FORM OR BY ANY MEANS, ELECTRONIC
OR MECHANICAL, INCLUDING PHOTOCOPY, RECORDING, OR ANY
INFORMATION STORAGE AND RETRIEVAL SYSTEM, WITHOUT
PERMISSION IN WRITING FROM THE PUBLISHER.

ACADEMIC PRESS, INC.
111 Fifth Avenue, New York, New York 10003

United Kingdom Edition published by
ACADEMIC PRESS, INC. (LONDON) LTD.
24/28 Oval Road, London NW1 7DX

LIBRARY OF CONGRESS CATALOG CARD NUMBER: 59–15761

ISBN 0–12–012120–4

PRINTED IN THE UNITED STATES OF AMERICA

81 82 83 84   9 8 7 6 5 4 3 2 1

Contents

CONTRIBUTORS vii
PREFACE ix

Management Information Systems: Evolution and Status
Gary W. Dickson

1. Introduction 1
2. Background 2
3. The MIS Concept 5
4. MIS Research 17
5. MIS Support Mechanisms 23
6. MIS Education 25
7. MIS—Quo Vadis? 27
   References 29

Real-Time Distributed Computer Systems
W. R. Franta, E. Douglas Jensen, R. Y. Kain, and George D. Marshall

1. Introduction 40
2. Hardware for Distributed Systems 45
3. Software for Distributed Real-Time Systems 62
4. Summary 79
   References 81

Architecture and Strategies for Local Networks: Examples and Important Systems
K. J. Thurber

1. What Is a Local Network? 83
2. Terminology and Nomenclature 87
3. Technology Trends and Their Influence 87
4. Decentralized versus Centralized Computation . . 88
5. Local Network Functions 89
6. Examples 89

CONTENTS

7. System Summaries	90
8. Hardware Availability	105
9. Computer Centers and Offices of the Future: Directions	109
10. The Future	110
References	111

Vector Computer Architecture and Processing Techniques
Kai Hwang, Shun-Piao Su, and Lionel M. Ni

1. Introduction	116
2. Vector-Processing Requirements	118
3. Pipeline-Processor Design Considerations	129
4. Multiple-Pipeline Computers	141
5. Recent Advances in Array Processors	164
6. Vector Processor Performance Evaluation	179
7. Conclusions and Future Trends	189
References	191

An Overview of High-Level Languages
Jean E. Sammet

1. General Introduction	200
2. Trends and Activities	208
3. Relationship of High-Level Languages to Software Engineering and Software Methodology	217
4. Some "Modern" Languages	227
5. Research and Advanced Development Language Topics	238
6. Future Trends	246
7. Summary and Conclusions	255
References	255

AUTHOR INDEX	261
SUBJECT INDEX	269
CONTENTS OF PREVIOUS VOLUMES	278

Contributors to Volume 20

Numbers in parentheses indicate the page on which the authors' contributions begin.

GARY W. DICKSON, *Department of Management Sciences, University of Minnesota, Minneapolis, Minnesota 55455 (1)*

W. R. FRANTA, *Department of Computer Science and Center for Microelectronic and Information Sciences, University of Minnesota, Minneapolis, Minnesota 55455 (39)*

KAI HWANG, *School of Electrical Engineering, Purdue University, West Lafayette, Indiana 47907 (115)*

E. DOUGLAS JENSEN,* *Honeywell Systems and Research Center, Minneapolis, Minnesota 55455 (39)*

R. Y. KAIN, *Department of Electrical Engineering, University of Minnesota, Minneapolis, Minnesota 55455 (39)*

GEORGE D. MARSHALL,† *Honeywell Systems and Research Center, Minneapolis, Minnesota 55455 (39)*

LIONEL M. NI, *Department of Computer Science, Michigan State University, East Lansing, Michigan 48824 (115)*

JEAN E. SAMMET, *IBM Federal Systems Division, Bethesda, Maryland 20034 (199)*

SHUN-PIAO SU, *School of Electrical Engineering, Purdue University, West Lafayette, Indiana 47907 (115)*

K. J. THURBER, *Architecture Technology Corporation, Minneapolis, Minnesota 55455 (83)*

---

* Present address: Department of Computer Science, Carnegie-Mellon University, Pittsburgh, Pennsylvania 15213.

† Present address: Intel Corporation, Santa Clara, California 95051.

Preface

Volume 20 of *Advances in Computers* achieves a milestone. It is the Twentieth Anniversary Volume of this serial publication. Volume 1 was published in 1960 and now Volume 20, published in 1981, continues a long and unbroken series. Twenty years in terms of computers comprise several generations. *Advances in Computers* permits the publication of in-depth articles of important current interest relating to computers, information technology, and applications. In addition to their vital current interest, subjects have been chosen for inclusion in *Advances in Computers* because of the expectation that they will be of significance for a considerable time to come. This publication provides an opportunity for highly regarded experts to write review or tutorial articles covering a major segment of their field. It permits the publication of longer survey articles that have been prepared in a leisurely fashion and that provide an overall perspective which would otherwise not be possible.

That this publication has continued unbroken until the present is a result primarily of the two former editors, who had the foresight and the initiative to establish it and who then took great pains to continue it until such time as it was able to stand alone. These two individuals, Franz Alt and Morris Rubinoff, deserve much credit. The fact that the series continues today is a tribute to their efforts and vision some 10 to 20 years ago.

Volume 20 is significant not only because it is the Twentieth Anniversary Volume, but because it is an important volume containing articles of current and long-range interest in their own right. Incorporated here are articles on both the hardware and software aspects of computers as well as on some important applications. Included are three articles primarily on hardware aspects: vector computing architecture, architecture for local networks, and real-time distributed computer systems. Also included is an article on high-level languages and their development over the past 20 years. As for applications, there is a significant contribution on management information systems and their development primarily since 1960.

In the first article, Gary Dickson points out that data processing budgets in the United States are expected to amount to about 78 billion dollars by 1983, and that within the first part of the twenty-first century almost 90% of the work force will be performing jobs involving the processing of information. He reminds us in contrast that only 25 years ago, processing of information by both public and private organizations was largely manual. Without question, major growth has taken place in the level of support devoted to information processing and its technology. Over the past 25 years the provision of information within organizations has become recognized as a major field of both academic and professional concern. Dickson's article traces the evolution of the area called management information systems and discusses the current status of this area. He places emphasis on the development of "MIS thought." He traces, appropriately for the twentieth volume of this series, the historical development of MIS and gives consideration to its future directions. He explores the area more from the flavor of a managerial perspective rather than a technical perspective.

One of the most important areas of current activity is that of real-time distributed computer systems. These systems are discussed by Franta, Jensen, Kain, and Marshall. It is pointed out that distributed computer systems containing several computers may provide increased system availability and reliability. However, the design of these systems is complex. On the other hand, these complex design issues may have simple solutions in well-understood application environments, particularly in real-time control environments. Because of this, the authors cover real-time distributed computer systems from promise through design implementation. They discuss the motivation for distributed computer systems and they characterize the real-time control application environment. The options and issues related to hardware and software designs are reviewed. The details of the design and implementation of the Honeywell Experimental Distributed Computing Processor system known as HXDP are summarized in the article. The authors conclude that the trend toward distributed systems is driven by technical, psychological, and economic reasons. The use of the HXDP as an advanced test-bed system is discussed. As more experience is obtained it will undoubtedly increase understanding of the design of distributed computer systems and of their use in many different environments.

K. J. Thurber discusses "Architecture and Strategies for Local Networks" and gives some important examples. He points out that interest and activity in local computer networks is growing rapidly. The primary objectives of Thurber's article are to provide an introduction to architectures in the area of local networks, to discuss some typical systems, and to describe the future of the technology. Thurber states that although there is still a great deal of debate over what exactly constitutes a local computer network, he defines it as having three explicit, basic properties described in his article. He ends his contribution by noting that a conclusion would really be inappropriate as there is nothing now approaching any conclusion to the saga of local networks. A large number of systems has been developed experimentally and a small number of products has been introduced, either as part of a larger system or as building blocks designed to allow systems designers to build systems. Local network technology is causing a reassessment of network architecture concepts and is pushing the designer into a view of a network as a hierarchically organized group of cooperating local networks. Development and implementation of such networks are just now beginning.

The article on "Vector Computer Architecture and Processing Techniques" by Hwang, Su, and Ni is devoted to reviewing architectural advances in vector processing computers. Both pipeline computers and array processors are studied and compared. Problems associated with designing pipeline computers are presented with examples from a number of current systems. They also report on the architectures of recently developed array processors with appropriate examples. They summarize recent research on these processors. Finally, Hwang, Su, and Ni evaluate the performance of pipeline and array processors and investigate various optimization techniques for vector operations. They include hardware, software, and algorithmic issues, and also discuss future trends.

In the final article, Jean Sammet writes a comprehensive article on high-level languages. She has provided an overview of all of the issues which she believes are worth mentioning in 1980. As a consequence, the coverage of many of the sections is fairly broad. However, many bibliographic citations are included so that more information on any topic can easily be found. It is quite appropriate, inasmuch as this is the twentieth volume of the *Advances,* that she incorporates in her contribution a brief history of major language developments over the past 20 or so years. She points out that research in languages pervades the entire programming process. Because of the importance currently attached to software engineering and methodology, a large section of the article is devoted to the involvement of languages in this area. Her major conclusion is that the only way to make maximum use of computer power we have available to us is to have an easy means of communicating with the computer. She believes that the ease of this communication will become *the pervasive* factor. Language research she believes will continue to be one of the cores of research and development in the computer field.

It is my pleasure in this, the Twentieth Anniversary Volume of *Advances in Computers,* to thank the two previous editors, Franz Alt and Morris Rubinoff, who were instrumental in establishing and continuing the series until it was able to develop on its own. This series owes its existence to their foresight and their strong interest and efforts on its behalf. I also thank the contributors to this volume. They have given extensively of their time and energy, and thus have made this book an important and timely contribution to the profession. Their participation ensures that this volume achieves a high level of excellence worthy of the series and that it will be of value for many years to come. It has been a rewarding experience to edit this volume and to work with these authors.

MARSHALL C. YOVITS

Management Information Systems: Evolution and Status

GARY W. DICKSON

Department of Management Sciences
University of Minnesota
Minneapolis, Minnesota

1.	Introduction	1
2.	Background	2
	2.1 Technological Environment for MIS Development	3
	2.2 Definitional Environment for MIS Development	4
3.	The MIS Concept	5
	3.1 Genesis	6
	3.2 Takeoff and Maturity	12
4.	MIS Research	17
	4.1 MIS Research Frameworks and Methodological Issues	18
	4.2 Organizational Studies	20
	4.3 Experimental Studies	22
5.	MIS Support Mechanisms	23
6.	MIS Education	25
7.	MIS—Quo Vadis?	27
	References	29

1. Introduction

Data-processing budgets in the United States amounted to $17 billion in 1970, $48 billion in 1978, and are estimated to be $78 billion by 1983 (International Data Corporation, 1978). Total spending on data processing, which adds "office automation" and first-time users of small business computers, will burgeon from over $60 billion in 1979 to in excess of $140 billion in 1985 (International Data Corporation, 1980). The budgets, corrected for inflation, continue to grow at a rate in excess of 10% per year. Most large business corporations spend from 0.5% to 7% of revenue on expenses associated with computing. Estimates have been made that within the first part of the twenty-first century, 80–90% of the work force will be performing jobs involving the accumulation and processing of information (*Business Week*, 1979; Murdick, 1980).

Considering that only 25 years ago the processing of information by public and private organizations was largely manual, one can gain some appreciation from the above data concerning the growth in the level of resources devoted to information processing and the technological support thereof. Over the past quarter century, the provision of information within organizations has become recognized as an area of academic and professional concern. To support this activity, educational programs have evolved, research is being conducted to enhance our understanding of how to better support information provision to organizations, and mechanisms such as professional societies and journals have appeared to facilitate communication among practitioners, researchers, and academicians in the area.

The purpose of this article is to trace the evolution of the area called *Management Information Systems* (MIS),[1] and to discuss the current status of this area. Emphasis will be placed upon: (1) the development of what can be called "MIS thought," (2) the body of knowledge that exists through the performance of research, and (3) the evolution of support mechanisms (e.g., professional societies, educational programs, periodical literature) in the area. To provide a perspective for the reader, first some background will be provided with regard to the evolution of the technology associated with information system development and some definitional discussion of the "MIS concept."

2. Background

Since a historical approach is being taken in this article in relation to the area of activity now generally referred to as Management Information Systems, one must have some appreciation for the technological era during which MIS evolved. As with any new area of academic interest, much controversy existed (and exists) as to what is the MIS area in a definitional sense. The following brief sections provide perspective on these issues. The emphasis in the technology section is upon the general, or macro, aspects of the technology which influence organizational use, in contrast to a detailed, or micro, discussion of technological characteristics.

---

[1] There is controversy over what constitutes an academic discipline or field, so to avoid problems of agreement the subject of this contribution will be designated as an area of common interest, or "area."

2.1 Technological Environment for MIS Development

Organizational processing of information goes back over 5000 years (see Sanders, 1970, pp. 13–18, for a historical overview). Mechanical aids to expedite information use by organizations have been documented as existing as early as 100 B.C. (Vitalari, 1978, p. 7), but better known are the devices of Pascal (1642), Babbage (1871), and Hollerith (1890). The first electronic computer used for business data processing, the UNIVAC I, was installed by the General Electric Company in 1954. According to Buckingham (1961), there were only a few dozen computers installed in the United States in 1955, with perhaps 4000 computers in place by the end of the decade of the 1950s (Association for Computing Machinery, 1971).

Computers in the late 1950s and early 1960s tended to be special purpose in nature, being devoted either to character-oriented business data processing or to scientific applications requiring high processor speed. During this period, the larger, more advanced machines tended to be scientifically oriented, with the largest proportion of computer expenditure in this area. Electromechanical tabulating machines, directed by wired plug board logic, were prevalent for business applications.

It was during the late 1950s and early 1960s that the IBM scientific line of computers, the 650, 704, 709, 7090, and 7094, was successful in capturing a large share of the market from UNIVAC. The IBM 1401 business computer was, in the early 1960s, the first business data-processing machine for many organizations. Computers of this era tended to be card oriented for input, produced printed output, and used magnetic tape for secondary data storage.

In 1963, IBM announced the S/360 computer family based upon an architecture allowing both scientific and business applications to be performed on computers within the family. These so-called "third-generation" computers took advantage of improved direct-access storage devices and the associated concept of multiprogramming.

Between 1963 and 1970, worldwide computer installations increased from 15,000 to 85,000 (Waldman, 1975). Aggressive marketing supplemented by education and strong service brought IBM to a dominant worldwide market position. Burroughs, UNIVAC, Honeywell, and NCR also developed substantial business in the general-purpose computer market, while a new corporate entity, CDC, appeared as a result of the growing demand of computerization. Two major firms, RCA and General Electric, produced general-purpose computers during the period, but prior to 1970 they either sold or merged their computer business with others.

Thus, as a backdrop to the MIS concept and the evolution of thought in this area, the reader should appreciate that there was virtually no organizational computer use in 1955, growing but fragmented use by 1965 (about 20,000 computers installed), and widespread use by 1970. It was by the latter date that some $17 billion was being spent in the United States alone on computer equipment, people, supplies, and data communication. As will be seen in a subsequent section, it was after 1967–1968 that the concept of MIS began to flourish. Activity and thought prior to that period was preliminary and of a stage-setting nature.

2.2 Definitional Environment for MIS Development

In this article dealing with the question: "What is MIS?" is a recursive process. On the one hand, MIS is defined by the thought and work conducted in the area. On the other hand, a discussion of the evolution of the area is greatly facilitated by a definition of the area about which we are writing.

Before providing some definitional background for the discussion of MIS, it is worth noting that a substantial amount of effort was devoted to this activity early in the evolution of the area. Although this concern has faded somewhat lately, one still hears the question, "What is MIS?" (Society for Management Information Systems, 1970). One of the motivations underlying this article is to provide insight to this question.

In the simplest, most straightforward terms, MIS deals with all informational and decision-making activity associated with operating an organization. It is the desire of those working in the MIS area to encourage better organizational efficiency and effectiveness through facilitating information provision and decision support to management.

Consider the following definitions of MIS, which are associated with various times in the evolution of the area. An early definition of "Information Technology" was provided by the landmark article of Leavitt and Whisler written in 1958:

> It is composed of several related parts. One includes techniques for processing large amounts of information rapidly, and it is epitomized by the high speed computer. A second part centers around the application of statistical and mathematical methods to decision-making problems; it is represented by techniques like mathematical programming, and by methodologies like operations research. A third part is in the offing, though its applications have not yet emerged very clearly; it consists of the simulation of higher-order thinking through computer programs (Leavitt and Whisler, 1958, p. 41).

Ten years later, in 1968, the author provided a framework for what were termed "Management Information–Decision Systems." Several levels of systems were identified which have survived the test of time as a way of identifying types of systems (or activity). Clerical systems represent mechanized processing of transactions. Information systems are those having as their purpose the provision of information for *use* in a management decision. Decision systems affect the *way* in which decisions are made. Programmed systems are those in which the system "makes" the decision. It was noted that although most systems in practice are clerical in nature, many higher level systems have some of the various attributes above. Also, concerning the framework:

> Speaking functionally, management information–decision systems is a blend of organizational theory, accounting, statistics, mathematical modeling, and economics, together with exposure in depth to advanced computer hardware and software systems. This field is centered on expanding the horizons and integrating the decisions of organizations, both public and private, which must operate within the dynamics and functional demands imposed by their organizational size and degree of complexity (Dickson, 1968, p. 18).

One should note that the above definitions deal with the MIS concept, in contrast to defining what a specific management information system is. Two commonly referenced definitions of the latter are:

> (1) A management information system is an organized method of providing past, present, and projection information relating to internal operations and external intelligence. It supports the planning, control, and operational functions of an organization by furnishing uniform information in the proper time-frame to assist the decision-making process (Kennevan, 1970, p. 21).

> (2) An integrated, man/machine system for providing information to support decision-making functions in an organization. The system utilizes computer hardware and software, manual procedures, management and decision models, and a data base (Davis, 1974, p. 5).

It is the MIS concept (or philosophy/process, if one prefers) that produces the systems of the type defined in 1970 by Kennevan and 1974 by Davis. It is conceptually helpful if one separates the process from the product, but in the following discussion of the former, be mindful of the contemporary view of what a management information system is as well as the organizational precomputer era, which existed prior to the middle 1950s. Section 7 of this article will deal with the question "What is MIS?" from a contemporary perspective and in view of the chronicle of the area, which follows.

3. The MIS Concept

The reader may have noted from the definitional discussion that in some of the earlier definitions titles such as "information technology" or "management information–decision systems" were used when addressing the body of knowledge and functions associated with the area now called MIS. These differences, which existed in the years prior to 1969–1970, serve to point up the fact that although there was consistency regarding a "concept," there was little agreement as to what its title should be.

One can trace many foundations for the "MIS Concept." The fields of management, cybernetics, operations research, behavioral science, economics, and computer science all can be shown to have contributed to the concept. As with many phenomena, MIS has undergone various evolutionary stages. The genesis of the MIS concept can be traced back at least to the 1930s. Much stabilization had occurred by 1967–1968, and the period from that time until 1975 can be called a "takeoff" stage in the area. From about 1975 until the present, the MIS area has been maturing but, as will be pointed out, this stage is far from complete. In the following sections the MIS area will be discussed in terms of these three stages.

3.1 Genesis

A case can be made that one logical starting point for the MIS concept was the work of Barnard published in 1938. In his book, *Functions of the Executive,* Barnard was the first management writer to emphasize the key role of decision making in the process of managing an organization. During World War II, little related publication took place in the field of management, but in 1947 the first edition of *Administrative Behavior,* written by Herbert Simon, was published. It was here that Simon first hypothesized a theory of management founded upon decision making. In subsequent work (Simon, 1957, 1960a,b, 1965; Simon and Newell, 1958; Newell *et al.,* 1958; March and Simon, 1958), Simon and his colleagues enriched and elaborated upon management vis-à-vis decision making and information.

During the same period two concepts, automation and cybernetics, evolved, which were related to the field of management. Automation and management were addressed by several authors (Diebold and Terbough, 1952; Bright, 1958), and, even more relevant, cybernetics and management were related by Wiener (1948, 1950) and Beer (1959). The concepts expressed by the cyberneticians are especially relevant to the development of MIS thought. As will be shown shortly, early views of MIS and organizations consisted of viewing the management process as a cybernetic control system within the organization, relying heavily upon the computer as the control mechanism.

Also significant in the period of the late 1950s in setting the stage for MIS is the fact that electronic computers were appearing in organizations and authors were writing computer-related texts for managerial and professional workers. These books tended to be factual in nature, with a focus on the technical details of a computer, rather than (despite some of their titles) discussion of the use of computers in managing (Canning, 1956; Kozmetzky and Kircher, 1956; Chapin, 1957; Bell, 1957; Vazsonyi, 1958).

In November of 1958, the charter issue of *Machine Accounting and Data Processing* appeared. The publisher stated the focus of the periodical to be important to management: "Management will be interested in principles that are important in establishing a most effective data processing activity. Management will gain better control through more accurate and timely reports at a reduced cost (Gille, 1958)." By its fifth issue, the name of this periodical was changed to *Data Processing,* which it has remained. In 1957, a data-processing periodical appeared that today has the greatest circulation in the United States (*Datamation*) among periodicals of its type. It was originally titled *Research and Engineering: The Magazine of DATAmation.*

Locating management-oriented articles concerning the computer prior to 1958 is a difficult process, leading one to some fairly obscure sources. At that time, few authors pointed in glowing phrases to the opportunities presented by the computer. Comments from two of the earlier of these articles are illustrative:

> We know that the path of technology is before us and that we have the opportunity to travel far. And we know, too, that no matter how twisting the course or steep the climb, it is a path which will lead to a brighter and stronger tomorrow (DuPont, 1954, p. 406).

> Then there is paperwork—automation coming to the office. Figures are marshalled to demonstrate that paperwork is really doing us in, unbeknownst. By tomorrow, business machines will take over ... Robots everywhere, and the old man all alone, watching pointers on the dials (Collins, 1954, p. 660).

The latter quote confirms the carryover between cybernetic concepts and early thinking concerning managerial computer use. Other early works tend to be predictive/evangelistic (e.g., Astrahan, 1958; Ebdon, 1958; Finke, 1957; Johnson, 1958; Salveson, 1957) and descriptive of computer use (e.g., Aswen, 1958; Carlin, 1958; Guest, 1956; Knox, 1958; Maynard, 1958).

It was in late 1958 that the first widely available article appeared that integrated the various streams of thought mentioned above. The article, entitled "Management in the 1980's," was published in the popular and highly read *Harvard Business Review* (Leavitt and Whisler, 1958). In addition to specifying the nature of "information technology" (see Section 2.2), the authors forecast what would be the impact of the new support to management on the organization and on management itself. To a large extent, Leavitt and Whisler should be given credit for describing an MIS concept and coalescing the material from other areas, for example, management, operations research, computer science.[2]

Following soon upon the publication of Leavitt and Whisler's article were two significant conferences, both of which published proceedings in book format. In February, 1959, a seminar on Management Organization and Computers was held at the University of Chicago (Shultz and Whisler, 1960). Later that year, in July, the Management Information and Control Systems Symposium was held at the System Development Corporation (SDC) in Los Angeles (Malcomb and Rowe, 1960). At the former, the following was noted:

> Rapid and extensive progress has been made during the last decade in the application of quantitative techniques and computers to the analysis of the problems of business management. These developments amount to an important technological change affecting the techniques of managing (Shultz and Whisler, 1960, p. xiii).

Among the significant contributions made at the seminar were papers by Simon and Newell, Whisler and Shultz, and Orden. The paper titles are indicative of the topical coverage at the seminar: "What Have Computers To Do With Management?" (Simon and Newell, 1960); "Information Technology and Organization" (Whisler and Shultz, 1960); "Man-Machine-Computer Systems" (Orden, 1960).

The SDC symposium is notable for two reasons. First, the System Development Corporation played an important role in the development of early military command and control systems (e.g., SAGE), which were cybernetic systems based upon concepts having analogies to organizational management. Second, these concepts led early information systems theorists toward the direction of a "total" system. The symposium paper by Donald Malcomb, "Exploring the Military Analogy—Real-Time Management Control" (1960), is an example of both of the above concepts. Malcomb (1960, p. 187) stated: "Many writers have described the era of "information technology" our society is now entering as one wherein the capability to formulate decision criteria precisely and to process information electronically will create markedly new patterns in management." The relationship among decision making, information, and management was clearly stated by Malcomb. It is this relationship that is at the heart of the MIS Concept. Other related work from the same period includes: the introduction of the decision supporting system entitled "industrial dynamics" by Forrester (1958), an article focusing on management decision making, which related to the earlier cited ideas of Bernard published in

---

[2] It was also in 1958 that the first known published reference to the term "Management Information System" was made (Stoller and Van Horn, 1958).

the late 1930s (Salveson, 1958), and an early article dealing with worker reaction to computer systems (Elliot, 1958). Surprisingly, it was more than a year before other significant work related to MIS began to appear.

During the early and mid-1960s, writing in the area was somewhat sparse compared with what appeared in the last part of the decade. The literature referenced below from the early 1960s includes almost all of that appearing, but, by the mid-1960s, references are made either to significant work or to works illustrating a point being made.

During the early to mid-1960s, several themes can be found in the literature related to MIS. First, there are the evangelical and definitional writers forecasting what is to come and defining the "new management tools" and explaining what their impact on organizations will be. Also clearly identifiable is another stream of thought put forth by more pessimistic writers. Those persons warn of the shortcomings of data processing and suggest that some of the proponents of computer support to management are overly optimistic.

Another group of writings are addressed to those applying data processing to management and direct their efforts to attempting to make the application more efficient and effective. The role of people in systems and behavioral problems is also articulated by a group of writers. Finally, a radical subgroup of the very positive information systems visionaries are the proponents of "total systems."

3.1.1 Information Systems—Definitions and Forecasts

Hoos, writing in 1960 about computers taking over offices, is typical of those forecasting the impact of computers. The impact on the organization (actually a response to prognostications by Leavitt and Whisler) (Anshen, 1960), a description of using the computer in management control (Malcomb and Rowe, 1961; Weinwurm, 1961), and the impact of computer technology on decentralization of organizations (Burlingame, 1961) are examples of articles of this type.

Other examples of forecasts involving computers and management involved integrated information systems (Hockman, 1963), electronics in management (Hertz, 1965), the "Firm of the Future" (Ansoff, 1965), joint man/machine decisions (Thompson, 1965), and the future of information technology (Diebold, 1965). Even Peter Drucker (1966), the well-known management professor, contributed toward what the computer would be "telling" managers. The trends in data processing within organizations was summarized by Canning (1966), whereas management science was related to information systems by Beged-Dov (1967). That advances had been made by 1967 can be seen by the fact that writers were beginning to address the use of computers by managers of middle-sized organizations (e.g., Couger, 1967).

A number of books were written about the computer and management with a managerial rather than a technical focus. In 1961, the first book with management information systems in the title was published (Gallagher, 1961). Others dealt with "information economics" and management systems (McDonough, 1963) and management and general systems theory (Johnson *et al.*, 1963). More typical books on organizations and computers covered *Management and the Corporation, 1985* (Anshen and Bach, 1960), *The Computer Revolution* (Berkeley, 1962), and *The Computer Age* (Burck, 1965).

It was not until after the mid-1960s that textbooks on computers, management, and information systems began to appear (Dearden, 1966; Richards and Greenlaw, 1966; Dearden and McFarland, 1966; Prince, 1966). As they were the first textbooks with MIS in the title, the latter two books are notable because of their probable contribution toward the general acceptance of this term as the most popular one for the area.

3.1.2 Information Systems—Caveats

It was not long after computers had been installed in organizations for managerial use that rumbles of dissatisfaction began to be heard and warnings were given as to problems that might occur. Daniel, in 1961, brought attention to the lack of managerial information available within organizations as a "management information crisis." A year later, managers were warned of the "seven deadly dangers of EDP" (Fiock, 1962). In the mid-1960s, a number of articles appeared pointing out that the expected managerial benefits from computer systems were not being realized (e.g., Dearden, 1964; Diebold, 1964; Garrity, 1964).

In a classic article appearing in 1967, Russell Ackoff called attention to the lack of payoff from information systems and listed what were, in his opinion, five inappropriate design assumptions. Until the appearance of the Ackoff article, little had been written concerning a theoretical basis for MIS or the lack thereof. Ackoff's work, probably the most reprinted article in the MIS area to date, provided one structure upon which research in the area could be based.

3.1.3 Information Systems—Applications and Techniques

In the early 1960s, there was relatively little concern as to how organizations ought to use computers in a managerial sense or how the process of developing systems ought to be done. The work by McKenney (1962) on the simultaneous processing of jobs on a computer published in *Management Science* is among the first to appear addressing the former area. Better management of the systems development process is exemplified by the Evans and Hague (1962) article on master planning for MIS, and was an early example in the latter area.

An article in 1963 on the subject of getting managers to use computer systems once they are installed, written by Garitty, was the first publication of ideas that later came to represent a major managerial concern for MIS managers. Other publications aimed at managing MIS development during this time dealt with the structure of the organizational systems function (Dearden, 1965), with intraorganizational information systems (Kaufman, 1966), and managing the computer function itself (Taylor and Dean, 1966).

3.1.4 Information Systems—Behavioral Aspects

The beginnings of a stream of work existing within the MIS area, that of concern with people interacting with systems, can also be found in the literature of the early 1960s. A very significant research project was reported by Mann and Williams concerning data processing and change in 1960. Other articles following shortly reported upon the reaction of office workers to "office automation" (Hardin, 1960; Blum, 1961). The concern with the people in systems was shown by a call to provide training for systems analysts (Schlosser, 1964).

3.1.5 Information Systems—Total Systems

The notion of applying cybernetic concepts to organizations was mentioned earlier. A body of thought very influential in MIS thinking during the formative years was based upon these concepts and reflected in the "total systems approach" (Neuschel, 1960; Lach, 1960; Rosenzweig, 1960; Dickey and Senewseib, 1963). The following statement made in 1965 by a data-processing manager is an excellent example of the total systems concept that was being suggested by many:

> In discussing the subject of management information systems, let us visualize a room completely equipped with the latest in electronic display devices, connected to a gigantic real time computer system and having the entire company's information on line and programmed to give information in the form of charts and graphs as well as reports and isolated items of data. Couple this with closed circuit television connecting key managers and the principle locations in the plant, and this room could truly be called a "command headquarters." This utopian setup is *now* available to the EDP manager who has sold management on the potential uses of the computer (Dyer, 1965, p. 27).

One should note not only what was being proposed, but that systems such as these should be "sold" to management. Management control in real time (Hartman, 1965) and the implementation of totally integrated cybernetic systems (Wendler, 1966) were much in vogue in the literature during this period of MIS development.

The beginnings of the MIS concept were in place, by and large, prior to the 1967–1968 time period. During the next several years work in the area burgeoned, leading us to where MIS is today. In the following section MIS will be discussed in a contemporary sense, drawing upon significant developments occurring between the late 1960s and the present.

3.2 Takeoff and Maturity

Activity and writing began in the MIS area in the late 1960s and flourished during the 1970s. During this period, educational institutions began offering degree programs in MIS and much curriculum development took place. Research centers/institutes were formed at two major United States universities to concentrate on MIS, while research, in general, was performed by multiple units within the MIS community. Additionally, many mechanisms emerged to support MIS activity, e.g., professional societies and periodical publications aimed at both practitioners and academics.

The amount of activity within the MIS area between the late 1960s and the end of the 1970s precludes the author from being as exhaustive as was possible in the previous section in identifying the major contributions, so only the highlights are treated. The appearance of conceptual material was of very great significance during this period.

3.2.1 *Conceptual Development*

There are any number of ways in which to approach the conceptual development of the area of MIS. One is to highlight those key contributions to the MIS literature which have attempted to provide a structure for MIS. An early example of this type of activity was the article by this author on the subject of Management Information–Decision Systems (Dickson, 1968). In this article, which is kindly called a "classic" by Dock and his colleagues (1977, p. 80), a hierarchy of systems are identified and described (clerical systems, information systems, decision systems, interactive systems, and programmed systems). Problems and issues as seen at the time in the MIS area are also discussed in the article.

Other key articles of this genre include those by Aron (1969), Pounds (1969), and Kriebel (1972). Aron identifies three levels of systems: data-

TABLE I

POPULAR MIS TEXTBOOKS (1970–1980)

Title	Author
Computer-Based Management Information Systems	Krause (1970)
Computerized Management Information Systems	Kelly (1970)
Management Information Systems: Progress and Perspectives	Kriebel et al. (1971)
Management Information Systems: Conceptual Foundations, Structure, and Development	Davis (1974)
Management-Oriented Management Information Systems	Kanter (1977)
Introduction to Management Information Systems	Murdick and Ross (1977)
Information Systems Concepts for Management	Lucas (1978b)
Information Systems in Management	Senn (1978)
Information Systems for Strategic Decisions	Radford (1978)
Information Systems: Theory and Practice	Burch et al. (1979)
MIS: Concepts and Design	Murdick (1980)

processing systems, information retrieval systems, and management information systems. The latter is characterized by "a foreknowledge of what decisions the manager will have to make" (Aron, 1969, p. 215). Pound's article concentrates on the issue of how managers "find" problems. Although not discussing MIS *per se,* the article is directly related to MIS if management information systems are to assist managers in becoming aware of potential problems. Kriebel, writing some years later, also focuses on levels of systems. He names four levels: data only, data plus inference, data plus inference and evaluation, and, finally, a decision level.

A second approach to the conceptual development of the MIS area is to examine the growth and evolution of major textbooks on MIS. In Section 3.1.1, a reference was made to early books on MIS (all published in 1966). Beginning in the late 1960s, a number of textbooks on MIS began to appear, until today there are probably more than 100 books that could be classified as MIS textbooks (this does not, of course, include the vast number of data-processing and technical books that are related to MIS). Several of the most popular MIS texts and their dates of publication are listed in Table I. Examination of the references and bibliographies of all the above texts as well as other books and articles leads one to conclude that the Davis text is the most frequently cited.

In addition to texts on the subject of MIS, there have been many efforts directed at collecting the most significant articles together and publishing books of readings. In chronological order, the most significant MIS readings books have been Sanders (1970), Coleman and Riley (1973), Sanders

(1974), Davis and Everest (1976), and Dock *et al.* (1977). The readings books are useful in examining two related issues: (1) repeated reprinting of some of the articles helps to identify works thought to have made a significant contribution, and (2) the structure of the books into parts and sections gives clues as to the topical coverage of the MIS area. Both of these considerations were taken into account as material was selected for inclusion in this contribution.

Many conceptual and procedural contributions have been made within subareas of MIS. Of note have been systems planning, analysis, design and development, and managing MIS activity.

3.2.1.1 Systems Planning, Analysis, Design, and Development.

Stanford Optner (1960) wrote one of the early books related to MIS, featuring the relationship between "systems theory" and business problem solving. The process called "systems analysis," which grew out of the relationship, was to guide the development of both manual and electronic systems that would aid managerial problem solving. An examination of Optner's ideas and his references fits in with the development of the MIS concept described in Section 3.1. For example, Optner references data processing (Canning, 1956; Kozmetzky and Kircher, 1956), operations research (Vazsonyi, 1958), and cybernetics (Wiener, 1948).

Optner published a second edition in 1968, and many other authors added to the list of books oriented toward the process of building systems, covering tools and techniques for facilitating the process. An important addition to the literature occurred in 1969 when Sherman Blumenthal wrote a book on planning and developing management information systems. Blumenthal developed a framework for encompassing basic information common to all business into an information system. It is unfortunate that Blumenthal passed away before he had an opportunity to elaborate on his early ideas.

There followed a number of important contributions in this area. Orlicky, in 1969, authored a book on the planning, development, and design of successful computer systems. In 1970, Borje Langefors contributed a very advanced book on the theoretical aspects of information systems design. These concepts are related to work by Tiechroew and his colleagues on automatically designing information systems (Tiechroew and Sayani, 1971). Many relevant books on systems analysis are in the literature of the area (Martin, 1967; Joslin, 1971; Yourdon, 1972; Couger and Knapp, 1974; Yourdon, 1975; Wetherbe, 1979).

Once the processes of information and systems analysis have been performed, systems development takes place. Efficiency in this process has been of concern within the MIS area. Project management and control (Schwartz, 1969; Cleland and King, 1975) and the efficient development of computer programs (Yourdon, 1975) illustrate contributions in this area.

The area of MIS Planning and its subarea, project selection, are other areas in which substantial work has been performed in the conceptual development of the area. MIS planning has been discussed by several authors (Schwartz, 1970; Zani, 1970; McFarlan, 1971; Head, 1978). One complete book has been devoted to "strategic planning for MIS" (McLean and Soden, 1977).

3.2.1.2 Managing MIS Activity. The major contributor to work on managing MIS activity has been Richard Nolan. Nolan (1973a) first contributed a "stage hypothesis" in which he postulated that organizations pass through various stages as they computerize. Originally four stages were identified and each was discussed in terms of: the data-processing budget, the way in which the computer is used (the applications portfolio), the way in which the computer resource is managed, and the role of the user in the computerization process (Gibson and Nolan, 1974). He later added two more stages to the growth pattern as practice changed and his own views evolved (Nolan, 1979). Although there has been controversy among academicians as to whether Nolan's hypothesis has been supported, the Nolan framework is widely known and appreciated by MIS practitioners. If general awareness is a major criterion, Nolan's stage theory can be argued to be the major contribution of work in the conceptual area to date.

Nolan has also written and edited two books on MIS administration (McFarlan *et al.*, 1973; Nolan, 1974), has written articles on allocating computer use through the chargeout mechanism (Dearden and Nolan, 1973; Knutsen and Nolan, 1974), and has written in general about managing MIS (Nolan, 1973b). Although other books and articles on managing MIS have appeared (Sweda, 1972; Hartman *et al.*, 1972), it is Nolan who is by far most frequently associated with the management of MIS.

3.2.1.3 Other Contributions. Not fitting precisely within the sections above are several other important conceptual contributions that have been made during the growth and maturation of MIS that are worthy of mention. As has been pointed out frequently in this article, concepts from general systems theory and control theory are a good part of the intellectual MIS foundations. The book on organizational planning and control by Emery (1969) is one of the first to deal in depth with the role of information in these processes.

In addition to systems and control theory, two other disciplines, information theory and information economics, have contributed to MIS thought. Shannon first proposed an "information theory" in 1949 (Shannon, 1948; Shannon and Weaver, 1949). Their work dealt with the probability of receipt of a "message" under various conditions of the transmission system rather than with the context of the message in relation to a management process. Although not directly relevant to MIS, Shannon and Weaver's notions of a theory of information have guided others.

Davis (1974), for example, treats information concepts in some depth in his basic MIS textbook. Yovits and his colleagues at Ohio State University have devoted considerable effort to the definition of an information science and the relationship between information and decision making (Yovits, 1969; Whittemore and Yovits, 1973, 1974). Information theory has found other applications in MIS-related work, especially in accounting information (Gregory and Atwater, 1957; Bostwick, 1968).

Measuring the value of information, information systems, the function of information systems in an organization, and computers has been of major concern to MIS scholars and practitioners for some time (Stigler, 1961). The works of Feltham, (1968; Feltham and Demski, 1970) concerning the value of information, although theoretical in nature, are highly regarded as contributions to how one ought to approach the problem of valuing a piece of information. An earlier work addressed the problem of attempting to attach value to a piece of information using simulation as a vehicle for investigation (Bedford and Onsi, 1966).

Work concerning how one ought to measure the value of an information system rather than a piece of information has been performed by several persons (Kriebel, 1971; Emery, 1971; Gallagher, 1974). Carlson (1974) won a cash prize offered by the Society for Management Information Systems for his work on measuring the cost/effectiveness of information. Attempting to evaluate the value of the information systems function within an organization has also been of much interest (Matlin, 1977, 1979). As did Carlson, Matlin also won a prize given by the Society for Management Information Systems. His paper on the evaluation of the information systems function won the SMIS Award Paper Contest in 1979.

The economic evaluation of computers and of computer systems has also been treated by several authors (Sharpe, 1969; Kleijnen, 1979). Another area receiving consideration is that dealing with charging for computer services (Bernard *et al.*; 1977, Hootman, 1977; Statland, 1977; Wetherbe and Dickson, 1979).

Thus, information theory and information economics have both contributed to the conceptual basis of MIS. The areas represent a theoretical foundation upon which much applied work has been performed. Although they did not spring from a support discipline as in the cases cited above, other works are worthy of mention to complete this section on MIS conceptual development.

Among the many persons attempting to define and describe MIS, the works of Robert Head stand out. In Section 2.2 reference was made to early attempts at sharpening the picture of what MIS is. Head, who was in 1969 to become the first president of the Society for Management Information Systems (see Section 5), wrote on the definitional/conceptual aspects of MIS a bit later than did others, but provided useful frameworks (Head, 1967, 1970, 1972). In his article, "Critical Appraisal of MIS," Head (1967) viewed the organization as a pyramid and examined the information requirements and systems needed at various levels. To do so he borrowed some of the notions of Robert Anthony (1965) concerning organizational functions and levels. The Anthony framework has been very useful to MIS writers and has helped to delineate differences in the organizational use of information. Anthony's framework and Head's applications to MIS were brought to their most complete form by Emery (1973) when he listed eleven properties of information systems for three levels of the organization (strategic, tactical, operational).

Finally, when discussing conceptual contributions to MIS one should not overlook the report issued in 1968 by McKinsey and Co., a management consulting organization that has been very active in the area. This report presented the results of a survey of 36 large computer users. The report was the first of its kind to examine computer expenditures and the results, in terms of successful use, of those expenses. In particular, the report stressed the importance of planning, evaluation, and the involvement of management in the systems-building process. Several useful surveys of computer use were conducted later in the MIS growth period (e.g., Churchill *et al.*, 1969; Ference and Uretsky, 1976). Other surveys have been conducted regarding the attitudes of managerial users of computers in both the private sector (Guthrie, 1974; Adams and Schroeder, 1973; Adams, 1975) and public sector (Danziger, 1977). The private sector studies appear to indicate much higher levels of user satisfaction with information systems than do the public sector studies. Thus, there is evidence that business organizations have overcome some of the problems of information systems, the effects of which were described in the late 1960s (see Section 3.1.2).

4. MIS Research

The growth and maturity of the MIS area is reflected by the research[3] performed during the last decade. In addition to the research itself, there has also been work that has facilitated the research. Research frameworks

---

[3] The reader may note that the more technical material related to MIS (such as data structures and data-base management, automated system design, aids to the productivity of

and discussions of research methodology particular to MIS are examples of the latter. Research in MIS can be categorized as being of several types. In following discussion, a breakdown of research studies will be employed that will categorize projects as to whether they are organizational studies or experimental studies. It should be noted that a very important area, technical MIS research, is being purposely excluded from this discussion.

4.1 MIS Research Frameworks and Methodological Issues

Key contributors to the performance of MIS research in the 1970s have been the research frameworks developed by a number of persons (Gorry and Scott Morton, 1971; Mock *et al.*, 1971; Chervany *et al.*, 1972; Lucas, 1973; Mason and Mitroff, 1973; Jenkins, 1977). The summary framework by Mason and Mitroff has frequently been referenced and is illustrative of the objective of MIS research frameworks. They proposed that an information system consists of:

1. A PERSON of a certain PSYCHOLOGICAL TYPE who
2. faces a PROBLEM
3. within some ORGANIZATIONAL CONTEXT for which he needs
4. EVIDENCE to arrive at a solution, where the evidence is
5. made available through some MODE OF PRESENTATION (Mason and Mitroff, 1973, p. 475).

The framework of Chervany *et al.*, later embellished and elaborated upon by Jenkins, suggested that certain decision-oriented outcome variables (e.g., profit, cost, time) are influenced by combinations of several types of input variables. The latter include the characteristics of: (1) the decision maker(s) (e.g., cognitive style, type of education), (2) the decision environment (e.g., its stability, the managerial level of the Anthony framework), and (3) the information system (e.g., graphical versus tabular output, built-in decision aids).

The research framework by Lucas took an organizational approach, which identified various potential outcomes and related variables that could influence the outcomes. He went on to suggest various ways of measuring the hypothesized relationships. In summary, Lucas presented a descriptive model of situational, personal, and attitudinal variables and

---

the design process, and systems software) are not covered in this section, not because these topics are unimportant, but rather because they are more a part of the field of computer science and their coverage is widely available in the literature of that more well-developed field. The same argument applies to material from the fields of behavioral science and organizational behavior that relate to MIS.

TABLE II

NOLAN–WETHERBE RESEARCH CLASSIFICATION TAXONOMY

MIS inputs	MIS outputs
Data	Transactions processing
Information requests	Information reporting
Resources	Decision support
MIS feedback	Programmed decisions
Efficiency	*MIS environment*
Effectiveness	Goals and values
MIS technology	Managerial
Hardware	Technical
Software	Structural
Database	Psychological
Procedures	
Personnel	

their impact upon usage of the system and performance of the information system user. Much of Lucas' work, which is described in the following section, grew out of his framework for research. In a similar way many of the experimental studies conducted at the University of Minnesota (Section 4.3) were performed according to the Chervany *et al.*/Jenkins frameworks described above.

These frameworks have guided many of the research studies that will be reported upon in the next two sections. As we enter the 1980s, summary articles have begun to appear that evaluate MIS research contributions. The existence of such works illustrates the trend of the MIS area in a very dramatic way. Whereas major research contributions in the early and middle part of the 1970s dealt with frameworks to assist doing MIS research, now attention has turned to classifying the research that has been done.

Nolan and Wetherbe (1980) build a comprehensive framework for MIS that attempts to define a domain for MIS research. These authors take samples from the MIS literature and classify it according to the framework that is summarized in Table II.

Davis, Ives, and Hamilton also have recently built a framework for classifying MIS research. Rather than mapping MIS literature into their framework as Nolan and Wetherbe did, these authors categorize 331 doctoral dissertations related to MIS. The Ives *et al* (1980) framework is shown in Table III.

Davis and his colleagues identify five types of research with regard to variables tested as well as four types of research strategies. Given the

TABLE III

DAVIS–IVES–HAMILTON RESEARCH
CLASSIFICATION TAXONOMY

Environmental variables
External environment
Organizational environment
User environment
Information systems (IS)
  IS development environment
  IS operations environment

Process variables
Development process
Operations process
Use process

Information systems subsystem (ISS)
ISS content
Presentation form
Time of presentation

---

mapping of the dissertations into the framework, the authors suggest cells into which additional research is needed. In their discussion of research type, they utilize another MIS research facilitator that identifies several ways of performing research: (1) the case study, (2) the field study, (3) field tests, and (4) laboratory studies (Van Horn, 1973). The first three categories represent organizational studies and the latter has tended to take an experimental approach.

4.2 Organizational Studies

Much of the MIS research that has been performed has been done in an organizational setting. In some cases, hypotheses have been tested using data from a number of organizations, whereas other research on MIS has been done using data from a single organization.

One example of hypothesis-testing research in an organizational setting is the study to find out what practices and organizational factors are associated with successful MIS project implementation (Powers and Dickson, 1973). This research found that many of the so-called "success factors" did not prove to be significant on the basis of studying 20 projects in 10 organizations. Further, the research did not support the factors that a number of MIS managers thought were related to MIS project success.

One area receiving a substantial amount of study has been the relationship between information systems and attributes of the organization. These studies have examined the impact of an MIS on the organization as well as investigated the impact of organizational factors on an MIS. The study by Whisler (1967) on the impact of computers on organizational control is an example of the former type. There have also been studies of the relationship between the degree of centralization/decentralization of an organization and its information system (Olson and Chervany, 1980) and of employee reactions to the introduction of an information system (Argyris, 1971).

Another example of a large study using organizational data is the one that was performed to investigate the "quality of working life" of MIS managers and analysts (Couger and Zawacki, 1978; Couger et al., 1979). This study utilized a popular and validated testing instrument, the Job Diagnostic Survey, and compared data-processing (DP) jobs to a number of previously tested occupations. A major finding was that both DP managers and analysts are much more highly goal oriented than their counterparts in other jobs, while at the same time they display significantly lower needs for social interaction.

A substantial number of organizational studies have been performed by Lucas (summarized in Lucas, 1978a). Over a ten-year time period, Lucas conducted nine studies of the implementation of systems and models. The nine studies involved testing hypotheses based upon various implementation success measures and a number of individual and organizational variables. In most of his studies, Lucas utilized only one organization, but two of the studies were multiorganizational research designs. Overall, Lucas found many relationships between organizational and individual variables that influence the successful implementation of a system.

In addition to Lucas, other researchers have focused upon systems implementation. Some important literature has been the building of implementation frameworks (e.g., Dickson and Simmons, 1970; Ginzberg, 1978). Another worthwhile contribution to this topic is the insightful critique of the entire implementation research area provided by Keen (1977). Relevant implementation studies include:

(1) A series of large scale projects examining the influence of organizational factors on the implementation of operations research projects (Rubenstein et al., 1967).

(2) An examination of the factors and practices associated with successfully implementing decision supporting systems (Alter, 1976).

(3) Determination of the degree of successful use of computers by local government (Kraemer and King, 1976).

4.3 Experimental Studies

An area attracting MIS research has been the relationship between various characteristics of information systems and decision outcomes (e.g., the quality of decisions made). The most popular approach to research of this type has been laboratory experimentation. The method has been to construct detailed "environmental simulators," which resemble business games but are especially constructed to allow experimenters to control the informational outputs. Subjects then play the role of decision makers in the simulated environment and utilize the information system to make their decisions. The decision outcomes (profits, costs, time to make decisions) are recorded and analysis is performed to examine the effect of the nature of the information system on decision-making behavior. Many simulated "environments" have been used including: (1) aggregate production planning, (2) inventory management, (3) purchasing management, and (4) commodities purchasing.

The best-known research studies of the experimental type have been conducted at the University of Minnesota. A set of ten experiments conducted over an eight-year period are known as "the Minnesota Experiments" (Dickson *et al.*, 1977). These experiments involved several simulated decision-making environments, a variety of types of subjects ranging from students to business managers, and tested many information systems characteristics. Among the latter, graphical versus tabular output, detailed versus summary data, and on-line versus batch outputs are examples. These experiments suggest that decision outcomes are significantly influenced by the nature of the information system utilized for decision support. Further, the experiments support the position that individual characteristics such as cognitive style, apptitudes, and past experience must be considered when designing an information system.

Although the Minnesota Experiments form the most comprehensive set of experiments involving MIS, they are not the only such studies. Other examples of MIS research involving experimental examination of the decision maker/machine interface include studies taking roughly the same approach to the study of the design problem (Ferguson and Jones, 1969; Prokop and Brooks, 1970; Mock *et al.*, 1971; Mock, 1973; Firth, 1980).

Much of the experimental work has addressed the issue of whether or not different decision-making styles must be taken into account by attributes of the information systems (Huysmans, 1970; Bariff and Lusk, 1977; Benbasat and Taylor, 1978). In particular, the work of Benbasat and Schroeder have shown how persons with different cognitive styles react to alternative information system characteristics (Schroeder and Benbasat, 1975; Benbasat and Schroeder, 1977).

As can be seen by examination of this discussion, which touches only the highlights of work performed, the 1970s were active years for MIS researchers. One aspect of the environment that changed dramatically during these years and facilitated the research activity was the support mechanisms that evolved for MIS activity. Support mechanisms include journals in which to publish research results, professional societies at which to make research presentations, and MIS research centers.

5. MIS Support Mechanisms

One of the problems in the MIS area during the formative years was a lack of ways for both practitioners and academics to communicate within their groups and with each other. In particular, professional societies that directed themselves to the MIS area were unavailable and journals devoted primarily to MIS material were lacking.

Several professional societies existed prior to 1960 that were tangentially related to MIS. The Institute of Management Science (TIMS), the Academy of Management, and the Association for Computing Machinery (ACM) are examples. During the 1960s the Data Processing Management Association (DPMA) and the Association for Systems Management (ASM) grew to serve many practitioners.

The professional societies prior to the late 1960s were diverse: TIMS served management scientists, ACM computer scientists, and DPMA and ASM were oriented toward practicing data processors. Thus, a person interested in the total aspects of the MIS area had to belong to several of these societies. Similarly, presentation of MIS material at society meetings was difficult since it only peripherally addressed the main focus of any society.

Much the same situation existed regarding journals until the late 1970s. One can scan the journal references used in this article and see the wide variety in the sources of the cited material. Persons attempting to publish their work in MIS were faced with the problem that MIS did not "fit" in many journals. *Management Science,* for example, was mainly quantitative in orientation, *The Communications of the ACM* published computer science (technical) material, and decision-making research or organizational studies were not "pure" enough to fit into the behavioral science journals. Periodicals such as *Datamation* and *Infosystems* had the proper focus, but were practitioner oriented. Thus, the MIS researcher had difficulty publishing MIS material and the scholar interested in MIS was forced to search widely for relevant material.

Matters in this area have improved somewhat, especially regarding journals. In 1977, two new journals emerged, the *MIS Quarterly,* and *In-*

TABLE IV

CITATIONS TO MIS PERIODICAL LITERATURE[a]

Journal	1955–1980
Harvard Business Review	24
Management Science	18
Management Information Systems Quarterly	12
Datamation	6
Data Base	5
Information and Management[b]	4
Sloan Management Review[b]	4
Communications of the ACM	3

[a] From the reference list at the end of this article, having three or more citations.
[b] Including predecessor journals.

formation and Mangement,[4] specifically oriented to MIS material. Although these journals are still gaining academic respectability, they do provide a focus for MIS material. Another MIS journal has recently been announced by New York University that will deal with case studies of MIS systems and an analysis of the success/failure of the system. This journal will be called *Systems, Objectives, Solutions*.

Since in this article we deal with a time period of approximately 25 years of MIS history, an analysis of its rather extensive bibliography provides some insight into the major periodicals publishing significant MIS-related material. Table IV lists citations to journals taken from the list of references at the end of this article. It is noteworthy that since 1977 the preponderance of the citations come from the *Management Information Systems Quarterly* (but it must also be noted that the author serves as Senior Editor of this journal). Thus, with some qualifications it appears that a journal is emerging to serve the needs of the MIS academic community while at the same time appealing to the practitioner community.

The MIS practitioner is well served by the professional societies listed above, but the same situation does not exist for the MIS academician. The societies either have a special focus or a membership bias that does not enhance interchange with the practitioner. Two relatively new profes-

---

[4] *Information and Management* evolved from the journal, *Management Datamatics*, which in turn came from *Management Informatics*. The latter two journals are no longer published and *Information and Management* has a new editorial focus. The journal has a European flavor and is not widely circulated in the United States.

sional societies, The American Institute for Decision Sciences (AIDS) and the Society for Management Information Systems (SMIS), were formed in the late 1960s. Unfortunately, AIDS has an almost exclusively academic membership, whereas SMIS is virtually all MIS managers. Furthermore, AIDS incorporates MIS only as one small subset of its overall activities.

Perhaps the First Conference on Information Systems (Philadelphia, December 1980), primarily for MIS academicians but with invited MIS practitioners, can remove the vacuum. This conference, supported by SMIS, TIMS, and ACM has as its purpose to solidify the MIS area and to move into the 1980s with an improved sense of direction.

Another support mechanism to activity in the MIS area has been the evolution of research centers devoted to MIS. Two research centers in the area now exist at major universities in the United States, the MIS Research Center is at the University of Minnesota and the Center for Information Systems Research is at the Massachusetts Institute of Technology. Examples of the work being done at these two centers plus research in MIS at the University of Michigan and at the Wharton School of the University of Pennsylvania are given by Canning (1979) in an issue of the *EDP Analyzer*. Other schools have formed or are forming associate/affiliate programs to facilitate interaction with industry and government. In addition to the Massachusetts Institute of Technology, and Minnesota, programs of this sort have been started at universitites such as New York University, the University of California at Los Angeles, and the University of Colorado.

One problem which is exacerbated by the lack of MIS support mechanisms is proper development of MIS educational programs and curricula. As a result, MIS programs cannot meet the demand for student output.

6. MIS Education

Educational programs in MIS were first announced in the late 1960s. Purdue University and the University of Minnesota began offering specialty programs in the area in 1969 (Journal of Data Management, 1969; *Business Week,* 1971). John Dearden, writing in 1972 that "MIS Is a Mirage" (one of the caveat school), questioned the ability to create an organizational information systems specialist. In making his argument, Dearden referenced the Minnesota program and research center.

In 1972, the Association for Computing Machinery (ACM) published a curriculum guide for information systems education (Ashenhurst, 1972). The curriculum specified two products from the educational program, a technically oriented design analyst and a managerially oriented information analyst. In 1973, a committee chaired by Couger made recommendations concerning undergraduate MIS education. A committee headed by Nunamaker, the ACM Curriculum Committee on Computer Education for Management, is presently studyi .g MIS curricular issues. Unfortunately, their report has not been published at this writing.

It is beyond the scope of this contribution to go into detail on specific MIS programs. There have been several MIS programs described in the *MIS Interrupt* edited by M. C. Munro at the University of Calgary. Anyone wishing to see specific programs should consult this source, but some general comments may be helpful.

Throughout the 1970s, MIS curricula have evolved along with specific MIS degree programs. Most institutions place MIS within the business school, a few have tried MIS as a free-standing department, some use a joint computer science/business school approach, and some place the area within computer science departments. Only a few MIS programs are "deep" in that they produce MIS specialists with a blend of computer science, business training, and computer-related skills not usually found within computer science. There are probably 20–25 programs of this sort. More frequently business schools offer a core data processing or MIS course with two or three more advanced electives in the area.

According to one published report there are 24 business schools offering a Ph.D. major in MIS (Munro, 1979), but the author suspects that about half of these are programs severely limited in students, faculty, and a structured curriculum with substantial depth. There is a great excess of demand for MIS Ph.D.s to assume professorial positions over the supply of such persons. Although no formal count has been made, the author estimates that the United States educational system produces fewer than ten MIS Ph.D. graduates yearly. In 1978, one professional organization active in placement listed over 200 academic positions in MIS/data processing.

There are many sources that document the need for trained MIS professionals. *Money* magazine, for example, lists the occupation of "computer systems analyst" as the best of "sunny" occupations for the 1980s, based upon job growth and salaries (*Money*, 1980). They go on to say, "Add management skills and you can write your own program for advancement." Another source lists systems analysts third after medical doctors and veterinarians among the career areas projected to experience the greatest shortage of professionals for the next several years (Bureau of Labor Statistics, 1978). It is a fair estimate that MIS programs will not produce graduates to fill one-tenth of the forecasted job openings. Most entry-level analysts will be trained by vendors, trade schools, or be schooled internally by organizations desperately needing their skills.

7. MIS—Quo Vadis?

The previous sections of this article have provided a substantial amount of detail concerning the area called management information systems. In doing this, a historical approach has been taken that has emphasized the academic and professional development of the MIS area. Among several potential topics that have not been covered in this contribution is a discussion of organizational computer use. The feeling is that it is more important to explore MIS as an area of study and to present the area as it is seen by educators, researchers, and, to some extent, by practitioners. As can be seen by noting the flavor of the previous material, a managerial (in contrast to a technical) perspective has been taken.

In presenting so much material there is always the danger of losing sight of the main ideas in the detail. Thus, in understanding what MIS is, it is important to return to the notions expressed in Section 3 and to update the MIS "concept" in view of all that has been presented.

We have seen that many names have been applied to what we have been addressing as MIS. Information technology and management information–decision systems were titles heard several years ago and now one hears about "Decision Support Systems" (DSS). Like MIS, DSS is a term that is awkward because it is applied to both the area and to a specific system; DSS is defined as:

> Decision Support Systems (DSS) represent a point of view on the role of the computer in the management decision making process. Decision support implies the use of the computer to:
> 1. Assist managers in their decision processes in semistructured tasks.
> 2. Support rather than replace, managerial judgment.
> 3. Improve the effectiveness of decision making rather than its efficiency. [Keen and Scott Morton, 1978, p. 1.]

There are persons who suggest that one major reason to concentrate on DSS and to throw out MIS is that MIS has failed. The claims are that MIS has not been effective (remember the "caveat" school of Section 3.1.2). The argument can be advanced that DSS is much different than MIS (Couger, 1979). That this is not the case can be shown quite easily. In the Foreword to the series on DSS, Keen and Scott Morton speak of the concept of DSS. They base the concept upon the Carnegie School of Simon and his colleagues. They also reference the "behavioral" school of management sciences as related to DSS. Thus, if one looks closely, the material presented in this article, although not overlapping DSS completely is, at the conceptual level, very closely related.

Both terms, MIS and DSS, refer to a product produced by a process. Unfortunately, both terms have been applied to the process as well as the product, which has caused no end of confusion. As presented here, MIS is used as an "umbrella" term, which applies to an entire area of inquiry. We can return to Section 2.2 to generalize the nature of the inquiry:

> In the simplest, most straightforward terms, MIS deals with all the informational and decision making activity associated with operating an organization. It is the desire of those working in the MIS area to encourage better organizational efficiency and effectiveness through facilitating information provision and decision support to management.

This is not at all inconsistent with the DSS concept. About the only substantive differences are that MIS is associated, to some extent, with operating an organization and with organizational efficiency, whereas DSS excludes those concerns. Thus, while decision support for management is very important to MIS, nonmanagerial activity such as data processing is also of concern because of its contribution to organizational efficiency. Certainly data processing feeds the managerial decision support systems that are part of MIS.

The systems hierarchy given earlier as clerical systems, information systems, decision systems, and programmed systems in the author's opinion still holds. A definition for an "umbrella" term, call it MIS or anything else, is:

A *process* for building systems that have as their purpose (1) the collection of information having the correct content, having the correct form, transmitted through the proper media, and available at the right time; and/or (2) the provision of aids to the managerial decision process itself.

If MIS is criticized for failing to achieve its aims because of an inappropriate focus, it is due to a belief in a concept different from that above. Clearly the focus of MIS as presented by this author emphasizes decision support. Persons associated with DSS have made substantial contributions to MIS (e.g., Scott Morton, 1971). Thompson (1965), for example, wrote an early book on joint man–machine systems. The research on the installation and evaluation of support for stock portfolio decision making in banking is, likewise, a contribution to our area (Gerrity, 1971). Similarly, the work by Carlson and his colleagues (1977) at the IBM Research Laboratory on graphics support of unstructured decisions is a part of the contributions to the MIS area.

Although new terms will come along that may be substituted for MIS as the umbrella term for the area, one must keep in mind that virtually all proponents are speaking of similar concepts. Only the misguided and severe critics misdefine terms to support their arguments. If the reader has carefully examined the detail provided in this contribution, the definition of MIS given above should be comfortable. Further, the growing amount of MIS-related work should be able to be placed in the framework provided by this article.

REFERENCES

Ackoff, R. (1967). Management misinformation systems. *Manage. Sci.* **14**(4), B147–B156.
Adams, C. (1975). How management users view information systems. *Decision Sci.* **6**(2), 337–345.
Adams, C., and Schroeder, R. (1973). Managers and MIS: They get what they want. *Bus. Horiz.*, December, pp. 63–69.
Alter, S. (1976). How successful managers use information systems. *Harv. Bus. Rev.* **54**(6), 97–104.
Anshen, M. (1960). The manager and the black box. *Harv. Bus. Rev.* **38**(6), 85–92.
Anshen, M., and Bach, G., eds. (1960). "Management and the Corporations, 1985." McGraw-Hill, New York.
Ansoff, H. (1965). The firm of the future. *Harv. Bus. Rev.* **43**(5), 162–174.
Anthony, R. (1965). "Planning Control Systems—A Framework for Analysis." Graduate School of Business, Harvard University, Cambridge, Massachusetts.
Argyris, C. (1971). Management information systems: Challenge to rationality and emotionality. *Manage. Sci.* **17**(6), B275–B292.
Aron, J. (1969). Information systems in perspective. *Comput. Surv.* **1**(4), 213–236.
Ashenhurst, R., ed. (1972). A report of the ACM curriculum committee on computer education for management. *Commun. ACM* **15**, 363–398.
Association for Computing Machinery (1971). A quarter century look back at the computer. *Commun. ACM* **14**(8), 614–616.
Astrahan, M. (1958). Automated library soon? *Mach. Des.* **30**(4), 40–44.
Aswen, D. (1958). Why are we using an automatic data collection system? *Power Ind.* **74**(3), 4–10.
Bariff, M. and Lusk, E. (1977). Cognitive and personality tests for the design of management information systems. *Manage. Sci.* **23**(8), 820–829.
Barnard, C. (1938). "The Function of the Executive." Harvard Univ. Press, Cambridge, Massachusetts.
Bedford, N. M., and Onsi, M. (1966). Measuring the value of information—an information theory approach. *Manage. Serv.* January–February, pp. 16–25.
Beer, S. (1959). "Cybernetics and Management." Wiley, New York.
Beged-Dov, S. (1967). An overview of management science and information systems. *Manage. Sci.* **13**(12), B817–B831.
Bell, W. (1957). "A Management Guide to Electronic Computers." McGraw-Hill, New York.
Benbasat, I., and Schroeder, R. G. (1977). An experimental investigation of some MIS design variables. *Manage. Inf. Syst. Q.* **1**(1), 37–50.
Benbasat, I. and Taylor, R. (1978). The impact of cognitive styles on information system design. *Manage. Inf. Syst. Q.* **2**(2), 43–53.

Berkeley, E. (1962). "The Computer Revolution." Doubleday, Garden City, New York.
Bernard, D., Emery, J. C., Nolan, R. L., and Scott, R. H. (1977). "Charging for Computer Services: Principles and Guidelines." Petrocelli, New York.
Blum, A. (1961). Electronic data processing and the office worker. *Data Process.* **4**(6), 11–15.
Blumenthal, S. (1969). "Management Information Systems: A Framework for Planning and Development." Prentice-Hall, Englewood Cliffs, New Jersey.
Bostwick, C. L. (1968). The use of information theory in accounting. *Manage. Account.* June, pp. 11–17.
Bright, J. (1958). "Automation and Management." Division of Research, Harvard University, Cambridge, Massachusetts.
Buckingham, W. (1961). "Automation: Its Impact on Business and People." Harper Brothers, New York.
Burch, J., Strater, F., and Gradnitski, G. (1979). "Information Systems: Theory and Practice." Wiley, New York.
Burck, G. (1965). "The Computer Age." Harper & Row, New York.
Bureau of Labor Statistics (1978). "Occupational Outlook Handbook," 1978–1979 ed., Bur. Labor Stat. Bull., 1955, pp. 5, 111–117. U.S. Department of Labor, Washington, D.C.
Burlingame, J. (1961). Information technology and decentralization. *Harv. Bus. Rev.* **39**(6), 121–126.
Business Week (1971). Business takes a second look at computers—special report. *Bus. Week* June 5, pp. 59–136.
Business Week (1979). New growth industries and some dropouts. *Bus. Week* September 3, pp. 188–193.
Canning, R. (1956). "Electronic Data Processing for Business and Industry." Wiley, New York.
Canning, R. (1966). Trends in the use of data systems. *EDP Analyzer* **4**(8), 1–12.
Canning, R. (1979). How to prepare for the coming changes. *EDP Analyzer* **17**(4), 1–13.
Carlin, F. (1958). The use of a large scale computer for manufacturing control. *Manage. Sci.* **4**(2), 177–182.
Carlson, E. D. (1974). Evaluating the impact of information systems. *Manage. Inf.* **3**(2), 57–67.
Carlson, E., Grace, B., and Sutton, J. (1977). Case studies of end user requirements for interactive problem solving. *Manage. Inf. Syst. Q.* **1**(1).
Chapin, N. (1957). "An Introduction to Automatic Computers." Van Nostrand-Reinhold, Princeton, New Jersey.
Chervany, N., Dickson, G., and Kozar, K. (1972). "An Experimental Gaming Framework for Investigating the Influence of Management Information Systems on Decision Effectiveness," MISRC Working Pap. No. 71-12. Management Information Systems Research Center, University of Minnesota, Minneapolis.
Churchill, N., Kempster, J., and Uretsky, M. (1969). "Computer Based Information Systems for Management: A Survey." National Association of Accountants, New York.
Cleland, D., and King, W. (1975). "Systems Analysis and Project Management." McGraw-Hill, New York.
Coleman, R., and Riley, M. (1973). "MIS: Management Dimensions." Holden-Day, San Francisco, California.
Collins, J. (1954). Will cybernetics do away with people? *Public Utilities Fortnightly* May 27, pp. 660–666.
Couger, J. D. (1967). Computer-based management information system for medium-sized firms. *J. Data Manage.* August, pp. 18–22.
Couger, J. D., ed. (1979). "Computing Newsletter," October. College of Business Administration, University of Colorado, Colorado Springs.

Couger, J. D. and Knapp, R. (1974). "Systems Analysis Techniques." Wiley, New York.
Couger, J. D., and Zawacki, R. (1978). What motivates DP professionals? *Datamation* **24**(9), 22–24.
Couger, J. D. (ed.) (1973). Curriculum recommendations for undergraduate programs in information systems. *Commun. ACM* **16**(12), 727–729.
Couger, J. D., Zawacki, R. A., and Oppermann, E. B. (1979). Motivation levels of MIS managers versus those of their employees. *Manage. Inf. Syst. Q.* **3**(3), 47–56.
Daniel, R. (1961). Management information crisis. *Harv. Bus. Rev.* **39**(5), 111–121.
Danzinger, J. (1977). Computers and the frustrated chief executive. *Manage. Inf. Syst. Q.* **1**(2), 43–54.
Davis, G. (1974). "Management Information Systems: Conceptual Foundations, Structure and Development." McGraw-Hill, New York.
Davis, G., and Everest, G. (1976). "Readings in Management Information Systems." McGraw-Hill, New York.
Dearden, J. (1964). Can management information be automated? *Harv. Bus. Rev.* **42**(2), 128–135.
Dearden, J. (1965). How to organize information systems. *Harv. Bus. Rev.* **43**(2), 65–73.
Dearden, J. (1966). "Computers in Business Management." Dow Jones-Irwin, Homewood, Illinois.
Dearden, J. (1972). MIS is a mirage. *Harv. Bus. Rev.* **50**(1), 90–91.
Dearden, J., and McFarlan, F. (1966). "Management Information Systems: Text and Cases." R. D. Irwin, Homewood, Illinois.
Dearden, J., and Nolan, R. (1973). How to control the computer resource. *Harv. Bus. Rev.* **51**(6), 68–78.
Dickey, E., and Senewseib, N. (1963). The total systems concept. *In* "Encyclopedia of Management" (C. Hegel, ed.), pp. 150–167. Van Nostrand-Reinhold, Princeton, New Jersey.
Dickson, G. (1968). Management information-decision systems. *Bus. Horiz.* December, pp. 17–26.
Dickson, G., Chervany, N., and Senn, J. (1977). Research in MIS: The Minnesota experiments. *Manage. Sci.* **28**(9), 913–923.
Dickson, G. W., and Simmons, J. K. (1970). The behavioral side of MIS. *Bus. Horiz.* **13**(8), 59–71.
Diebold, J. (1964). ADP—The still sleeping giant. *Harv. Bus. Rev.* **42**(5), 60–65.
Diebold, J. (1965). What's ahead in information technology. *Harv. Bus. Rev.* **43**(5), 76–82.
Diebold, J., and Terbough, G. (1952). "Automation—The Advent of the Automatic Factory." Van Nostrand-Reinhold, Princeton, New Jersey.
Dock, V., Luchsinger, V., and Cornette, W. (1977). "MIS: A Managerial Perspective." Science Research Associates, Palo Alto, California.
Drucker, P. (1966). What the computer will be telling you. *Nation's Bus.* August, pp. 84–91.
DuPont, H. (1954). Frontier unlimited: The promise of technology. *Manage. Rev.* July, pp. 406–407.
Dyer, A. (1965). Management information systems opportunity and challenge for the data processing manager. *Data Process. Mag.* **8**(6), 16–25.
Ebdon, J. (1958). Trends for 1958: Increased use of computers. *Gas* **34**(1), 99–101.
Elliot, J. (1958). EDP—its impact on jobs, procedures, and people. *Ind. Eng.* **9**(5), 41–56.
Emery, J. C. (1969). "Organizational Planning and Control Systems." Macmillan, New York.
Emery, J. C. (1971). "Cost/Benefit Analysis of Information Systems." SMIS Workshop Rep. No. 1. Society for Management Information Systems, Chicago, Illinois.

Emery, J. C. (1973). An overview of management information systems. *Data Base* **5**(2–4), 1–15.

Evans, M., and Hague, L. (1962). Master plan for information systems. *Harv. Bus. Rev.* **40**(1), 92–104.

Feltham, G. A. (1968). The value of information. *Account. Rev.* **43**(4), 684–696.

Feltham, G. A., and Demski, J. S. (1970). The use of models in information evaluation. *Account. Rev.* **45**(4), 623–640.

Ference, T., and Uretsky, M. (1976). Computers in management: Some insights into the state of the revolution. *Manage. Datamatics* **5**(2), 55–63.

Ferguson, R., and Jones, D. (1969). A computer aided decision system. *Manage. Sci.* **15**(10), B550–B561.

Finke, W. (1957). New giant brain for businessmen. *Franklin Inst. J.* **264**(12), 456–467.

Fiock, L., Jr. (1962). Seven deadly dangers of EDP. *Harv. Bus. Rev.* **40**(3), 88–96.

Firth, M. (1980). The impact of some MIS design variables on managers. *Manage. Inf. Syst. Q.* **4**(1), 45–54.

Forrester, J. (1958). Industrial dynamics: A major breakthrough for decision makers. *Harv. Bus. Rev.* **36**(4), 37–66.

Gallagher, C. A. (1974). Perceptions of the value of a management information system. *Acad. Manage. J.* **17**(1), 46–55.

Gallagher, J. (1961). "Management Information Systems and the Computer." American Management Association, New York.

Garrity, J. (1963). "Getting the Most Out of Your Computers." McKinsey Co., New York.

Garrity, J. (1964). The management information dream—the end or a new beginning. *Financ. Exec.* September, pp. 11–17.

Gerrity, T., Jr. (1971). Design of man-machine decision making: An application to portfolio management. *Sloan Manage. Rev.* **12**(2), 59–75.

Gibson, C., and Nolan, R. (1974). Managing the four stages of EDP growth. *Harv. Bus. Rev.* **52**(1), 76–88.

Gille, F. (1958). Observations from the publisher. *Mach. Account. Data Process.* Nov.–Dec., 1.

Ginzberg, M. (1978). Redesign of managerial tasks: A requisite for successful decision support systems. *Manage. Inf. Syst. Q.* **3**(1), 39–52.

Gorry, A., and Scott Morton, S. (1971). A framework for management information systems. *Sloan Manage. Rev.* **13**(1), 55–70.

Gregory, R. H., and Atwater, T. V., Jr. (1957). Cost and value of management information as functions of age. *Account. Res.* **8**(1), 42–70.

Guest, L. (1956). Centralized data processing for decentralized management. *Syst. Mag.* **20**(5), 6–7.

Guthrie, A. (1974). Attitudes of the user-managers towards management information systems. *Manage. Datamatics* **3**(4), 221–232.

Hardin, E. (1960). The reaction of employees to office automation. *Mon. Labor Rev.* September, pp. 925–932.

Hartman, H. (1965). Management control in real time is the objective. *Systems*, Sept., pp. 45–57.

Hartman, W., Matthes, H., and Proeme, A. (1972). "Management Information Systems Handbook." McGraw-Hill, New York.

Head, R. (1967). Management information systems: A critical appraisal. *Datamation* **13**(5), 22–28.

Head, R. (1970). The elusive MIS. *Datamation* **16**(10), 22–27.

Head, R. (1972). "Managers Guide To Management Information Systems." Prentice-Hall, Englewood Cliffs, New Jersey.

Head, R. (1978). Strategic planning for management information systems. *Infosystems* **25**(10), 19–25.
Hertz, D. (1965). Electronics in management. *Manage. Sci.* **11**(6), B59–B68.
Hockman, J. (1963). An integrated management information system. *Syst. Proced. J.* **14**(1), 40–41.
Hoos, I. (1960). When the computer takes over the office. *Harv. Bus. Rev.* **38**(4), 102–112.
Hootman, J. T. (1977). Basic considerations in developing computer charging mechanisms. *Data Base* **8**(4), 4–9.
Huysmans, J. H. (1970). The effectiveness of the cognitive style constraint in implementing operations research proposals. *Manage. Sci.* **17**(1), 92–104.
International Data Corporation (1978). Computing for business into the 1980's. *Fortune* **99**(10), 56–83.
International Data Corporation (1980). Trends in computing: Applications for the 1980's. *Fortune* **101**(10), 29–70.
Ives, B., Hamilton, S., and Davis, G. (1980). A framework for research in computer based management information systems. *Manage. Sci.* **26**(9), 910–934.
Jenkins, A. (1977). A framework for MIS research. *Proc. 9th Annu. Conf. Am. Inst. Decision Sci.* p. 573.
Johnson, J. (1958). Electronics to start revolution in office. *Franklin J.* **266**(5), 437–438.
Johnson, R., Kast, F., and Rosenzweig, J. (1963). "The Theory and Management Systems." McGraw-Hill, New York.
Joslin, E. (1971). "Analysis, Design, and Selection of Computer Systems." College Readings, Inc., Arlington, Virginia.
Journal of Data Management (1969). Purdue University's MIS graduate program. *J. Data Manage.* April, pp. 24–26.
Kanter, J. (1977). "Management-oriented Management Information Systems." Prentice-Hall, Englewood Cliffs, New Jersey.
Kaufman, F. (1966). Data systems that cross company boundaries. *Harv. Bus. Rev.* **44**(1), 141–155.
Keen, P. (1977). "Implementation Research in OR/MS and MIS: Description vs. Prescription," Res. Pap. No. 390. Graduate School of Business, Stanford University, Stanford, California.
Keen, P., and Scott Morton, M. (1978). "Decision Support Systems." Wiley, New York.
Kelly, J. (1970). "Computerized Management Information Systems." Macmillan, New York.
Kennevan, W. (1970). MIS universe. *Data Manage.* September, pp. 62–64.
Kleijnen, J. P. C. (1979). "Computers and Profits: Quantifying Financial Benefits of Information." Addison-Wesley, Reading, Massachusetts.
Knox, C. (1958). Computer simplified purchasing decisions. *SAE J.* **66**(7), 29–31.
Knutson, H., and Nolan, R. (1974). Assessing computer costs and profits. *J. Syst. Manage.* **25**(2), 28–34.
Kozmetzky, G., and Kircher, P. (1956). "Electronic Computers and Management Control." McGraw-Hill, New York.
Kraemer, K. L., and King, J. L. (1976). "Computers Power, and Urban Management: What Every Local Executive Should Know." Sage Publications, Beverly Hills, California.
Krause, L. (1970). "Computer-based Management Information Systems." American Management Association, New York.
Kriebel, C. H. (1971). The evaluation of information systems. *I. A. G. J.* **4**(1), 2–14.
Kriebel, C. H. (1972). The future MIS. *Infosystems* **19**(6), 18–42.
Kriebel, C. H., Van Horn, R., and Heames, T., eds. (1971). "Management Information Systems: Progress and Perspectives." Carnegie-Mellon Press, Pittsburgh, Pennsylvania.

Lach, E. (1960). The total systems concept. *Syst. Proced.* November, pp. 6–7.

Langefors, B. (1970). "Theoretical Analysis of Information Systems." Barnes & Noble, New York.

Leavitt, H., and Whisler, T. (1958). Management in the 1980's. *Harv. Bus. Rev.* **36**(6), 41–48.

Lucas, H., Jr. (1973). Descriptive model of information systems in the context of the organization. *Data Base* **5**(2), 27–39.

Lucas, H., Jr. (1978a). Empirical evidence for a descriptive model of implementation. *Manage. Inf. Syst. Q.* **2**(2), 27–42.

Lucas, H., Jr. (1978b). "Information Systems Concepts for Management." McGraw-Hill, New York.

McDonough, A. (1963). "Information Economics and Management Systems." McGraw-Hill, New York.

McFarlan, F. (1971). Problems in planning the information system. *Harv. Bus. Rev.* **49**(2), 147–156.

McFarlan, F., Nolan, R., and Norton, D. (1973). "Information System Administration." Holt, New York.

McKenney, J. (1962). Simultaneous processing of jobs on a computer. *Manage. Sci.* **8**(3), 344–354.

McKinsey & Co., Inc., (1968). "Unlocking the Computer's Profit Potential: A Research Report to Management." McKinsey & Co., New York.

McLean, E., and Soden, J. (1977). "Strategic Planning for MIS." Wiley, New York.

Malcomb, D. (1960). Exploring the military analogy—real-time management control. *In* "Management Control Systems" (D. Malcomb and A. Rowe, eds.), pp. 187–208. Wiley, New York.

Malcomb, D., and Rowe, A., eds. (1960). "Management Control Systems." Wiley, New York.

Malcomb, D., and Rowe, A. (1961). An approach to computer based management control systems. *Calif. Manage. Rev.* **3**(3), 4–15.

Mann, F., and Williams, L. (1960). Observations on the dynamics of change to electronic data processing equipment. *Admin. Sci. Q.* **5**(2), 217–256.

March, J., and Simon, H. (1958). "Organizations." Wiley, New York.

Mason, R., and Mitroff, I. (1973). A program for research on management information systems. *Manage. Sci.* **19**(5), 475–487.

Martin, J. (1967). "Design of Real Time Systems." Prentice-Hall, Englewood Cliffs, New Jersey.

Matlin, G. L. (1977). How to survive a management assessment. *Manage. Inf. Syst. Q.* **1**(1), 11–17.

Matlin, G. L. (1979). What is the value of investment in information systems. *Manage. Inf. Syst. Q.* **3**(3), 5–34.

Maynard, A. (1958). Automation for small-lot producers: Systems approach. *Automation* **54**(3), 8–15.

Mock, T. (1973). A longitudinal study of some information structure alternatives. *Data Base* **5**(2–4), 40–49.

Mock, T., Estrin, T., and Vasarhelyi, M. (1971). Learning patterns decision approach, and value of information. *J. Account. Res.* Spring, pp. 129–153.

Money (1980). The right stuff for careers in the eighties. *Money* May, pp. 64–76.

Munro, M., ed. (1979). MIS doctoral programs. *MIS Interrupt* **6**, 4.

Murdick, R. (1980). "MIS: Concepts and Design." Prentice-Hall, Englewood Cliffs, New Jersey.

Murdick, R., and Ross, J. (1977). "Introduction to Management Information Systems." Prentice-Hall, Englewood Cliffs, New Jersey.

Neuschel, R. (1960). "Management By System." McGraw-Hill, New York.

Newell, A., Shaw, J., and Simon, H. (1958). Elements of a theory of human problem solving. *Psychol. Rev.* **65**(3), 151–166.

Nolan, R. (1973a). Managing the computer resource: A stage hypothesis. *Commun. ACM* **16**(7), 399–405.

Nolan, R. (1973b). Plight of the EDP manager. *Harv. Bus. Rev.* **51**(3), 143–152.

Nolan, R., ed. (1974). "Managing the Data Resource Function." West Publishing, St. Paul, Minnesota.

Nolan, R. (1979). Managing the crises in data processing. *Harv. Bus. Rev.* **57**(2), 115–126.

Nolan, R., and Wetherbe, J. (1980). Toward a comprehensive framework for MIS research. *Manage. Inf. Syst. Q.* **4**(2), 1–18.

Olson, M., and Chervany, N. (1980). The relationship between organizational characteristics and the structure of the information systems function. *Manage. Inf. Syst. Q.* **4**(2), 57–68.

Optner, S. (1960). "Systems Analysis for Business Management." Prentice-Hall, Englewood Cliffs, New Jersey.

Optner, S. (1968). "Systems Analysis for Business Management," 2nd. ed. Prentice-Hall, Englewood Cliffs, New Jersey.

Orden, A. (1960). Man-machine-computer systems. *In* "Management Organization and the Computer" (G. Shultz and T. Whisler, eds.), pp. 67–86. Free Press, Glencoe, Illinois.

Orlicky, J. (1969). "The Successful Computer System: Its Planning, Development, and Design." McGraw-Hill, New York.

Pounds, W. (1969). The process of problem finding. *Ind. Manage. Rev.* **11**(1), 1–19.

Powers, R., and Dickson, G. (1973). MIS project management: Myths, opinions, and reality. *Calif. Manage. Rev.* **15**(3), 147–156.

Prince, T. (1966). "Information Systems for Management Planning and Control." R. D. Irwin, Homewood, Illinois.

Prokop, J., and Brooks, F., Jr. (1970). Decision making with computer graphics. *Proc. Full Jt. Comput. Conf.*

Radford, K. (1978). "Information Systems for Strategic Decisions." Reston Publishing Co., Reston, Virginia.

Richards, M., and Greenlaw, P. (1966). "Management Decision Making." R. D. Irwin, Homewood, Illinois.

Rosenzweig, J. (1960). The weapons systems management concept and electronic data processing. *Manage. Sci.* **6**(1), 149–164.

Rubenstein, A., Radnor, M., Baker, N., Heimen, O., and McColley, J. (1967). Some organizational factors related to the effectiveness of management science groups in industry. *Manage. Sci.* **13**(8), B508–B518.

Salveson, M. (1957). High speed operations research. *Harv. Bus. Rev.* **35**(4), 89–99.

Salveson, M. (1958). An analysis of decisions. *Manage. Sci.* **4**(3), 203–217.

Sanders, D. (1970). "Computers and Management," 1st ed. McGraw-Hill, New York.

Sanders, D. (1974). "Computers and Management," 2nd ed. McGraw-Hill, New York.

Schlosser, R. (1964). Psychology for the systems analyst. *Manage. Serv.* November-December, pp. 29–36.

Schroeder, R. G., and Benbasat, I. (1975). An experimental evaluation of the relationship of uncertainty in the environment to information used by decision makers. *Decis. Sci.* **6**(3), 536–567.

Schwartz, M. (1969). Computer project selection in the business enterprise. *J. Acc.* April, pp. 35–43.
Schwartz, M. (1970). MIS planning. *Datamation* 16(10), 28–31.
Scott Morton, M. (1971). "Management Decision Systems: Computer Based Support for Decision Making." Graduate School of Business, Harvard University, Cambridge, Massachusetts.
Senn, J. (1978). "Information Systems in Management." Wadsworth, Belmont, California.
Shannon, C. E. (1948). A mathematical theory of communication. *Bell Syst. Tech. J.* 4(2), 379–423.
Shannon, C. E., and Weaver, W. (1949). "The Mathematical Theory of Communication." Univ. of Illinois Press, Urbana.
Sharpe, W. (1969). "The Economics of Computers." Columbia Univ. Press, New York.
Shultz, G., and Whisler, T., eds. (1960). "Management Organization and the Computer." Free Press, Glencoe, Illinois.
Simon, H. (1947). "Administrative Behavior." Macmillan, New York.
Simon, H. (1957). "Models of Man." Wiley, New York.
Simon, H. (1960a). The corporation: Will it be managed by machine? *In* "Management and Corporations 1985" (M. Anshen and G. L. Bach, eds.), pp. 37–63. McGraw-Hill, New York.
Simon, H. (1960b). "The New Science of Management Decision." Harper & Row, New York.
Simon, H. (1965). "The Shape of Automation for Men and Management." Harper & Row, New York.
Simon, H., and Newell, A. (1958). Heuristic problem solving: The next advance in operations research. *Oper. Res.* 6(1), 1–10.
Simon, H., and Newell, A. (1960). What have computers to do with management? *In* "Management Organization and the Computer" (G. Shultz and T. Whisler, eds.), pp. 39–60. Free Press, Glencoe, Illinois.
Society for Management Information Systems (1970). "What is a Management Information System," SMIS Res. Rep. No. One. Society for Management Information Systems, Chicago, Illinois.
Statland, N., ed. (1977). Guidelines for cost accounting practices for data processing. *Data Base* 8(3), 2–20.
Stigler, G. J. (1961). The economics of information. *J. Political Econ.* 69, 213–225.
Stoller, D., and Van Horn, R. (1958). "Design of a Management Information System. Rand Corp. Doc. AD 400-353. Rand Corporation, Santa Monica, California.
Sweda, R. (1972). "Information Processing Management." Auerbach, New York.
Taylor, J., and Dean, N. (1966). Managing to manage the computer. *Harv. Bus. Rev.* 44(5), 98–110.
Thompson, H. (1965). "Joint Man/Machine Decisions." Systems and Procedures Association, Cleveland, Ohio.
Tiechroew, D., and Sayani, H. (1971). Automated system design. *Datamation* 7(16), pp. 25–30.
Van Horn, R. (1973). Empirical studies of management information systems. *Data Base* 5 (2–4), 173–182
Vazsonyi, A. (1958). "Scientific Programming in Business and Industry." Wiley, New York.
Vitalari, N. (1978). "The Evolution of Information Systems Support for Management," MISRC Working Pap. No. 78-01. Management Information Systems Research Center, University of Minnesota, Minneapolis.

Waldman, H., ed. (1975). "Computer Yearbook 76." International Electronic Information Services, Detroit, Michigan.
Weinwurm, G. (1961). Computer management control systems through the looking glass. *Manage. Sci.* **7**(4), 411–419.
Wendler, C. (1966). "Total Systems: Characteristics and Implementation." Systems and Procedures Association, Cleveland, Ohio.
Wetherbe, J. C. (1979). "Systems Analysis for Computer-Based Information Systems." West Publishing, St. Paul, Minnesota.
Wetherbe, J. C., and Dickson, G. W. (1979). Zero-based budgeting: An alternative to chargeout systems. *Inf. Manage.* **2**(4), 203–213.
Whisler, T. (1967). The impact of information technology on organizational control. *In* "The Impact of Computers on Management" (C. Meyers, ed.), pp. 16–49. MIT Press, Cambridge, Massachusetts.
Whisler, T., and Shultz, G. (1960). Information technology of management organizations. *In* "Management Organization and the Computer" (G. Schultz and J. Whisler, eds.), pp. 1–36. Free Press, Glencoe, Illinois.
Whittemore, B., and Yovits, M. C. (1973). A generalized conceptual development for the analysis and flow of information. *J. Am. Soc. Inf. Sci.* **24**(3), 221–229.
Whittemore, B., and Yovits, M. C. (1974). The quantification and analysis of information used in decision processes. *Inf. Sci.* **7**, 171–184.
Wiener, N. (1948). "Cybernetics." John Wiley, New York.
Wiener, N. (1950). "The Human Use of Human Beings: Cybernetics and Society." Doubleday, Garden City, New York.
Yourdon, E. (1972). "Design of On-line Computer Systems." Prentice-Hall, Englewood Cliffs, New Jersey.
Yourdon, E. (1975). "Techniques of Program Structure and Design." Prentice-Hall, Englewood Cliffs, New Jersey.
Yovits, M. C. (1969). Information science: Toward the development of a true scientific discipline. *Am. Doc.* **20**, 369–376.
Zani, W. (1970). Blueprint for MIS. *Harv. Bus. Rev.* **48**(6), 95–100.

Real-Time Distributed Computer Systems

W. R. FRANTA

Department of Computer Science and
Center for Microelectronic and Information Sciences
University of Minnesota
Minneapolis, Minnesota

E. DOUGLAS JENSEN*

Honeywell Systems and Research Center
Minneapolis, Minnesota

R. Y. KAIN

Department of Electrical Engineering
University of Minnesota
Minneapolis, Minnesota

GEORGE D. MARSHALL[†]

Honeywell Systems and Research Center
Minneapolis, Minnesota

1.	Introduction	40
	1.1 Distributed Processing	40
	1.2 The Real-Time Environment	43
	1.3 An Experimental System	45
2.	Hardware for Distributed Systems	45
	2.1 General Structure Alternatives	46
	2.2 HXDP Hardware Architecture	50

* Present address: Department of Computer Science, Carnegie-Mellon University, Pittsburgh, Pennsylvania 15213.
† Present address: Intel Corporation, Santa Clara, California 95051.

	2.3 General Communication Subnet Structure Options	51
	2.4 HXDP Hardware Design Details	53
	2.5 Remarks on the HXDP Hardware Design	60
3.	Software for Distributed Real-Time Systems	62
	3.1 Nonfunctional Objectives Affecting Real-Time Software	62
	3.2 HXDP Software Architecture	64
	3.3 General Design Options in Message-Based Systems	65
	3.4 HXDP Software Message Handling	66
	3.5 Remarks on the HXDP Software Design	75
4.	Summary	79
	References	81

1. Introduction

Distributed computer systems, containing several computers, may provide increased system availability and reliability. Their design is complex, involving the design of communications mechanisms in hardware and software and the selection of policies and mechanisms for distributed system control. The complex design issues may have simple solutions in well-understood application environments; the real-time control environment is one such environment. For these reasons, some early distributed computer system development projects have focused on the real-time application environment.

In this contribution we cover real-time distributed computer systems from promise through design and implementation. First, we discuss the motivation for distributed computer systems in terms of possible system characteristics attained by distributing the computational resources and then we characterize the real-time control application environment. In subsequent sections we review the options and issues related to hardware and software designs for distributed systems, and accompany the general discussions with the details of the design and implementation of the Honeywell Experimental Distributed Computing (Processor) system, known as HXDP. The HXDP project hardware design began in 1974, was realized in 1976, and system software design and realization were completed in 1978. Applications experiments are continuing in 1980.

1.1 Distributed Processing

Distributed systems consist of a federation of nearly autonomous processing elements (nodes) that cooperate to achieve the coherency necessary to realize a system. Both hardware and software are distributed. The following three sections provide the motivations for distributed systems, characterization of their nature, and problems in their realization.

1.1.1 Characterization of Distributed Systems

Distributed systems consist of a collection of nearly autonomous processing elements that communicate to realize a coherent computing system. Each processing element has (at least) a processor operating out of a private memory. The operation of each element is asynchronous with respect to the other elements. Communication is effected through an interconnection network whose topology can be a generalized network graph, but which is usually a bus or ring structure. Under the latter options the nodes share a so-called multiaccess (shared) channel provided by the bus or ring. Distributed systems use a distributed control strategy consistent with the objective of nearly autonomous nodes. With distributed control, nodes are equal; that is, no node is subject to the direction of a higher level authority, e.g., a centralized controlling node. Thus, system coherency is achieved by node cooperation; cooperation that extends from rules for access to the shared communication channel to rules for application process communications and synchronization (LeLann, 1977).

1.1.2 Promises of Distributed Systems

Distributed computer system development is motivated by several realized and promised benefits. The importance of these benefits and our ability to actualize them depend upon the application environment. More experience in design and application, most easily obtained from test-bed systems such as HXDP, is needed to better understand how to realize these promises.

First, distributed computer systems have the potential to provide better *system reliability* than do centralized computer systems. Second, they allow load-dependent or functional system *extensibility*. Third, distributed computer systems offer the potential for improved *performance* beyond that of centralized systems. Fourth, this improved performance could potentially be achieved at *lower cost* than centralized systems. Finally, distributed computer systems have the potential to be *easier to program*, and hence easier to use to realize an application system. This potential advantage has not been verified in practice, partly due to our primitive understanding of the relationships between applications processing requirements and the interprocess communication mechanisms necessary to support communication among the constituent processes.

These potential advantages of distributed computer systems over centralized computer systems are important in real-time applications; in addition, certain characteristics of the real-time control problem permit a close match between the distributed computer system and the application environment. Reliability, performance, and cost are important for all applications. Extensibility permits the design of generic distributed computer systems for real-time applications, using functional and capacity extensions to accommodate particular applications without redesigning the basic system. Ease of programming permits a low-cost, timely realization of the system. For real-time applications, distributed systems offer an additional *positioning advantage* over centralized systems. Processing power can be placed at "natural" sites in the system. For example, radar data can be collected and processed at the point of reception rather than at a centralized node, reducing communications bandwidth needs. Similarly, intelligence can be associated with actuators physically distributed from the sensors.

1.1.3 Problems Associated with Implementing Distributed Computer Systems

There are problems in implementing distributed computer systems, ranging from interconnection hardware, through executive software, to application software. Some of these problems admit solutions using well-established techniques, whereas others challenge our understanding of the issues.

At the hardware level, the design of processing elements and interconnection devices is well understood, but complex trade-offs exist between the functionality assigned to hardware and the cost and complexity required to provide that functionality. We need more experience with both test-bed and deployed systems to quantify such trades.

At the executive software level, we need to better understand basic intercommunication mechanisms. Should, for example, interconnections be based on virtual circuit or datagram communications (Davies *et al.*, 1979)?

We also need to better our understanding of the match between the design of the underlying mechanisms and a model of a potential application. Specifically, how should the software components be physically distributed among the physical nodes of the system, and what are the consequences of those strategies on the communication pattern among those components? This issue is critical as it ultimately determines the performance of the system. What we need, then, are models that reflect the consequences, in terms of required message traffic, of a given process distribution. From this information, we could generate a description of the communication patterns at the message-generation level so that we could characterize the communication loadings and hence the communication delays.

In the applications area, we need experience in the use of languages that support distributed systems, including experience with message-based interprocess communication mechanisms and devices. For example, those interprocess communications mechanisms wherein a process references an object in its own address space to communicate with a process at another node better support modularization than do those schemes wherein the process references an object in the address space of the destination process (Franta and Chlamtac, 1981). Furthermore, we need experience with system-generation tools, interprocess communication mechanisms, debugging aids, instrumentation strategies, and diagnostics. In short, although considerable progress can be made via paper and pencil projects, there is definitely a need for the kind of experience realized by having built distributed computing systems including hardware, executive software, and applications software. In short, the proof of the pudding is in the eating, and additional experience must be obtained to make formidable advances in the design and construction of distributed computing systems.

1.2 The Real-Time Environment

Many real-time control systems have top-level feedback loops divided between a "controller" and the outside environment. The controller accepts data from sensors, performs a computation, and uses the results to move actuators. The consequences of actuator movement are fed back to the controller through the outside environment and the sensors. For example, an autopilot accepts inertial position and air data, computes, and moves control surfaces as needed to achieve the desired aircraft state (e.g., constant altitude). The control surface movement affects subsequent airspeed, altitude, and/or position sensor readings.

Digital real-time control systems are typically designed to regularly sense conditions within the controlled process (or system) and to regularly respond with signals to actuators that control the process. The regularity of process sensing and actuator signalling is an important influence simplifying computer system design. As a consequence, our initial efforts in distributed computer system design were directed towards the real-time environment. Real-time system activity regularity allows static allocations, which are simpler to select and implement than dynamic ones.

The real-time environment can be demanding, however, in terms of performance. Performance in real-time systems is measured more in terms of response time than throughput—violation of an application time constraint often constitutes a system failure. In addition, events may occur in bursts after exceptions arise, requiring a large and immediate increase in processing over that needed under steady-state conditions.

High-performance requirements often dictate the use of a large centralized processor. The real-time control environment has enough structure that the system performance requirements can be met by a confederation of smaller processors.

A real-time control computer performs specific functions, which are known at the time of system configuration. The ratio of cyclic to event-driven functions depends very much on the application, but the former always constitute a significant percentage. The basic feedback structure, in fact, suggests that the controller subsystems can be viewed as a pipeline that can be realized by a chain of modules through which information flows unidirectionally. The pipeline structure may be inherent to many real-time control problems, or it may be an artifact of the traditional views taken by feedback control system designers. Using this view, the processing can be performed by 10–100 processes, which are usually pipelined and can operate concurrently. The decomposition of the processing into a set of concurrent processes is presently done *a priori,* manually, and heuristically. The decomposition criteria include minimizing interprocess communication bandwidth, permitting interprocess communication in simple messages subject to reasonableness tests (rather than raw data), allowing the assignment of physical or functional meaning to processes and interprocess communication messages, and process simplicity.

A good decomposition will result in a system using processes that require a modest 30K–300K instructions to be executed per second on small operands (1–6 bits). The space for code and local operands for each process can be relatively compact, fewer than 64K 16-bit words. Process references, furthermore, tend to be highly localized, both spatially and temporally. Therefore, the performance and space requirements of each process can be met by a minicomputer, even though a simple minicomputer may not meet the total system needs. Processes can be loosely synchronized through message exchange, access to shared variables, and signaling to maintain execution precedence constraints. The required interprocess communication rates may vary from hundreds of bits to tens of kilobits per second per process. Messages usually contain on the order of 1–100 data words. Physical inertia in the application makes interprocess communication latencies from hundreds of microseconds to tens of milliseconds tolerable. These latency requirements, coupled with the loose coupling among the constituent processes, suggest that the system be realized by a set of processors coupled through a message-passing mechanism. In many cases there are clusters of processes requiring more intra-cluster communication; if so, all processes in the cluster might be assigned to the same processor.

1.3 An Experimental System

In this article we summarize issues that concern the design of real-time computer systems and then present details of the Honeywell Experimental Distributed Process (HXDP) system (Jensen, 1978): a test-bed system designed, built, and used in experiments to determine its effectiveness. Since HXDP was designed as a test-bed for laboratory experiments about the design and operation of future high-performance distributed real-time control systems, the system had to meet flexibility and data-collection requirements that make the system viable as a laboratory test vehicle, in addition to the real-time distributed computer system requirements discussed above. Experimental systems should be easily reconfigurable. Moreover, it should be easy to change operating policies and mechanisms within the system. Finally, it should be easy to monitor system operation under various experimental conditions.

The HXDP system incorporates standard minicomputer hardware for processing elements but otherwise uses components specifically designed for distributed computation in real-time environments. Novel interconnection hardware, system control software, and system policies were developed for the HXDP system. The system hardware was constructed, microcode controlling the hardware was implemented, a software kernel for interprocess message communication was designed and implemented, computer models of important system behavioral characteristics were developed, and experimental application systems were implemented. This complete sequence of implementation, modeling, and evaluation provides guidance for future distributed computer system design and implementation.

2. Hardware for Distributed Systems

In this section we describe the architecture of distributed computer systems in general and of HXDP in particular, emphasizing the functional operation and implementation of the HXDP system. We first discuss the general range of system configuration and organization alternatives, with some discussions of the trade-offs. We present the overall HXDP system architecture, including HXDP hardware characteristics. Finally, we offer some lessons learned from the project and recommendations for future

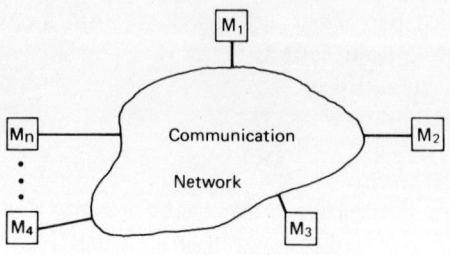

Fig. 1. A distributed system.

projects of a similar nature, in terms of both general system features and internal design details.

2.1 General Structure Alternatives

Distributed systems are collections of modules interconnected through a communications mechanism, as depicted in Fig. 1. This view is appropriate at both hardware and software levels. At either level, the major system design questions concern the nature of the modules and of their interconnection, including the view of the interconnections as seen from the modules. In Section 2.1 we cover these issues at the physical level; the software level is covered in Sections 3.2 and 3.3

2.1.1 Module Granularity Selection

The designer of a distributed system must carefully consider what functions and modules are to be distributed and, in particular, the degree of granularity. At the low end of granularity, systems in which the subcomponents of a uniprocessor are physically distributed are sometimes called "distributed systems." This architecture suffers from performance and modularity drawbacks, leading to lower system reliability than might be available within distributed architectures. Using complete computers as system nodes moves highest bandwidth communications to within nodes, improving system performance. Reliability is also increased as sharing is restricted to communications paths, so that the effects of node failure could be limited, by proper design, to those processes assigned to the failed node. Additionally, decoupling the individual processes running within the system relieves software complexity, improving the chances of developing correct software with minimum effort. Furthermore, standard computer modules, augmented with communication facilities, can be used to construct such systems. This approach is compatible with the real-time environment, in particular, with the view of a real-time system as a collection of small, fairly autonomous processes with relatively low intercommunication needs. In addition, a system structure with a variable number of identical, autonomous processing element components can be made highly configurable: the number of system nodes is a design parameter, and can be tailored to the application without a complete redesign of the system.

2.1.2 Connection Topologies

The physical connection topology of a distributed computer system must be carefully selected as it impacts a number of important properties of the distributed system. System reliability and expandibility are strongly influenced by topological selection; with certain topologies single points of failure exist, and system reliability will be severely and adversely affected by failure at these points. System expandability is also affected by similar topological considerations. The system physical topology also affects the mechanisms required to correctly route messages among the processes in the system and consequently impacts the complexity of both hardware and software interfaces between processors or processes and the complexity of the interconnection mechanism.

A variety of interconnection topologies could be used (Anderson and Jensen, 1975). For simplicity of implementation and regularity of design, however, several categories of topological structures are commonly considered for the construction of loosely coupled computer systems. These are illustrated in Fig. 2, which shows the bus, the ring (loop), the star, the fully interconnected structure, and the partially interconnected structure. In the bus a single communication link is shared by all nodes. In the loop messages traverse the individual links of the ring and are actively relayed at each node around the ring. In the star topology, the communicating processes are at the "leaves" of the star, and every message must pass through the central node, where it is routed to the appropriate destination node. The fully interconnected topology provides a branch for every possible path, and no relaying is necessary. Partial interconnections, as illustrated in Fig. 2e, reduce the cost of the full interconnection at the expense of requiring message relays for certain messages, while other messages can be passed from source to destination in one hop.

System reliability is affected by system topology in important ways. With some topologies, such as the ring and the star, the signal must be actively relayed between the source and the destination. If the active relaying module fails, the communication link may be lost. In particular, in the star, if the central node fails, no interprocessor communication is pos-

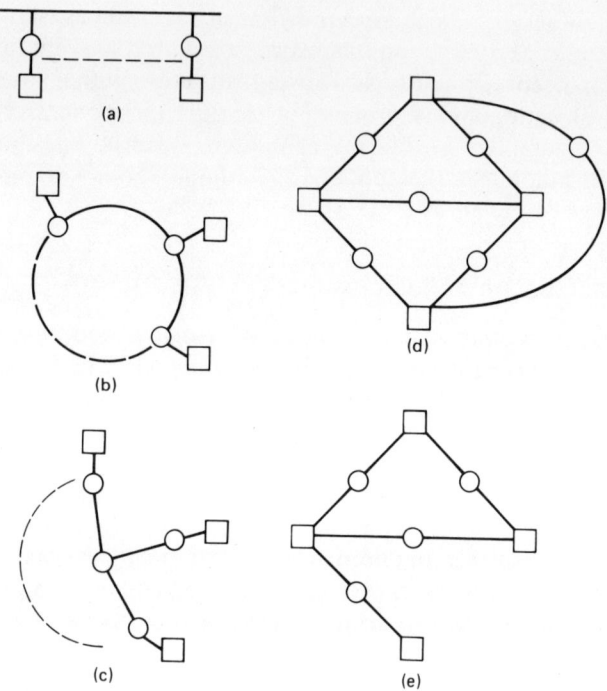

FIG. 2. Interconnection options: (a) bus; (b) ring (loop); (c) star; (d) fully interconnected (four modules); (d) partially interconnected (four modules). (○) Interface module; (□) computing modules.

sible. In the loop, the failure of one active relay causes failure of the loop, unless a bypass is used. With full interconnection, failure of any link or interface used in any link disables only one interconnection path, and the system may in fact be able to construct an alternate path using multiple hops with message relay. The bus system can be constructed so that the bus itself is entirely passive and therefore highly reliable, although this requires special interface techniques to reduce the probability that failures at the interface disable the bus.

System topology affects system expandability. In the loop topology, every node is connected to the system through the same small number of interfaces, but in order to expand the system the loop must be broken, disrupting the system. The star topology, on the other hand, allows the inclusion of additional leaves as long as the interface capability of the central node is not exceeded. The fully interconnected topology requires that every new node supply a communication link to every old node, which makes expansion difficult and certainly places a low upper bound on the feasible number of fully interconnected nodes. This consideration drives one to the partial connection compromise in which complete interconnection need not be provided for all nodes, but messages therefore may have to be relayed, introducing failure points, as previously discussed. The passive bus topology provides the simplest expandability, as every new node only need connect to the bus, independent of the remainder of the system. Notice, however, that as the system expands, more communication must be handled on the same links, and therefore the system size may be limited not only by its expandability but also by the bandwidth of the links.

System topology also affects the complexity of the interface and message routing mechanisms. In loop and bus systems the interface need only recognize which messages are destined for the attached node and which are not, whereas in star, fully, or partially interconnected systems, the message passing interface must make routing decisions to determine how best to relay messages destined for other nodes within the system. In the star topology, the ring topology, and the full interconnection topology the physical interface is quite simple, as each link is point to point and no routing decisions need be made.

Due to reliability, expandability, and complexity considerations, real-time distributed computer systems usually use either bus or loop interconnection structures.

Bus systems can utilize a single conductor with serial data transmission (Metcalf and Boggs, 1976) or multiple conductors with parallel data transmission (IEEE Instrumentation and Measurements Group, 1975). Serial transmission is usually preferred over all but the shortest distances, because the cost of the connectors, cables, and interface electronics per signal is high in parallel transmission schemes. Nodes can be connected passively to the bus cable in such a way that a failure in one node is unlikely to cause the failure of the entire bus. A bus topology is highly flexible, since no other node is directly affected by the addition or deletion of a node; the incremental cost of a new node is a single connection. There will typically be some upper limit on the number of nodes that can be connected to the same global bus, for reasons involving the analog design of the bus; this limit can generally be made high with respect to the needs of any specific class of applications.

In ring topologies (see Fig. 2) the signal cable is broken at each node, and some delay and buffering logic is introduced to allow the node to recognize and remove or change the passing data. The buffering may be a few bits or an entire message. One loop design (Farmer|and|Newell, 1969) operates the loop much like a bus: there can be at most one packet in transit at a time. Another loop organization (Pierce, 1972) introduces packet-size buffers in-line in each node and exploits this additional buffering to gain some data transmission concurrency; there can be different packets circulating simultaneously in the loop. With either scheme, because each node on the loop has active components "in line" with the data, the loop has additional failure modes (beyond those of a bus) which can cause the failure of one node to bring down the entire network; additional features must be added to compensate for them. The ring topology is highly flexible, since the addition of a new node requires only that the ring be cut at one point, and the new node added. Rings do not have an analog-design-imposed limit on the number of nodes in the system, since each node transmits to exactly one other node. The delay through the system increases with each additional node, and so there may be a practical limit on the number of nodes determined by the response time requirements of an application.

2.2 HXDP Hardware Architecture

The HXDP system uses an interconnected set of computer processing elements connected to a global serial bus.

2.2.1 Physical Structure

The HXDP system is a collection of processing elements (PEs), each containing a mini- or microcomputer with its own private memory, and some peripheral devices (see Fig. 3). The processor address spaces do not

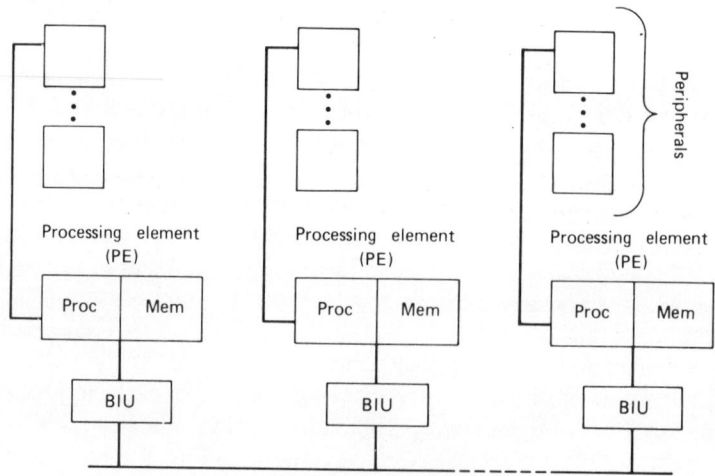

Fig. 3. HXDP hardware architecture.

interset. Each PE is connected to a single global serial bus via a special interface device called a bus interface unit (BIU), which provides a powerful set of message-based communication services. Each computer supports a small number of resident nonconflicting processes, each interacting with other processes in the system through messages passed along the bus.

2.2.2 The Bus Interface Unit

Interprocess message handling functions could be supported entirely by software, but hardware modules that handle basic message passing functions greatly ease software complexity and improve system performance. The HXDP bus interface unit (BIU) is the hardware module supporting message passing from the memory of one computer to the memory of another. Since the BIU interface with the computer is directly to the memory, the functionality provided by the BIUs and the message communication mechanism is applicable to numerous host computer architectures. The BIU functionality, therefore, is crucial to system success; in addition, due to the difficulty of implementing system diagnostic and monitoring functions entirely in software, hardware support provided by the BIU is essential to the success of HXDP as a test-bed system. A detailed description of the BIU is presented in Section 2.4.

2.3 General Communication Subnet Structure Options

In this section we describe the general structure of communication subnets implemented by communication interface units (CIUs) connecting processors to communication links. We examine the functions provided by this net and suggest the distribution of functionality between the local pieces of the system executive and the communication interface units. As the links do not perform information processing, they will be ignored in the remainder of the discussion.

2.3.1 Functional Overview

The following discussion is based on the process view of communications, in which all communication is effected by messages that originate in some process and are destined to another (possibly the same) process. This view is flexible and applies directly to many message-based interprocess communication system designs; it does not, however, apply to systems using communications through shared memory objects. According to this view, an interprocess communication is initiated when the sending process executes a primitive system call requesting that a communication be initiated. At that time an indivisible (as far as the process can tell) operation of sending the message is performed by the communication subnet. Whether the sending process "blocks" (waits for confirmation of completion of the message transmission) or not is a distributed systems software design decision, which has only minor effects on the communications subnet. The system call executed by the sending process initiates activities in the system's message-handling software, which typically will queue the message, pending the availability of the communications interface unit to handle the message. Later the communications interface unit will pick up the message and transmit it through the communications links. The receiving communications interface unit will accept the message, check it for errors, and queue it for the receiving process or the receiving system's message-handling software. The relative timing of these events may be different from the foregoing descriptions; one could design a system, for example, in which communications on the link are initiated by the receiver rather than by the sender.

The general message flow just described is complemented by a number of support functions provided by the communication subnet. These include message formatting (different formats will be required at different stages of the communication), error control, system monitoring, and diagnostic handling when monitoring indicates the need for a diagnostic. In addition, the communications modules must map message addresses, manage queues, allocate the communications bandwidth, and perform other functions necessary for correct operation.

2.3.2 Function Allocation

The functions performed by the communications subnet are, as mentioned above, performed by cooperation between system software and communication interface units. The system designer must determine the allocation of functions between these two classes of modules.

Message addresses must be used by the senders and receivers to ensure correct routing. Different system policies can be utilized. Typically the system software will perform some logical-to-physical address mapping, and the CIU hardware may use physical or logical addresses to distinguish messages for local destinations from other messages on the communications link or to determine proper routing for messages that must be forwarded to other links.

Typically both the system software and the communication interface unit will reformat messages passing through the subnet; the system software will combine the message contents with the destination address to form a message that can be handled by the communication interface unit, which will add control signals and redundancy check codes before transmitting the message on the communication link. Upon reception, message formats are verified and the message taken apart in a complementary manner. In some structures control messages may be generated and passed among modules within the communications subnet in order to determine or synchronize system state or to select routing choices; those messages are never be seen by applications processes and may not be visible to the system executive either.

Queues in the interfaces (between application processes and the system software and between the system software and the communication interface unit hardware) must be managed by the units using those queues.

Message flow control, which may be required as a consequence of queues being full, is handled by the units detecting the fact that a queue may be full. Since a queue may be found to be full, the sending module must await a positive acknowledgment of message reception before deleting its copy of the message. After receiving a negative acknowledgement or no response within an appropriate response interval, the sender might request retransmission of the message at a later time. Such message flow control functions may be performed either by the communication interface unit or by the system software. Message flow control among the application processes may be necessary; it will not impact the design of the communications mechanisms, however.

Error control in response to the failure of redundancy checks in arriving messages is handled by units detecting the errors. Communication interface units, for example, might automatically retry the transmission of a message if its reception appears erroneous, although after some number of retries the operating system should be notified so that appropriate action can be taken. At the system executive level, few error control functions will be found in typical systems.

System status monitoring and consequent diagnostic information production, like error control, are handled by all the modules in the system.

The details of these management functions and their implementation will differ from system to system; in the next section we discuss the details of how these functions were performed in the HXDP design. The HXDP design is characterized by the placement of many of these communication functions in the communication interface unit, called the BIU. The functions assigned to the BIU could have been performed by systems software, with a consequent loss of message communication bandwidth.

2.4 HXDP Hardware Design Details

In this section we describe the policies and mechanisms used in the HXDP design, concentrating on those influencing the structure of the bus interface unit. We also discuss the structure and functionality internal to the HXDP bus interface units.

2.4.1 HXDP Policies

The policies utilized in the HXDP system affect the algorithms for addressing, queue management, flow control, bus allocation, and error checking and status monitoring.

2.4.1.1 Addressing. Processes in the HXDP system communicate messages through "windows" such that the identity of a window implies the identity of the destination for messages sent through that window. The operating system module invoked when a message is sent through a window consequently must know the logical connection of the sending window to a receiving window, so that it can construct a 16-bit logical address for the outgoing message. The ideal HXDP system design would allow the system to utilize this address throughout the message communication process. In the realistic HXDP system, a speed limitation restricts the receiving bus interface units to recognizing not more than about 25 different logical addresses. The original BIU firmware was coded to recognize up to eight different logical addresses; the subsequent system software design uncovered this limit, and the decision was made to overcome the limitation by system software and not by microcode changes, so that the operating system could not, in fact, use the logical destination address on the message, as the number of destinations resident at one physical location may exceed eight. Consequently, the software in the sending executive software must place the message in an envelope addressed to the receiving executive system, rather than to the destination user process. The 16-bit logical address placed in the message in this manner is used unchanged by the hardware communication mechanisms.

2.4.1.2 Queue Management. Queues are used in the HXDP system as interfaces between the BIUs and the rest of the system. Each BIU has one queue of outgoing messages (leaving the local processor) and eight queues for incoming messages. These queues are managed by manipulating pointers held in the memory of the local processing element and in the BIU hardware. Queue size and locations are specified by the software and can be changed to match any application environment. The queues are implemented in a circular space; read and write pointers are used cooperatively by the BIU hardware and the executive software to permit noninterferring access. Figure 4 depicts the information structure of these queues.

2.4.1.3 Message Flow Control. Significant message flow control activities in the HXDP system occur at both the BIU and the executive software levels. At the BIU level, messages are refused at the receiving end if

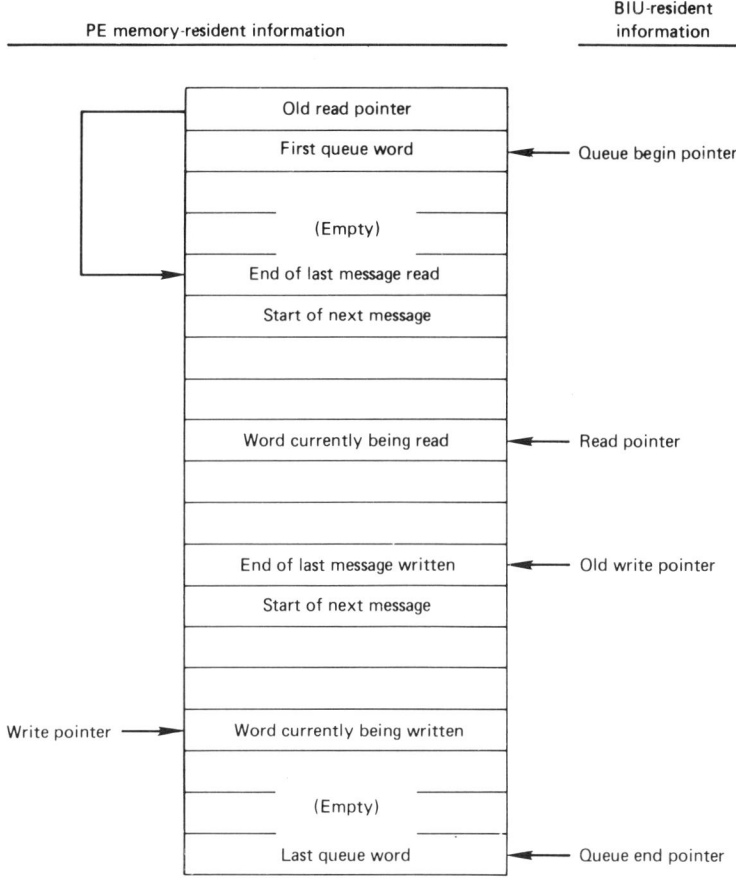

FIG. 4. Example output queue structure.

the appropriate queue for receiving the message does not have enough space to hold the message; message refusal is indicated by sending a negative acknowledgment to the sender, indicating that the reason for the negative acknowledgment is the fullness of the input queue. At the executive level, messages can be rejected if the receiving process no longer exists or if the process was assigned to a processor of a node that has failed. In this case, the originating executive process will attempt an alternate disposition of the message, as discussed in Section 3.4

2.4.1.4 Bus Allocation. The HXDP bus is managed by using a fully decentralized method of bus allocation called vector-driven proportional access (VDPA). VDPA allows the system configurator to assign fractional bus bandwidth individually to each source node, according to the application requirements, without wasting significant bandwidth on processors temporarily without need of their assigned share. Conceptually, a single system-wide arbitrary-length circular allocation list defines the order and the frequency with which each BIU is allowed an opportunity to transmit a message. The list contains BIU identifications (IDs) in arbitrary order with arbitrary duplication allowed. The number of times a BIU ID appears on the list determines its fractional bandwidth allocation when every BIU has a message to send in every available slot. Since the slot width is variable, this VDPA scheme is not a traditional time-division multiplex scheme, in which each transmitter receives a constant bandwidth; rather, in VDPA, any BIU can use almost all of the bus bandwidth if no other BIU has a message to transmit.

2.4.1.5 Error Checking. Error checking is handled in the HXDP system by both parity bit and cyclic redundancy check (CRC) techniques. The destination address included in the message is checked with two parity bits, while the entire message is checked with a 16-bit CRC checkword. All these redundancies are generated and checked at the BIU level; the sending BIU inserts the parity checks on the destination address and also generates the CRC code for transmission at the end of the message. The receiving BIU checks these redundancies and, if they do not check properly, responds appropriately; on CRC failure, a message indicating the failure is sent, but the BIU does not respond if the destination address appears incorrect. The latter policy is designed to prevent multiple responses to a message whose address has been incorrectly transmitted or received. Unless the sending BIU receives a positive acknowledgment within a short time after sending a message, it will retry the transmission several times; the number of automatic retries is a BIU firmware constant (in our experiments, three retries were allowed).

2.4.1.6 Status Monitoring. Status monitoring in the HXDP system is extensively used to reduce the probability of error and to prevent loss of synchronization among active BIUs. Each BIU in the system tracks every transaction on the bus, performing every operation of the receiver except the actual copying of the message contents into a memory queue associated with the BIU. If a BIU detects an illegal transaction in this manner, it logs the condition and optionally interrupts the attached processor. Status monitoring features such as these are very useful as instrumentation and diagnostic aids, especially when experimenting with prototype systems such as HXDP.

2.4.2 HXDP Hardware Mechanisms

The HXDP hardware directly implements several unique mechanisms to support logical message addressing, bus allocation, and status monitoring.

Logical message addressing is supported within the BIUs. Each BIU holds a list of logical addresses corresponding to the message destinations resident in the associated PE. The BIU compares the destination address field of each message passing on the bus against the list; the BIU thereby selects messages it should copy and which it should acknowledge.

Bus allocation is supported by a distributed implementation of the VDPA policy; there is no centralized allocation list in HXDP. The same effect is achieved by a set of bit-wide "time-slot vectors," one in each BIU. If the selected bit in a BIU's time-slot vector is "1," that BIU may transmit a message in the current bus slot. Bit selection is controlled by a local pointer. On initialization, all pointers are set to the same value. During normal operation, all pointers are advanced by a special control signal sent over the bus when a BIU relinquishes bus control. Since pointer synchronization errors would be disastrous, the BIUs are designed to detect and recover from loss of synchronization. Pointer information is sent in each message. Each BIU maintains an allocation history and current state information. Whenever a BIU detects an unresolvable error, it disables its transmitter temporarily while monitoring the bus to gain enough information to resynchronize.

The HXDP message transfer protocol was designed to be as reliable as practically possible within the constraints of response time and the amount of system state information kept within BIUs. The basic message transfer protocol used to send a single message is rather conventional, with exceptions discussed in the following text. Figure 5 shows the basic format used in transmitting one message. The BIUs employ an explicit acknowledge/negative acknowledge protocol to reliably transfer messages from sender to receiver. A successful message transfer consists of the message transmission, an acknowledgment (ACK) from the receiver, and an end-of-transaction signal (EOT) from the sender which is both a response to the ACK and a bus reallocation signal to all BIUs. A BIU can transmit at most one message (and its retries) in each of its time slots. If no outgoing messages are waiting in the queue, it sends only the EOT signal, initiating immediate bus reallocation. Typically, bus reallocation will allow another BIU to send a queued message, though the VDPA vector may allocate consecutive slots to a BIU with high-traffic requirements.

An important part of HXDP BIU status monitoring is the checking of the pointer used in the VDPA allocation policy implementation. Every time a BIU transmits a message, it inserts its current value of the index

| SOT | Destination | Parity | Index Value | Word Count | Message | CRC Check | EOT |

FIG. 5. Bus message format.

pointer into the header of the message. Every BIU checks this value against its current pointer value; if they do not match, the receiving BIU updates its index pointer if it is only off by one; otherwise it turns off its transmitter and resynchronizes after the consistent observation of two successive transmissions of index values (i.e., in two messages, possibly separated by empty slots). This particular status monitoring and correction feature is extremely important for an allocation algorithm such as VDPA, in which the distributed internal states of BIUs must be consistent to avoid chaos.

Because BIUs may disable their transmitters and because they may fail, a reliable communications protocol implementation must include a mechanism for recovering to "normal" operation after an expected signal does not arrive. Every BIU monitors every transaction; after every message or control signal every BIU starts a time-out timer. If a BIU's timer reaches time-out without a signal arriving, the BIU transmits an EOT signal to terminate the allocation slot. Each BIU's time-out value differs from all others by at least the sum of the round trip bus transit time and the time to execute firmware to select the consequent action (the latter dominates the timing); therefore, only one BIU will transmit an EOT.

2.4.3 HXDP Hardware Structure

The BIU is implemented as a set of seven cooperating hardware controllers with one of them, the input controller, implementing a firmware engine, which executes the algorithms for all receive functions, bus allocation, and overall BIU management and control. The BIU interfaces with a single serial bus that uses Manchester bit encoding for message contents and Manchester coding violations for low-level system control signals.

2.4.3.1 BIU Structure. The input controller (IC) has overall control of BIU functions. It monitors all bus traffic, determines when the BIU has control of the bus, and either transmits an EOT to relinquish control (if it has no message to send) or causes the output controller to send a message. The IC also passes input messages from the bus to the input queue. The IC performs BIU diagnostic and recovery functions, including detecting errors and handling retry requests, generating PE interrupts for exceptional conditions detected by the microcode, and maintaining system status lists.

The most complex hardware controller is the input controller (IC); it implements the BIU firmware engine, executing vertical microcode at 3–4 million instructions per second. The IC has a 64-word register file, a parameter memory, an arithmetic/logic unit (ALU), a 16-word microprogram address stack for the instruction sequencer, and a number of dedicated input and output control lines to the rest of the BIU. The microprogram memory is a read/write memory to allow flexibility in the test-bed system; this memory can be written into only by the PE. There are but two instruction types: jump and control. During a control instruction the input controller can, in one cycle, read two 16-bit operands, perform a logical or arithmetic operation on them, write the result to a possibly different third location, and perform a conditional skip. A jump instruction is similar, but substitutes a full-range conditional jump, call, or return for result writing.

The output controller (OC) handles the transmission of messages from the output queue (OQ) to the global bus. It is controlled by the IC; each time the OC is started, it sends one complete message from the OQ, reading the message from PE memory via DMA.

The direct memory access (DMA) controller coordinates all DMA requests arising from within the BIU; DMA operations are requested independently by the IC and the OC through dedicated, noninterfering address and data registers and request flags. There actually are two distinct parts of the DMA controller; one acquiring the processor/memory bus of the PE, the other controlling the actual data transfers once the bus has been acquired. The modulator interface (MI) controls the transmitting bus driver and does parallel-to-serial data conversion. It accepts word-by-word transmit requests and control (sync) signal transmit requests from the input controller and the output controller. To send messages the MI takes the parallel data, converts it to serial data, and passes the serial data stream to the bus driver, inserting check bits where required. The bus driver performs Manchester encoding and generates synchronization signals on request.

The demodulator interface (DI) receives serial data and bus sync signals from the bus receiver, which has decoded the Manchester codes and separated the sync signals from the data stream. The bus sync signals are passed directly to the IC; the serial data is converted in the DI to parallel words and then buffered to the IC. The DI also removes check bits from the incoming data stream and controls the flags (read by the IC) which indicate the status of the received data (i.e., parity error or coding violation).

The interrupt controller (ITC) is used by the IC to cause interrupts in the PE; the ITC is an interface controller isolating the IC from the specific interface requirements of the PE hardware. The BIU firmware can generate ten different vectored interrupt levels, nine of them individually armed and enabled (the tenth is an automatically generated "catastrophic hardware failure" signal, which is always armed). The design of the interrupt controller is unusual in that it can remember up to two occurrences of all nine interrupts (a total of 18 events) while administrating a (potentially) third occurrence of one interrupt for the processor.

The programmed input/output (PIO) controller provides an interface giving the PE software the capability to initialize, control and monitor the BIU. Through the PIO interface, the PE can read the IC register file, the IC address stack and address stack pointer, the microprogram memory, the OC pointer registers, and a 16-bit status vector. The PE can write into the register file, the top of the stack, the microprogram memory, the OC pointer registers, and a BIU control register. The PIO interface provides an extensive BIU diagnostic capability to the PE since it can read and modify BIU registers and memory both while the BIU is operating and when it is idle. In addition, the PE can use the PIO interface to change policy parameters within the BIU.

2.4.3.2 Bus Details. The HXDP global bus can be up to approximately 1000 m long, and can have up to 64 physical nodes connected via short (1-m) stubs. The data rate of the bus is 1.25 M bits/sec. The BIUs use synchronous data transmission, with Manchester encoding of the data bits; a special coding violation waveform at the beginning of each block establishes bit synchronization. HXDP was designed to exploit the error detection potential of the Manchester encoding to detect and flag any invalid bit at the receiver, thus greatly reducing the probability that noise on the bus would be accepted as valid data.

The sync waveform is a special Manchester code violation that all receivers scan for when the bus is idle; scanning is disabled when a valid sync signal is detected. The two bits immediately following the sync signal specify its class (EOT, etc.). Data transfers in HXDP are synchronized by message, not by word, as in MIL-STD-1553B (U.S. Air Force, 1973). This results in a higher data rate, since there is no time devoted to interword idle gaps and sync waveforms between successive words of the same message. This trade-off requires a high-stability clock, since HXDP must correctly decode a longer string of bits from one synchronization signal than 1553, and since the receiver design favors error detection over adaptive clocking.

2.5 Remarks on the HXDP Hardware Design

Two separate prototype HXDP systems were built, one with two nodes and one with three nodes; the two systems have been combined to form a five-node system.

The design decision to off-load message handling functionality from the

REAL-TIME DISTRIBUTED COMPUTER SYSTEMS

processors to the bus interface units was a good decision. In this implementation the BIUs supported message handling mechanisms, but did not make any policy decisions. With a single communication link, the significant policy decisions concern whether messages should have priorities and should be transmitted ahead of queued messages if their priorities are high enough. Our bus bandwidth was high enough relative to the number of processors and their speed that message queueing was not significant and priority policies would have had little effect on system performance.

Message queues in HXDP hold actual messages, rather than pointers to messages. This design decision may not have been so good; the basic trade compares the complexity of allocating message buffer space against message copying overhead. Designers of future systems might consider using queues containing pointers, rather than message contents.

The VDPA bus allocation mechanism was a good design for real-time applications in which message loading patterns can be accurately anticipated. Dynamic changes of the allocation vectors during system operation, while possible in principle, were not attempted during our experiments, partly because erroneous incompatible vector settings could result in overlapping ("colliding") bus transmissions. Synchronization of vector updates would be necessary to insure no overlap. Protocols to guarantee no overlap can be designed using messages passed among support software kernels in the processing elements.

Bus allocation patterns with multiple slots for single processors can be used in VDPA to allocate more bandwidth for selected processors. The application system designer should allocate slots to BIUs in proportion to their message transmission demand rates. Within this constraint, determining optimal VDPA slot assignments seems a complex problem, requiring consideration of a combinatorial number of assignments, although in our experience an even spacing of slots within the VDPA vector always produced good results (high correlations in traffic patterns might suggest an uneven spacing).

Use of logical destination names (rather than physical ones) supports system flexibility and reconfigurability and is, therefore, helpful. Some applications may require messages to be "broadcast" to several (or all) destinations. It is difficult to insure correct, reliable recognition of, and recovery from an unsuccessful broadcast. In HXDP we emphasized reliability and a small number of BIU states, which precluded implementing broadcasts. They could have been added by changes to BIU microcode. Designers of other systems may wish to provide low-level support for message broadcast; in HXDP we supplied it through library processes (see Section 3.4.3).

3. Software for Distributed Real-Time Systems

Contemporary software practices, especially those derived from operating systems research, may not be applicable in real-time environments, due to nonfunctional objectives for real-time systems. Since different applications may require different system functional capabilities to support the differing objectives, general test-bed software might be designed to provide only the basic mechanisms supporting system distribution—specifically, interprocess communication. In this section, after discussing nonfunctional system requirements that impact the structural design and support message-based interprocess communications, we turn to the general design options for message-based interprocess communication mechanisms. We describe the mechanisms developed and implemented for the HXDP executive kernel. We informally evaluate this design to close the section.

3.1 Nonfunctional Objectives Affecting Real-Time Software

All real-time control systems must satisfy the constraint that a given amount of processing be performed in a fixed interval of time. The degree to which this constraint affects the executive software appears to be a function of processor speed: when the processor is fast relative to the computational requirements, then simple, iterative program control structures can be used; when the processor is slow, event or interrupt-driven structures must be used, with a corresponding increase in complexity and difficulty of verification (Post, 1978; Bender, 1976). Due to this relationship between the complexity of program control structure and processor speed, different program control structures may be appropriate for different applications. Distributed computer systems can be a cost-effective way to provide sufficient processing capability to permit simple program control structures in real-time applications.

3.1.1 Device Control

In the Dijkstra hierarchical operating system model (Dijkstra, 1968) devices are managed at a level of abstraction between the hardware and the applications programs. In the classical realization of real-time control applications, however, most devices are functionally dedicated and therefore managed directly by application programs. As a consequence, typical real-time executive software has not provided elaborate resource management functions. Furthermore, the structure of a typical real-time software system exhibits a much "flatter" hierarchy than a representative general-purpose operating system: one or two levels as opposed to 10 or 12. This difference may be the result of an isolation of real-time control software developers from contemporary software practices, as observed by Rubey (1978).

3.1.2 Fault Isolation

Fault tolerance is important in real-time control environments due to the possible catastrophic consequences of faults. Distributed systems may provide greater fault tolerance than centralized systems, owing to the ability to disperse processing elements and perform redundant processing. System recoverability may be limited by the intimate relationships between devices and PEs.

A moderate fault-tolerance objective is fault isolation. With fault isolation the loss of a PE may result in the loss of the function performed by that PE but may not cause the system as a whole to cease functioning. Fault isolation lies in the middle of a spectrum of techniques that range from elaborate dynamic reconfiguration to ignoring fault tolerance. Complete dynamic reconfiguration may not be viable, owing to the coupling of devices to PEs in distributed real-time control systems; complete reconfiguration is thus rendered ineffective by the inability to move the function of the external devices, though processes not directly coupled to devices may be moved during reconfiguration.

3.1.3 Functional Modularity

The objective of functional modularity means that a functional capability can be added to or replaced within an applications system without extensive modification of the existing executive and applications software. This objective supports modular system construction and growth.

3.1.4 Decentralized Control and Partitioned System State

To support functional modularity and fault isolation, the system executive must be at least as decentralized as the system hardware; no single PE may contain a "global executive" that has configuration-wide authority (Jensen, 1980). Two implementation objectives support the necessary decentralization: "decentralized control" and "partitioned system state." Under decentralized control, system control functions are performed by groups of cooperating PEs, rather than by a single PE having some established "authority." Partitioned system state requires that essential control tables be partitioned or replicated and distributed among the PEs.

3.1.5 Independent Verifiability and Context Independence

System organization and kernel primitives should support and encourage "clean," "structured," "clear," and verifiable applications software. Levin's (1977) criterion of independent verifiability applies: it should be possible to determine the correctness of a given application software module without recourse to the text of other modules with which it may interact.

A closely related objective is context independence: with context independence the act of interconnecting modules does not require knowledge or alteration of the implementations of the modules, and the act of implementing a module requires only a minimum knowledge of the context in which it is to be used.

3.1.6 Minimum Number of Primitives

It is desirable to minimize the number of kernel primitives and to ensure that the selected primitives are "orthogonal" to each other. Meeting this objective minimizes the size of kernel run-time packages. Second, orthogonality among the primitives insures that each is necessary, i.e., the power of one is not contained in the rest of them. Primitives must be selected such that they can be freely used to implement more elaborate executive functions.

3.2 HXDP Software Architecture

Software system designers must carefully select the system structure to support appropriate applications modularity that meets the software design goals. The HXDP software executive supports independent processes communicating via message passing; the design permits a hierarchical decomposition of individual processes into a set of communicating processes. The message passing primitives that support this communication are described in Section 3.4.

3.2.1 Modules

Application modules known to the HXDP executive are called virtual processing elements, or VPEs. A VPE has a visible part and a hidden part, from the viewpoint of the HXDP executive.

3.2.1.1 Visible Part. The visible VPE interface consists of an information interface and a signal interface. The information interface is a set of objects of type *rawstorage* (such as bytes or words), called *windows*. The signal interface is a set of objects of type *Boolean,* called events. The visible VPE semantics need to be known to effect programming in the large (i.e., VPE interconnection). The appropriate notation of Kramer and Cunningham (1978) and Boebert *et al.* (1979) expresses the semantics of asynchronous modules as a list of precondition–action pairs, specifying both a condition and an action that should ensue after the condition becomes true; this notation is especially useful when the preconditions and actions are defined as functions in a suitable specification language.

3.2.1.2 Hidden Part. The hidden part of a VPE consists of the implementation of the VPE semantics in some programming language. This language should be able to incorporate the communication primitives supported by the kernel. A VPE may have other hidden parts; these include the internal control structure of the VPE, the types of internal data objects, and special features (such as a local interrupt structure) used to handle external devices that are not visible to the executive.

3.2.2 Structures of Modules

Application structures constructed from interconnected VPEs are called virtual architectures (VAs). A VA may be redefined as a VPE at a still higher level of abstraction, in which case its constituent VPEs and all their associated parallelism and interactions become hidden and a new visible interface (containing events and windows) is defined to permit interconnection of the VA to other VPEs.

3.3 General Design Options in Message-Based Systems

Within the context of message-based interprocess communications, significant software design decisions concern the message addressing techniques and whether processes block or not when executing message-handling primitives. Similar issues are of concern at both the hardware and software levels; here we concentrate on the process level.

3.3.1 Addressing

Message addressing schemes usually use either source object addressing or destination object addressing. With source object addressing, a sending process specifies a local object (whose name implies a message destination) in initiating a message transmission. With destination object addressing, on the other hand, a sending process specifies an object in the destination process.

Destination object addressing necessitates globally unique object names, and promotes compile time (static) checking for legal communication exchanges, but hinders reconfiguration in the face of failure. Source object addressing promotes modularity and reconfiguration, but requires a separate binding step to associate objects in different modules to effect a communication (HXDP addressing, described in Section 3.4, uses source object addressing).

3.3.2 Process Blocking

Blocking refers to suspending the progress of a module that has attempted a message exchange until some stage of that exchange is completed. Typical stages seen from the sending process are transfer to the system, receipt by the destination process, and response from the destination process. A receiving process might be blocked pending message arrival or pending receipt of the acknowledgment at the sending process; whatever the selection, a module executing a "receive" operation must either be blocked or be notified of an exception if an appropriate message is not available.

Various combinations of blocking/nonblocking send/receive policies are possible; the choice of blocking options determines the level of node autonomy and the level of asynchrony and parallelism amongst nodes. By selecting nonblocking options and including a "wait for message" primitive the designer obtains a flexible design within which various blocking variants can be realized. Exception handling complicates the design of communicating processes, and therefore it is best avoided, if possible, when designing communication primitives.

3.4 HXDP Software Message Handling

In this section we present the message communication primitives supplied by the kernel of the HXDP executive. In keeping with the objective of language independence, we will emphasize the semantics of the primitives and largely ignore syntax; the reader should visualize the primitives as calls to separately compiled procedures. The primitives are presented first without motivation; later we discuss the design issues and the reasons for the design choices, and in Section 3.5 we describe how the design meets the stated objectives.

3.4.1 HXDP Message Addressing

The HXDP executive uses source object addressing; when a VPE sends a message, the system call's parameter list includes one of its windows, which implicitly designates the destination for the message. The source window–destination window relationships, which determine message routing among VPEs, are established prior to process execution. The act of constructing a VA, or programming in the large, relates each (source) window of each VPE unidirectionally to another (destination) window, generally in another VPE. In addition, the VA constructor may specify a set of related windows to serve as alternate destinations. The use of alternate destinations will be described more fully in Section 3.4.2.

3.4.2 HXDP Communication Primitives

The HXDP executive kernel provides three primitives supporting interprocess communication—*display, view,* and *wait. Display* and *view* support message passing, while *wait* is available for processes to synchronize progress based on events caused by external (to the VPE) activities.

We illustrate basic message transmission using *display* and *view* through an example. Consider two VPEs. Suppose that VPE_1 has an interface consisting of (an output) window ($window_1$) and an event ($event_1$), and its implementation defines some hidden object ($object_1$), such as a table or an array. Furthermore, VPE_2 has an interface consisting of (an input) window ($window_2$) and an event ($event_2$), and has a hidden object ($object_2$). Suppose that $event_2$ has been associated with $window_2$. Finally assume that these two VPEs have been combined into an elementary VA by relating $window_1$ unidirectionally to $window_2$, with $window_1$ the message source, as indicated by the interconnection arrow shown in Fig. 6.

Owing to the asynchrony between the two communicating VPEs, either the *display* or the *wait* related to a message transmission could occur first. We assume that the *display* is first, so that the message interaction begins when VPE_1 invokes the primitive:

> *display* $object_1$ *as* $window_1$ *acknowledge event* is $event_1$.

This causes the value of $object_1$ to be moved in *rawstorage* form through $window_1$ to $window_2$. The acknowledge event ($event_1$) is reset to *false* immediately, and the arrival event ($event_2$) is set to *true* when the message arrives in $window_2$, producing the situation shown in Fig. 6.

VPE_2 detects the arrival of the message by means of $event_2$, either by executing a clause of a conditional statement governed by $event_2$ or by

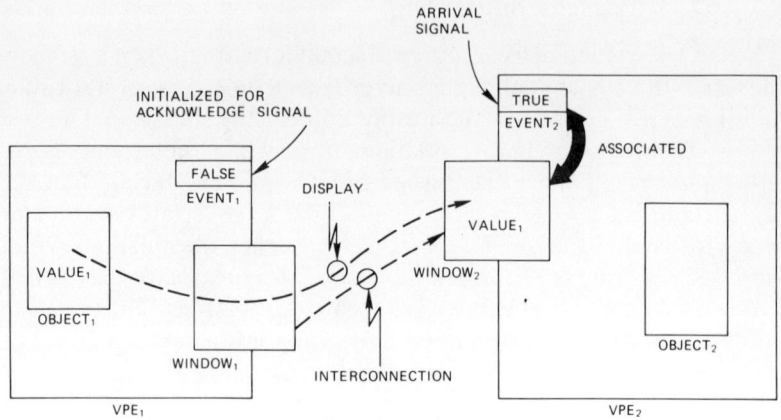

Fig. 6. Consequences of a *display*.

resuming execution after a *wait* primitive that has event$_2$ as a parameter. After detecting the arrival of a message, VPE$_2$ invokes the primitive:

view window$_2$ *as* object$_2$.

This causes the *rawstorage* message in window$_2$ to be moved to the storage area assigned to object$_2$. Invocation of the *view* by VPE$_2$ eventually causes event$_1$ to be set to *true*; this is the acknowledgement signal, which VPE$_1$ can detect in the same ways that VPE$_2$ detected the arrival event. Also, the *view* sets event$_2$ to *false*, ready for arrival of the next message. This set of events produces the status shown in Fig. 7.

If VPE$_1$ invokes a second *display* through window$_1$ and the second mes-

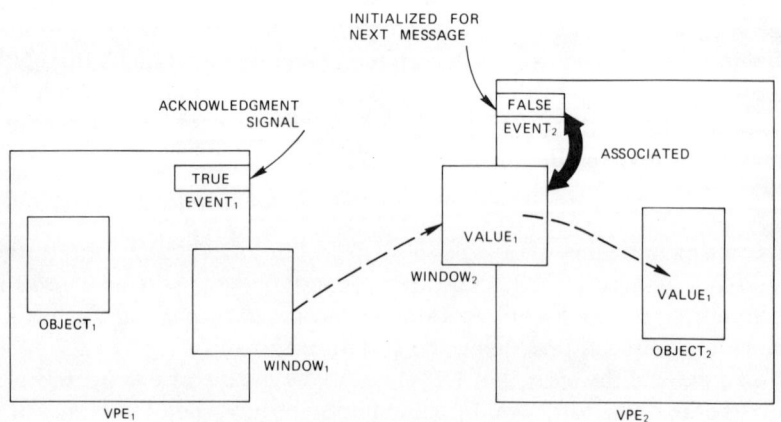

Fig. 7. Consequences of a *view*.

sage arrives at window$_2$ before VPE$_2$ invokes the first *view*, the second message replaces the first one in window$_2$ and the first will thereby be lost. This circumstance can be guarded against during module implementation by using the acknowledgment events to serialize *views* and *displays*; alternately, it can be guarded against during VA construction by inserting an "intermediary" VPE, which implements a desired queueing discipline.

The use of the arrival event and the acknowledgment event are optional. If the acknowledgment event is not used, messages may be lost and are delivered on a "most recently arrived" basis, as noted above. If, on the other hand, the arrival event is not used, the receiving VPE must test for message arrival by executing repeated *views* and examining the results; this will generally be a complex and unreliable practice.

Since events are (from the viewpoint of the VPE implementation) Boolean variables, they may be manipulated directly by the VPE. Such usage might occur if a VPE expects a message that will act as stimulus or signal with no associated message; in this case, setting the arrival event to *true* represents the complete information transfer to the receiving VPE. Since there is no message body, the receiving VPE does not need to *view* it, and can complete the transaction (from its viewpoint) by resetting the event by assigning it the value *false*. This coding, however, subverts the synchronization mechanism because the sender never sees an acknowledgment—acknowledgments can be produced only by a *view* executed by the receiving VPE.

3.4.2.1 Undeliverable Messages. Three degrees of certainty can be associated with each attempt by the kernel to deliver a message:

Case 1: The kernel can be certain that the message arrived.
Case 2: The kernel can be certain that the message did not arrive and will never arrive.
Case 3: The kernel cannot be certain whether the message has arrived or will ever arrive.

The uncertainty arises because message delivery may require actions by two physically dispersed kernel subsystems. One subsystem may send a message and receive, instead of an acknowledgment, indication that the destination has failed. The sending subsystem cannot know whether the message arrived before or after the failure. Uncertainty may arise in other ways—for example, if the sender has not received any response from the transmission request; there may be no way to set time outs to guarantee reliable detection of this case, since the system does not guarantee response times. The design decision to minimize the BIU state precluded the implementation of a reliable message delivery service at the BIU level; reliable delivery could be effected by an interVPE protocol.

If the kernel is certain that the message arrived (Case 1), the *display* is complete. If either of the other two cases occurs, the kernel will examine the VA definition to see if a set of alternate windows has been related to the source window. In defining such relationships, all alternate windows are included within *oralternate* groups. The first window in an *oralternate* group is an *oralternate* window. Other windows within each *oralternate* group are declared to be *andalternate* windows. The kernel will try successive alternate windows according to the following rules.

(1) If the kernel is certain that the message arrived at a window, the *display* is complete.

(2) If there are no remaining alternate windows, the *display* is complete.

(3) If the next alternate window is an *andalternate* window, the kernel will try to send the message to that window if Case 2 (above) or Case 3 applied to the previous attempt.

(4) If the next alternate window is an *oralternate* window, and if Case 1 or Case 3 applied to any previous attempt, the *display* is complete; otherwise, the kernel will try to send the message to that window.

The *andalternate/oralternate* qualifiers are required because strategies that minimize the probability of message loss (e.g., retransmit to an *andalternate* window) raise the probability of message duplication, and those that minimize the probability of message duplication (e.g., not retransmitting to an *oralternate* window) raise the probability of message loss.

3.4.2.2 *Extended Functionality.* The three kernel primitives *display, view,* and *wait* can be used in intermediary VPEs to provide functionality (such as timing, queueing, or broadcast) not provided by the kernel's minimum set of primitives. Intermediary VPEs may perform functions (such as copying messages for broadcast) that are independent of the meaning that applications VPEs associate with message contents. Such intermediary VPEs may be cataloged and reused in a variety of applications. Providing enhanced functionality by means of intermediary VPEs should not be much more expensive than incorporating those functions directly in the kernel if the number of VPEs per processor is small.

3.4.3 Rationale

Several basic design decisions underlying the HXDP Executive Kernel derive from the design requirements, while others were a consequence of project complexity constraints.

3.4.3.1 *Type Enforcement.* Should the system enforce type consistency in messages, requiring that the source object ($object_1$ in Fig. 7) be of the same type as the destination object (object$_2$ in Fig. 7)? Such type enforcement would require either run-time processor support (e.g., from descriptor or capability hardware), or compile-time support (e.g., from object type checking). As both approaches greatly increase overall system complexity, messages are considered typeless by the HXDP kernel.

3.4.3.2 Message Buffers. Should the kernel create a dedicated virtual object to act as a message buffer for every window? Having such a buffer would allow a slight simplification of the primitives, but would increase the expense of broadcast or message-routing VPEs, which would have to copy messages from arrival buffer to departure buffer. We anticipate that such message-routing VPEs will be common, and so the HXDP executive does not require dedicated buffers.

An object related to the window by the *as* clause of the *display* primitive is the equivalent of a buffer for a departure window. This object can be an arrival window, permitting an invocation such as

display inwindow *as* outwindow:

which permits a message to be passed along without the need to copy it within the forwarding VPE.

3.4.3.3 Blocking. Should the kernel force a VPE executing a *display* or *view* to block until a message can be successfully transmitted? If both sender and receiver were to block, reliable message delivery would be enforced on every transaction (Hoare, 1978). The resulting close synchronization between the sender and receiver would be a problem in real-time systems, however. A VPE processing sensor data might not be able to meet sampling rate requirements if a later VPE does not, in turn, meet the requirements. The selected mechanism—no blocking, with synchronization signals—allows applications coders to implement blocking when needed and to permit looser coupling to meet response time requirements.

3.4.3.4 Separate Signal Interface. Should the kernel provide an interface signal that flags message arrival? Although it is possible to mechanize inter-VPE signals by means of messages, the lack of an explicit signal that a message has arrived would force a VPE to implement algorithms to discover indirectly whether a new message has arrived (e.g., because the current contents of a given window differ from the contents there at the last examination). Since consecutive identical messages create ambiguities that cannot be resolved by the receiver alone, such indirect techniques may compromise the verifiability objective, and so a separate signal interface was included.

Now we turn to the two parts of the signal mechanism: the conditions under which signals are raised, and a way a raised signal is detected by a VPE.

A designer could include an explicit primitive *raise* function, or could couple the raising of signals to the movement of messages, making signal raising a by-product of the use of *display* and *view*.

We selected the latter option principally because it subsumes the case of the *raise* primitive; any VPE can signal any other VPE by sending it a (possibly empty) message. This option also reduces the number of primitives and provides a structure consistent with that of the hardware, as isolated signals would probably be mechanized as messages even if they were raised by a distinct *raise* primitive.

How should signals be raised? A signal might be raised only upon arrival of a message in a window (as a consequence of a distant *display*), only upon assignment of a message value to a local object (as a consequence of a *view*), or upon either event. Any of these options could be used in conjunction with a separate mechanism to signal negative acknowledgements. Consider the consequences of these different options.

If signals are raised only upon message arrival, then all acknowledgments must be sent as messages (by means of an explicit *display*). This requires that the receiving VPE know when the sender requires an acknowledgment, which severely compromises the context-independence objective, or that the receiving VPE always send an acknowledgment, which doubles the message traffic, increasing system overhead.

If signals are only raised distantly as a consequence of a *view* (i.e., acknowledgment signals only), then there is no arrival signal and a VPE must explicitly test for the arrival of a new message. This option is thus discarded because it compromises verifiability.

In the HXDP design, a negative acknowledgment can be obtained by appropriate use of alternate windows. If an alternate window belongs to the sending VPE, undeliverable messages will be returned to the sender and their receipt can be interpreted as negative acknowledgments.

The above decisions resulted in the current kernel message facility, in which a distant *display* causes a local event variable to be set to *true* as a signal of message arrival and a local *view* causes a distant event variable to be set to *true* as a signal of acknowledgment (only once for each *display* despite possibly multiple *views*). This arrangement also simplifies the coordination between signals and messages when a VA needs to enforce a complete and strict pattern of message transmissions.

How should signals be detected? We considered five ways:

(1) A VPE could explicitly test for the signal in a busywait loop.
(2) A VPE could wait by suspending virtual progress until the signal arrives.
(3) A VPE could be allowed to either test or wait for the signal.
(4) A VPE could be forced to execute a goto when the signal occurs.

REAL-TIME DISTRIBUTED COMPUTER SYSTEMS 73

(5) A VPE could be forced to execute a procedure call when the signal occurs.

A busy waiting strategy may not be affordable. Restricting signal detection to *wait*, however, prevents a VPE from waiting for a disjunctive combination of signals.

The option of testing or waiting is attractive; it allows the VPE designer to select a signal detection technique appropriate for the application environment. The forced goto, on the other hand, exemplifies unstructured programming.

The commonly used forced procedure call has many attractive atributes; we attempted for some time to define a version of the forced call that was consistent with the objectives and constraints of the project. Levin (1977) made it clear that this consistency requirement was an unresolved research question. We identified three specific reasons for declining the forced procedure call option:

(1) Verifiability requires that the side effects of such a call be constrained; to do so requires both language facilities and associated compiler or run-time (processor) support (Levin, 1977).

(2) A common reason cited for requiring a forced procedure call is "response time" or "speed in handling interrupts." This requirement is concerned with stimuli sent to a VPE from external devices (interrupts) and not with stimuli propagated through a distributed system (signals). From the viewpoint of a signaled VPE, the signal is the local manifestation of distant event, and any response delay by the receiving VPE will be in addition to an indeterminate and possibly sizable delay in propagating the signal from its source to that VPE. The kernel primitives do not, however, prevent a VPE from using interrupts to serve the needs of some local, external device.

(3) Forced procedure calls can occur during the execution of a procedure whose call was forced by an earlier signal. As a result there may exist several called but not completed procedure executions, and a scheduler must be introduced to resolve the demands for the processor (Brinch Hansen, 1978). One simple scheduling policy is to run all procedures to completion, resulting in highly variable response times. Complex scheduling policies to reduce this variance were not feasible.

3.4.3.5 Interconnection Specifications. How should the paths taken by interprocess messages be specified? This issue admits a wide range of positions, including schemes, e.g., "ports" (Walden, 1972), in which messages move by way of virtual rendezvous locations, and schemes in which messages move through fixed and unchangeable interconnections. We rejected Walden ports because that design compromises context independence and independent verifiability; a complete message transfer requires that both VPEs know the same port name, and verification that a receiving VPE does indeed receive its input messages requires checking the sender's and receiver's implementations for consistency in the use of global port names. Two recent variants on ports (Liskov, 1979; Mao and Yeh, 1980) also require inter-VPE consistency in the use of port names.

We also considered an interconnection specification technique that used an explicit run-time *link* primitive that specified a named window of some distant VPE. This technique requires language support for windows as abstract data types with VA-global names, which was not feasible within the language constraints of the project. This approach also hides interconnect operations within VPE implementations, compromising context-independence and complicating verification.

The selected specification technique incorporates enough flexibility through alternate windows to permit a degree of fault isolation while remaining close to the fixed interconnect end of the spectrum. Within this structure we can effectively emulate other interconnection techniques (ports, for example).

3.4.3.6 Executive Status Information. What mechanism should be used to communicate status information between the executive and the applications VPEs? How, for example, does the executive notify a VPE that another distant VPE is no longer operational? Such status information can be transmitted through executive windows dedicated to system status communications. This approach not only forces a uniform interface for interprocess communication but is also compatible with introducing VPEs to perform additional executive functions. Thus a more complete system executive can easily be built on top of the message-passing facility provided by the executive kernel.

3.4.4 Kernel Implementation

The kernel was implemented in assembly language using a PASCAL variant as a design language. The implementation comprised an Executive module and *display, view,* and *wait* procedures for each processing element. The Executive's cycle time under no load was $(180 + 36n)$ instructions for a PE with n display windows. The real time expended by the Executive delivering a message was $(1000 + 80n)$ instructions for a message of n data words. The time was split equally between send and receive. Most of this time, $(450 + 80n)$ instructions, was spent copying the message between object, window, and an internal queue. The kernel occupied 1300 words of storage in each PE. We believe the instruction times could be cut by two-thirds and the storage by half in a revised implementation.

REAL-TIME DISTRIBUTED COMPUTER SYSTEMS

3.5 Remarks on the HXDP Software Design

We present observations on how well the system met the general objectives of real-time software outlined in Section 3.4.1. We also remark on our key software design decisions. These observations are based on our experiences in designing, implementing, and experimenting with the HXDP message-passing kernel.

3.5.1 General Observations

The HXDP system meets the five nonfunctional objectives of real-time systems discussed in Section 3.1.

3.5.1.1 Fault Isolation. After loss of a PE, the HXDP system loses the functionality assigned to the failed PE, but communications among the surviving processors and their software modules are not affected unless the failure disables bus communication, a remote possibility. Interprocess communication among survivors does not depend upon failed processors, processes, or bus interface units. Although the kernel does not support dynamic reconfiguration, it does attempt to deliver messages to alternate destinations, as directed by the application program. The alternate destination facility can be used for limited fault detection and reconfiguration by applications software that routes messages through backup windows after a failure.

3.5.1.2 Functional Modularity. The HXDP executive kernel supports functional modularity—neither the executive nor the application processes need be modified to add processes to an application. Module interconnection specifications (the "program in the large") would, of course, be altered to incorporate new modules.

3.5.1.3 Decentralized Control and Partitioned System State. The combination of a bus interconnection topology and logical destination addressing appears to relieve the executive of the requirement of knowing the location of the destination VPE. In the current implementation, each BIU provides for eight input queues with the intention that the BIU perform the first level of demultiplexing from the bus. Since we did not wish to modify the BIU microcode to increase the limit, we had to handle multiple destinations at a single PE with software, so the executive was able to make use of only two queues, for separating VPE/VPE messages from subnet traffic. The next level of useful demultiplexing would occur on the window level, but eight is clearly too small a number. Thus, each kernel subsystem must know the executive process number corresponding to each applications process or window, and, therefore, there exists a distributed process–processor allocation table. Bus control, on the other hand, is decentralized, with certain state synchronization information placed in control messages; this information is used to silence wayward bus interface units.

3.5.1.4 Independent Verifiability. The HXDP executive kernel primitives support simple input/output ports that transmit messages among processes; the resulting visibility of all interprocess interactions clarifies the code structure. Furthermore, module correctness proofs should be simplified by using specifications of all possible interaction patterns.

It should be noted, however, that the high visibility of the communications mechanisms makes it possible to subvert interprocessor synchronization mechanisms. A receiving process could, for example, refuse to *view* an incoming message (or simply reset the window's status bit), with the result that the message sender never receives an acknowledgment. After this sequence, the overall system state is inconsistent and the obscure error may be difficult to track down. On the other hand, if the sender were designed to continue to send messages without checking for acknowledgments, the system would not hang up. This could be viewed as a context dependency of either the sender or the receiver. We should note, however, that designs having this problem arise naturally in response to the requirement for pipelined processing in real-time control systems.

The automony of VPEs is consistent with the fault isolation objective (conversely, "call-by-message" arrangements are not). VPEs receive messages at their own discretion, and so their behavior or control flow cannot be forcibly altered by another VPE. A malfunctioning VPE can neither block the progress of a functioning one by refusing to respond to a "call" nor forcibly preoccupy a functioning one by "calling" it in a pathologically frequent fashion.

All HXDP VPEs communicate via messages that do not contain the identities of the processes communicating those messages (such information could be included in a higher level protocol). Thus, each HXDP process communicates and performs functions in response to messages independent of their origins. This decoupling from the context supports independent verifiability.

3.5.1.5 Minimum Number of Primitives. The kernel provides one input primitive, one output primitive, and one synchronization primitive —certainly a small number. Without *wait*, the set would clearly be minimum. Due to the nature of the real-time environment and the existence of applications in which it is better to have the most recently received input rather than waiting for a new input, the *wait* primitive is necessary to provide explicit process synchronization when required. Hence, three is a minimum number of primitives. It is possible, even in a minimum system, to create obscure applications modules and message-passing patterns.

3.5.2 Specific Observations

The following specific remarks are based on our experience in implementing the executive kernel and in using it in test applications.

3.5.2.1 The Send and Receive Message Primitive.
The semantics of *display* and *view* have been entirely adequate for our applications. Some executive designs have placed the burden of message acknowledgment at a level above the executive kernel level; HXDP does not. The acknowledgment protocols in the HXDP Executive seem well placed and easy to use. Some application programs have been written using explicit messages for acknowledgments, but this complicated the programming task.

3.5.2.2 Efficiency of Message Transmission.
Message-transfer efficiency is affected by several considerations, including management overhead and copying. In the HXDP design, the following copying actions are required to move message M from process P to process Q:

(1) window (P):   = M (in P)
(2) OQ(PE(P)):   = window (P)
(3) IQ(PE(Q)):   = OQ(PE(P))   (Message passed via bus)
(4) window (Q):   = IQ(PE(Q))
(5) M (in Q):   = window (Q)

Here OQ, IQ, M, and PE denote the output queue, input queue, memory, and processing element, respectively. If copying a message across the global bus is viewed as a copy, then sending an n-word message from P to Q requires copying $5n$ words.

For inter-PE communications Step (3) is always necessary. The extra $4n$ words of copying are needed because messages are passed within a PE by value rather than by reference; that is, the contents of messages are copied between buffers and queues, rather than copying pointers to messages. This copying is unavoidable in the current implementation because BIU queues require message values and not message references. With BIU changes and adding memory management to the PE, the extra copying overhead could be exchanged for memory management overhead.

Since the HXDP system was designed for a test bed, its design requires that every message transmission be placed on the bus, even if both source and destination are, in fact, coresident in the same PE. This design is helpful in system debugging both because all message traffic can be monitored on the bus and because all VPE message interactions work identically. As a consequence, applications can be debugged with some arbitrary assignment of processes to PEs and then the system deployed without rechecking. This design decision does have consequences, however. Consider the minimum steps needed to transmit a message between two VPEs located in the same PE. Using HXDP windows, one might expect intra-PE message transmission to involve:

(1) window (P): = M (in P)
(2) window (Q): = window (P)
(3) M (in Q): = window (Q)

Thus, an n-word message requires copying only $3n$ words. The same effect could be achieved by pointer manipulation at the cost of mamory management complexity without any message copying. Such efficiency improvement may be necessary to meet response time requirements in deployed systems.

There are other interesting logical consequences of this message routing design. Suppose, for example, that an interrupt handler is implemented as a VPE and communicates with the Executive via messages. Then communications between the interrupt handler and the Executive pass over the global bus. But if the interrupt VPE receives an interrupt signaling that the global bus is malfunctioning, it may be impossible for the Executive to be notified of the error.

3.5.2.3 VPE/VA Construction. To gain experience with distributed computing systems using message-based interprocess communication, we implemented several examples, including Lamport's bakery algorithm (Lamport, 1979). It was easier to construct VAs out of VAs, called VA nodes, rather than writing VAs composed of a single level of VPEs. Applications thus took the form of two-level hierarchies (or, considering library VPEs, e.g., the interrupt VPE, three-level hierarchies) of VPEs. For example, for each instance of a process executing the bakery algorithm in a conventional multiprocessor system, we used a VA node made up of five VPEs. A "manager" VPE performed simple system control and monitoring. Three "service" VPEs—broadcast, queue, and timer VPEs —handled message traffic. Finally, a "sharer" VPE actually executed the bakery algorithm. We believe the manager and service VPEs to be "standard" and reusable, and expect that often a VA will require such standard supporting VPEs in addition to specialized application VPEs.

Our application was written incrementally, the manager and timer VPEs being added in the second version. Minimal changes were required in the sharer, broadcast, and queue VPEs to integrate the manager and timer VPEs into the VA node.

The fact that VAs are often constructed from sets of VPEs, with some VPEs common to every set, allows one to view VPEs as a sort of abstract data type, where the loading of a VPE into a PE constitutes an instantiation of the type. As with the general theory of abstract data types, a very useful feature would be the incorporation of parameters within VPE definitions. Although we want the specification of VPE interconnections to remain external to individual VPEs (programming in the large), parameterized VPEs would allow for the reflection of certain attributes of configurations in the instantiation of general-purpose VPEs.

As a simple example, a queue VPE may be placed in a configuration with a varying number N of view windows, which define N VPEs able to send the queue a message. The queue VPE might be written as

```
vpe queue (N: integer);
  I: integer;
  {viewevent definitions};
  cycle
    for I: = 1 to N do
      if viewevent [I] = true
        then view window [I] as object;
          {process message}
    end for
      {deliver queued messages}
  endcycle
end vpe
```

Here, N is passed as a parameter at load (instantiation) time. It would be very useful to have such a VPE parameterization facility.

4. Summary

The trend toward distributed systems is driven by technical, psychological, and cost reasons.

Technology mates computing with communication; this mating has made the development of distributed systems possible. This mating comes at a time when microprocessors are increasing in capability as rapidly as they are decreasing in cost. These technological developments would allow us to realize new HXDP BIUs at a fraction of the cost associated with the existing HXDP BIU units. In fact, microcomputer costs have decreased so much that a next generation HXDP BIU could be organized as a microcosm of the distributed system they support; i.e., as multiple microprocessors interconnected by a bus internal to the BIU. Individual internal microprocessors could be assigned tasks corresponding to the function of the seven controllers (Section 2.4.3) in the current design. Additional BIU functionality could be added without undue cost, or extensive revision of extant BIU firmware or software.

Psychologically, distributed systems are attractive because they may provide efficiency, modularity, robustness to failure, and extensibility. Additionally, for real-time environments, they allow physical distribution of functionality, placing computing power at places where its needed. In this way, the designer can reduce the overall necessary communication bandwidth and improve system response times.

The *costs* of both processing elements and interconnection mechanisms are declining rapidly, permitting the development of cost-effective distributed systems. Microcomputers are cheap. Broadcast communication technology is becoming cheap, especially cable-based communication technology developed for the CATV market. Designers can use these low-cost building blocks to construct efficient, flexible, powerful systems that are also robust in the face of failures. For similar reasons, we can design BIUs that support the major portions of the functionality necessary to provide both a message passing service and high-level interprocess communications. This functional division reserves PE processing power for applications code; this decision is shown to be viable and attractive by the HXDP system.

Relegating communication functions to the BIU does not complete design, as a myriad of options remain concerning how the BIU meets its functional requirements. In the real-time environment these design decisions might be simpler than in more complex environments. For instance, since the real-time environment is structured, designers can ascertain *a priori* the consequences of various software modularization decisions on message traffic patterns. Typically message communication needs will be different for different nodes, but nevertheless the node message transmission needs will exhibit more of a cyclic than a "bursty" nature. The access protocols for many distributed systems are designed for environments with significant bursty transmission needs. Other access protocols, such as time-division multiplexing, are inappropriate for at least two reasons. First, they assign substantial bandwidth to nodes which do not have messages to transmit, leaving the channel idle. Second, many protocols cannot efficiently handle unequal channel bandwidth needs of different system nodes. Polling can eliminate the deficiencies, but the price includes the centralization of the control, degrading system reliability, and the addition of polling messages, degrading system performance. The VDPA access protocol is responsive to the differing bandwidth needs of nodes and employs distributed control. Both modeling and experimentation have shown that the VDPA access protocol effectively meets differing node bandwidth requirements. The VDPA pointer update algorithm is extremely robust; the pointer recovery algorithm can reestablish pointer synchronization even after the most unlikely disasters. Thus,

VDPA is a viable, efficient, and general access protocol applicable to distributed real-time systems. Its design, development, and verification contribute to the state of the art in distributed real-time system design.

Attention to software concerns is very important in designing distributed computer systems. One must pay attention to mechanisms that promote modularity and independent verifiability. The HXDP window concept and mechanism, wherein VPE addresses (names) a window in its own address space to communicate with a remote VPE, contribute to modularity, independent compilation, and the creation and use of library VPEs (Bullis and Franta, 1979). Furthermore, the signaling, acknowledgment, and message overwrite philosophies have been sufficient and convenient in the realization of real-time applications. The ability to use library VPEs has been helpful, and the combination of alternate destination windows and a system (executive) connected window have been adequate for error control. Additionally, overwriting messages rather than buffering them is both appropriate and effective for some real-time systems using "update" messages transmitted on a cyclic basis.

Finally, the ability to load the entire system into a single node facilitates application system debugging. After debugging is completed, the same modules can be redistributed among multiple nodes without modification. This feature is supported by the built-in mechanism which places every inter-VPE message on the system bus. This feature was included for flexibility and for observability in the test-bed environment.

Further experiments and the development of future advanced test-bed systems based on the HXDP experience will undoubtedly increase our understanding of the design of distributed computer systems and of their use in many environments.

Acknowledgments

The development of HXDP's hardware and software required the efforts of many individuals, including W. E. Boebert, Tammy Chan, Dennis Cornhill, Mike Gutman, and George Anderson. We also acknowledge the efforts of R. Y. Kain in preparation of this version of the chapter from an earlier version prepared jointly by the authors. The development also required the support given by the U.S. Navy Ocean Sciences Center under contract N00123-74C0891, and the Honeywell Systems and Research Center.

References

Anderson, G. A., and Jensen, E. D. (1975). Computer interconnection structures: Taxonomy, characteristics, and examples. *Computing Surveys* 7(No. 4, Dec.), 197–213.

Bender, M. A. (1976). "Software Development Study," Rep. 46704. Honeywell Aircraft Flight Systems Engineering Department, Honeywell, Minneapolis, Minnesota.

Boebert, W. E., Franta, W. R., and Berg, H. K. (1979). NPN: A finite-state specification technique for distributed software. *Proc. Conf. Specification Reliable Software, 1979*, pp. 139–149.

Brinch Hansen, P. (1978). Distributed processes: A concurrent programming concept. *Commun. ACM* **21**, 934–941.

Bullis, K., and Franta, W. (1980). Implementation of eventcounts in a broadcast network. *Comput. Networks* **4**, No. 2, 57–69.

Davies, D. W., Barber, D. L. A., Price, W. L., and Solomonides (1979). "Computer Networks and their Protocols." Wiley, New York.

Dijkstra, E. W. (1968). The structure of the T. H. E. multiprogramming system. *Commun. ACM* **11**, 341–346.

Farmer, W. D., and Newell, E. E. (1969). An experimental distributed switching system to handle bursty computer traffic. *Proc. ACM Symp. Probl. Optim. Data Commun. Syst.*, pp. 1–33.

Franta, W. R., and Chlamtac, I. (1981). "Local Networks: Motivation, Technology and Performance." D. C. Heath & Co., Lexington, Mass.

Hoare, C. A. R. (1978). Communicating sequential processes. *Commun. ACM* **21**, No. 8, 666–677.

IEEE Instrumentation and Measurements Group (1975) IEEE standard digital interface for programmable instrumentation. *IEEE Stand.* **488**.

Jensen, E. D. (1978). The Honeywell experimental distributed processor—An overview. *Computer* **11**, No. 1, Jan., 28–39.

Jensen, E. D. (1980). Decentralized control. *In* "Distributed Systems: An Advanced Course." Springer-Verlag, Berlin and New York.

Kramer, J., and Cunningham, R. J. (1978). Towards a notation for the functional design of distributed processing systems. *Proc. Int. Conf. Parallel Process., 1978*.

Lamport, L. (1979). A new approach to proving the correctness of multi-process programs. *ACM Trans. Programm. Lang. Syst.* **1**, No. 1, 84–97.

LeLann, G. (1977). Distributed systems—toward a formal approach. *Proc. IFIP Cong., 1977* pp. 155–160.

Levin, R. (1977). Program structures for exceptional condition handling. Ph.D. Thesis, Carnegie-Mellon University, Pittsburgh, Pennsylvania.

Liskov, B. (1979). Primitives for distributed computing. *Proc. 7th Symp. Oper. Syst. Princ., 7th*, pp. 33–42.

Mao, T. W., and Yeh, R. T. (1980). Communication port: A language concept for concurrent programming. *IEEE Trans. Software Eng.* **SE-6**, No. 2, 194–204.

Metcalfe, R. M., and Boggs, D. R. (1976). Ethernet: Distributed packet switching for local computer networks. *Commun. ACM* **19**, No. 7, 395–404.

Pierce, J. R. (1972). Network for block switching of data. *Bell System Tech. J.* **51**, No. 6, July–Aug., 1133–1145.

Post, D. L. (1978). Executive architecture for digital avionics systems. *Proc. NAECON 1978* pp. 714–724.

Rubey, R. J. (1978). Higher order languages for avionics software—a survey, summary, and critique. *Proc. NAECON 1978* pp. 945–951.

U.S. Air Force (1973). "MIL-STD-1553: Military Standard Aircraft Internal Time Division Multiplex Data Bus." USAF, Washington, D.C.

Walden, D. C. (1972). A system for interprocess communication in a resource sharing computer network. *Commun. ACM* **15**, No. 4, 221–230.

Architecture and Strategies for Local Networks: Examples and Important Systems

K. J. THURBER

Architecture Technology Corporation
Minneapolis, Minnesota

1.	What Is a Local Network?	83
2.	Terminology and Nomenclature	87
3.	Technology Trends and Their Influence	87
4.	Decentralized versus Centralized Computation	88
5.	Local Network Functions	89
6.	Examples	89
7.	System Summaries	90
	7.1 Ethernet	91
	7.2 AN/USQ-67	97
	7.3 HYPERchannel	99
	7.4 Rings	102
8.	Hardware Availability	105
	8.1 Application-Embedded Hardware	106
	8.2 Turnkey Systems	106
	8.3 Subsystem Building Blocks	106
	8.4 Components/Modules	107
	8.5 Chips	107
	8.6 Hardware Overview	107
9.	Computer Centers and Offices of the Future: Directions	109
10.	The Future	110
	References	111

1. What Is a Local Network?

Interest and activity in the area of Local Computer Networks (LCNs) is growing rapidly (*1*). Workshops and symposiums entirely devoted to LCNs are held (*2–4*). The IEEE Computer Society in conjunction with the University of Minnesota now sponsors an annual conference on local computer networks (*5*), and most of the major conferences in the computer or communications fields have at least one session devoted to this topic. The purpose of this article is to provide an introduction to architectures in the area of local networks, discuss some example systems, and describe the future of this technology.

There is still a great deal of debate over exactly what constitutes an LCN. A number of "introductory" papers have been written in which an LCN is defined (6–12), and definitions based upon such factors as speed, transmission medium, switching technology, percentage of traffic not passing through a gateway, single-organization ownership, single-function usage, use for distributed processing, network configuration, and/or relationship to I/O channels have been proposed. For example, Clark *et al.* (7) feel that local networks are defined by the distance over which inexpensive high-speed digital communication technologies can be used. Ownership of the network is not part of their definition. Technological

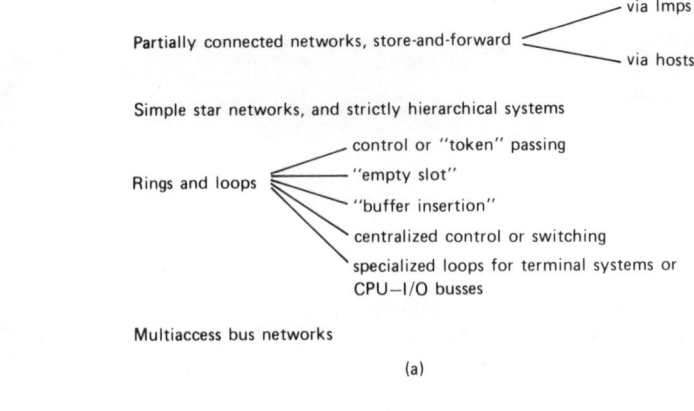

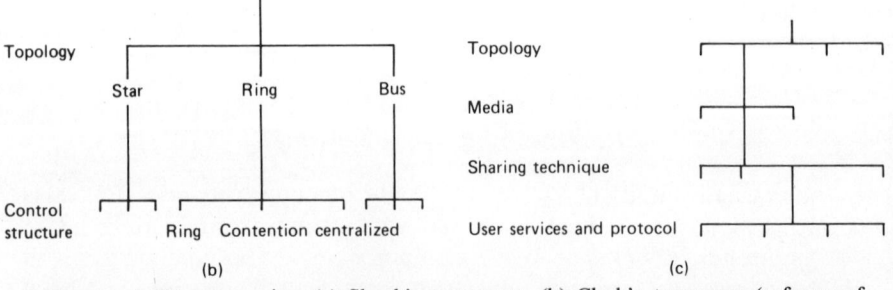

FIG. 1. LCN taxonomies: (a) Shoch's taxonomy; (b) Clark's taxonomy (a frame of $M + 1$ slots will contain M reservation slots and a slot used for reservation requests); (c) Cotton's taxonomy.

factors that they use to distinguish local networks from long-haul networks and from buses include high bandwidth and low delay. The major classification schemes developed to date for local networks are shown in Fig. 1.

In this article, we will use the definition of LCNs given in Thurber and Freeman (6). Local computer networks constitute the class of network-like systems which satisfy the following basic properties:

(1) They are generally owned by a single organization.
(2) They are generally local; that is, the distances involved are on the order of a few miles.
(3) They contain some type of switching-element technology.

These definitions are not totally precise, but all of the systems that are identified as local network architectures are thought generally by researchers to be in the LCN class and also satisfy the above three postulates (Fig. 2) (12–70).

The interest in and the whole concept of local computer networks appears to stem from two diverse groups. The first is composed mainly of those people who are reaching the limits of their current systems and are seeking ways to extend and improve them. Further, some nets in this group evolved because owners decided to connect together some computers that they owned or evolve some products that they built. Some

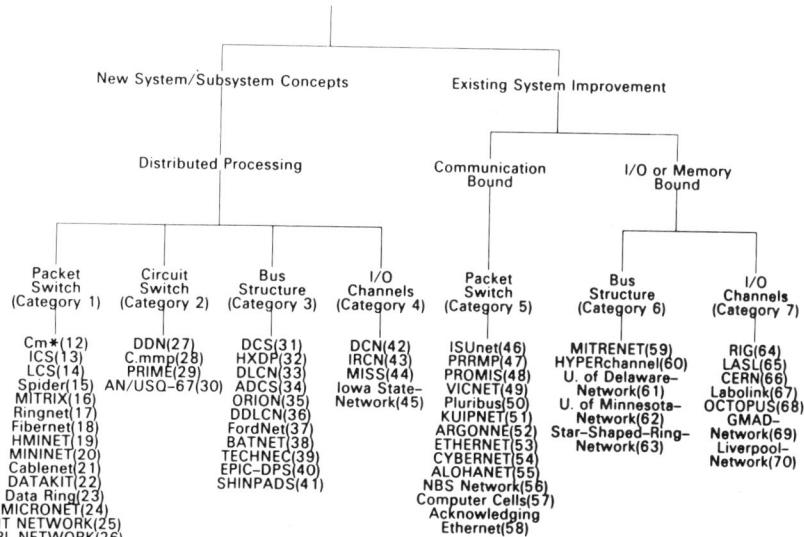

FIG. 2. Thurber–Freeman LCN taxonomy (numbers in parentheses are reference numbers).

groups had specific applications and problems with particular requirements, and thus chose a local network as a system solution. The performance of these existing systems can be improved and their useful life extended by forming networks of the various mass storage devices or networks of the various communication devices. Generally such systems are typified by the Network Systems Corporation HYPERchannel®.

A second group has been recognized as those looking to incorporate and use such new system concepts as distributed processing. Specialized functions such as fast-Fourier transform, data base, or array processing can be off-loaded from a single host, developed as separate devices with architectures optimized for their particular function, and used by others in the network. Further, in this category we have included systems which were not originally designed as local nets, but have been or will be used as local networks.

In developing Fig. 2, an attempt was made to determine the reason for development of the network or its status and then place the network under the most appropriate category. Therefore, some unusual classifications occurred; e.g., Ethernet appears as an existing system improvement. Everyone recognizes Ethenet as an experiment in distributed processing; however, in the current state of the art at Xerox PARC, multiple Ethernets have evolved into separate networks connected via gateways into an internet environment.

Thus, it is felt that the current state of Ethernet is that of a system improvement,[1] whereas Fibernet, a fiber optic, media-based version of Ethernet at PARC, is listed as a distributed processing evolution because it is an attempt to apply fiber optics as the connection mechanism in a system concept based upon Ethernet and as such is still in the distributed processing category.

Clearly, in developing Fig. 2 many opinions as to the status and intent of various local networks have been interpreted. It is believed that Fig. 2 accurately represents the facts as of mid-1980; however, many of the designers of the systems may not agree completely with the represented view.

Further, there were difficult questions to answer about broadcast-based (contention channel) systems and rings: "Where should they be placed?" If we made a place for every unique technique, we would lose our higher level perspective. Thus, it was decided that because contention channels are used primarily to support packet-switching communication networks they would be classified in that category. Since there are an extremely

---

[1] An Ethernet connection is also currently announced as an integral part of future Xerox products, the Xerox 860.

wide variety of rings, some of which support packet switching and some of which do not, we would include these in the most rudimentary class—bus structures—since the most fundamental parameter of the wide variety of rings is that they can be viewed as a set of point-to-point links.

2. Terminology and Nomenclature

We now define the terms used in this article, and as we proceed, other terms will be defined as needed. This section LCNs will be placed in their appropriate context with respect to geographic networks and distributed systems.

A distributed processor is a system consisting of at least two processor–memory pairs (hosts) in which all communication takes place via messages over a communication subnetwork and there is no shared memory. It is assumed that the processor–memory pairs cooperate to complete jobs. A network is one form of a distributed processor in which communication on the subnetwork is usually via switches. A *local network* as defined previously is a specialized form of a network. A packet is a fixed-length subpart of a message and packet switches transmit packets using a store-and-forward technique. Circuit switches build a connection between communicating processor–memory pairs and generally do not contain a storage capability. Architecture refers to the functional view of a system as opposed to how it is implemented based upon technology/cost trade-offs. Distributed processors may be viewed as a set of layers. Each layer appears to communicate with its corresponding layer on another host via a set of agreements called protocols. Agreements between unlike layers are called interfaces.

3. Technology Trends and Their Influence

In recent years data-processing costs have declined faster than communication costs in general and data communications costs in particular. Thus, there is a tendency, in a system design, to try and decentralize computation; i.e., provide remote processing to effectively substitute computation for communication. Between 1967 and 1977 bipolar logic costs were down two orders of magnitude (measured in cents per gate)! Between 1973 and 1979 bipolar memory costs were down two orders of magnitude (measured in cents per bit)! Communication costs were stable or increasing. In the future we may expect communication costs to come down. The advent of private satellites, fiber optics, and/or private carriers may cause communication costs to decrease. However, in comparison to logic and memory costs, the cost of communications has remained stable. As logic and memory costs decline even further, the push to decentralize will become even stronger. We should note that rapidly declining costs of logic and memory do not automatically mean similar performance/cost increases. There are other design and manufacturing costs that modify the decrease, with the net result that system costs decrease at a rate of 15–25%/year; i.e., the price per instruction per second decreases at a rate of 15–25%/year. Further, developments in technologies for logic and systems may alter this rate.

The effect of technology is a desire to build hierarchially structured networks with a LCN as the most basic system building block.

4. Decentralized versus Centralized Computation

There are many reasons supporting either centralized or decentralized architectures. These are summarized below. LCNs are decentralized. The primary reason for their existance is local resource sharing.

Proponents of centralized systems claim that the concepts of distributing a system are not well developed; thus, it will be difficult to actually deploy this technology. How will large data bases be distributed, updated, and synchronized? Clearly, centralized concepts are proven and well developed. Further, their development costs are reasonably well known. The cost of centralized systems is claimed to grow at a rate of the square root of n; i.e., if the cost of a system doubles, the performance goes up by a factor of four. This observation is known as Grosch's law. It is an empirically observed law that has held up for over 30 years, regardless of architecture.

Distributed systems, local networks in particular, offer a number of advantages. They have the possibility of resource sharing, thus enabling a user to obtain special features/facilities without direct ownership. It is claimed that communication costs are a major cost in large systems, and therefore technology economics is on the side of decentralization. The desire for interactive computation only increases the potentially high communication costs. It is claimed that microprocessors do not follow Grosch's law, and thus the cost balance would change drastically if large systems could be built from such small processors (which grow in complexity daily). Distributed systems also exhibit promise for improved system maintenance, availability, and reliability. Last, it may be possible to update a distributed system in a piecemeal manner as technology improves. If such systems are developed as a hierarchy consisting of local networks connected via satellites and common-carrier networks, a major system user could evolve from currently centralized systems at separate locations into a single integrated system based around local networks.

5. Local Network Functions

Probably the most important example of a distributed processing architecture is that of a network. The functional nature of a local network architecture is described in this section. Like an operating system, a local network architecture can be viewed as a set of embedded architectures or layers performing a set of increasingly complex functions. For local networks, these functions are summarized as follows:

Access path. Provides physical connections between system hosts.
Analog/digital conversion. Provides modulation/demodulation and analog/digital (A/D) signal conversion functions for the connections.
Data links. Develop a protocol to transmit messages across the paths.
Multiplexing. Overlays a switching regime on the data links to allow for multiplexing for economic purposes.
Communication subnetwork. Its topology and switches provide for end-to-end protocols, error control, buffering, flow control, addressing, and routing to ensure that messages are sent and received by the correct hosts.
Switch interface. Provides message assembly/disassembly, buffering, and flow control to interface hosts to the communication subnetwork.
Dialogue manager. Sets up the "connections" between end users.
Internetting/protocol conversion. Ensures that messages and their formats are compatible among hosts/networks/other local networks, etc.
Network control. Controls levels and their setup, parameters, etc.

These functions may be viewed as operating in a peer fashion and exist in all systems in which two processors must communicate with messages.

6. Examples

With the widespread interest in local computer networks, it is becoming increasingly important to categorize them to aid in their evaluation and to determine their features. As the attempts to date indicate, LCNs are difficult to categorize. Many features of LCNs are common to distributed processors and geographically distributed networks. Other LCNs have features that make it difficult to distinguish them from that of a centralized computer site. In many cases, the differences between LCNs, distributed processors, and geographically distributed networks are in an issue of degree rather than kind. Further, networks are being devised that contain a number of interconnected local networks.

Thurber and Freeman have developed a taxonomy that is based on the evolution context of the systems, the reasons for this development, and the subnetwork communication technology involved. Many local computer networks exist within a building or complex of buildings and have evolved as an experiment in distributed processing in which new system concepts were tried and developed. Others evolved out of a need to embrace the existing computer systems to improve system usage, extend communication capabilities, or to provide more memory at a reasonable cost. I/O channels and bus structures are included as subnetwork communication technologies because they are extremely cost competitive over the few miles that LCNs are thought to extend. As with long-haul networks, packet and circuit switching are also appropriate subnetwork communication technologies.

The taxonomy that was developed was shown in Fig. 2. At the lowest level, seven categories have been identified. For each category, the major local computer networks that were identified are listed. The systems range from those that have been designed but whose implementation has not been completed [e.g., DDLCN (37)], to those working networks [e.g., Ethernet (54), OCTOPUS (69)], to those commercially available LCNs [e.g., HYPERchannel (61), RINGNET (18), SHINPADS® (42)]. If the intention was to construct the network, it is included. System designs that were the result of Masters or Ph.D. theses were excluded as were systems that fell into the "wouldn't it be nice to have this type of network" category.

7. System Summaries

Four important local network concepts will be covered in this section. Three of these will be specific system concepts: Ethernet, AN/USQ-67, and HYPERchannel. The fourth will be rings. In the description of rings, general strategies to develop rings will be described due to the extreme importance of this system concept and the large number of extant example systems which are built around various ring structures. Ethernet will be discussed because it is a very good example of three points: (1) a contention channel approach to the communication architecture, (2) an "available product" from Xerox Corporation, and (3) a very well documented system, with major results that are available in the public literature. The AN/USQ-67 will be discussed because it is an example of a circuit switch-based local network in which software operating systems are used to build a set of virtual multiprocessors. Last, the HYPERchannel concept is described to illustrate the state of the art with respect to purchasing hardware components that will allow a designer to interconnect a number of computers built by various manufacturers.

7.1 Ethernet

Ethernet is a concept that evolved at the Xerox Palo Alto Research Center (PARC) over a period of years. It started as a single local network and evolved into an experimental system consisting of several local Ethernets connected together via an internetting technique, or set of gateways, and also connected via a gateway to the Advanced Research Projects Agency Network (ARPANET) and into the Bay Area Packet Radio Network. In late 1979, Xerox introduced an Ethernet connection as part of a product, the 860.

Ethernet is shown in Fig. 3. The concept of a contention channel is illustrated in Fig. 4.

Physically, the Ethernet can be viewed as a set of nodes connected onto a coaxial cable. Each node consists of a cable connector, transceiver, cable to a processor interface, and the processor. Most of the processors on the network are ALTOs; however, DEC, Data General, and Hewlett Packard processors are also available as hosts. ALTOs are custom designed minicomputers designed at PARC, and a typical network may have upward of 100 nodes on it.

Access of a processor to the communication channel is via a contention concept. Each node monitors the state of the coaxial cable. If the cable is not in use, then the node can transmit. This monitoring is known as car-

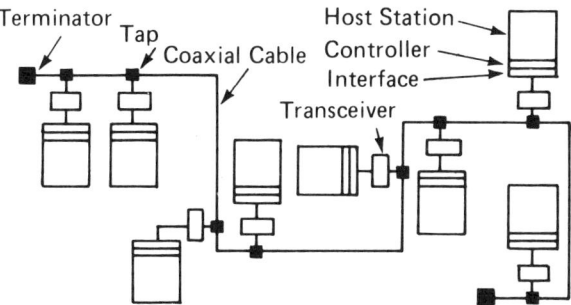

FIG. 3. Ethernet.

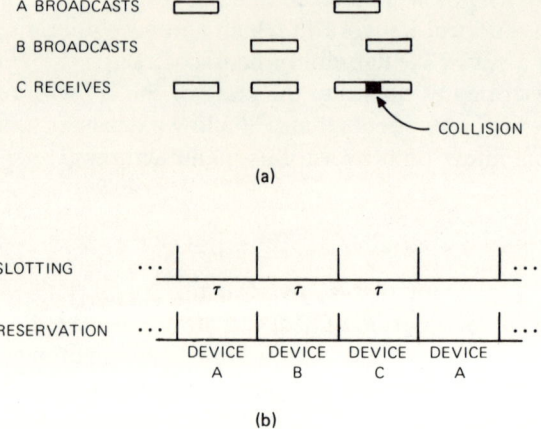

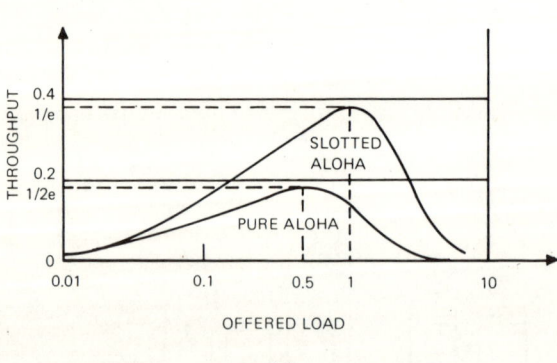

FIG 4. Contention channels: (a) broadcast concept, (b) options; (c) characteristics; (d) throughput versus load; (e) Ethernet test result: linearity due to listen before talk orientation of design; (f) effect of packet size on Ethernet contention channel utilization; (g) Franta's simulation of delay versus channel throughput on a parametric model ($K = 10$, $a = 0.01$).

LOCAL COMPUTER NETWORKS

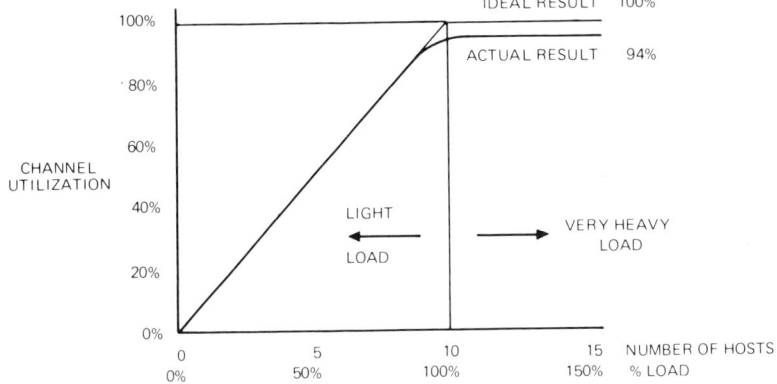

OFFERED LOAD WITH EACH HOST ATTEMPTING TO GENERATE A 10% LOAD

(e)

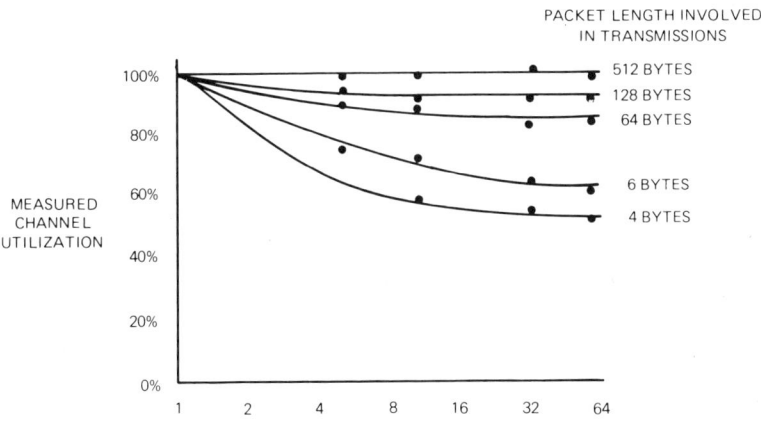

NUMBER OF HOSTS TRYING TO GENERATE A 100% CHANNEL UTILIZATION LOAD

(f)

FIG 4. (*Continued*)

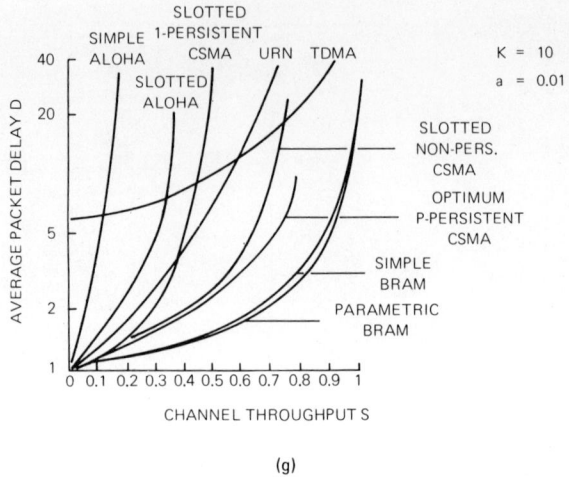

(g)

FIG 4. (*Continued*)

rier sensing. Clearly, two nodes may try to transmit at about the same time, at which point a collision may occur. In such a case of collision, the nodes go into a jamming procedure, which is designed to ensure that all nodes see the collision. After the jam procedure, each processor involved in the collision determines the time at which it will again try to broadcast. This is done by generating a start time within a particular interval. Each time a transmission attempt fails, then the interval size is changed (doubled from the previous size). This is known as a binary exponential back-off scheme. If the interval gets to a maximum size, an error routine is called.

A node broadcasts a datagram.[2] The datagram mechanism is unreliable, and some datagrams may not be delivered. In such cases, the appropriate acknowledgments will not be received and the datagram will be rebroadcast. A reliable communication mechanism is built upon this unreliable datagram facility using higher level protocol structures (*71*).

The protocol hierarchy of PUP and Ethernet is shown in Fig. 5 (*71*). The overall internetwork strategy of Ethernet is that of the PUP datagram shown in Fig. 6. The basic PUP datagram is encapsulated for various internetwork transmissions in the forms shown in Fig. 6. Routing is performed via a decentralized adaptive router, as in ARPANET (*71*).

---

[2] A datagram is an individual packet of information. A datagram interface between processors promises a best-effort transmission, and thus does not guarantee delivery, order of delivery, time taken for delivery, status or existance of duplicates, error-free delivery, etc.

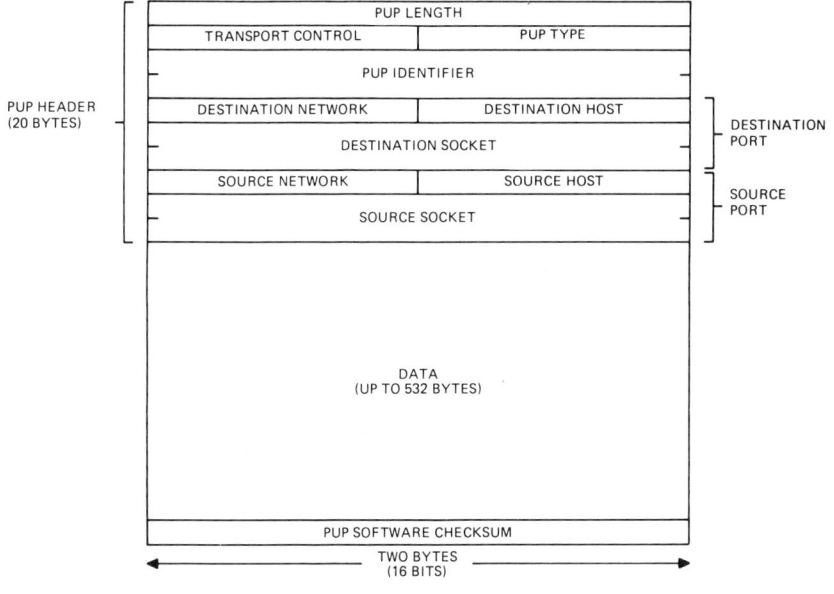

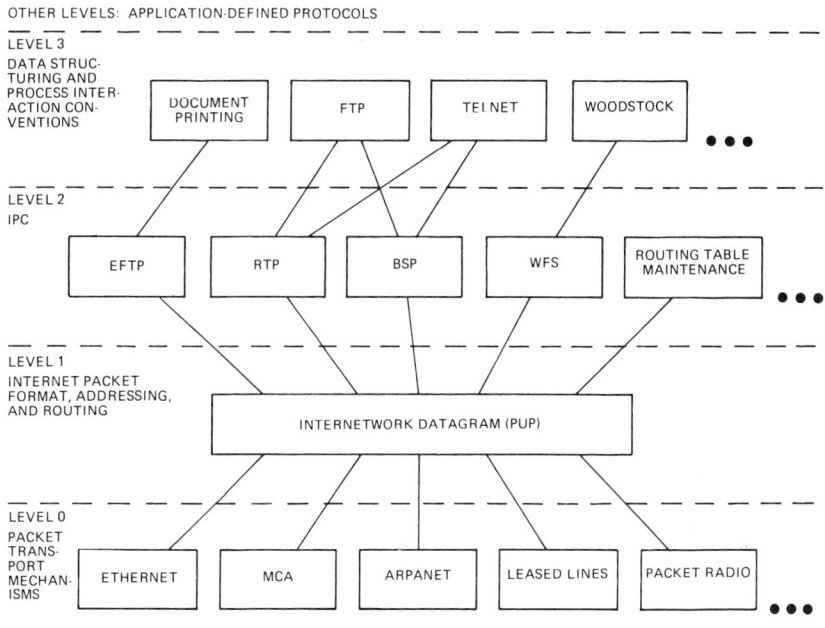

FIG. 5. PUP: (a) PUP datagram; (b) protocol hierarchy.

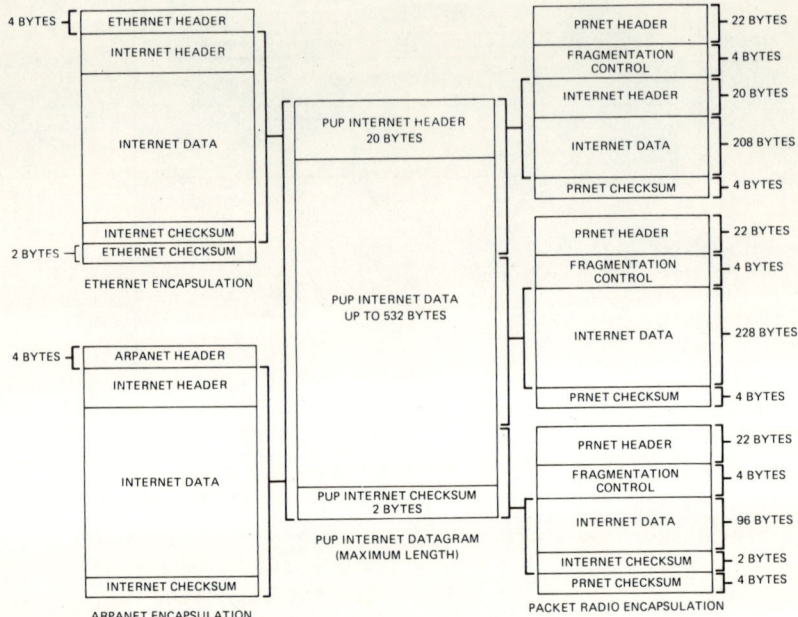

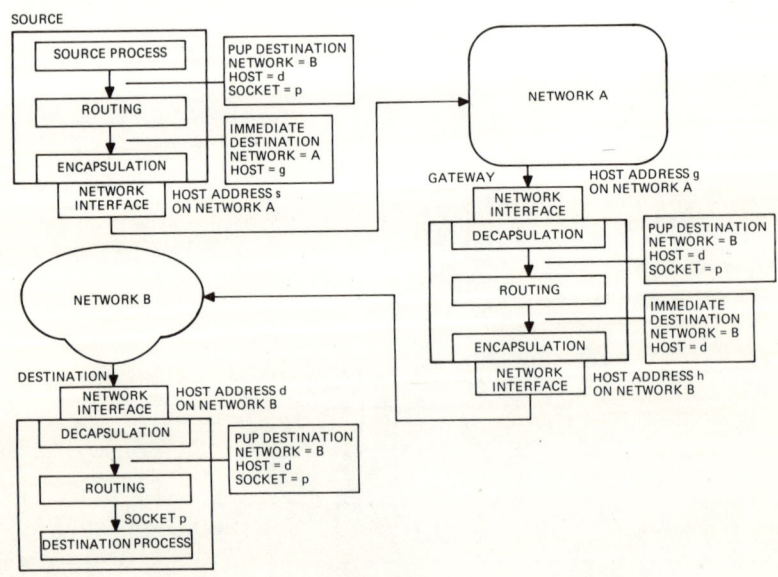

FIG. 6. Use of PUP: (a) internet encapsulation; (b) internet routing.

Typical performance of the Ethernet communication scheme is quite important. At peak periods, single nets with almost 130 nodes have exhibited communication loads near 40%, whereas overall average loads have been on the order of 2–3% (71). Shoch's measurements (71) of the communication mechanism have shown that the combination of carrier sense for collision avoidance, and exponential backoff provide a stable linear communication mechanism in comparison to pure Aloha strategies, which become unstable at large loads (see Fig. 4).

The use of Ethernet strategies in future system concepts such as office automation systems promises to provide a new dimension in system design.

7.2 AN/USQ-67

AN/USQ-67 is the nomenclature for a large circuit switch (crossbar switch) shown in Fig. 7. The switch has a size of 640 elements and consists of 640 high-speed serial links. Each link can interface to an I/O channel via a serial/parallel conversion device. Thus, the system may be modeled as shown in Fig. 7. There are a number of important features of the system concept. First, the switch acts essentially as a set of direct point-to-point connections whenever it is set in a given state. Second, the topology of the switch tends to look like a star; i.e., a set of devices surround-

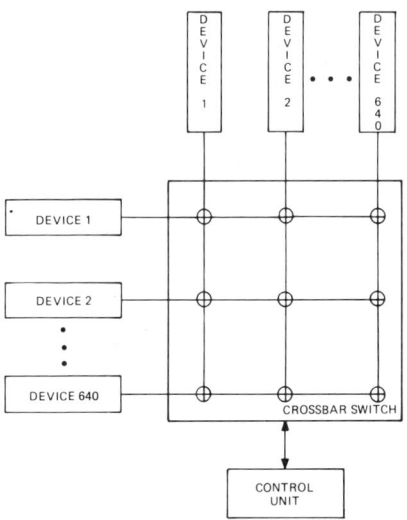

FIG. 7. AN/USQ-67.

ing or eminating from a central point. Last, because of the nature of the interface between processors, the links must be high speed. Typically, interfaced to a circuit is a 32-bit parallel I/O channel capable of operating at a rate in the microsecond range. This forces the individual serial circuits going through the switch to have a bandwidth requirement over 32 times the bandwidth of the fastest I/O channel assuming the following:

(1) The interfaces connect to only I/O channels;
(2) all circuits in the switch are serial; and
(3) the basic word size of a channel is 32-bits plus some error-correction bits.

The circuits in the switch are serial instead of multiple line to cut down the amount of hardware in the switch. The ramification of this is that the line circuits must be very high speed.

The system can be envisioned as operating as follows. At some time point, a setting of the switch (or set of routes through the switch) is determined and the setting is made. The switch setting then effects a set of interconnections of processors via either their I/O channels or via hardware which looks like their I/O channels, as shown in Fig. 7. This switch setting specifically describes a set of hardware connections which gives a set of hardware processor interrelationships. It is conceivable that a number of disjoint groupings of the hardware are specified, in which case a number of disjoint system configurations may be simultaneously supported. It is thus possible that this one local network (from the hardware perspective) may be able to support multiple virtual systems.

Assuming that the specified interconnections have been made, then software is placed upon the processors. If, for example, the switch setting provides an interconnection pattern that looks like a set of multiprocessors (implemented via I/O channel interconnections), then the appropriate operating systems may be placed on each separate multiprocessor, and a set of individual multiprocessors operating without knowledge of each other may be in operation. It now is clear why the circuits must be so fast. If the circuits were slower than the fastest I/O channel rate, then delays would be inserted, which would not allow the systems to have the illusion of physical proximity. The clear advantage of this system is that by using local networking concepts a facility has been built which allows hardware to be shared such that a number of multiprocessor configurations can be used for development, simulation, or performance monitoring without actually building all the configurations. The hardware to simultaneously build all configurations is not necessary, assuming that all possible systems are not required to be operational at all times.

7.3 HYPERchannel

The HYPERchannel of Network Systems Corporation is a concept for a set of building blocks to be used to build both local computer networks and back-end storage networks. Originally, the goal of the company was to build back-end storage networks for the "computer center of the future"; however, due to funding constraints in starting a new company, the products originally developed by the company were involved with the communication mechanism for local networks. A number of years after the original product announcements, the HYPERcache®, a mechanism that can be used in conjunction with HYPERchannel to build a back-end storage network, was introduced. The concept and availability of HYPERchannel products is summarized in Fig. 8. Figure 9 summarizes the HYPERcache concept, and Figure 10 shows a typical configuration of these products as a local network back-end storage network.

The HYPERchannel itself consists of a tapped coaxial cable capable of transmitting signals over distances on the order of about 1000 m at rates of up to 50 MHz. Connected onto this cable are devices called adaptors. Each adaptor consists of a buffered storage area along with a microprogrammed processor designed to interface to a device, accept data from the device, and transmit the data to another adaptor. The adaptors transmit the data between each other in a special protocol (or format). This format was originally based upon a zero-insertion protocol, but was later changed to a length-oriented protocol. Each adaptor can connect to up to

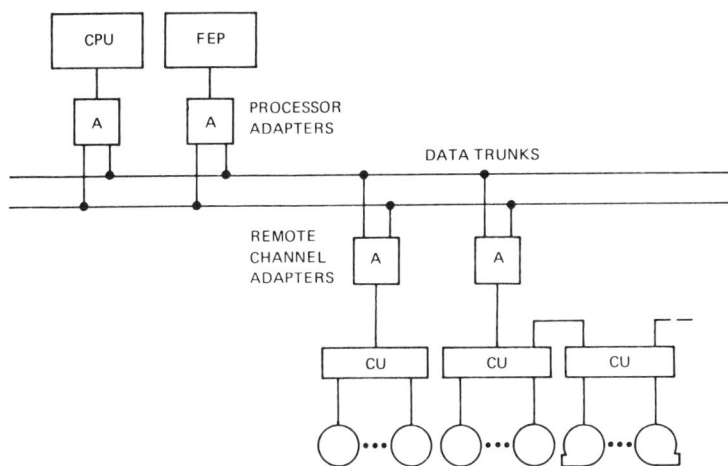

FIG. 8. HYPERchannel concept.

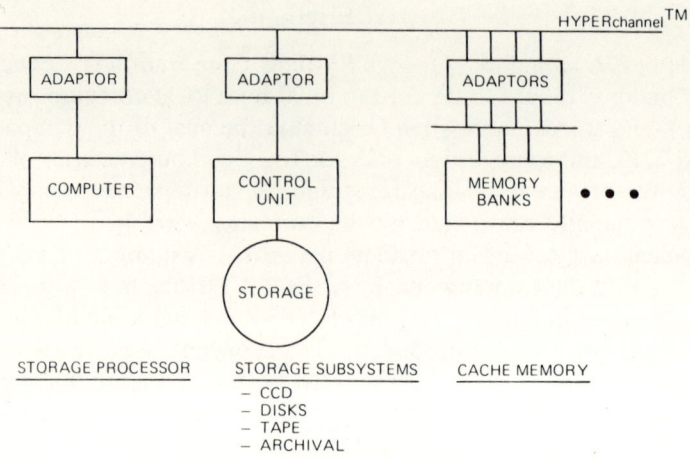

Fig. 9. HYPERcache concept.

four coaxial cables in parallel. On the device side, each adaptor connects to a specific type of device in a specific way. Some adaptors connect to processors via I/O channels; others connect to memories via DMA (direct memory access) channels. The adaptor buffers information transfers from the processor memory and places the data into the proper format for transfer to another adaptor. Additional adaptor types are available that allow for connection to a channel control unit. These adaptors allow for unit record equipment to be interfaced directly onto the coax via an adaptor connected to their channel control unit. As indicated in Fig. 11, such a connection may be made remotely. In such cases, the adaptor connected

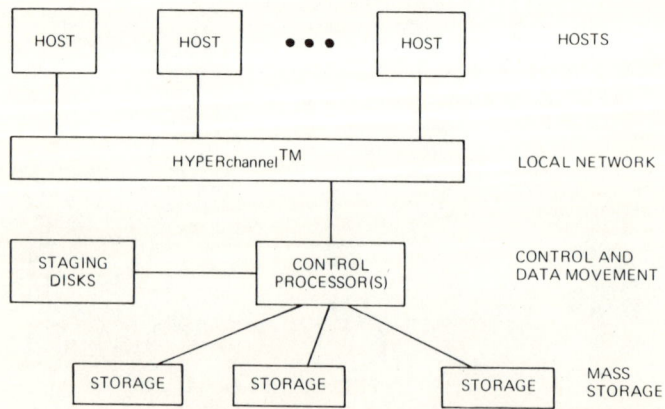

Fig. 10. Shared VSS from MASSTOR: A backend storage network.

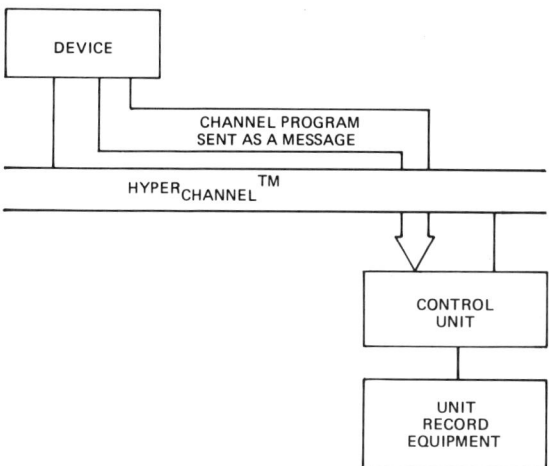

FIG. 11. Remote channel usage on HYPERchannel.

to the processor desiring to use the unit record equipment will transfer the channel program to the adaptor, which will look like the channel to the channel control unit. In some cases, the operating system of the processor may be modified so that the channel program can reside on the remote adaptor and be called from the processor. The HYPERchannel bus allocation scheme is based upon a prioritized carrier sense concept; i.e., any device can access the bus if no device is transmitting. If a device is locked out from transmitting for an extended period of time, a priority bias eventually asserts itself to ensure bus access. The carrier sense concept is modified by a collision detection scheme and no acknowledgement of a transmission, a faulty ACK, or a detected collision all cause a transmission retry. Actual data transmission is done bit serial, using a Manchester code.

The HYPERcache is a large, high-speed buffer memory, which connects to the HYPERchannel using a set of adaptors. It is used primarily to buffer a transmission when a sender is ready but the destination is busy. It may, however, have many other uses. For one, it can be used as a centralized store-and-forward buffer pool. If multiple HYPERcaches are included in a network, they can be used as packet switches distributed on the HYPERchannel. Another use is to form a back-end storage network where the HYPERcache is used as a buffer or staging device, as shown in Fig. 10. A product developed around this concept is that of the shared VSS® of MASSTOR Corporation.

One complaint about the HYPERchannel has been its cost in comparison to a minicomputer. Part of this "problem" results from the extensive cost to develop and build high-speed hardware. With respect to minicomputers, e.g., the PDP-11, up to four PDP-11s can be multiplexed onto an adaptor. Further, it can be expected that Network Systems Corporation will begin to develop products that meet the competitive cost constraints of large user bases.

7.4 Rings

There are a wide variety of ring networks available. One reason for this is the relative ease with which a ring (or loop) can be implemented. Most of the differences in ring system are due to algorithm differences in the detailed implementation. There are really two primary ring strategies: The Pierce loop (72) and the DLCN loop of Liu (34). Another important case, the Newell loop (73), is an extension of the Pierce concept. The general strategy of the ring concept is summarized in Fig. 12. Figures 13–15 illustrate the concept of the Pierce loop (73), Newell loop (74), and Liu's DLCN (34).

The Pierce loop can be thought of as the cylinders of a revolver. Each (message slot) cylinder is well defined by an encoding indicating whether it is empty or full. If the slot is empty, a message may be placed in the slot and the slot marked as full. If the slot is full, it may not be filled. As the slots circulate (the cylinder spins), each slot passing a processor is examined to determine whether it is empty (messages can be transmitted) or full (check to see if message is for this processor). Usually a processor is interfaced to the ring by a specialized interface designed to perform such processing and called a ring interface. In the Pierce case, the messages transmitted on the ring are considered to be of a fixed length. The "message" being circulated in a ring slot may consist of several subparts of a

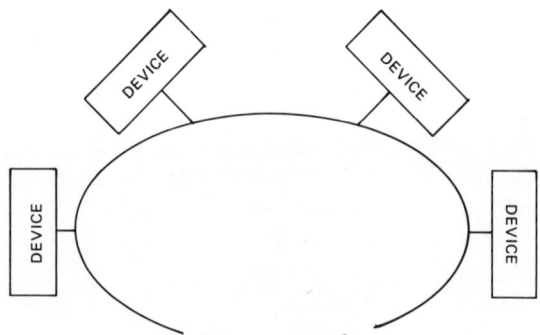

FIG. 12. Ring structure.

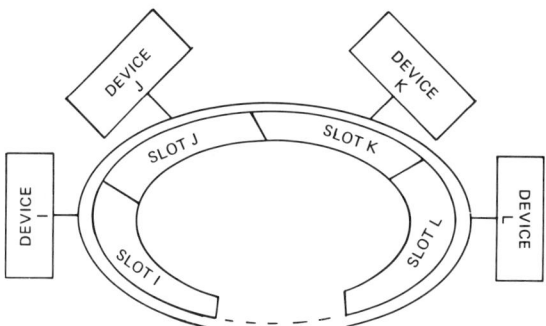

Fig. 13. Ring with fixed-size slots.

message that a process running on a processor is actually trying to transmit, thus necessitating software in the ring interface to reassemble the original message. It should be clear that the design of the ring protocols can be developed so that the ring acts as a circuit switch (provides a virtual circuit) or as a datagram-oriented network. Last, there may be several messages in transit on the ring at a given instance in time.

Newell loops operate much like a Pierce loop except that they allow for a variable-length message. Control of the loop is passed from processor to processor (commonly called "token passing"). When a processor has control of the loop and wishes to transmit a message, it transmits and then passes control. When a processor (or its ring interface) detects a message for itself, it removes the message from the ring. Because the message circulating on the ring is of variable length and the control token is passed from processor to processor, there can only be a single message on the loop at a given time.

The strategy of Liu for the DLCN loops is commonly known as the shift

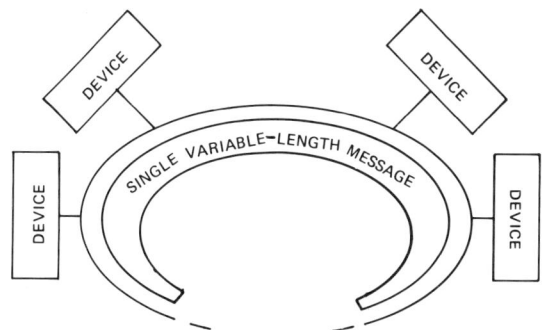

Fig. 14. Ring with single variable-length message.

DEVICE
DEVICE
DEVICE
DEVICE
RI
RI
RI
RI
M
M
M
M
M

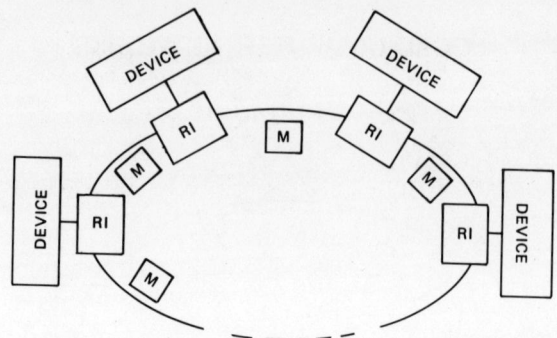

FIG. 15. Ring with shift register insertion capability in the ring interface (RI), where M is a message and RI is the ring interface that buffers incoming messages and inserts a new message if desired.

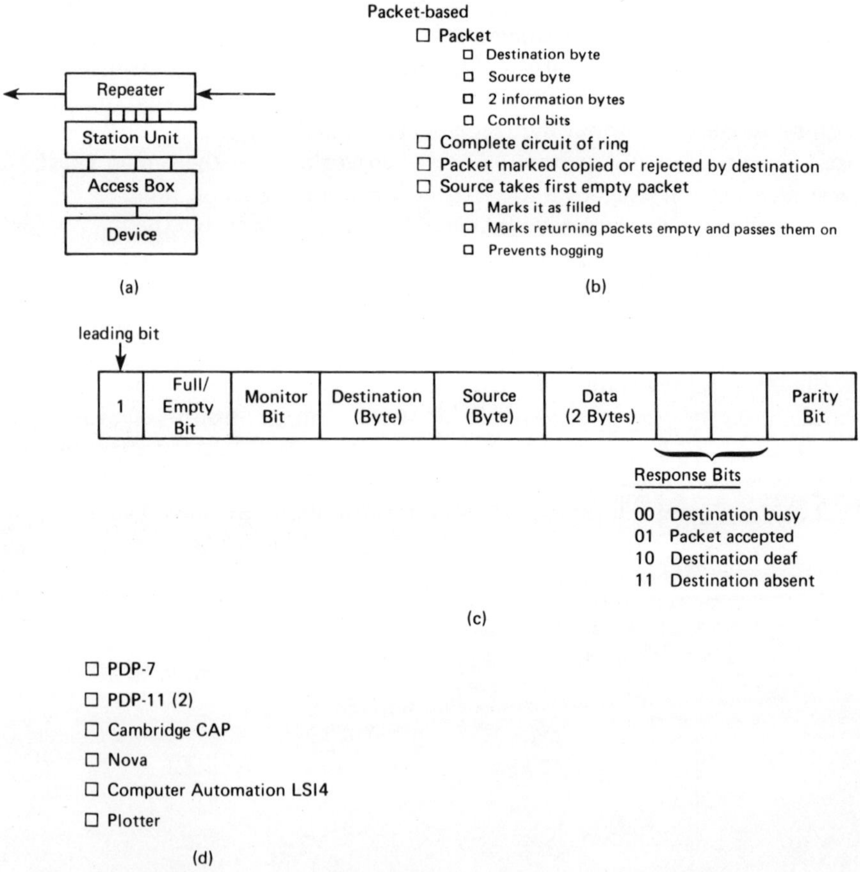

Repeater
Station Unit
Access Box
Device
(a)
Packet-based
☐ Packet
☐ Destination byte
☐ Source byte
☐ 2 information bytes
☐ Control bits
☐ Complete circuit of ring
☐ Packet marked copied or rejected by destination
☐ Source takes first empty packet
☐ Marks it as filled
☐ Marks returning packets empty and passes them on
☐ Prevents hogging
(b)
leading bit
1
Full/ Empty Bit
Monitor Bit
Destination (Byte)
Source (Byte)
Data (2 Bytes)
Parity Bit
Response Bits
00 Destination busy
01 Packet accepted
10 Destination deaf
11 Destination absent
(c)
☐ PDP-7
☐ PDP-11 (2)
☐ Cambridge CAP
☐ Nova
☐ Computer Automation LSI4
☐ Plotter
(d)

FIG. 16. Cambridge ring: (a) basic node; (b) concept; (c) packet format [packets follow head-to-tail maximum capacity and gap digits terminate a train of packets (establish frame)]; (d) node equipment.

register insertion strategy. This concept can be visualized as providing two buffers in the ring interface: an output buffer and a delay buffer. Messages produced at the processor that owns the ring interface are placed into the output buffer. The delay buffer is used to buffer incoming messages. If a processor desires to transmit a message, it finds the end of an outgoing message, inserts its outbound message (from the output buffer) while delaying any incoming message (in the delay buffer), and finally retransmits the accumulated messages in the delay buffer either to its own processor (if it is the destination) or else on to the next processor in the ring. This strategy allows multiple variable-length messages to be handled, but requires that the ring interfaces have a store-and-forward capability.

In addition to the previously mentioned concepts, there are a large number of ring strategies available: hierarchical, star shaped, etc. They vary in a number of details as to message length, whether traffic flows bidirectionally or undirectionally, whether bidirectional traffic can occur simultaneously, whether multiple rings are provided for reliability and redundancy reasons, etc., but most are variations on either the Pierce, Newell, or Liu DLCN rings. A particularly interesting ring, the Cambridge ring (24), is summarized in Fig. 16.

8. Hardware Availability

The previously mentioned taxonomies (6–8,11) identify about 80 different local network systems. Clearly, there is much interest in this area. The majority of these systems have an unfortunate property in that they are custom built and are thus not the type of equipment that one can go out and purchase. Many have grown out of experiments. Some, particularly at universities, have grown out of the necessity to connect together a large number of machines to achieve some specific computational goal.

Let us assume for the moment that you want a local network. You have a strong desire to get one for your computer center, office of the future, etc. Where can you get one right now? What kinds can you buy? Unfortunately, for all of the emphasis in this technology area, the majority of systems are experimental. In this section an overview of some of the hardware that can be purchased will be given. Note that we said "hardware," because in general you must build your own software. This should not discourage you, because at least hardware exists, and eventually software will be developed.

Let us get specific. We are interested in hardware, particularly, hardware that is in production. Where do we go? After looking around for a while, we decided that there are a variety of places to obtain hardware that could be a local network. This hardware exists at many system levels and thus is as hard to classify as a local network is to identify.

8.1 Application-Embedded Hardware

Some local network hardware is not available as a specific piece of hardware; i.e., it is embedded in a system and comes as part of the system and associated application—whether you want it or not. Such system hardware may be deeply embedded in the application system, or it may be accessible so that the hardware can be configured into a local network, or the application may be modified to exploit the known hardware characteristics.

An example of such a system is the Xerox 860 office automation system,[3] which contains an Ethernet interface embedded in the product. Many products in the area of communications or word processing have this type of characteristic.

8.2 Turnkey Systems

A number of groups provide turnkey systems made of their main frames (or minicomputers). It is to the manufacturer's advantage to provide such a product, and it is also easy. If you have a networking product currently, you can develop versions of the transport mechanism designed to work in a geographically local environment. In fact, this may even simplify the design. One ring-oriented structure that provides local networking capabilities is the RINGNET of Prime Computer Corporation. Other system concepts such as SNA (IBM) and DECNET (DEC) could be utilized in a local network framework. Zilog's Z-NET® provides local network capability for microcomputers.

8.3 Subsystem Building Blocks

With certain components, you may be able to build very interesting products. Such hardware may be the basis for a subsystem. Hardware available in the category of subsystems is now appearing. The most "well-known" subsystem is a back-end storage network known as Shared VSS (Virtual Storage System) (75) being built by the MASSTOR Corporation. This subsystem is based upon the Network Systems Corporation HYPERchannel and HYPERcache used in conjunction with the equiva-

---

[3] See Section 7.1 for a discussion of Ethernet.

lent of IBM 3850 and IBM 4341 systems to provide for a very large staged-memory subsystem. The concept is quite simple. Shared VSS provides for the on-line capability to share a back-end storage network with several nonhomogeneous hosts. The large data base is stored in archival storage, and its movement into a host is controlled via a control processor from the archival and backing storage into a HYPERcache and eventually via the HYPERchannel into the appropriate host.

8.4 Components/Modules

The most exciting area for local networking is the problem of interconnecting a number of nonhomogeneous computers into a network. Since the machines come from a variety of manufacturers, there is most probably no available software, and the manufacturers probably try to discourage this procedure for obvious reasons. But the fact remains that a majority of the hardware produced for local networking falls into this category. Competition is increasing in this area and can be expected to intensify.

To date, the most significant commercial-grade hardware components or modules available to assist in the development of local networks are available from Network Systems Corporation. Almost 20 adaptor types are available for the HYPERchannel, in addition to the HYPERcache (76). Control Data Corporation (77) is in the process of announcing competitive hardware to Network Systems Corporation adaptors, and Sperry Univac has introduced military hardware to construct bus-oriented local networks. A number of manufacturers provide hardware products in this category.

8.5 Chips

Chips and chip sets are now becoming available that may be used to support local network construction. Western Digital is producing an X.25 chip, while Harris is developing hybrid and single-chip 1553 military bus interfaces. A number of other semiconductor manufacturers are planning to introduce local network bus chips. In particular, Intel, DEC, and Xerox have announced plans to jointly develop a standard local network interface chip based upon the Ethernet concept.

8.6 Hardware Overview

We have briefly discussed a set of categories of local network hardware and some of the types of hardware that might be available in a category.

Table I

Available Off-the-Shelf Hardware for LNI

Application Embedded Hardware
  ROLM REMS (ROLM Electronic Mail System): an electronic mail concept based around application extension of ROLM PBX (Private Branch Exchange) Systems
  Wang Mailway: an electronic mail concept based on application extensions of Wang word processors
  Xerox 860: a word-processing system containing an Ethernet interface

Turnkey Systems
  DEC DNA: if the processors were placed in close (local) proximity, DNA could be considered a local net.
  IBM SNA and 8100 SDLC ring: if the processors were placed in close proximity, SNA and/or the 8100 SDLC ring could be a local net.
  Prime Computer RINGNET: a token-based ring system. A similar concept, "Computer Cells," is available for multiprocessors.
  Zilog Z-NET: a bus system that is used to connect MCZ 2 computers

Subsystem Building Blocks
  MASSTOR Shared VSS: a back-end storage network

Components/Modules
  AMDAX CDX: a modem-based local network concept
  Bolt, Beranek & Newman, Inc. (BBN) Pluribus IMP: a multiprocessor interface message processor originally designed for the ARPANET
  Control Data LCN: a high-performance set of local network interfaces
  Computer Megalink: multidrop bus based on DMA interfaces
  Digital Communications CAPAC®· Cable Access Packet Communications System for interfacing RS 232 devices using FSK modems
  Digital Equipment Corp. (DEC) PCL-11, DR11, etc.: a number of DEC devices, PCL-11 DR11 cards, etc.; could be used to build local networks

  Hewlett Packard (HP) DS 1000: packet switch connections for local networks
  IEEE 488 Bus: built by various manufacturers; could be used to build local networks
  NESTAR Systems Cluster/One®: local network hardware for use with personal computers
  Network Systems Corporation HYPERchannel and HYPERcache: the largest selection of adaptors and support hardware available to build nonhomogeneous networks of large main frames; a high-speed memory subsystem available to assist in the development of back-end storage networks and useful to add store-and-forward capability to HYPERchannel-based systems
  Network Systems LNI: a PDP-11-based ring concept
  Sperry Univac AN/USQ-67, SHINPADS®, and EPIC/OPS: AN/USQ-67, a 640 × 640 circuit switch for local nets; SHINPADS, a high-speed bus structure for local nets; EPIC/DPS, a ring-based local network that may be virtualized into a centralized system concept
  Three Rivers Computer Packet Stream Network: contention-based coaxial system
  Ungermann-Bass Net/One: local net based on microprocessor node hardware
  Wang WISE (Wang Inter System Exchange): can be used to build local networks of Wang equipments

Chips
  Harris 1553: the 1553 is a standard military serial interface. Harris is building such interfaces on modules and is developing such interfaces as single chips
  Western Digital X.25: Western Digital has announced an X.25 standard chip which primarily implements HDLC
  Xerox/Intel/DEC: announced a joint venture to develop a standard Ethernet protocol chip

LOCAL COMPUTER NETWORKS 109

What would we find if we tried to perform an exhaustive list of such hardware? It depends! Since we cannot define a local network precisely, we clearly cannot build an exhaustive survey. Table I provides a representative view of available off-the-shelf hardware. In each category, the hardware is listed alphabetically by manufacturer.

9. Computer Centers and Offices of the Future: Directions

The direction of networks and distributed processing is toward hierarchial linked groups of local networks. Local nets are the key to the future. Although there will still be computer centers, their character will be enhanced. Note that the doom of computer-center-type operations is not predicted; rather, their evolution in a fashion that is designed to make them more useful is predicted. This direction is oriented toward, but not limited to, a local network internetted to other local networks and providing enhanced capabilities. This complicates systems, and the process will be evolutionary rather than revolutionary. There is no need to throw away current system hardware in the hopes of finding a magical solution to system problems. Examples of the types of systems that can be expected are existing electronic fund transfer systems and military communication systems. Such systems have one major new system characteristic; they combine two important technologies, communications and computers, into a single integrated system. The characteristics of such systems are summarized below.

Electronic fund transfer (EFT) systems provide support to both retail and wholesale operations. Typical functions include money transfer (both domestic and international), cable messages, letter of credit instruments, federal reserve messages, and clearinghouse information. To adequately perform, the system must provide fast service, a log of all transactions, redundancy, and the ability to distinguish transfers that have been completed out of a set processed from a queue in case of a system failure. Because of the nature of the application, it does not require large amounts of flexibility and can be evolved from current hardware concepts.

Military networks must be designed to support voice and data traffic for messages. Generally, such networks must support both narrow- and wide-band applications over long-haul distances. The key design issues include extensive security and encryption requirements, the need to evolve from existing systems, system combination, and integration with up to 30 different existing "standard" systems.

Generally, based upon the requirements of EFT and military systems, the services required by the user will include:

Reliability
Security
Maintainability
Tested and proven system features
Simple user interfaces:
    Portable terminals
    Standard terminals (e.g., remote bank terminals)
    Ability to cross network boundaries
    Ability to access a hierarchy of services at varying costs
Voice service
Data service
Graphics service

The major application areas of the future will be houses, offices, and "computer centers."

The main functions associated with houses will be functions such as electronic mail, on-line libraries, electronic option polls, intruder detection, maintenance of family records, and energy management. Such services will be integrated into, or with, cable television and phone systems.

In the offices of the future, one can expect such functions as integrated documentation, storage, data collection, test services, graphics, and other utilities. All such services will be available from an on-line system.

Computer centers of the future will provide for the connection of many machines which in the past may have been dedicated to particular functions. The systems will provide for capabilities to hold very large data bases directly on line.

Houses, offices, and computer centers will be hierarchically linked to provide complete functions and service to a user group.

10. The Future

A conclusion to this article would be inappropriate as there is nothing approaching a conclusion to the saga of local networks. What has transpired to date is that a large number of systems have been developed experimentally, researchers have just begun to meet to discuss the future potential of local networks, and a small number of products have been introduced either as a part of a larger system (Xerox) or as building blocks designed to allow system designers to build systems.

What will transpire in the future is indicated in Fig. 17. Computer centers will be enhanced. Current main frames will be collected into local networks inside factories, offices, and corporations. Use of local networks in systems will bring about new concepts and meaning to the concept of office automation. It is truly feasible for every person in an office to connect into a local network for data-base access, text editing, etc. These local

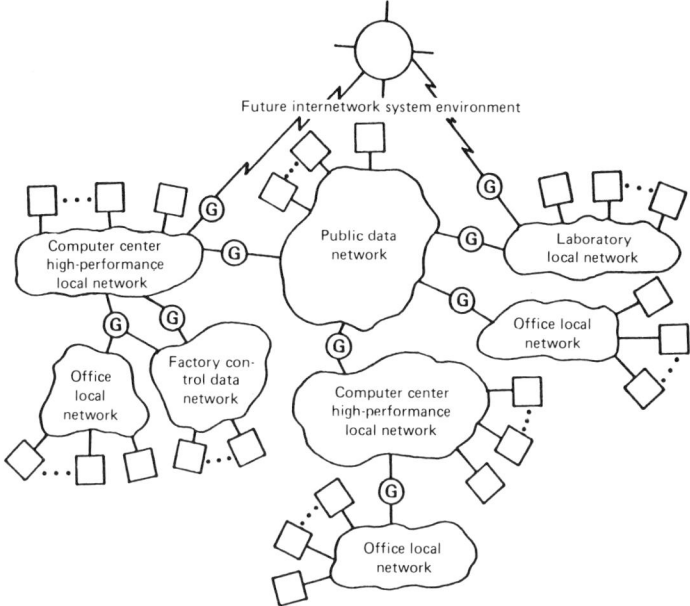

Fig. 17. Most probable future system environment.

networks may include back-end storage networks which will provide the function of massive amounts of on-line system storage to the local network. These local networks will be hierarchically grouped within regions comprising cities and countries through the use of public data networks or private data networks built using radio or microwave technologies. These networks will eventually be linked across nations and continents using public or private carrier and satellite facilities.

Local network technology is causing a reassessment of network architecture concepts and is pushing the designer into a view of a "network" as a hierarchically organized group of cooperating local networks. The development and implementation of such networks is just beginning.

ACKNOWLEDGMENTS

Special thanks go to John Shoch and Butler Lampson for their assistance with the section describing Ethernet, and to Harvey Freeman for his help in constructing the reference section.

REFERENCES

1. Thurber, K. J., and Freeman, H. A. (1980). "Tutorial: Local Computer Networks." IEEE Computer Society, Long Beach, California.

2. Cotton, I. W., ed. (1978). "Local Area Networking," Report of a Workshop Held at the National Bureau of Standards, August 22–23, 1977. U.S. Dept. of Commerce, National Bureau of Standards, Washington, D.C.
3. Patton, P. C., and Franck, A., eds. (1976–1978). "Proceedings of the University of Minnesota Workshop on Local Computer Networks. Sept. 16–17, 1976, Oct. 13–14, 1977, and Oct. 23–24, 1978. University of Minnesota, Minneapolis.
4. "Proceedings of the Local Area Communications Network Symposium. May 1979." Boston, Massachusetts.
5. "Proceedings of the 4th Conference on Local Computer Networks, Oct. 22–23, 1979." University of Minnesota, Minneapolis.
6. Thurber, K. J., and Freeman, H. A. (1979). Architecture considerations for local computer networks. *Proc. Int. Conf. Distributed Comput. Syst., 1st, 1979* pp. 131–142.
7. Clark, D. D., *et al.* (1978). An introduction to local area networks. *Proc. IEEE* **66**, No. 11, 1497–1517.
8. Cotton, I. W. (1979). Technologies for local area computer networks. *Proc. Local Area Commun. Network Symp., 1979* pp. 25–45.
9. Anderson, R. J. (1979). Local data networks—Traditional concepts and methods. *Proc. Local Area Commun. Network Symp., 1979* pp. 127–149.
10. Fraser, A. G. (1976). The present status and future trends in computer communication technology. *Communications* **14**, No. 5, 10–19, 27.
11. Shoch, J. F. (1979). "An Annotated Bibliography on Local Computer Networks," Xerox Parc Tech. Rep. SSL-79-5.
12. Swan, R. J., *et al.* (1977). Cm*—A modular, multi-microprocessor. *AFIPS Conf. Proc.* **46**, 637–644.
13. Hinton, O. R., et al. (1977). Distributed industrial control using a network of microcomputers. *COMPCON '77 Fall* pp. 316–319.
14. Pogran, K. T., and Reed, D. P. (1978). The MIT laboratory for computer science network. *NBS Spec. Publ. (U.S.)* **500-31**, 20–22.
15. Fraser, A. G. (1974). Spider-An experimental data communications system. *ICC '74 Conf. Rec.* pp. 21 F-1–21 F-10.
16. Willard, D. G. (1974). A time division multiple access system for digital communication. *Comput. Des.,* June, 1974.
17. Gordon, R. L., *et al.* (1979). Ringnet: A packet switched local network with decentralized control. *Proc. Conf. Local Comput. Networks, 4th, 1979* pp. 13–19.
18. Rawson, E. G., and Metcalfe, R. M. (1978). Fibernet: Multimode optical fibers for local computer networks. *IEEE Trans. Commun.* pp. 983–990.
19. Popescu-Zeletin, R. (1979). The data access and transfer support in a local heterogeneous network (HMINET). *Proc. Data Commun. Symp., 6th, 1979* pp. 147–152.
20. Manning, E. G., and Peebles, R. W. (1977). A homogeneous network for data sharing—communications. *Comput. Networks* **1**, No. 4, 211–224.
21. Wood, D. C., *et al.* (1979). A cable-bus protocol architecture. *Proc. DATACOM '79*, pp. 137–146.
22. Fraser, A. G. (1979). DATAKIT—A modular network for synchronous and asynchronous traffic. *ICC '79 Conf. Rec.* **2**, 20.1.1–20.1.3.
23. Hopper, A. (1978). Data ring at computer laboratory, University of Cambridge. *NBS Spec. Publ. (U.S.)* **500-31**, 11–17.
24. Wittie, L. D. (1979). MICRONET: A reconfigurable microcomputer network for distributed systems research. *Simulation,* Nov., 1978, 145–153.
25. Lin, K. (1978). Design of a packet-switched micro-subnetwork. *COMPCON '78 Fall* pp. 184–193.

26. Burnett, D. J., and Sethi, H. R. (1977). Packet switching at Philips Research Laboratories. *Comput. Networks* **1**, 341–348.
27. Springer, J. F. (1978). The distributed data network, its architecture and operation. *COMPCON '78 Fall* pp. 221–228.
28. Wulf, W., and Levin, R. (1975). A local network. *Datamation* Feb., 1975, pp. 47–50.
29. Quatse, J. T., *et al.* (1972). The external access network of a modular computer system. *AFIPS Conf. Proc.* **40**, 783–790.
30. Sperry Univac (1977). "AN/USQ-67 Converter—Switching System, Signal Data," Sperry Univac Prod. Description Bull. Sperry Univac, St. Paul, Minnesota.
31. Farber, D. J. (1975). A ring network. *Datamation* Feb., 1975, 44–46.
32. Jensen, E. D. (1978). The Honeywell experimental distributed processor—An overview. *Computer* **11**, No. 1, 28–38.
33. Liu, M. T. (1978). Distributed loop computer networks. *Adv. Comput.* **17**, 163–221.
34. Aramis, E., *et al.* (1979). ADCS: Aramis distributed computer system. *Comput. Networking Symp. Proc., 1979* pp. 139–151.
35. Aramis, E., *et al.* (1979). ORION: A new distributed loop computer network. *Comput. Networking Symp. Proc., 1979* pp. 164–168.
36. Wolf, J. J., and Lui, M. T. (1978). A distributed double-loop computer network (DDLCN). *Proc. Tex. Conf. Comput. Syst., 7th, 1978* pp. 6-19–6-34.
37. Biba, K. J., and Yeh, J. W. (1979). FordNet: A front-end approach to local computer networks. *Proc. Local Area Commun. Network Symp., 1979* pp. 199–215.
38. Gerhardstein, L. H., *et al.* (1978). The Pacific Northwest Laboratory Minicomputer Network. *Proc. Berkeley Workshop Distributed Data Manage. Comput. Networks, 3rd, 1978* pp. 144–158.
39. Huen, W., *et al.* (1977). A network computer for distributed processing. *COMPCON '77 Fall* pp. 326–330.
40. Anderson, D. R. (1975). The EPIC-DPS: A distributed network experiment. *EASCON '75 Rec.* pp. 121A–121G.
41. Kuhns, R. C., and Shoquist, M. C. (1979). A serial data bus system for local processing networks. *COMPCON '79 Spring Dig. Pap.* pp. 266–271.
42. Mills, D. L. (1976). An overview of the distributed computer network. *AFIPS Conf. Proc.* **45**, 523–531.
43. Rosen, S., and Steele, J. M. (1973). A local computer network. *COMPCON '73 Dig.* pp. 129–132.
44. Ashenhurst, R. L., and Vonderohe, R. H. (1975). A hierarchical network. *Datamation* Feb., 1975, 40–44.
45. Pohm, A. V., *et al.* (1979). A network of mini and microcomputers for experimental support. *Proc. Conf. Local Comput. Networks, 4th, 1979* pp. 91–96.
46. Lee, C. C., and Pohm, A. V. (1978). Interface processor for high speed recirculating data network. *COMPCON '78 Fall* pp. 194–200.
47. Mehra, S. K., and Majithia, J. C. (1979). A modified ethernet for multiprocessor intercommunications. *Proc. Comput. Network. Symp., 1979* pp. 132–138.
48. Hertzberg, R. Y., *et al.* (1979). The PROMIS network. *Proc. Local Area Commun. Network Symp., 1979* pp. 87–111.
49. Bowles, S. W. (1978). VICNET: An X.25 packet switching network. *Proc. N. Z. Comput. Conf., 6th, 1978* Vol. 1, pp. 83–99.
50. Mann, W. F., *et al.* (1976). A network-oriented multiprocessor front-end handling many hosts and hundreds of terminals. *AFIPS Conf. Proc.* **45**, 533–540.
51. Sakai, T., et al. (1977). Inhouse computer network KUIPNET. *In* "Information Processing" (B. Gilchrist, ed.), pp. 161–166. North-Holland Publ., Amsterdam.

52. Lidinsky, W. P. (1976). The Argonne intra-laboratory network. *Proc. Berkeley Workshop Distributed Data Manage. Comput. Networks, 1976* pp. 263–275.
53. Metcalfe, R. M., and Boggs, D. R. (1976). ETHERNET: Distributed packet switching for local computer networks. *Commun. ACM* **19**, No. 7, 395–404.
54. Sherman, R. H., et al. (1978). Current summary of Ford activities in local networking. *NBS Spec. Publ. (U.S.)* **500-31**, 22–23.
55. Binder, R., et al. (1975). ALOHA packet broadcasting—A retrospect. *AFIPS Conf. Proc.* **44**, 203–215.
56. Carpenter, R. J., et al. (1978). A microprocessor-based local network node. *COMPCON '78 Fall* pp. 104–109.
57. Nelson, D. L., and Gordon, R. L. (1978). Computer cells—A network architecture for data flow computing. *COMPCON '78 Fall* pp. 296–301.
58. Tokoro, M., and Tamaru, K. (1977). Acknowledging Ethernet. *COMPCON '77 Fall* pp. 320–325.
59. Hopkins, G. T. (1979). Multimode communications on the MITRENET. *Proc. Local Area Commun. Network Symp., 1979* pp. 169–177.
60. Thorton, J. E. (1980). Back-end network approaches. *Computer* pp. 10–17.
61. Szurkowski, E. (1978). A high bandwidth local computer network. *COMPCON '78 Fall* pp. 98–103.
62. Franck, A., et al. (1979). Some architectural and system implications of local computer networks. *COMPCON '79 Spring* pp. 272–276D.
63. Saltzer, J. H., and Pogran, K. T. (1979). A star-shaped ring network with high maintainability. *Proc. Local Area Commun. Network Symp., 1979* pp. 179–190.
64. Ball, J. E., et al. (1976). RIG, Rochester's intelligent gateway: System overview. *IEEE Trans. Software Eng.* **SE-2**, No. 4, 321–328.
65. Christman, R. D. (1973). Development of the LASL computer network. *COMPCON '73 Dig.* pp. 239–242.
66. Altaber, J. (1978). Real-time network for the control of a very large machine. *NBS Spec. Publ. (U.S.)* **500-31**, 5–6.
67. Yajima, S., et al. (1977). Labolink: An optically linked laboratory computer network. *Computer* pp. 52–59.
68. Fletcher, J. G., et al. (1975). Computer storage structure and utilization at a large scientific laboratory. *Proc. IEEE* **63**, No. 8, 1104–1113.
69. Smith, S. M. (1979). Use of broadband coaxial cable networks in an assembly plant environment. *Proc. Local Area Commun. Network Symp., 1979* pp. 67–74.
70. Innes, D. R., and Alty, J. L. (1975). An intra university network. *Data Commun. Symp., 4th, 1975* pp. 1-8-1-13.
71. Lampson, B. W. (1980). Ethernet, pup, and violet. Part E. Case studies. *In* "Lecture Notes Advanced Course: Distributed Processing Systems" (B. W. Lampson, ed.). Springer-Verlag, Berlin and New York.
72. Shoch, J., and Hupp, J. A. (1980). Performance of an Ethernet local network—A preliminary report. *COMPCON '80 Spring*.
73. Pierce, J. R. (1972). Network for block switching of data. *Bell Syst. Tech. J.* **51**, 1133–1143.
74. Farmer, W. D., and Newell, E. E. (1969). An experimental distributed switching system to handle bursty computer traffic. *Proc. ACM Symp. Data Commun. 1969* pp. 1–33.
75. Eller, W. R. (1979). "System Description," Product brochure describing MASSTOR Shared VSS handed out at 4th Conference on Local Networks, October 1979.
76. Christenson, G. S. (1979). A network storage system. *Proc. Con. Local Comput. Networks, 4th, 1979*.
77. Schiebe, L. H. (1980). LCN—A loosely coupled network system. *Proc. NCC, 1980*.

Vector Computer Architecture and Processing Techniques

KAI HWANG AND SHUN-PIAO SU

School of Electrical Engineering
Purdue University
West Lafayette, Indiana

AND

LIONEL M. NI

Department of Computer Science
Michigan State University
East Lansing, Michigan

1.	Introduction	116
	1.1 Vector/Array Computations	116
	1.2 Pipeline Processors	117
	1.3 Array Processors	117
2.	Vector-Processing Requirements	118
	2.1 Characteristics of Vector Operations	119
	2.2 Vector Processing in Array Processors	120
	2.3 Pipelined Vector Processing	122
	2.4 Vectorization in Pipeline/Array Processors	124
3.	Pipeline-Processor Design Considerations	129
	3.1 Classification of Pipeline Processors	130
	3.2 Collision-Free Task Scheduling	131
	3.3 Congestion and Branch Controls	135
	3.4 Dynamic Pipelines with Shared Resources	139
4.	Multiple-Pipeline Computers	141
	4.1 System Architecture of CRAY-1	141
	4.2 Multiple Functional Pipes in CRAY-1	145
	4.3 Pipeline Chaining and Vector Loops	146
	4.4 Pipeline Designs in STAR, ASC, and CYBER-205	150
	4.5 Floating-Point Systems AP-120B	160
5.	Recent Advances in Array Processors	164
	5.1 Interconnection Modeling of SIMD Computers	165
	5.2 Burroughs Scientific Processor	167
	5.3 Linear Vectorization to Parallelism	169
	5.4 The Massively Parallel Processor	171

5.5 Shared-Resource Multiple Array Processors		176
6. Vector Processor Performance Evaluation		179
6.1 Performance Modeling of Vector Processors		180
6.2 Optimization of Vector Operations		184
7. Conclusions and Future Trends		189
References		191

1. Introduction

This article is devoted to reviewing architectural advances in vector-processing computers. Two major classes of vector machines, namely, pipeline computers and array processors, are comparatively studied. We begin with vector/array-processing requirements and associated vectorization methods. Problems associated with designing pipeline computers are presented with examples from the Texas Instruments Advanced Scientific Computer (TI-ASC), Control Data STring ARay (STAR-100) and CYBER-205 Computers, Cray Research CRAY-1, and Floating-Point Systems AP-120B. Then we study the architectures of recently developed SIMD array processors. In particular, the development experiences of the Burroughs Scientific Processor (BSP) and the Goodyear Aerospace Massively Parallel Processor (MPP) are closely examined. Recent research works on array and pipeline processors are summarized. Finally, we evaluate the performance of pipeline/array processors and investigate various optimization techniques for vector operations. Hardware/software and algorithmic issues of vector-processing systems and future trends of vector computers are discussed.

1.1 Vector/Array Computations

In scientific or engineering computations, there exists an ever-increasing demand of high-performance computer systems that can be cost-effectively used to process long or short vectors and to perform large-scale computations over multidimensional arrays of data (Stokes, 1977; Higbie, 1978; Johnson, 1978). Vector/array-processing computers are designed to maximize the concurrent activities inside a computer and to match the bandwidth of data flow to the execution speed of various subsystems within a computer. Approaches to match effective bandwidths of computer subsystems include pipelining of interleaved parallel memories, using high-speed cache memory to close up the speed gap between CPU and main memory, provision of additional vector registers files and masking schemes, broadening or multiplicity of machine data paths, overlapped CPU and I/O operations through multiprogramming, and Direct Memory Access (DMA) techniques. Parallelism embedded in a computer can be explored in two levels of instruction/operand preparation and execution. Methods to enhance concurrency of operation in these two levels include instruction/operand prefetch, lookahead/lookaside logic, instruction pipelining for overlapped operations, loop entrapment and vectorization, branch and interrupt handling, utilization of multiple functional units, data forwarding and pipeline chaining, overlapped scalar and vector execution, etc. (Paul, 1978).

1.2 Pipeline Processors

Pipelining offers a cost-effective realization of concurrency in the form of overlapped parallelism (Chen, 1980). The concept of pipelined processing is similar to assembly lines used in industrial assembly plants. To achieve pipelining one must subdivide the input job (process) into a sequence of tasks (subprocesses), each of which can be executed by a specialized hardware segment that operates concurrently with other segments in the pipeline. Successive jobs are streamed into the pipe and get executed in an overlapped fashion at the task level. The proper subdivision of input jobs into sequential tasks becomes a crucial factor in determining the performance of a pipeline processor.

Both instruction and arithmetic pipelines appear in today's vector processors. Famous examples include IBM System/360 models 91 and 195 (Anderson *et al.*, 1967), Amdahl 470V/6 (Amdahl Corp., 1976), CDC 6600 and 7600 (Thornton, 1970), TI-ASC [Texas Instruments, 1971], CDC STAR-100 [CDC, 1973], CYBER-205 [Control Data Corp., 1980], CRAY-1 (Cray, 1977), and AP-120B (Floating-Point, 1978), etc. We shall classify various pipeline processors in Section 3.1. New research results on static or dynamic pipeline processors are discussed in Section 3. Two powerful multipipeline systems, CYBER-205 and CRAY-1, are examined along with pipeline designs in ASC, STAR, and AP-120B. For an earlier survey of pipeline architecture, readers are advised to consult Ramamoorthy and Li (1977).

1.3 Array Processors

The common term of a parallel computer refers, in general, to an array processor, which consists of multiple Processing Elements (PEs) under the control of one Control Unit (CU). The Array Processor can handle

Single Instruction and Multiple Data (SIMD) streams. In this sense, array processors are also known as SIMD computers. They are specially designed to perform vector computations over matrices or arrays of data.

Array processors became well publicized with the hardware/software development of the Illiac IV system (Barnes, *et al.*, 1968; Bouknight *et al.*, 1972). Ever since then, many SIMD machines have been constructed to satisfy various parallel processing applications. The Burroughs Parallel Element Processing Ensemble (PEPE) (Evansen and Troy, 1973) and the Goodyear Aerospace STARAN (Batcher, 1974) are two "associative" array processors. Extended from the Illiac IV design are the BSP (Burroughs, 1978), Goodyear Aerospace MPP (Batcher, 1980), and the Cellular Vector Computer (CVCVHP) developed in China (Gao and Zhang, 1979, 1980).

In addition to regular SIMD machines, several "algorithmic" array processors have been developed as back-end attachment to a host machine. Among them are IBM 3838 (IBM, Inc., 1977), Univac array processor (Sperry Rand, 1971), Floating-Point Systems AP-120B, and Datawest Array Transform Processor (Datawest Corp., 1979), etc. We shall describe only recently developed systems such as BSP and MPP in this contribution. Shared-resource multiple-array processors have been studied in Hwang and Ni (1980) for parallel vector processing. The remaining array processors have been described in Thurber (1976), Hayes (1978), Kuck (1978), and Baer (1980). Vectorization methods and performance evaluation of SIMD machines for vector processing will be treated in Sections 2 and 6.

2. Vector-Processing Requirements

In order to enhance the performance of vector processors, one should explore both spatial and temporal dimensions of system design to provide all possible processing concurrencies. Traditional serial computers operate on single-valued operands, called *scalers*. In vector processors, data objects are expressed as *vectors*. The term vector means an ordered set of values that is processed as a block of operands. A program written for a vector processor can be treated as a single-instruction stream processing data over vectors. These two types of vector processors differ in the internal implementation of vector operations.

For vector processing, data sets are structured in ordered forms of arrays or matrices and retrieved as rows, columns, or diagonals. In order to run a program more efficiently on a vector processor, the art of "vectorization" must be understood. A vectorizing compiler differs from conventional compiler in two important areas. As a language, it allows the user to express parallelism in his program explicitly. As a compiler, it provides automatic detection of parallelism within a program.

2.1 Characteristics of Vector Operations

A vector operand contains an ordered set of n elements, where n is the length of the vector. Each element in a vector is a scalar quantity, which may be a floating-point number, an integer, a logical value, a character (byte), etc. Vector operations can be classified into four primitive types:

$$f_1: V \to V, \quad f_3: V \times V \to V$$
$$f_2: V \to S, \quad f_4: V \times S \to V \tag{1}$$

where V and S denote vector and scalar operands, respectively. f_1 and f_2 are unary operations and f_3 and f_4 are binary operations. For examples, vector square rooting is an f_1 operation, sum of vector elements (vector summation) is an f_2 operation, scalar–vector product is an f_4 operation, and vector add is an f_3 operation. The dot product of two vectors is generated by applying f_3 (vector multiply) and then f_2 (vector sum) operations in a sequence. Table I lists some representative vector operations that can be found in modern vector processors.

Special instructions must be used to facilitate the manipulation of vec-

TABLE I

SOME REPRESENTATIVE VECTOR OPERATIONS

Type	Mnemonic	Description ($I = 1$ to N)
f_1	VSQR	Vector square root: $B(I) \leftarrow \sqrt{A(I)}$
	VSIN	Vector Sine: $B(I) \leftarrow \sin(A(I))$
	VCOM	Vector Complement: $A(I) \leftarrow \overline{A(I)}$
f_2	VSUM	Vector Summation: $S = \sum_{I=1}^{N} A(I)$
	VMAX	Vector Maximum: $S = \max_{I=1,N} A(I)$
f_3	VADD	Vector Add: $C(I) = A(I) + B(I)$
	VMPY	Vector Multiply: $C(I) = A(I) * B(I)$
	VAND	Vector And: $C(I) = A(I)$ and $B(I)$
	VLAR	Vector Larger: $C(I) = \max(A(I), B(I))$
	VTGE	Vector Test >: $C(I) = 0$ if $A(I) < B(I)$
		$C(I) = 1$ if $A(I) > B(I)$
f_4	SADD	Vector/Scalar Add: $B(I) = S + A(I)$
	SDIV	Vector/Scalar Divide: $B(I) = A(I)/S$

tor data. A bit vector can be generated as a result of comparing two vectors, and it can be used as a masking vector for the enable and disable of component operations in a vector instruction. A COMPRESS instruction will shorten a vector under the control of a masking vector. A MERGE instruction combines two vectors under the control of a masking vector. Compress and merge are special f_1 and f_3 operations because the resulting operand may have different length. Several examples are used to characterize these special vector operations.

Example 1

Let $\mathbf{X} = (2, 5, 8, 7)$ and $\mathbf{Y} = (9, 3, 6, 4)$. After a COMPARE instruction "$\mathbf{B} = \mathbf{X} > \mathbf{Y}$" is executed, the bit vector $\mathbf{B} = (0, 1, 1, 1)$ is obtained.

Let $\mathbf{X} = (1, 2, 3, 4, 5, 6, 7, 8)$ and $\mathbf{B} = (1, 0, 1, 0, 1, 0, 1, 0)$. After a COMPRESS instruction "$\mathbf{Y} = $ COMPRESS $\mathbf{X}, (\mathbf{B})$" is executed, the compressed vector $\mathbf{Y} = (1, 3, 5, 7)$ is obtained.

Let $\mathbf{X} = (1, 2, 4, 8)$, $\mathbf{Y} = (3, 5, 6, 7)$, and $\mathbf{B} = (1, 1, 0, 1, 0, 0, 0, 1)$. After a MERGE instruction "$\mathbf{Z} = $ MERGE $\mathbf{X}, \mathbf{Y}, (\mathbf{B})$" is executed, with the result $\mathbf{Z} = (1, 2, 3, 4, 5, 6, 7, 8)$. The first 1 in $\mathbf{B}$ indicates that $\mathbf{Z}(1)$ is selected from the first element of $\mathbf{X}$. Similarly, the first 0 in $\mathbf{B}$ indicates that $\mathbf{Z}(3)$ is selected from the first element of $\mathbf{Y}$.

Recurrence operations appear often in scientific application programs. For example, finding the sum of all the elements in a vector $\mathbf{A}$ is an f_2 operation. Let $S(i)$ be the sum after the ith iteration. We can write

$$S(0) = 0 \\ S(i) = S(i - 1) + A(i) \qquad (2)$$

This algorithm is essentially sequential, because each $S(i)$ depends on $S(i - 1)$ accumulated in previous execution of the recursion. Vector processors can be used to solve this type of recurrence problems.

2.2 Vector Processing in Array Processors

In general, array processors may assume two architectural configurations as shown in Fig. 1. Illiac IV is structured as in Fig. 1a. Each PE_i has its own local memory PEM_i in which distributed data sets are stored. Each PE_i contains several fast access registers and a *data-routing register* R_i. The R_i of PE_i is connected to R_j registers of other PEs via the interconnection network. Masking schemes are used to specify which PEs will be active. The program is stored in the CU memory. The function of a CU is to decode each instruction and to determine where the execution should

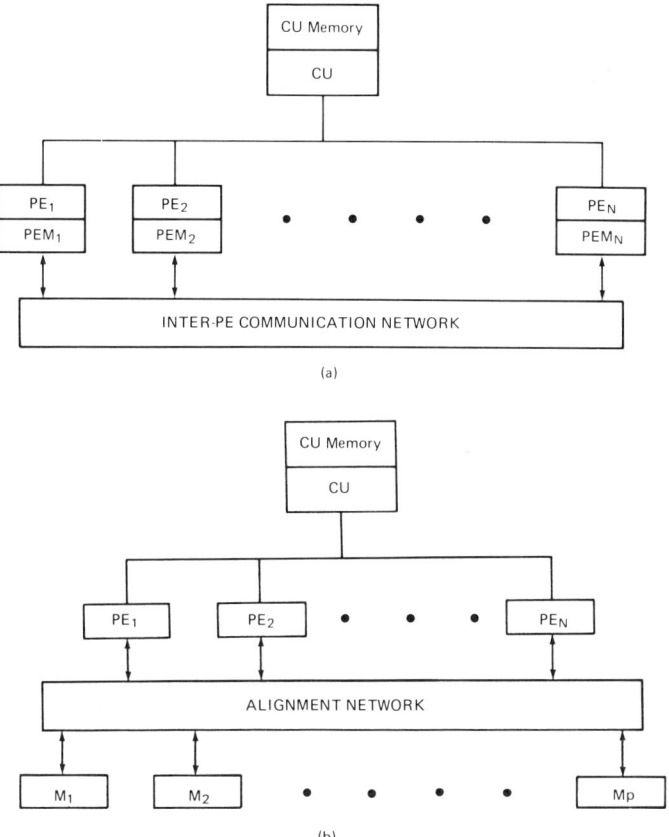

FIG. 1. Architectural configurations of SIMD array processors: (a) Illiac IV-like array processors; (b) BSP-like array processors.

take place. Scalar and control-type instructions are executed directly in the CU. Vector instructions are broadcast to the PEs for execution. A masking vector is used to enable or disable the corresponding PEs. Data routing among the PEs is done via the interconnection network. Figure 1b shows the BSP-like array processors. BSP uses a crossbar switch between its PEs and the shared parallel memory modules. Note that the number N of PEs and the number P of memory modules may not be identical in this case. The inter-PE communication network in Fig. 1a is essentially a permutation network for data routing, whereas the alignment network in Fig. 1b is a path-switching network between PEs and shared memories. Such a switching network is desired to allow conflict-free accesses of the shared memories by as many PEs as possible. We shall describe the operational requirements of Illiac-IV-like array processors below. The BSP-like array processors will be described in Section 5.

One can use register numbers or memory addresses to specify vector operands. For memory-reference instructions, each PE addresses its own PEM, offset by a *local index register*, D_i. The D_i register modifies the global address broadcast from the CU. Thus, different locations in different PEMs can be accessed simultaneously. From the hardware viewpoint, the physical length of a vector is determined by the number of PEs. The CU performs the sectioning of a long vector, vector loop control, setting of global base address, and offset increment.

How to distribute vector elements in different PEMs is crucial to the efficient utilization of an array processor. Ideally, the effective elements of a vector are retrieved from different PEMs simultaneously. In the worst case, the n elements are all in a single PEM, which must be fetched sequentially. A one-dimensional linear vector of n elements can be stored in all PEMs, if $n < N$. Long vectors ($n > N$) can be stored by distributing n elements cyclically among the N PEMs. Difficulty may arise in using high-dimensional vectors. For example, in matrix computations, rows and columns are both needed as vectors in intermediate calculations. The matrix must be stored in a way to allow parallel fetch of a row or of a column in one memory cycle. Skewed storage methods have been introduced to solve this problem (Kuck, 1968; Lawrie, 1975; Batcher, 1977).

The recursive summation in Eq. (2) can be implemented in an array processor in $\lceil \text{Log}_2 k \rceil$ steps as shown in Fig. 2 with different routing and masking practices. During the initialization, $A(i)$ is stored in PEM_i for all i. In the first step, $A(i)$ is routed from PE_i to PE_{i+1} and added to $A(i + 1)$ in PE_{i+1} for $i = 1$–7. The temporary results are obtained at the second column from left. In step 2, the temporary results in PE_i are routed to PE_{i+2} and added to the previous temporary results in PE_{i+2} for $i = 1$–6. In the final step, the temporary results in PE_i is routed to PE_{i+4} and then added to the previous results stored in PE_{i+4} for $i = 1$–4. Consequently, PE_k has the final value of $S(k)$ for $k = 1, 2, \ldots, 8$, as shown in the last column.

2.3 Pipelined Vector Processing

The execution of a vector instruction consists of two levels of pipelining in a pipeline processor. In the first level, a vector instruction is fetched, decoded, and the necessary control paths are connected before the needed elements are fetched from a specified address range in memory to a set of vector registers or directly into the pipe. Here a *vector register* is a collection of registers, each of which contains one element of the vector. The second level is the execution pipe, which carries out the specified

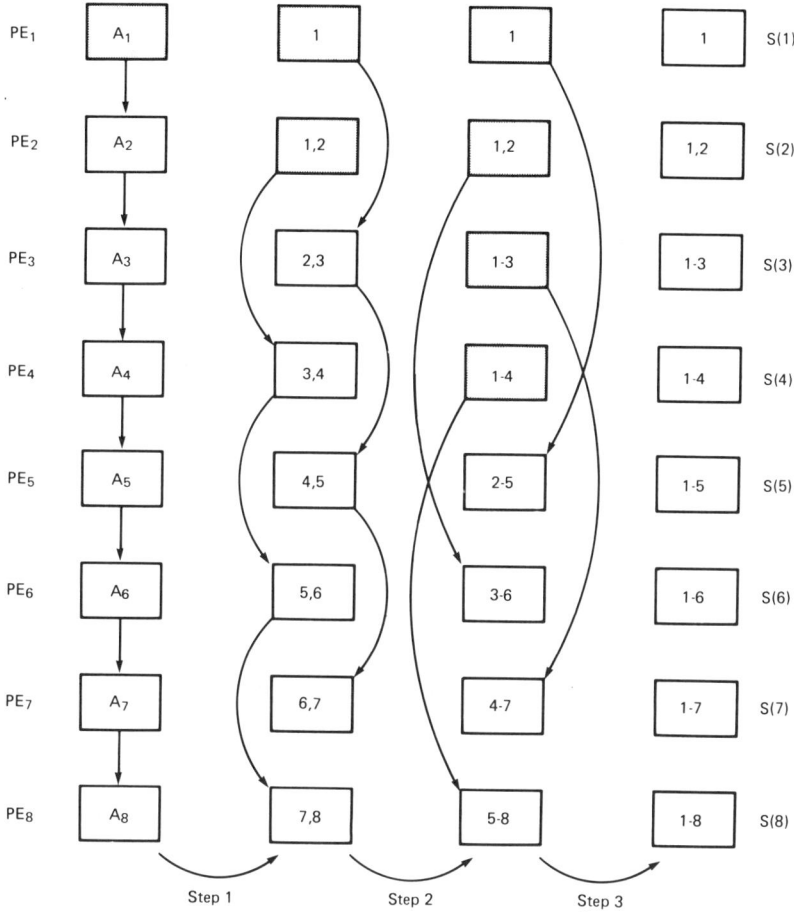

FIG. 2. A recurrence calculation of the summation $S(k) = \sum_{i=1}^{k} A_i$, $k = 1, 2, ..., 8$.

arithmetic or logic operations on these elements, normally supervised by a read-only control memory. Vector instructions for pipeline processors must specify, in general, the operation code, base addresses, increments, and offsets of source operands and results.

In order to maximize a pipe utilization, memory fetches must be fast enough to match the high pipeline speed. With interleaved memory organization, elements stored consecutively can be fetched simultaneously. In addition, memory buffering for each pipeline will smooth data flow between main memory and execution pipelines. Buffers provide storage areas for intermediate results. This will reduce the number of memory accesses. Moreover, a Vector Register File (VRF) can be used to reduce the data traffic between CPU and memory and the overhead caused by setup time for vector instructions.

Vector processing can be extended to high dimensions, such as the two-dimensional vector operations in the TI-ASC system. For sparse vectors or matrices, masking may result in poor space utilization and longer processing time. Vector compression operations should be used to alleviate the problem. By packing the active elements into consecutive memory locations, compressed vectors save both memory space and processing time. Which method is preferable depends on the density of the control vector (bit vector) and on the complexity of calculations. When the control vector is relatively sparse, it will be more efficient to deal with the compressed vectors. When the control vector is relatively dense, it is more efficient to calculate the entire vector with masking.

The execution of a VSUM vector instruction in a linear pipeline processor is used to illustrate pipeline operations. Vector **A** has 12 elements, each of which is a floating-point number. We want to calculate the sum of all the elements by using a four-segment floating-point adder. The block diagram of such a floating-point adder and its operation are illustrated in Fig. 3. The delay of intermediate results in a pipeline has the same affect as the delay due to data routing in an array processor.

Vector instruction format in a pipeline processor differs from that in an array processor. For memory-to-memory vector instructions, the information on base address, offset, increment, and the vector length must be specified. For register-to-register vector instructions, only the source and result register(s) need to be specified. Vector instruction formats in CDC STAR-100 and TI-ASC were described in Ramamoorthy and Li (1977). TI-ASC, STAR-100, and CYBER-205 are designed to execute memory-to-memory vector instructions (Kozdrowicki and Theis, 1980). CRAY-1 is designed mainly to execute register-to-register operations (Cray Research, Inc., 1977).

2.4 Vectorization in Pipeline/Array Processors

Substantial attention has been paid to high-level programming languages for vector processing; examples are the extended Fortrans in BSP (Burroughs, 1977), CRAY-1 (Cray, 1978), STAR (CDC, 1976), ASC (TI, 1972), and the VECTRAN developed by IBM (Paul and Wilson, 1978). Language aspects of vector processing and features of vectorizing compilers are addressed below. The desired features for extending standard Fortran are presented below with examples.

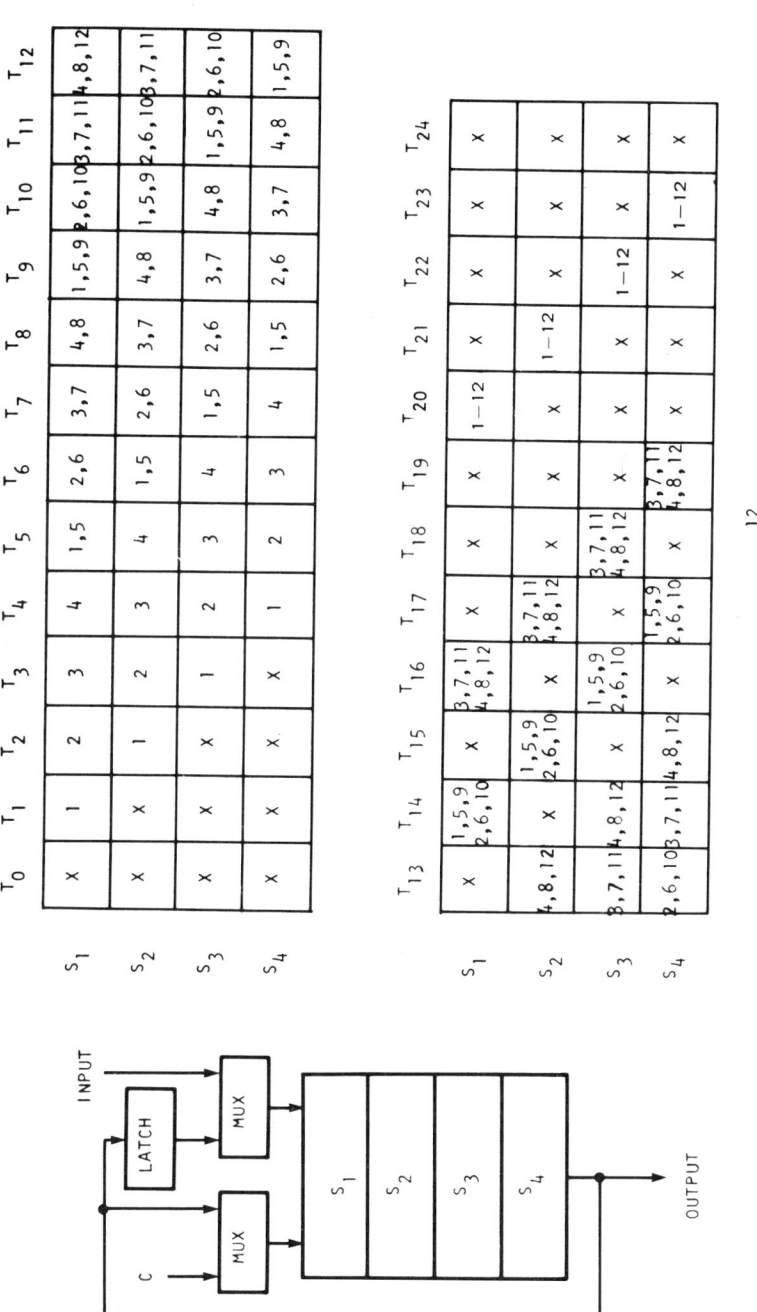

Fig. 3. A four-segment FLP adder and the contents of each segment during the execution of the vector summation instruction (VSUM).

$$S = \sum_{i=1}^{12} A_i$$

2.4.1 The Vector Identifiers

A vector may be identified implicitly by the appearance of an array name followed by specific subscripts. The extended notation may be specified through an implied DO notation as follows:

$$\begin{array}{c} e_1 : e_2 : e_3 \\ e_1 : e_2 \\ * \\ e_1 : * : e_3 \end{array} \quad (3)$$

where e_1, e_2, and e_3 are expressions of indexing parameters as they appear in a DO statement. e_1 indicates the first element or the *initial index* value, e_2 indicates the *terminal index* value, and e_3 is the *index increment* or skip distance. If e_3 is omitted, the increment is one; this includes all of the elements from e_1 to e_2. The single symbol * indicates that all of the elements are in a particular dimension. If the elements are to be used in reverse order, the notation $-*$ may be used.

Example 2

Given: DIMENSION X(8), Y(10, 4).
Then:

X(2 : 8 : 2) represents the elements X(2), X(4), X(6), X(8);
Y(3 : 5, 3) represents the elements Y(3, 3), Y(4, 3), Y(5, 3);
Y(*, 3) represents the third column of the matrix Y;
Y(5, 2 : *) represents the elements Y(5, 2), Y(5, 3), Y(5, 4).

2.4.2 The Vector Statements

The vector statement allows different portions of an array to be identified explicitly by separate names. No extra storage is allocated for an identified vector. Each identified vector is simply a virtual name for a collection of elements in the original vector.

Example 3

Given: REAL X(10, 10)
Then:

VECTOR X ROW 2(1 : 10) is a vector consisting of the second row of X;
VECTOR X DIAG(1 : 10) is a vector consisting of the main diagonal elements of X;

VECTOR X COL 5(1 : 10 : 3) is a vector consisting of X(1, 5), X(4, 5), X(7, 5);
VECTOR X ROW N(N : 10) represents the elements X(7, 7), X(7, 8), X(7, 9), X(7, 10), when N = 7.

2.4.3 The Vector Operations

For binary vector operations, the two operands must have equal length except the COMPRESS and MERGE operations. These operations are applied element by element to the operands. Each vector operation may be associated with a logical array that serves as a control vector. A WHERE statement may allow the programmer to indicate the assignment statements to be executed under the control of a logical array. The COMPRESS and MERGE operations must be provided to facilitate manipulating the vector operands. BSP uses PACK and UNPACK operations to provide such facilities.

Example 4

Given: DIMENSION A(6), B(6), C(6); DATA A/-3, -2, 1, 3, -2, 5/
Then:

PACK WHERE (A.GT.0) B = C causes elements of C in positions corresponding to "trues" in A.GT.0 to be assigned to B elements such that B(1) = C(3), B(2) = C(4), B(3) = C(6);
UNPACK WHERE (A.GT.0) A = B inserts the elements of B into A in positions indicated by A.GT.0. Thus, A(3) = B(1), A(4) = B(2), A(6) = B(3).

2.4.4 The Intrinsic Functions

The elemental intrinsic functions apply a computation to each element of a vector operand. For example A(1 : 10) = SIN(B(1 : 10)) extends the scalar intrinsic function to a vector intrinsic function.

Example 5

Given: DIMENSION A(50), B(50), C(50)
Then:

C(2 : 9) = VADD(A(2 : 9), B(1, 8)) performs the vector addition;
    S = SIZE(A(1 : 50 : 4)) equals the length of the sparse vector A(1 : 50 : 4);
    S = DOTPD(A, B) forms the dot product of vectors A and B;
    S = MAXVAL(A) finds the largest value of vector A.

An intelligent FORTRAN compiler is called a FORTRAN *vectorizer*, which has the capability of detecting parallelism from the serially coded FORTRAN programs. The function of a vectorizer is to recognize FORTRAN constructs that can be executed in parallel. Basic operations performed by the vectorizer program are precedence analysis and code generation. In performing the analysis, the vectorizer analyzes FORTRAN instruction sequences for possible translation into a vector syntax. This phase is extremely machine dependent, since it must consider special characteristics of the hardware. Key functions of a FORTRAN vectorizer include scheduling of vector and scalar operations concurrently, allocating registers efficiently, eliminating common subexpressions, and loop detection and conversion.

An ideal vectorizer performs sophisticated analysis of data dependencies and determines the possibility of vectorization. General guidelines in a vectorizer include: (1) determining the flow pattern between subprograms; (2) checking the precedence relationship among the subprograms; (3) checking the locality of variables; (4) determining loop variables; (5)

TABLE II

FORTRAN VECTORIZATION METHODS

FORTRAN vectorization method	Conventional FORTRAN statements	Vectorizing FORTRAN statements
1	DO 20 I = 8,120,2 20 A(I) = B(I + 3) + C(I + 1)	A(8:120:2) = B(11:123:2) + C(9:121:2)
2	A(0) = X DO 20 I = 1,N 20 A(I) = A(I − 1) * B(I) + C(I + 1)	A(0) = X A(1:N) = A(0:N − 1) * B(1:N) + C(2:N + 1)
3	DO 20 I = 1,N 20 IF(L(I).NE.0)A(I) = A(I) − 1	WHERE (L(I).NE.0)A(1:N) = A(1:N) − 1
4	DO 20 I = 1,N A(I) = B(I − 1) 20 B(I) = 2 * B(I)	B(1:N) = 2 * B(1:N) A(1:N) = B(0:N − 1)
5	DO 20 I = 1,N A(I) = B(I) + C(I) 20 B(I) = 2 * A(I + 1)	TEMP(1:N) = A(2:N + 1) A(1:N) = B(1:N) + C(1:N) B(1:N) = 2 * TEMP(1:N)
6	DO 20 I = 1,80 DO 20 J = 1,10 20 A(I,J) = B(I,J) + C(I,J)	DO 20 J = 1,10 DO 20 I = 1,80 20 A(I,J) = B(I,J) + C(I,J)

checking the independency of variables; and (6) replacing inner loop with vector instructions. Listed below are six known techniques for converting conventional FORTRAN statements into vectorized statements. These six vectorizing methods are illustrated by the examples in Table II.

(1) A simple DO loop containing independent operations and no branch statements can be converted to a single vector instruction.

(2) The recurrence problems can be converted into vector form subject only to precedence constraint.

(3) An IF statement in a loop can be eliminated by setting a corresponding control vector together with a WHERE statement.

(4) Exchanging the execution sequence sometimes will enable parallel computations.

(5) Temporary storage can be used to enable parallel computations.

(6) Prolonging the vector length is always desired for pipeline processing. In nested-loop statements, the vectorizing compiler attempts to code inner loops of programs as vector operations.

Other techniques, such as register allocation, vector hazard, and instructions rearrangement are also machine dependent. For example, in CRAY-1 all vector instructions operate on vector registers. How to allocate the vector registers so as to result in optimal execution time is a challenging issue. Rearranging the execution sequence to execute the same vector operations repeatedly can reduce the pipeline reconfiguration overhead in a multifunctional pipe. A vectorized Fortran enables the programmer to extend Fortran with minor efforts. It informs the programmer of the possibility of parallel operations. It provides also a learning tool in that the programmer can examine the output of the vectorizer and gain insight on the ways that algorithms can be restructured using parallel constructs. Vectorization enables programs to be transportable and reduces the amount of programming effort in developing programs for vector processors.

3. Pipeline-Processor Design Considerations

Key problems in designing pipeline processors are addressed below with accumulated development experiences from STAR-100, CYBER-205, TI-ASC, AP-120B, and CRAY-1 systems. First, we present two classification schemes that have been proposed for pipeline processors. Principles of task scheduling and associated control mechanisms are treated separately for unifunction and multifunction pipelines. Finally, we discuss techniques for resource sharing in designing dynamic multifunction pipelines.

3.1 Classification of Pipeline Processors

According to the levels of processing, Händler has proposed the following classification for pipeline processors, as depicted in Fig. 4 (Händler, 1977).

3.1.1 Arithmetic Pipelining at the Arithmetic/Logic Circuit Level

This refers to the segmentation of arithmetic/logic units for Add, Multiply, Divide, and Square Root in various data format. Famous examples

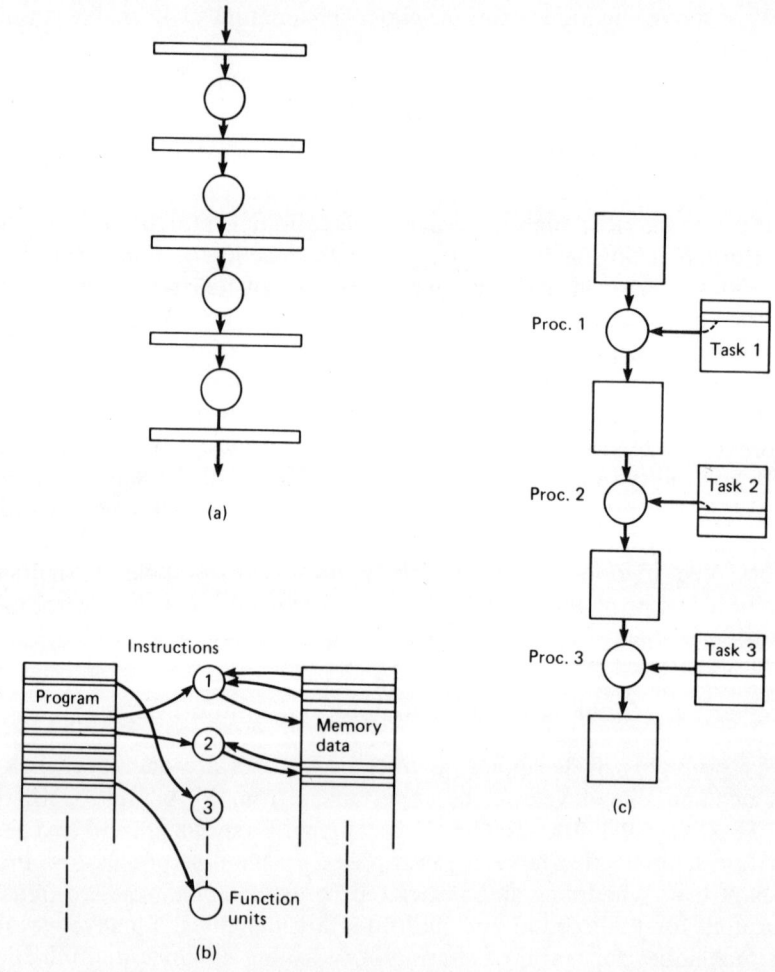

FIG. 4. Classification of pipeline processors: (a) arithmetic pipelining; (b) instruction pipelining; (c) macropipelining (Händler, 1977).

VECTOR-PROCESSING COMPUTERS

are the four-segment floating-point arithmetic pipelines used in STAR-100 and the eight-segment arithmetic pipelines used in TI-ASC.

3.1.2 Instruction Pipelining at the Instruction Execution Level

The execution of a stream of instructions can be pipelined by overlapping the execution of current instruction with the Fetch, Decode, and Operand Fetch of later instructions. IBM System 360/91 and Amdahl 470/V6 are two typical instruction pipelining machines.

3.1.3 Processor Pipelining at the Program Control Level

This refers to the pipelined processing of the same data stream by a cascade of linearly connected processors. The data stream passes the first processor, with results stored in a memory block, which is also accessible by the second processor. The second processor then passes the refined results to the third, and so on.

According to pipeline configurations and control strategies, Ramamoorthy and Li (1977) proposed the following classification scheme.

3.1.3.1 Unifunctional versus Multifunctional Pipelines. A pipeline processor with a fixed and dedicated function, such as a floating-point adder, is called unifunctional. A multifunctional pipeline may perform different functions, either at different time or at the same time, by interconnecting different segments in the pipeline.

3.1.3.2 Static versus Dynamic Pipelines. A static pipeline may assume only one functional configuration at a time. Static pipelines can be either unifunctional or multifunctional. Pipelining is made possible in static pipelines only if instructions of the same type are to be executed continuously. A dynamic pipeline permits several functional configurations to exist simultaneously. In this sense, a dynamic pipeline must be multifunctional. On the other hand, a unifunctional pipeline must be static. The dynamic configuration needs much more elaborated control and sequencing mechanisms than those for static pipelines.

3.2 Collision-Free Task Scheduling

Once a task is initiated in a pipeline, its data-flow pattern is fixed. When two or more tasks attempt to use the same segment at the same time, a collision results. Task scheduling of queued tasks awaiting initiation intends to avoid collisions and to achieve high throughput. A reservation table can be used to display the space–time flow pattern of sequential tasks through a pipeline.

Figure 5 shows the reservation table of a unifunction pipeline. The rows

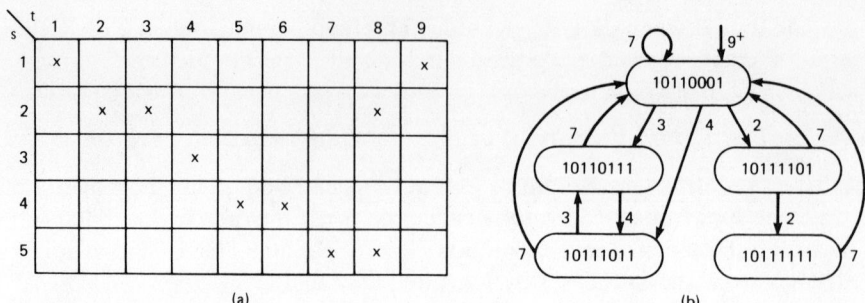

FIG. 5. Characterization of a unifunction pipeline. (a) Reservation table and related terms: forbidden list, $F = \{1, 5, 6, 8\}$; collision vector, $\mathbf{C} = (10110001)$. (b) State diagram with MAL = $(3 + 4)/2 = 3.5$ (Davidson et al., 1975).

in the table correspond to segments and the columns to time instances following the initiation. An **x** is placed in row i and column j if the task requires segment i at time j. Multiple **x**'s in a column indicate concurrent computations by different segments. Multiple **x**'s in a row indicate either a slow segment or a flow feedback (segment reusage). It is the multiple **x**'s in a row which pose the collision problem. A collision occurs when two tasks are initiated with a latency (initiation interval) equal to the column distance between two **x**'s on some row of the reservation table. The set of distances between all possible pairs of **x**'s on the same row, over all rows of the reservation table, is called the forbidden list of latencies and denoted by F. The collision vector, denoted by $\mathbf{C} = (C_n \ldots C_2 C_1)$, corresponds to an array of latencies such that $C_i = 1$ if $i \in F$ and $C_i = 0$ otherwise, where n equals the longest latency in set F. For the example in Fig. 5, the forbidden list $F = \{1, 5, 6, 8\}$, and the collision vector $\mathbf{C} = (10110001)$.

One can use an n-bit shift register to hold the collision vector for controlling successive initiation of tasks in the pipeline. Upon initiation of the first task, the collision vector is loaded into the shift register. The shift register is shifted one bit at a time to the right, entering 0 from the left end. An initiation is allowed at the next time instant, if and only if the bit being shifted out of the right end is 0. After a task is initiated, the collision vector is bitwise ORed with the shifted contents of the register to produce a new state vector. The shifted contents are used to prevent future task collisions with previously initiated tasks, while the collision vector prevents collisions with the very last task.

Since a shift register is a finite-state sequential machine, a state diagram is adequate to describe its behavior. Figure 5b shows such a state diagram corresponding to all possible state vectors that can be generated without collision. Arcs in the diagram correspond to initiations, each labeled with the latency between current task and the immediate successor task. The initial state vector is the collision vector itself. A state has an outbound arc for each 0 position in the vector coding of the state. In addition, there is an arc labeled $(n + 1)^+$ from each state to the initial state, indicating that the shift register will return to the initial state if more than n time units elapse between initiations.

Closed loops or cycles in the state diagram show the steady-state sustainable sequences of task initiations without collisions. Any cycle can be entered from the initial state. The cycle consisting of states (10110111) and (10111011) in Fig. 5b has two latencies, 3 and 4. The average latency of this cycle is $7/2 = 3.5$. Another cycle, which consists of the states (10110001), (10111101), and (10111111), has three latencies: 2, 2, and 7. The average latency of this cycle is $11/3 = 3.66$. The *throughput* of a pipeline equals the reciprocal of the average latency. Maximum throughput is achieved by an optimum scheduling strategy that achieves minimum average latency (MAL) without collisions. Thus, the task-scheduling problem is to find a cycle with MAL in the state diagram. A branch-and-bound search algorithm has been proposed in Davidson (1975) and Patel (1976b) to achieve this goal. Note that the maximum number of x's among any row of the reservation table is a lower bound of the MAL.

A pipeline processor, which can perform k distinct functions, can be described by k reservation tables overlaid together. In order to perform multiple functions, the pipeline must be reconfigurable. One example of static multifunction pipes is the arithmetic pipelines in ASC, which has 8 segments with about 20 possible functional configurations. Each task to be initiated can be associated with a function tag identifying its flow pattern. Collisions may occur between two or more tasks with the same function tag or from distinct function tags.

The segment-usage pattern for each function in a multifunction pipeline is displayed with a different tag in the overlaid reservation table. An overlaid reservation table for a two-function pipeline is shown in Fig. 6a, where A and B stand for two distinct functions. Each task requesting initiation must be associated with a function tag. A forbidden list for a multifunction pipeline is the collection of collision-causing initiation intervals. A task of function A may collide with a previously initiated task of function B, if the latency between these two initiations is a member of the forbidden list. The cross-collision vector V_{AB} marks the forbidden latencies for the function pair A and B. The vector $V_{AB} = (C_n \ldots C_2 C_1)$ may be calculated by overlaying the reservation tables for A and B. The component $C_k = 1$ if some row of the overlaid reservation table contains an A in column t (for some t) and a B in some column $t + k$; $C_k = 0$, otherwise. Four cross-collision vectors, $V_{AA} = (0110)$, $V_{AB} = (1011)$, $V_{BA} = (1010)$, and $V_{BB} = (0110)$ are shown in Fig. 6b. In general, there are k^2 cross-collision

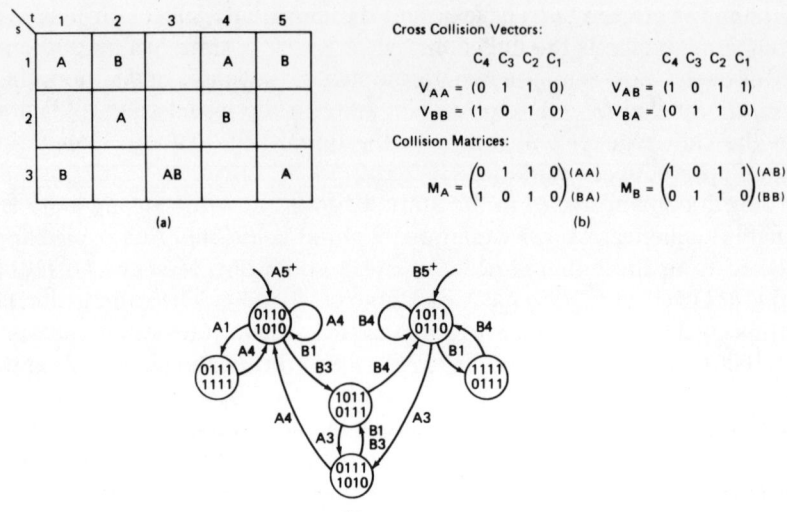

FIG. 6. Characterization of a two-function pipeline processor: (a) reservation table of a two-function pipeline; (b) cross-collision vectors and collision matrices; (c) state diagram. (Davidson *et al.*, 1975.)

vectors for a k-function pipeline. The k^2 cross-collision vectors can be rewritten as k collision matrices. Collision matrix M_R indicates forbidden latencies for all functions initiated after the function R. The ith row in matrix M_R is the cross-collision vector V_{IR}, where $I = 1, 2, \ldots, k$ are the k-function tags. A k-function pipeline can be controlled by a bank of k shift registers. Shift register I controls the initiation of function I. The control bit for function initiation is the rightmost bit of each shift register. Initiation of a task with function tag Q is allowed at next time instant if the rightmost bit of the corresponding shift register Q is 0. Immediately after initiation of a task with function tag Q, the collision matrix M_Q is ORed with the matrix formed after the shifting process in each shift register, in which the vector of shift register I is bitwise ORed with the cross-collision vector V_{IQ}, for all $1 \leq I \leq k$.

A state diagram is constructed with state vectors of the shift register bank. Arcs are labeled with latency and function tag of the initiation. The initial state can be one of the k collision matrices. Cycles in the state diagram correspond to collision-free patterns of task initiations. Any cycle can be entered from at least one of the initial states. For example, the cycle $(A3, B1)$ in Fig. 6c can be reached by an arc labeled $A3$ from initial state M_B or by an arc $B1$ from initial state M_A.

The method of finding MAL to achieve maximum throughput in a multifunction pipeline is similar to that of a unifunction pipeline. If the task arrival pattern is predictable and sufficient freedom in scheduling is allowed (i.e., when the controller desires a particular function, there is always a task of that function waiting in the input queue), then a globally optimum scheduling strategy may be evolved (Thomas and Davidson, 1974).

3.3 Congestion and Branch Controls

The processing speeds of segments in a pipeline processor are usually unequal. The throughput of a pipeline is constrained by the bottleneck segment. Therefore, we wish to remove the bottleneck which causes congestion. One obvious method is to subdivide the bottleneck, say dividing the bottleneck segment into subsegments, each of which has a shorter delay. If the bottleneck is not subdivisible, using duplicates of the bottleneck in parallel is another way to smooth congestions. The control and synchronization of tasks in parallel segments are much more complex than those for cascaded segments.

Another method to smooth traffic flow is to use buffers to prefetch instructions or operands for pipelined executions. The instruction buffers or operand buffers provide a continuous supply of instructions or operands to the appropriate pipeline units. In STAR-100 system, a 64-word (of 128 bits each) buffer is used to temporarily hold the data input stream until operands are aligned. In addition, an instruction buffer provides the storage of 32 64-bit instructions. The instruction buffer will be filled up with 8 64-bit words in one memory fetch. The buffer can supply a continuous stream of instructions to be executed, despite memory access conflicts. In the TI-ASC system, several buffers are used for essentially the same purposes. Two 8-word buffers are utilized to balance the stream of instructions from memory to the execution unit. A Memory Buffer Unit (MBU) has three double buffers called X, Y, and Z. Two of them (X and Y) are used for holding input operands and the third for output results. These buffers greatly alleviate the problem of mismatched bandwidths of the memory and of the arithmetic pipelines.

In the Floating-Point System AP-120B, there are two blocks of faster registers, namely Data Pads X and Y, serving as operand buffers for the pipelined FLP multiplier and adder. In the CRAY-1 system, 8 64-bit scalar registers and 64 64-bit intermediate scalar registers are used as operand buffers interfacing the central memory and function units for scalar operations. Eight 64-word vector registers are buffers for vector operations. There are also four instruction buffers, each consisting of 64 16-bit registers. These instruction buffers prestore substantial program segments on-line with the operation of functional pipes.

Concurrent operations are expected in a pipeline. Ideally, the subfunction being executed by one segment should be independent of all other subfunctions executed by other segments, otherwise some processes in the pipeline must be halted until the dependency is removed. For example, when one instruction waiting to be executed is yet to be modified by a future instruction, the execution of this instruction must be suspended until the dependency is released. Another example is the conflicting use of some registers or memory locations by different segments of a pipeline. These problems cause additional time delays. An efficient internal busing structure is desired to route results to the requesting stations with minimum time delays.

In the TI-ASC system, once instruction dependency is recognized, only independent instructions are distributed over the arithmetic units. Update capability is incorporated by immediately transferring the contents of the Z buffer to the X buffer or the Y buffer. With such a busing structure, time delays due to dependency are significantly reduced. The pipeline processors of STAR-100 can establish a direct route from the output segment to the input segment. Thus, no registers are used to store the intermediate results, which reduce the routing delays.

In the AP-120B system, the busing structure is even more sophisticated. Seven data buses provide multiple-data paths. The output of the floating-point (FLP) adder can be directly routed back to the input of the FLP adder, to the input of the FLP multiplier, to the data pad, or to the data memory. Similar busing is provided for the output of the FLP multiplier. This eliminates the time delays due to starting and fetching the intermediate results to or from the registers. In the CRAY-1 system, multiple data paths are also used among functional units and memory files.

Some functions like Interrupts and Branch produce damaging effects on pipeline operations. When Instruction I is being executed, the occurrence of an interrupt postpones the execution of the next Instruction $I + 1$ until the interrupting request has been serviced. Generally, there are two types of interrupts. Precise interrupts are caused by illegal operation codes in instructions, which can be detected during the decoding state. The other type, called imprecise interrupts, is caused by defaults from storage address and execution functions.

The effect of branching on pipeline performance is described below by a linear instruction pipeline, consisting of five segments: Instruction Fetch, Decode, Operand Fetch, Execute, and Store Results. Possible memory-access conflicts between overlapped fetches are ignored and sufficient large-cache memory (instruction/data buffers) is assumed. As illustrated in Fig. 7b, the instruction pipeline executes a stream of instructions continuously in an overlapped fashion if branch-type instruction does not occur, and once the pipeline is filled up, the pipeline completes execution

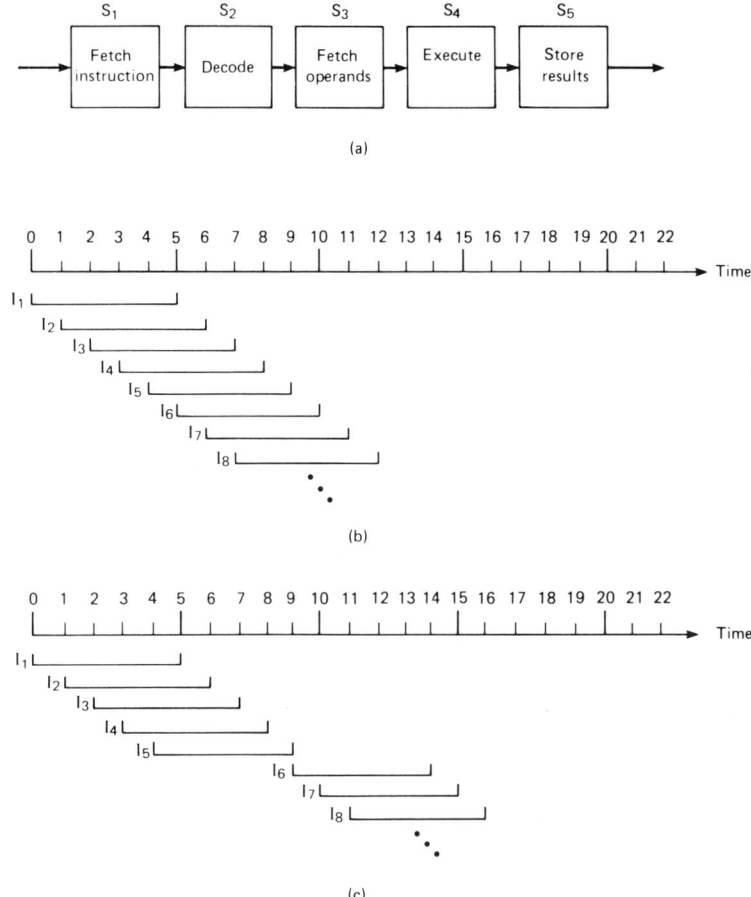

FIG. 7. The effect of branching on the performance of an instruction pipeline: (a) an instruction pipeline with $n = 5$; (b) overlapped execution of instructions without branching; (c) instruction I_5 is a branch instruction.

of one instruction per each clock period. When a branch-type instruction is executed, the pattern of overlapped executions is changed. A branch instruction entering the pipeline may be halfway down the pipe (such as a "successful" conditional branch instruction) before a branch decision is made. This will cause the program counter to be loaded with the new address of where the program should jump. Then all prefetched instructions (either in the cache memory or already in the pipeline) are useless. The next instruction cannot be initiated until the completion of the current branch instruction cycle. This causes extra delay penalty in order to drain the pipe. The overlapped action is suspended, and the pipeline must be drained at the end of the branch cycle. The continuous flow of instruction into the pipeline is thus temporarily interrupted.

In general, the higher the percentage of branch-type instructions in a program, the slower a program will run on a pipeline processor. This certainly violates the merit of pipelining. An analytical estimation of the effect of branching on an n-segment linear instruction pipeline is given below. Each instruction cycle here is assumed to be one time unit. For example, one time unit is equal to five pipeline clock periods in Fig. 7. Clearly if a branch does not occur, the performance would be n instructions processed per unit time. Let p be the probability that an instruction is a conditional branch and q be the probability that a branch is successful. Suppose that there are m instructions waiting to be executed. The number of instructions that cause successful branches is then $m \cdot p \cdot q$. Since an additional $(n - 1)/n$ time unit is needed for each successful branch instruction, the total time units required to process these m instructions are $(1/n)(n + m - 1) + (m \cdot p \cdot q)(n - 1)/n$. The performance of the n-segment linear instruction pipeline is defined by

$$\text{Performance} = \lim_{m \to \infty} \frac{m}{(n + m - 1)/n + m \cdot p \cdot q \cdot (n - 1)/n}$$

$$= \frac{n}{1 + pq(n - 1)} \quad \text{(instructions/unit time)} \quad (4)$$

In the STAR-100 system, the pipelines are dedicated to vector-oriented arithmetic operations. In order to handle interrupts during the execution of a vector instruction, special interrupt buffer areas are needed to hold addresses, delimiters, field lengths, etc. that are needed to restart the vector instructions after an interrupt. This establishment demands a capable recovery mechanism for handling unpredictable and imprecise interrupts.

For CRAY-1 computers, the interrupt system is built around an Exchange Package. To change tasks, it is necessary to save the current processor state and to load a new processor state. The CRAY-1 does this semiautomatically when an interrupt occurs or when a program encounters an EXIT instruction. Under such circumstances, CRAY-1 saves the eight scalar registers, the eight address registers, the Program Counter, and the Monior flags. These are packed into 16 words and swapped with a block whose address is specified by a hardware Exchange Address Register. However, the exchange package does not contain all the hardware-state information, so software Interrupt Handlers must save the rest of the states. "The rest" includes the 512 words of vector (V) registers, the 128 words of intermediate registers, the Vector Mask, and the real-time clock, etc.

3.4 Dynamic Pipelines with Shared Resources

Applications of a pipeline processor with specific function type are rather limited. Reconfigurable pipelines with different function types are more desirable. Such an approach requires extensive resource sharing among different functions. To achieve this, a more complicated structure of pipeline segments and their interconnections control are needed. Bypass techniques can be used to avoid unwanted segments. This may cause collision when one instruction, as a result of bypassing, attempts to use the operands fetched for preceding instructions. To alleviate this problem, one solution is that each instruction activates a number of consecutive segments down the pipeline, which satisfy its need.

A dynamic pipeline allows several configurations to be simultaneously present. For example, a dynamic pipeline arithmetic unit can perform addition at the same time perform multiplication. However, due to the tremendous overhead caused by control, interconnection of segments, etc., none of the existing pipeline processors can achieve this capability. It is much easier to design a static pipeline that has only one configuration at a time.

In TI-ASC, the desired control allows different instructions to assume different data paths through the arithmetic pipeline at different times. All path control information is stored in a Ready-Only Memory (ROM), which can be accessed at the initiation of an instruction. Three different functional configurations for the arithmetic pipeline in ASC that share the use of the ADD Segment are depicted in Fig. 8. Note that the input operands in all configurations are from the Receiver Segment. Only one ROM word is required to supply the control signals necessary for fixed-point addition. An identical pipeline configuration is used for fixed-point subtraction, but a different ROM address is accessed since a selection signal indicating SUBTRACT must be obtained.

The configuration for floating-point addition requires four ROM words for its path innerconnection information. This forces the instruction execution logic to access the ROM for control signals. The ROM words for an FLP Add may be located at 100, 101, 102, 103, while for a FLP Subtract, they could be located at 200, 101, 102, 103. The common ROM words (101, 102, 103) used by FLP Add and FLP Subtract represent similar suboperations contained in these two instructions. The starting ROM address is supplied by the instruction execution logic directly after the decode of the instruction.

The pipeline configuration for a floating-point Vector Dot Product is depicted in Fig. 8c. If the Vector Dot Product operated upon 1000 operands, the pipeline would be in this configurations for 1000 clocks. Scalar instructions in ASC use different control sequences. When several scalar

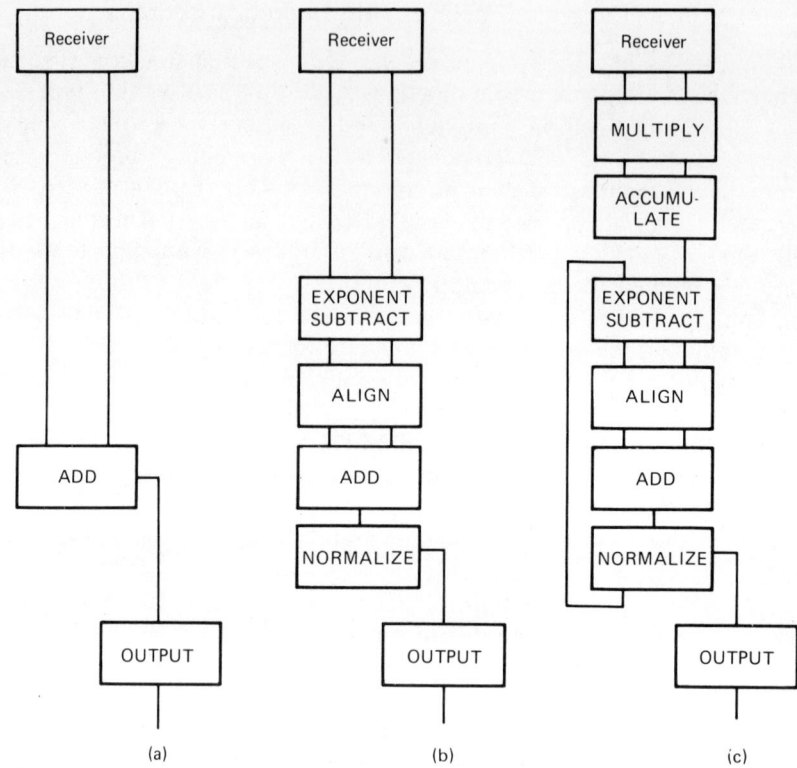

FIG. 8. Three operational configurations for the arithmetic pipeline in ASC: (a) fixed-point add; (b) floating-point add; (c) floating-point vector dot product.

instructions in a sequence are of a common type, the instructions streaming through the arithmetic pipeline can be treated as vectors. This requires a careful selection of ROM output signals to allow maximum overlapping of instructions. The ability to overlay instructions of the same type is implemented by graphically studying utilization of each pipeline segment. Overlaying identical patterns gives the minimum number of clocks per result. The two arithmetic pipeline processors in STAR 100 computer are also reconfigurable with variable structures. Variable structure and resource sharing are of central importance to designing multifunction pipelines. Systematic procedures are highly demanded to design dynamically reconfigurable pipelines.

Two methods for improving the throughput of dynamic and multifunctional pipeline processors have been proposed by Davidson et al. (1975) and Patel (1976, 1978). The collision characteristics of a pipeline can be modified with the insertion of noncompute delays or with the use of internal buffers at each segment. The utilization of the segments and hence the throughput of the pipe can be greatly enhanced with the use of noncompute delays and internal buffers. Interested readers may refer to Patel (1976a,b; 1978a,b) for necessary and sufficient conditions to build efficient dynamic pipeline processors with these two mechanisms.

4. Multiple-Pipeline Computers

Most of today's pipelined computers contain multiple number of dedicated arithmetic pipes in addition to instruction pipe in the central processor. Among these pipeline computers, CRAY-1 is the most powerful one, containing multiple scalar and vector arithmetic pipes. It can execute 140–200 million floating-point operations per second in scientific and industrial computations. CRAY-1 utilizes a large number of working registers, large instruction and data buffers, and 12 functional pipeline units. With the "chaining" of pipeline units, interim results are used immediately once they are available. The clock period of 12.5 nsec in CRAY-1 is by far the fastest among all supercomputer systems. CRAY-1, CYBER-205, STAR-100, and ASC all display its high-speed computational power by use of multiple pipelined processors. We shall consider each of these computers separately. The low-cost pipeline system AP-120B will be studied at the end in contrast with the design of vector supercomputers.

4.1 System Architecture of CRAY-1

CRAY-1 is not a stand-alone computer. A front-end host computer is required to serve as the system manager. A Data General Eclipse computer or a Cray Research "A" processor has been used as the front end. The system manager is connected to CRAY-1 via I/O channels. Three sections in the CPU of CRAY-1 include the Computation Section, Memory Section, and I/O Section. Twenty-four I/O channels are connected to the front-end computer, I/O stations, peripheral equipment, mass storage subsystems, and a Maintenance Control Unit (MCU). The front-end system collects data, presents them to CRAY-1 for processing, and receives output from CRAY-1 for distribution to slower devices.

The Memory Section in CRAY-1 computer is organized with 16 banks. Each memory bank consists of 72 modules. Bipolar RAMs are used in the main memory with 1 million words of 72 bits each. Each memory module contributes 1 bit of a 72-bit word, out of which 8 bits are parity checks for Single-Error Correction and Double-Error Detection (SECDED). A logical data word has only 64 bits. Sixteen-way memory interleaving is incorporated in the system with low-access conflicts. The bipolar memory has a cycle time of 50 nsec (four clock periods). The transfer of information from the bipolar memory to the computation section can be done in half-word, one word, or four words per clock period (12.5 nsec). Such high-speech data transfer rates are necessary to match the high-processing bandwidth of the functional pipelines in the computation section.

The I/O section contains 12 input and 12 output channels. Each channel has a maximum transfer rate of 80 Mbytes/sec. The channels are divided into four channel groups with each containing either six input channels or six output channels and each served equally by all memory banks. One 64-bit word can be transferred per channel during each clock period. Four input channels or four output channels can operate simultaneously to achieve the maximum transfer of instructions/data to the computation section. The MCU handles system initiation and monitors the system performance. The Mass Storage Subsystem provides large secondary storage, in addition to the one million words of bipolar main memory.

A functional block diagram of the computation section is shown in Fig. 9. It contains four Instruction Buffers, over 800 registers for various purposes, and 12 functional units, all of which are pipelined with few clock delays. Arithmetic operations include both integer and floating-point computations. Integer arithmetic is performed in 24-bit two's complement mode. Floating-point numbers are 64 bits each, with a signed-magnitude mantissa. Operation codes can distinguish scalar from vector instructions. The use of large numbers of high-speed (6-nsec) operating registers contribute significantly to the vector/scalar processing capability of CRAY-1. Without these registers, the functional units cannot operate with a clock rate of 12.5 nsec. There are five types of registers: three primary types and two intermediate types. The primary registers are the Address Registers (**A**), Scalar Registers (**S**), and Vector Registers (**V**). The functional units can directly access primary registers. To extend the Scalar and Address Registers, intermediate registers are used between the primary registers and the main memory as buffers. These intermediate registers are not accessible directly by the functional pipes. The Address-Save Registers (**B**) and Scalar-Save Registers (**T**) are used to support the **A** and **S** registers, respectively. Block transfers are made possible between the **B**, **T** registers and the bipolar memory banks.

There are eight address registers with 24 bits each. They are used for memory addressing, indexing, shift counting, loop control, and I/O channel addressing. Data are moved directly between bipolar memory and **A** registers or can be placed in **B** registers first and then moved into **A** registers. There are 64 24-bit **B** registers. The **B** registers hold data to be referenced repeatedly over a sufficiently long period. It is not desirable to

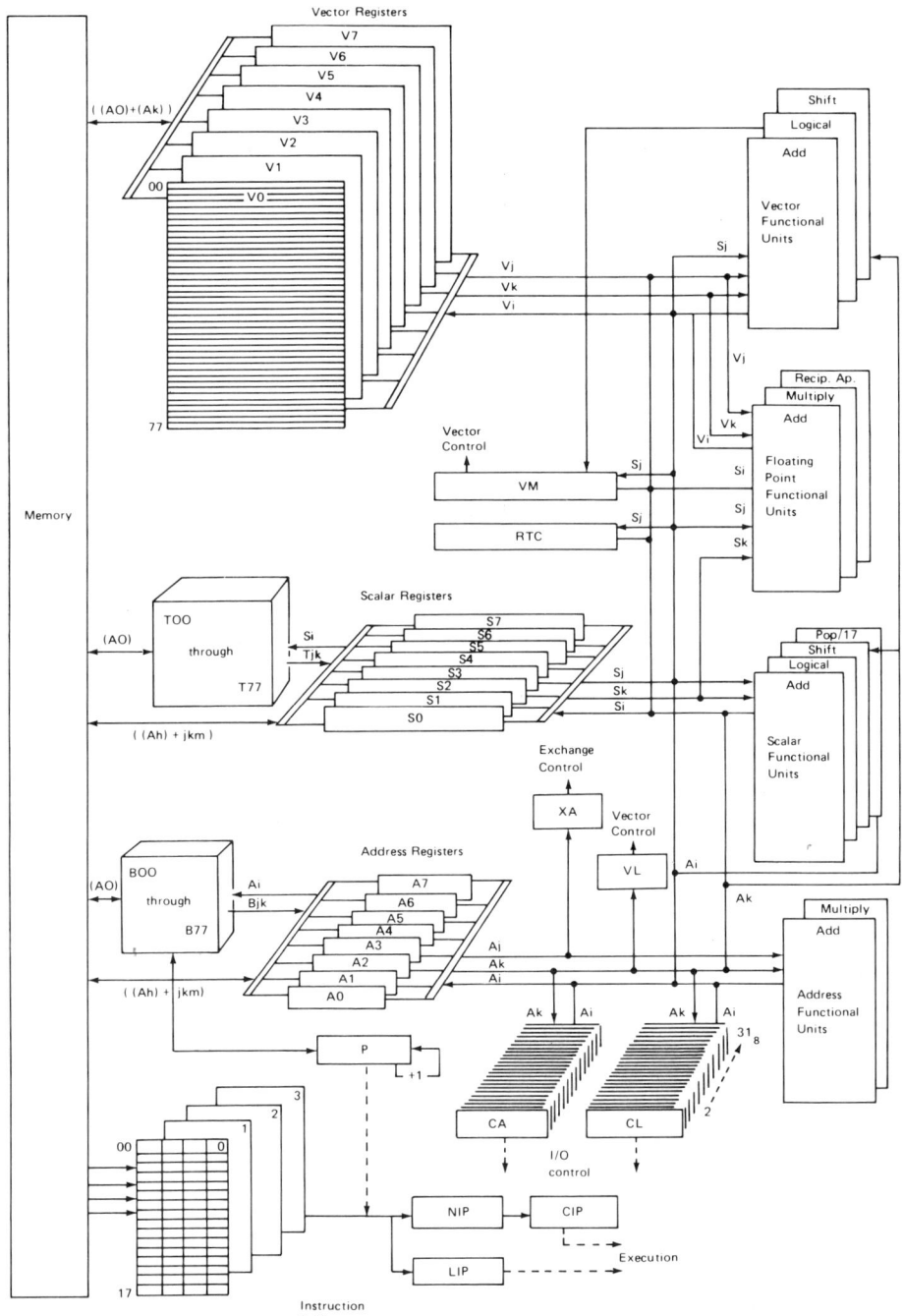

FIG. 9. Functional block diagram for the computation section of CRAY-1 system (Cray Research, Inc., 1977).

retain such data in the **A** registers or in the bipolar memory. Examples of such uses are shift counts, loop counts, variable-array base addresses, and dimension control.

There are eight 64-bit **S** registers for storing and source and destination operands used in scalar arithmetic and logical instructions. **S** registers may furnish one operand in scalar–vector instructions. Data can be moved directly between memory and **S** registers or can be placed in **T** registers as an intermediate step before transferring to **S** registers. There are 64 64-bit **T** registers. T Registers access the bipolar memory by Block Read or Block Write instructions. Block transfers occur at a maximum rate of 1 word per clock period.

There are eight **V** registers; each has 64 Component Registers. A group of data are stored in successive Component Registers of a **V** register to form a vector operand. Vector instructions demand the iterative processing of components in the registers. A vector operation begins with fetching operands from the first components of **V** registers and ends with delivering the vector result to a **V** register. Successive component operands are supplied in each clock period, and the result is delivered to successive elements of the result **V** register. The vector operation continues until the number of operation performed equals a count specified by the Vector Length (VL) register. Vectors having a length greater than 64 are handled under program control in groups of 64 plus a remainder. The contents of a **V** register are transferred to or from memory in a block mode by specifying the address of the first word in memory, an increment for the memory address, and a vector length.

All instructions, either 16 or 32 bits long, are first loaded from memory to the instruction buffers, each buffer having 64 16-bit registers. With the large instruction buffers, substantial program segments may be prefetched. Forward and backward branching within the buffers are possible. When the current instruction does not reside in a buffer, one instruction buffer, which is least recently used, is replaced with a new block of instructions from memory. Four memory words are fetched per clock period to this least recently used instruction buffer. To allow the fast issue of instructions, the memory word containing the current instruction is the first to be fetched.

The **P** register is a 22-bit Program Counter indicating the next parcel of program code that is supposed to enter the Next Instruction Parcel (NIP) register in a linear program sequence. The **P** register is entered with a new value on a branch instruction or on an exchange sequence. The Current Instruction Parcel (CIP) register holds the instruction waiting to be issued. The NIP register holds a parcel of program code prior to entering the CIP register. If an instruction is a two-parcel instruction, the CIP register holds the upper half of the instruction, while the Lower Instruction

Parcel (LIP) register holds the lower half. Other registers, such as the Vector Mask (VM) registers, the Base Address (BA) registers, the Limit Address (LA) registers, the Exchange Address (XA) registers, the Flag (F) register, and the Mode (M) register, are used for masking, addressing, and other program control purposes.

4.2 Multiple Functional Pipes in CRAY-1

The 12 functional units in CRAY-1 are organized into four groups, namely, Address, Scalar, Vector, and Floating-Point Units, as shown in Fig. 9. Each functional unit is pipelined with several segments. The register-to-register usages and the processing delays of these pipes will be illustrated by pipeline chaining in the next section. The number of required clock periods corresponds to the number of segments in each functional pipeline. Each functional unit can operate independently of the rest. A number of functional units can operate at the same time, as long as there exists no register conflicts. A functional unit receives operands from the connected source registers and delivers the result to a destination register. These pipelines operate essentially in three-address mode with direct source and destination register addressing.

The address functional pipes perform 24-bit two's complement integer arithmetic on operands obtained from **A** registers and deliver the results back to **A** registers. There are two such integer pipes; the Address Add unit and the Address Multiply unit. The Scalar functional pipes are the Scalar Add, Scalar Shift, Scalar Logic, and Population/Leading Zero Count units, performing operations on 64-bit operands from S registers, and in most cases deliver the 64-bit results to an S register. The Population/Leading Zero Count pipe delivers a 7-bit integer result to an **A** register. The Scalar Shift unit can shift either the 64-bit contents of an **S** register or the 128-bit contents of two **S** registers concatenated together to form a double precision quantity. The Population Count unit counts the number of nonzero bits in an operand, while the Leading Zero Count units counts the number of zeros preceding the first nonzero bit in an operand. The Scalar Logical unit performs mask and Boolean operations.

The vector functional units are the Vector Add, Vector Logical, and Vector Shift pipes performing vector operations. These pipes obtain operands from one or two **V** registers, or from a **V** register and an **S** register. Results from a Vector pipe are delivered to a **V** register. When a floating-point pipe is used for a vector operation, it functions in a way similar to a vector functional pipe. Three floating-point pipes, FLP Add, FLP Multiply, and Reciprocal Approximation units, perform, respectively, floating-point arithmetic over both scalar and vector operands. The Reciprocal Approximation pipe finds the approximated reciprocal of a 64-bit operand in floating-point format. Note that CRAY has no Divide unit. It performs floating-point division by multiplying the reciprocal of the divisor with the dividend. The Reciprocal Approximation pipe has the longest delay, 14 clock periods. The rest have 1–7 clock delays.

4.3 Pipeline Chaining and Vector Loops

While STAR-100 and ASC are designed to handle long vectors, CRAY-1 handles both long and short vectors efficiently. Vector instructions in CRAY-1 are classified into four types. A Type 1 vector instruction is handled by vector registers and the vector functional pipes. A Type 2 vector instruction contains one operand from an S register and one from a V register. The other two types of vector instructions transmit data between memory and the V registers. A path between memory and a V register may be considered as a Data Transmit pipe when time delay is counted.

When a vector instruction is issued, the required functional pipe and operand registers are reserved for the number of clock periods determined by the vector length. Subsequent vector instructions using the same set of functional pipe or operand registers cannot be issued until the reservations are released. Two or more vector instructions may use different functional pipes and different vector registers at the same time, if they are mutually exclusive. For example, vector instructions $V0 \leftarrow V1 + V2$ and $V3 \leftarrow V4 * V5$ present no conflict in resources. However, the same demand of the Vector Add pipe by the two following vector instructions $V3 \leftarrow V1 + V2$ and $V0 \leftarrow V4 + V5$ is obvious. When the first Add instruction is issued, the Vector Add unit is reserved. Therefore, the issue of the second Add instruction is delayed until the pipe is freed. The two vector instructions $V3 \leftarrow V1 + V2$ and $V6 \leftarrow V1 * V5$ share the use of the same operand register V1. The first Add instruction reserves the operand register V1, causing the issue of the Multiply instruction to be delayed until operand register V1 is freed. Another example with instructions, $V0 \leftarrow V1 + V2$ and $V3 \leftarrow V1 + V5$, illustrates the reservations of both the Vector Add pipes and the operand register V1. Like the reservation required for operand registers, the result register need be reserved to ensure the proper transfer of the final results.

The result register may become the operand register of a succeeding instruction. In CRAY-1, a technique called pipeline chaining is used. Basically, chaining is a linking process that occurs when results obtained from one functional pipe are immediately fed into the operand registers of another functional unit. In other words, intermediate results do not have to be stored back into memory and can be used even before the current vector operation is completed. Chaining permits successive instruction to be issued, as soon as the first result becomes available as its operand. Of course, the desired functional pipes and operand registers must be properly reserved, otherwise chaining operations have to be suspended until the demanded resources become available.

Consider a sequence of four instructions below, which demonstrates the implementation and timing requirements of pipeline chaining:

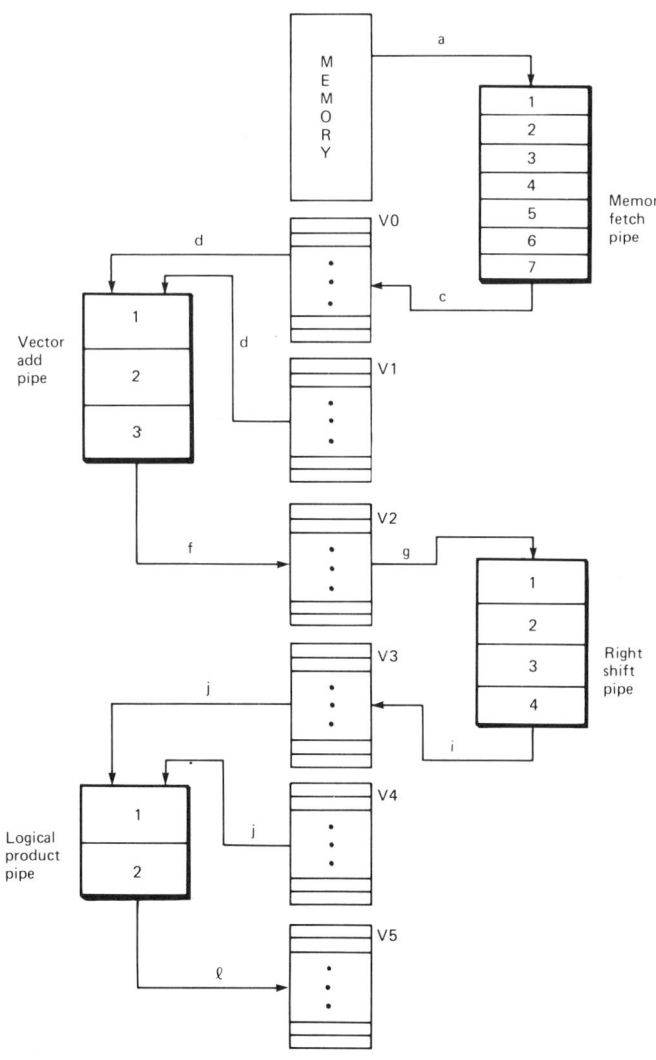

FIG. 10. A pipeline chaining example in CRAY-1 (Johnson, 1977).

(1)	V0 ← Memory	(Memory Fetch)	
(2)	V2 ← V0 + V1	(Vector Add)	
(3)	V3 ← V2 > A2	(Right Shift)	(5)
(4)	V5 ← V3 * V4	(Logical Product)	

A pictorial illustration is given in Fig. 10 which shows the chaining of the Memory Fetch pipe, the Vector Add pipe, the Vector Shift pipe, and the Vector Logical pipe into a single long pipeline processor. The contents of address register A2 determine the shift count. A timing diagram of the chaining operations is shown in Fig. 11. The Memory Fetch instruction is issued at time t_0. Each horizontal line shows the production of one component of the results in register V5. The time span in each of the four pipelines is indicated by solid heavy line segments (such as those made by b, e, h, and k). The dashed lines represent the transit time (such as those marked by a, c, d, f, g, i, j, and 1) between the memory and functional pipelines or between vector register and functional pipelines. One operand is fetched from memory to enter the cascaded pipelines at each clock period. The first result emerges at clock period t_{24} and a new component results enters the V5 register for every clock period thereafter. For long vectors of length greater than 64, the remainder section of the vector length is processed first through the chain, and followed by the processing of every 64-component loop, until all of the vector components are processed in an overlapped fashion. The segmentation of a long vector into loops is done by the system hardware and software control, which is unknown to the programmer. The program construct for processing long vectors is called a vector loop. Each pass through the loop processes a 64-element (or smaller) segment of the vector. Loop control is performed in the scalar registers.

Consider the following example of a FORTRAN loop:

$$\text{DO } 10 \text{ I} = 1, \text{N}$$
$$10 \text{ A(I)} = 5.0 * \text{B(I)} ; \text{C}$$

When N is 64 or less, a sequence of 7 instructions generates all the values of **A** array in memory:

(1)	S1 ← 5.0.	Set Constants in Scalar Register
(2)	S2 ← C	Load Constant C in Scalar Register
(3)	VL ← N	Set Vector Length into VL register
(4)	V0 ← B	Read **B** Vector into Vector Register
(5)	V1 ← S1 * V0	Multiply each component of the **B** array by 5.0
(6)	V2 ← S2 + V1	Add C to 5.0 * B(I)
(7)	A ← V2	Store the result vector in **A** array

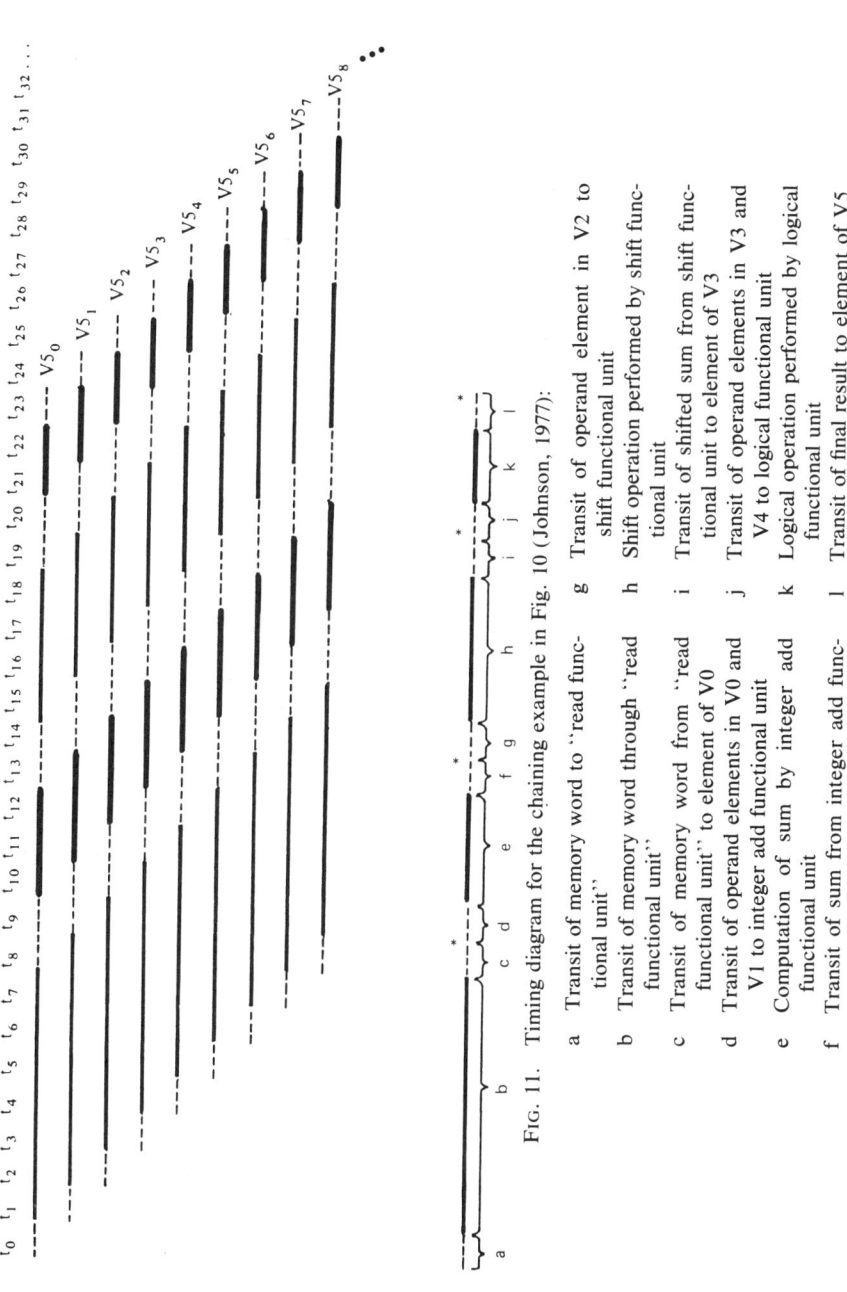

FIG. 11. Timing diagram for the chaining example in Fig. 10 (Johnson, 1977):

a Transit of memory word to "read functional unit"
b Transit of memory word through "read functional unit"
c Transit of memory word from "read functional unit" to element of V0
d Transit of operand elements in V0 and V1 to integer add functional unit
e Computation of sum by integer add functional unit
f Transit of sum from integer add functional unit to element of V2
g Transit of operand element in V2 to shift functional unit
h Shift operation performed by shift functional unit
i Transit of shifted sum from shift functional unit to element of V3
j Transit of operand elements in V3 and V4 to logical functional unit
k Logical operation performed by logical functional unit
l Transit of final result to element of V5

Instructions 4–6 use different functional pipelines with shared intermediate registers. They can be chained together. The outputs of the chain are finally stored in **A** array. When N exceeds 64, vector loops are set up. Before entering the loop, N is divided by 64 to determine the loop count. The remainder (less than 64 elements of **A**) is processed in the first pass through the loop. The loop executes instructions 4–7 for a segment of **A** and **B** arrays. The last vector instruction at the loop stores the current segment of **A** array in memory. This operation must be done before the next segment of **B** array is fed into the chain (Instructions 4–6) of the vector loop.

In CRAY-1, the startup time for vector operations is nominal; therefore, even for short vectors the performance is quite impressive. Because of the low overhead, the loss of speed in processing short vectors is not crucial. Clearly any vector operation can be processed as an iterative scalar operation, as it is done on any scalar processor. The "scalar mode" refers to operations performed in an iterated scalar loop, instead of in a vector operation. According to Johnson (1978), vectors of length three or less may run faster in scalar mode, while those having four elements or more may run faster in vector mode. In addition, the vector mode is about five times faster than the scalar mode on long vectors.

4.4 Pipeline Designs in STAR, ASC, and CYBER-205

Control Data STAR-100 is a vector-oriented processor with two nonhomogeneous arithmetic pipelines. It is structured around 4 million bytes of high-bandwidth core memory for stand-alone operations. The core memory has a cycle time of 1.28 μsec. It has 32 interleaved memory banks. Each bank has 2048 words of 512 bits each. The memory cycle is divided into 32 minor cycles of 40 nsec each. This implies the arithmetic bandwidth of 512 bits per minor cycle. The two pipelined arithmetic processors are designed for sequential and parallel operations on the single bits, 8-bit bytes, and 32-bit or 64-bit floating-point operands and vectors. In streaming mode, the system can produce 100 million floating-point operations per second (Mflops) with 32 bits per result.

The system architecture of CDC STAR-100 is shown in Fig. 12. The memory banks are organized into eight groups of four banks each. The width of the memory data bus for each group is 128 bits. During streaming operations, four buses will be active, with each bus transferring data at a rate of 128 bits per minor cycle. Two of the buses are used for transferring operands to the pipeline processors. The third bus is used by the result stream, and the fourth bus is shared between input/output storage requests and control vector references. These data buses allows the pipelines to operate at a maximum rate of 100 million results per second.

VECTOR-PROCESSING COMPUTERS

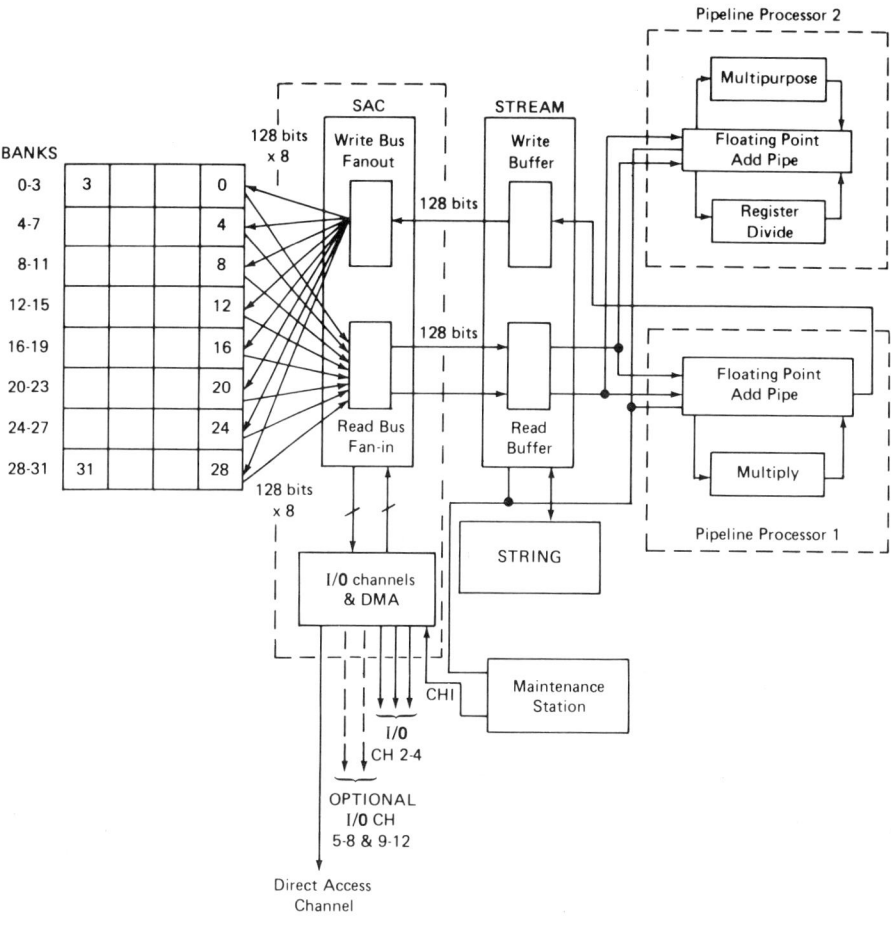

FIG. 12. The system architecture of CDC STAR-100 (Control Data Corp., 1973).

The Storage Access Control Unit controls the transmission of data to and from the memory. One of its principal functions is to perform virtual memory address comparison and translation. All memory references control signals originate from the Stream Unit. It has the facilities for instruction buffering and decoding. The read and write buffers in the stream unit are used to synchronize the four active buses to maintain a smooth data flow. The memory requests are buffered eight banks apart to avoid memory access conflicts. As a result, the maximum pipeline rate can be sustained, regardless of distribution of addresses on the four active buses. Register file in the stream unit supplies necessary addresses for operands and results. The String Unit processes strings of decimal or binary digits and performs bit-logical and character-string operations. It contains several adders to execute binary coded decimal (BCD) and binary arithmetic. The two pipelined processors are independent and have different structures. Pipeline processor No. 1 (Fig. 13a) consists of a 64-bit Floating-Point (FLP) Adder and a 32-bit pipelined FLP Multiplier. The FLP Adder on the right contains four segment groups in cascade. The Exponent Compare compares exponents and saves the larger. The difference between the exponents is then saved as a shift count by which the fraction with the smaller exponent is right-shifted in the Coefficient Alignment. In the Add segment, the shifted and unshifted fractions are added. The sum and the larger exponent are then gated to the Normalize. The Transmit selects the desired upper or lower half of the sum, checks for any fraction overflow, and transmits results to the designated data bus. There is a path from the output of the Transmit Segment to the input of the Receive. This feedback is especially useful for continuous addition of multiple FLP numbers. It is possible to split the 64-bit FLP adder into two independent 32-bit adders. Consequently, the availability for halfwidth (32-bit) arithmetic can be greatly enhanced. The 32-bit multiplier is a pipeline implemented with multiplier recoding logic, multiplicand gating network, and several levels of carry save adders. The product of a multiplication is formed by adding the final partial sum and carry vector. The required postnormalization after FLP multiply is done by the Normalize segment of the Add pipe.

Pipeline Processor No. 2 is depicted in Fig. 13b. It contains a pipelined FLP adder, nonpipeline FLP divider, a pipelined Multipurpose Unit, and some pipelined Merge Units. The FLP adder in Processor No. 2 is similar to that in Processor No. 1. The multipurpose pipe has 24 segments and is capable of performing a FLP Multiply, Divide, Square Root, and a number of other arithmetic/logic operations. The register divider is a nonpipelined unit, which also performs BCD arithmetic. When the pipeline enters streaming operations, it is possible to maintain a 40-nsec output rate from these pipes. The delay of the FLP adder is 160 nsec, because there are four segments in this pipeline. The time delay of the FLP multiplier equals 320 nsec. The maximum throughput for performing Add/Subtract is 100 Mflops (32-bit operands) or 50 Mflops (64-bit operands). For Multiply, the maximum speed is 100 Mflops (32-bit operands) or 25 Mflops (64-bit operands). Double-precision FLP operations require more execution time. We shall describe the CYBER-205, an upgraded LSI-version of STAR-100, at the end of this section.

The ASC system is another supercomputer that incorporates with a high degree of pipelining in both instruction and arithmetic levels. The central processor contains up to four arithmetic pipes. The Peripheral Processing Unit is used by the operating system. The Disc Channels and

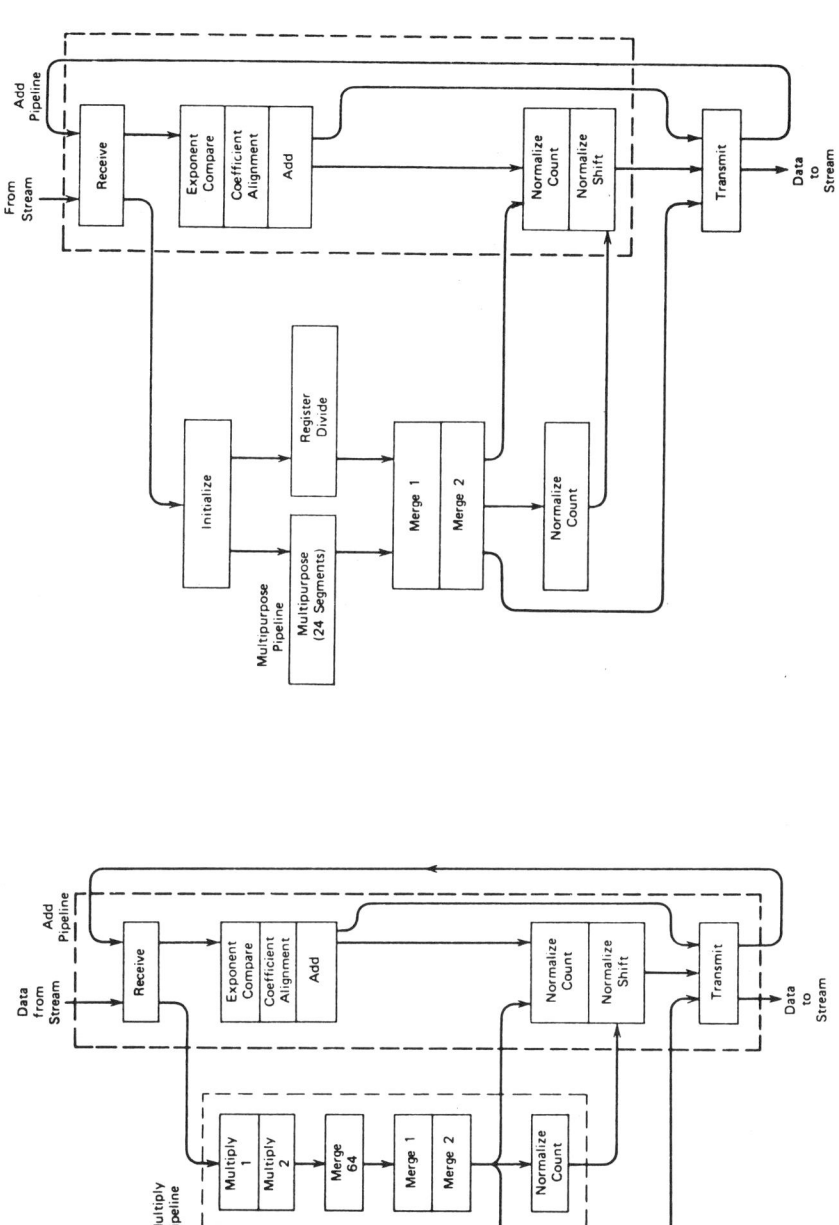

FIG. 13. Structures of two arithmetic pipes in STAR-100: arithmetic pipeline processors 1 (a) and 2 (b) (Control Data Corp., 1973).

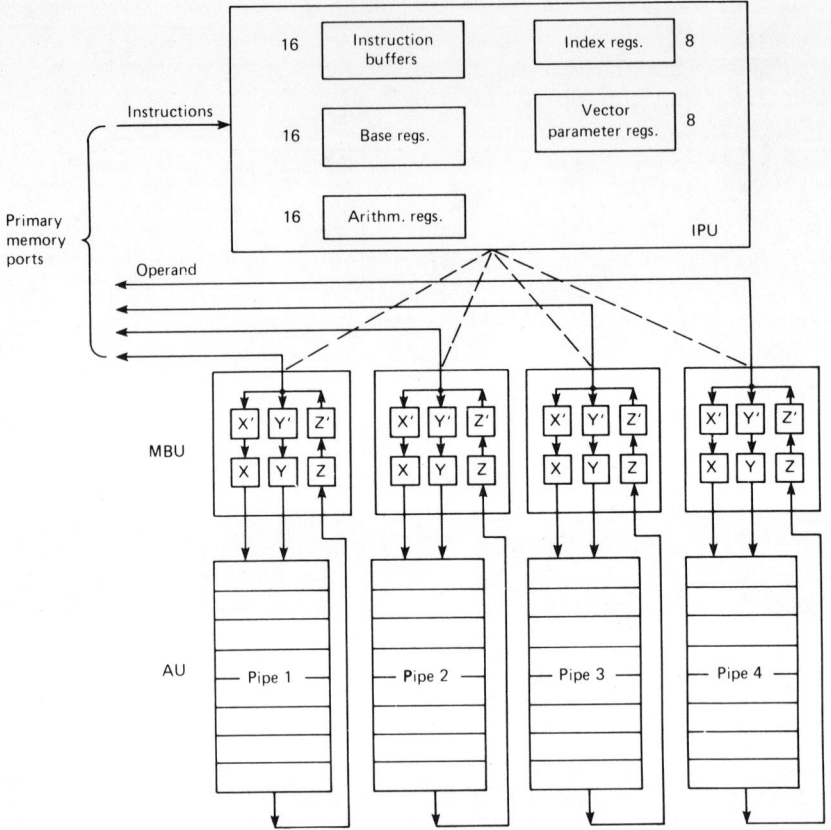

FIG. 14. Functional block diagram of the ASC central processor (Texas Instruments, Inc., 1971).

Tape Channels support a large number of storage units. Data concentrators are included for support of remote batch and interactive terminals. The memory banks and an optional Memory Extension are managed by the Memory Control Unit.

The main memory in ASC has eight interleaved modules, each with a cycle time of 160 nsec and a word length of 32 bits. With interleaving, eight memory words can be accessed in one memory cycle. The Memory Control Unit interfaces eight independent processor ports with nine memory buses. Each processor port has full accessibility to all memories. The sharing of memories among eight processor ports is controlled by the Memory Control Unit. The nine memory buses are organized so that the first eight buses are eight-way interleaved and the ninth bus is used for memory extension.

The Central Processor can execute both scalar and vector instructions at the machine level. Basic instructions are 32 bits each using 16-, 32-, or 64-bit operands. Figure 14 shows functional block diagram of the Central Processor. The processor has three types of functional units: the Instruction Processing Unit (IPU), the Memory Buffer Unit (MBU), and the Arithmetic Unit (AU). Up to four MBU–AU pairs can be built into the Central Processor. The primary function of the IPU is to supply the rest of the Central Processor with a continuous stream of instructions. Internally, the IPU is a multisegment pipeline, which has 48 program-addressable registers. Instructions are first fetched from memory in Octets (eight words) into the instruction buffers of 16 registers. The IPU assigns instructions to the MBU–AU pairs to achieve parallel processing in the arithmetic pipes. The MBU is an interface between Main Memory and the arithmetic pipes. Its primary function is to support the arithmetic pipes with continuous streams of operands. "X" and "Y" buffers in the MBU are used for inputs, and the "Z" buffer is used for output. The fetch and store of data are made in eight-word increments. The arithmetic units are static multifunctional pipes, which are reconfigurable for different function at different time. There are eight segments in each pipe, which can execute a number of fixed-point (FXP) or floating-point (FLP) arithmetic operations. The output of the arithmetic pipeline can be routed back to the input. The basic pipe clock has a period of 60 nsec. Vector results of up to 4 can be produced for every 60 nsec, depending on the number of AUs used.

The eight segments of each arithmetic pipeline are specified in Fig. 15a. The interconnection routes for the execution of FLP Add and FXP Multiply are specially marked in the drawing. According to the design, this arithmetic pipeline operates statically with one function at a time. Different arithmetic instructions use different segments. Possible segment interconnections are shown in Fig. 15b for executing different arithmetic functions. The Receiver Register segment receives the input operands from the MBU. The Exponent Subtract segment determines the exponent difference and supplies the shift count to the Align segment which aligns the fractions for FLP operations. The Add segment is a 64-bit carry look ahead adder. The Normalized segment normalizes FLP results before sending them to the Output segment. The Multiply segment performs 32×32 multiplication. It produces two 64-bit digital vectors referred to as pseudosum and pseudocarry, which are added by the Accumulator segment to produce the desired product. Finally, the Output segment provides a common point for results of all instructions. Simple instruction, such as LOAD and STORE use only the Output segment.

The STAR-100, ASC, and Illiac-IV marked the first generation of vector supercomputers. The second generation of vector processors began with CRAY-1 in 1976. There were 20 CRAY-1 computer installations as of

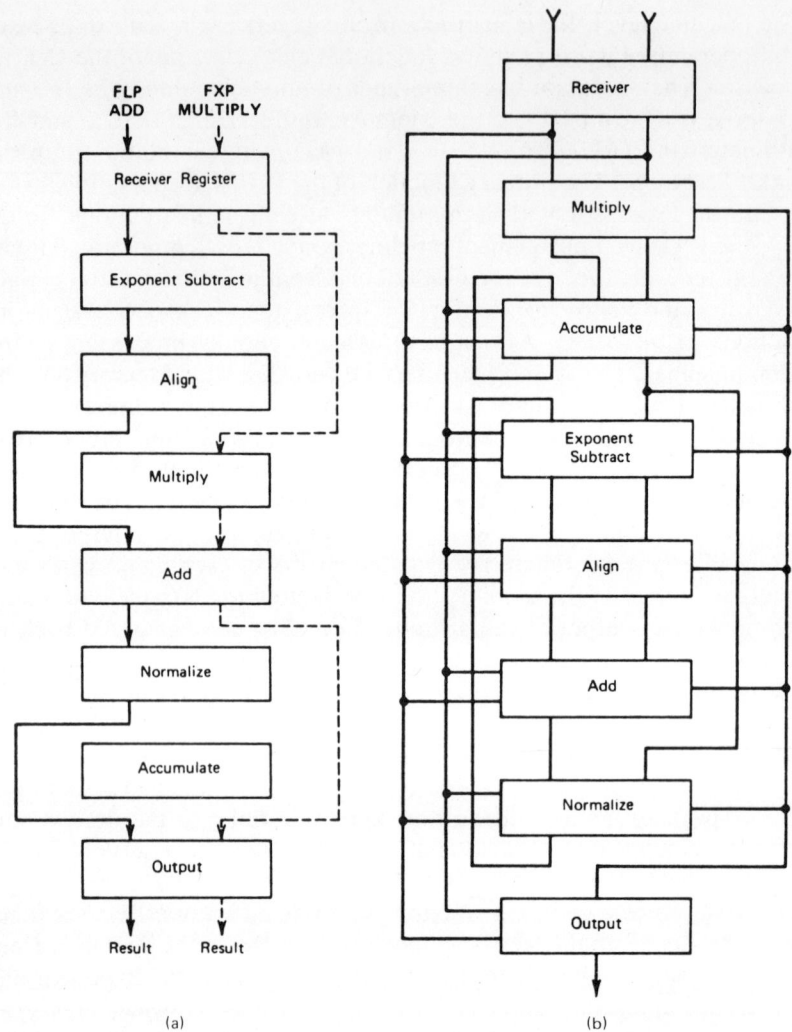

FIG. 15. The structure of the arithmetic pipeline in ASC system (Hwang, 1970): (a) segment connections for fixed Multiply and FLP Add; (b) segment interconnections of the ASC arithmetic pipeline.

October 1980. Burroughs announced the BSP in 1977, which evolved from the Illiac-IV and PEPE. In 1980, Control Data announced its CYBER-205, which is an LSI version of the earlier CYBER-203, a significantly improved design upgrading CDC's basic STAR-100 architecture (Kozdrowicki and Theis, 1980; Control Data Corp., 1980).

The system architecture of CYBER-205, as depicted in Fig. 16, differs

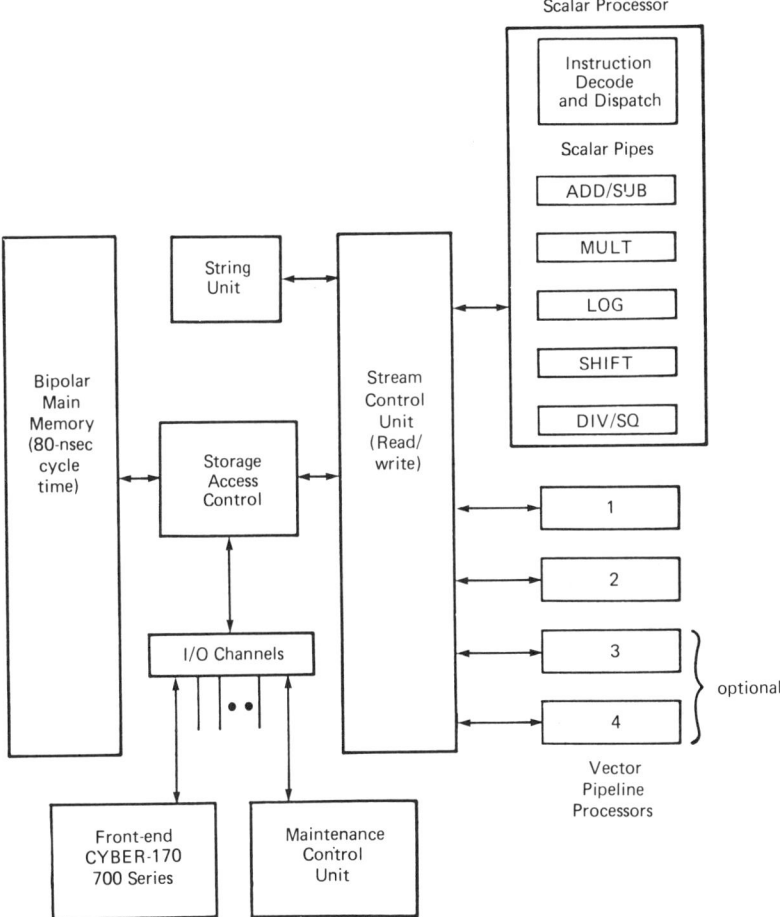

FIG. 16. System architecture of Control Data CYBER-205 (Control Data Corp., 1980).

basically from that of STAR-100 (Fig. 12) in the addition of a powerful scalar processor and two optional pipeline vector processors (with a total of four vector pipes). The basic clock rate of CYBER-205 pipelines is now 20 nsec, half of that of STAR. Only 29 distinct LSI chip types are used in the whole system construction, which significantly increases the system reliability and maintainability. Instead of using slow core memory, bipolar main memory of up to 4 million 64-bit words is used in CYBER-205 with an 80-nsec cycle time. Memory access patterns include 512-bit super words (eight 64-bit words) for vector operands and full word (64 bits) and half word (32 bits) for scalars.

Instruction execution control is now residing in the scalar processor,

TABLE III

ARCHITECTURAL FEATURES OF THREE LATEST VECTOR SUPERCOMPUTERS[a]

Characteristics	CRAY-1	CYBER-205	BSP
Instruction repertoire types	10 vector instruction types 13 scalar instruction types	16 vector instruction types 10 scalar instruction types	16 vector instruction types 19 scalar instruction types plus special instructions for system control use.
Instruction word length	16/32 bits	32/64 bits	48 bits
Pipeline clock rate	12.5 nsec	20 nsec	320/16 = 20 ns
Memory word length	64 bits (+8 bits SECDED)	64 bits (+7 bits SECDED/32 bit half word)	48 bits (+8 bit SECDED)
Memory cycle time	50 nsec	80 nsec	160 nsec
Address field	24-bit address	48-bit address	24-bit address
Programming addressable registers	72 24-bit registers 584 64-bit registers	256 64-bit registers	16 48-bit registers 16 120-bit registers
Instruction stack	64 64-bit words	64 64-bit words	256 48-bit words
Functional (arithmetic) pipelines	12 pipes (3 vector: VADD, VLOGICAL, VSHIFT, 4 scalar: SADD, SSHIFT, SLOGICAL, PCOUNT; 3 floating point: FADD, FMPY, FRECIP-ROCAL; 2 integer: ADD, MPY)	11 pipes (6 Vector: 2 FLPT, 1 string; 5 Scalar: ADD/SUB, MULT, LOG, SHIFT, DIV/SQ).	16 (AE's) + 1 Control processor
Number of segments in pipeline	Up to 14 segments each	Up to 26 segments each	4 × 16 (where each stage contains 16 variables for a total of 64 pipeline slots).
CPU computation rates	80 Mflops 32-bit addition 25 Mflops 64-bit division etc.	200 Mflops 32-bit addition 12.5 Mflops 64-bit division, etc.	50 Mflops 48-bit addition 6.7 Mflops 96-bit division, etc.
Maximum memory capacity	4M words	4M words	16M words (parallel)
Maximum virtual capacity	16×10^6 words (2^{24} words)	4×10^{12} words (2^{42} words)	16×10^6 words (2^{24} words)

Degree of memory interleaving	16 banks	32 banks	16 banks
Maximum memory bandwidth	320M 64-bit words (80 M per bank × 4 banks)	400M 64-bit words	100M 48-bit words.
Technology chip types	4 chip types	29 chip types, (7303 chips total)	(Chip type unknown)
Logic family	SSI/ECL with 1-nsec gate delay	LSI/ECL	MSI/CML—current mode
Front-end host computer	IBM, CDC, UNIVAC, others	CYBER 170 series, IBM 303X	B7800/7700
Maximum I/O transfer rates	50M bits per second for standard channel,	50M bits per second for standard channel,	12M bits per second for standard channel
	850M bits per second for DMA channel	50M bits per second on 16 DMA channels (total 800M bits per second)	DMA access not applicable
Operating system features	CRAY-1 has its own operating system (48K words) exclusive of main memory. It is a table-driven, multiprogramming system with several priority scheduling algorithms options.	Majority of operating system virtually addressable (i.e., automatically moved in and out of 64K words)	All system functions are executed in front end B7800
FORTRAN IV features	ANSI 66 (77 imminent), AUTOMATIC, compiler override, directives available, Compiler executes in CRAY-1 itself and it has automatic vectorization with programmer override in both directions.	ANSI 66 (77 Development), Vector arithmetic, Vector compare, order; min–max index; dot product; gather, scatter; control store bit map. Option-automatic vectorization.	ANSI 66, Array Extensions (where, pack, unpack, if, then, else), and vectorizer analyzes data dependencies and generates parallel code executable constructs
Peripheral models	Model 3350 Disk/Drum	Model 885/844-41 Disk/Drum	Model 9494-44/9373-21 Disk/Drum
	Model 3420 Mod 8 Magnetic tape unit	Model 679-7 Magnetic Tape Unit	Model 9495-24 Magnetic Tape Unit
	Model 3800/3211 line printer	Model 580-200 Line Printer	Model 9246-20 Line printer
	Model 3505 Card reader	Model 405 card reader	Model 9112 card reader
	Model 3525P3 card punch unit	Model 415 card punch unit	Model 9213 card punch unit

[a] Compiled from information reported by Kozdrowicki and Theis (1980).

which receives and decodes all instructions from memory, directly executes scalar instructions, and dispatches vector instructions to the four vector pipeline processors for execution. The scalar processor has itself five independent floating-point pipeline units for scalar *Add/Subtract*, *Multiply*, *Log*, *Shift*, and *Divide/Sort*. Up to 50 megaflops can be done in the scalar processor. The four vector pipeline processors can perform up to 800 megaflops through linked vector streaming processing. Table III is a summary of architectural features of three of the latest vector supercomputers, CRAY-1, CYBER-205, and BSP. BSP will be described in Section 5. An impressive comparison of these three systems can be found in the recent article by Kozdrowicki and Theis (1980).

4.5 Floating-Point Systems AP-120B

Floating-Point Systems AP-120B is a high-speed floating-point arithmetic processor, specially designed to process large vectors or arrays (matrices) of data. AP-120B must work with a host computer, which can be either a minicomputer (PDP-11 Series) or a main frame computer (IBM 360/370 Series). While the host computer handles the overall system control and supervises I/O and peripheral devices, the AP-120B is responsible for heavy floating-point arithmetic computations. Such a functional distribution could result in a speedup of 200 times over a minicomputer, and a speedup of 20 times over a main-frame computer.

The combination of an AP-120B and a host computer is shown in Fig. 17. All the peripheral devices, such as printers, display terminals, disk and tape units, are attached to the host computer. In fact, AP-120B array processor is itself a back-end peripheral attachment to the host. Since the host and back end may have different data format (and even unequal word lengths), an Interface Unit is needed to convert the data on the fly and to help implementing the Direct-Memory Access (DMA) and Programmed Input/Output (PI/O) data transfers. There are two sets of registers in the interface unit; one set is devoted to control functions via programmed I/O, the other to block data transfer via DMA. The programmed I/O section of the Interface Unit provides the array processor with a simulated front panel of the host. It contains a Switches Register used by the host to pass control or parameter data and addresses to the array processor. A Light Register is used to display the contents of registers in the array processor. A Functional Register is used for front panel commands, such as start, stop, or reset.

The DMA section includes the Host Memory Address register, AP Memory Address register, Word Count register, Control register, and

VECTOR-PROCESSING COMPUTERS

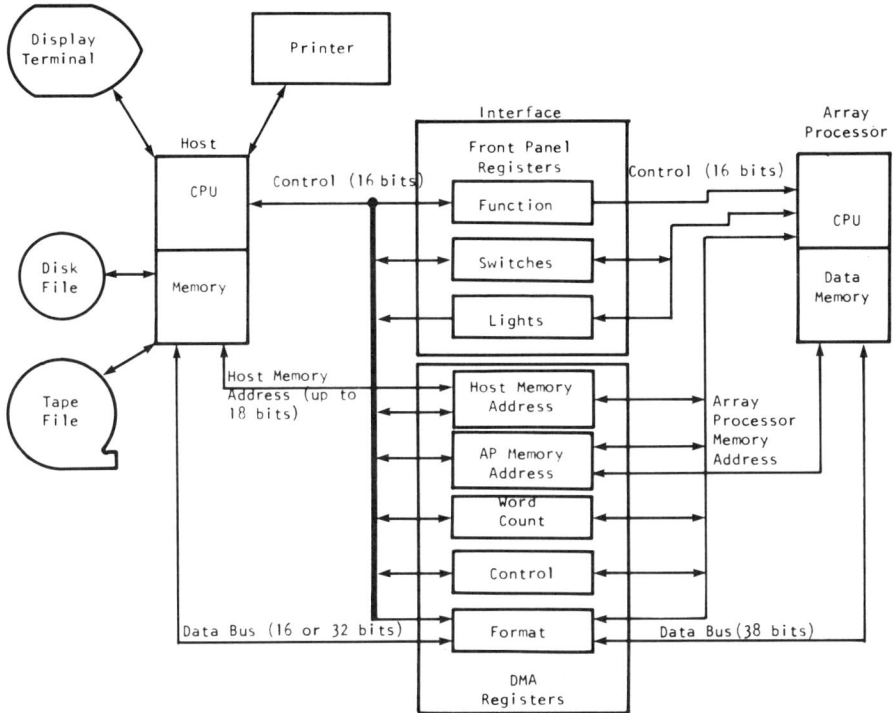

FIG. 17. Interface between AP-120B and the host computer attached with other peripheral devices. (Floating Point Systems, Inc., 1976.)

Format register. The control register governs the direction of data transfer and mode of transfer. The format register provides conversion between the FLP format of the host and that of AP-120B. Interface logic permits data transfer to occur under control of either the host or the AP-120B. The floating-point format in AP-120B is 38 bits long, with a 28-bit two's complement mantissa and a 10-bit exponent biased by 512. Using such a format, the precision and dynamic range are improved over the conventional 32-bit floating-point format. If the host has different floating-point data formats, the format conversion is done "on the fly" through the interface, so that the processing in AP-120B will not be used for format conversion. Consequently, the AP-120B can concentrate on useful computational tasks.

A block diagram of AP-120B processor is shown in Fig. 18. The processor can be divided into six sections, namely, the I/O Section, Memory Section, Control Memory, Control Unit, Data Bus, and two Arithmetic Units. The Memory Section consists of the Data Memory (MD), Table

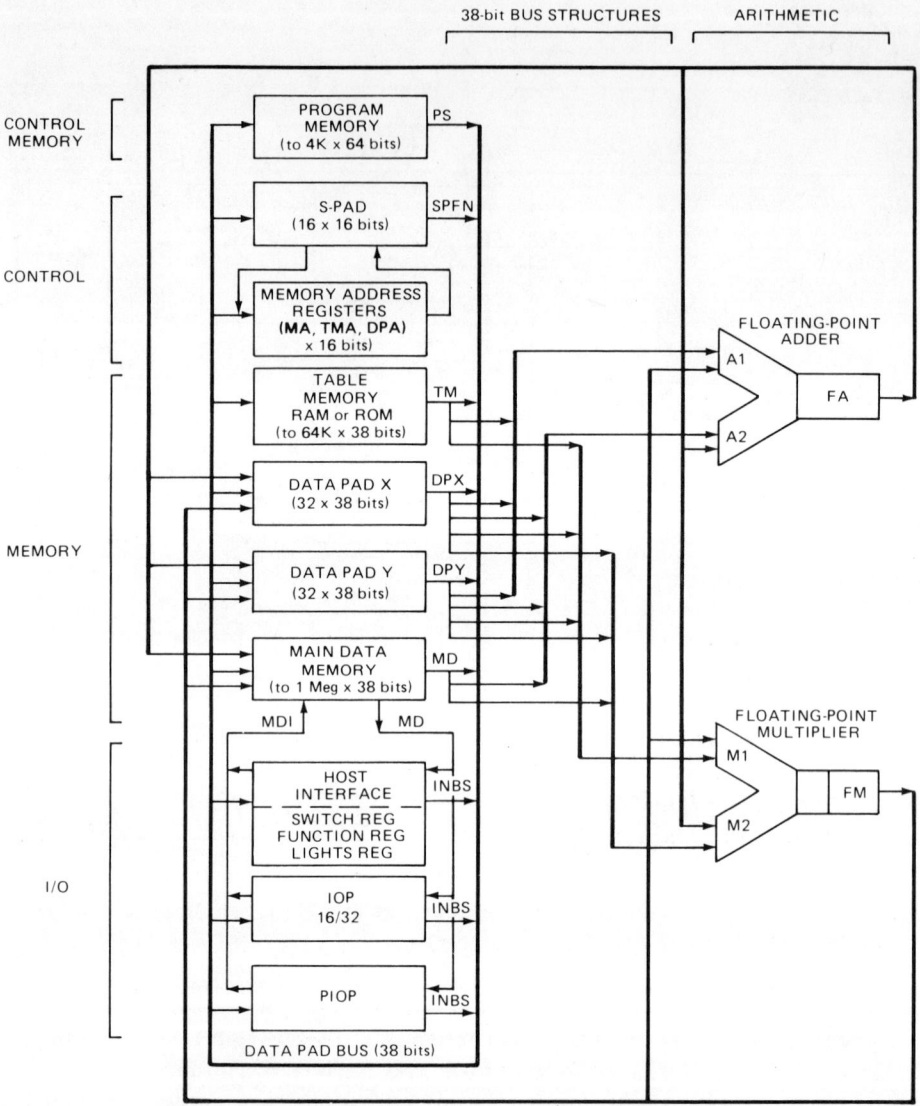

FIG. 18. Block diagram of the AP-120B processor (Floating Point System, Inc., 1976).

Memory (TM), and two Data Pads (DPX and DPY). The control memory or Program Memory (PS) has 64-bit words with 50-nsec cycle time. The program memory consists of up to 4k words in 256-word increments. Instructions residing in the PS are fetched, decoded, and executed in the control unit. The data memory is interleaved with a cycle time of either

167 or 333 nsec. The choice of a particular speed depends on the trade-off between cost and performance. The data memory is the main data storage unit with 38-bit words. It is directly addressable up to 1 million words in 2k words (167 nsec) or 8K words (333 nsec) increments. The TM has up to 64k 38-bit ROM or RAM words of 167 nsec cycle time. The table memory is used for the storage of frequently used constants (e.g., FFT constants). It is associated with a special data path which does not interfere with the data path associated with the data memory. The data pads X and Y are two blocks of 38-bit accumulators. There are 16 accumulators in each block. These accumulators are directly addressable by the AP processor. Any accumulator can be accessed in a single machine cycle of 167 nsec. Simultaneous read and write are possible in each data pad within the same cycle.

The S-pad in the control unit contains two parts: S-pad Memory and an Integer ALU. The S-pad memory has 16 16-bit directly addressable integer registers. These registers feed the integer ALU to produce effective operand address. The integer ALU performs 16-bit integer arithmetic. The outputs of the address ALU can be routed to any one of the following address registers: MA for the data memory, TMA for the table memory, and DPA for the data pads. Other functions of the integer ALU include Clear, Increment, Decrement, logical AND, and logical OR, etc. The bus structure of AP-120B contain 7 data buses (data paths), which speed up the data routing among different sections/units.

Two Arithmetic Units are the Floating-Point Adder (FA) and the Floating-Point Multiplier (FM). The FA consists of two input registers, A1 and A2, and a two-segment pipeline, as shown in Fig. 18. In the first segment, the exponents are compared, the fraction of the smaller number is shifted to the right, and the fractions are added. In the second segment, the resulting fraction is normalized and convergently rounded. Due to the different processing speeds in the two segments, a buffer is inserted to hold the intermediate result. The output of the FLP Adder, denoted by FA, can be routed to one of five different destinations. Possible source connections to the input registers A1 and A2 are shown at the top of the figure. The FM has M1 and M2 input registers and a three-segment pipeline, as shown in Fig. 18. In the first segment, the 56-bit product of the two 28-bit fractions are partially completed. The second segment completes the product of the fractions. The third segment adds the exponents, rounds, and normalizes the fraction of the product. All possible source and destination connections to the FLP Multiplier are identified in the figure. Once the pipeline is full, a new result (sum or product) is produced for every machine cycle of 167 nsec. Consequently, the maximum throughput rate for AP-120B is 12 mega-floating-point computations per second.

AP-120B has been applied extensively in the field of digital signal processing. The execution sequence of Fast Fourier Transform (FFT) in AP-120B is selected as an illustrative example. The FFT program resides in the Program Memory of the AP-120B. The array of data is stored in the main memory of the host computer. The FFT computation sequence consists of the following steps:

(1) The host computer issues an I/O instruction to initiate the FFT program in AP-120B.

(2) The AP-120B requests host DMA cycles to transfer the array of data from host memory to Data Memory in AP-120B. The floating-point format is converted during the fly of data through the interface unit.

(3) The FFT computations are performed over 38-bit floating-point data array.

(4) The AP-120B requests the host DMA cycles to return the results of the FFT frequency-domain coefficients array. Again, the data format conversion is done by the interface unit.

The entire process is accomplished in the host by only four FORTRAN statements:

```
CALL  APCLAR        //clear AP-120B
CALL  APPUT (···)   //transfer data to AP-120
CALL  CFFT  (···)   //perform FFT
CALL  SPGET (···)   //transfer results back to host
```

where "···" denotes the parameters used in the routines.

The AP-120B, unlike the super pipeline processors (STAR-100, ASC, and CRAY-1), does not have vector instructions. Instead, microinstructions are used to explicitly specify the parallel activities. More than 200 application software packages have been developed. Important FORTRAN callable routines for AP-120B can be found in the AP-120B Processor Handbook (Floating Point System Inc., 1977).

5. Recent Advances in Array Processors

In general, an SIMD computer can be characterized by the fourtuple (N, F, I, M), whose N is a positive integer representing the number of PE's in the system; F is a set of routing functions (bijections defined over the set $A = \{0, 1, \ldots, N - 1\})$, which determines the interconnection network among the PE's; I is the set of machine instructions for scalar/vector and data routing operations; and M is the set of masking schemes, where each mask partitions the set A into disjoint subsets of enabled and disable

VECTOR-PROCESSING COMPUTERS

PE's. This model of SIMD machine provides a common formal basis for evaluating different SIMD machines (Siegel, 1979). In this section, only two of the most recently announced SIMD array processors, namely, the BSP and MPP, will be described as working examples. Descriptions on earlier array processors, such as Illiac IV and STARAN, can be found in those texts mentioned in Section 1.3.

5.1 Interconnection Modeling of SIMD Computers

The interconnection network can be described by a set of routing functions over the set A of PE addresses. When a routing function f is applied, PE_i copies the contents of data-routing register R_i into $R_{f(i)}$ of $PE_{f(i)}$. This occurs for all active i in set A simultaneously. An inactive PE may receive data from another PE if a routing function is executed but it cannot send data. To pass data between two PEs that are not directly connected, the

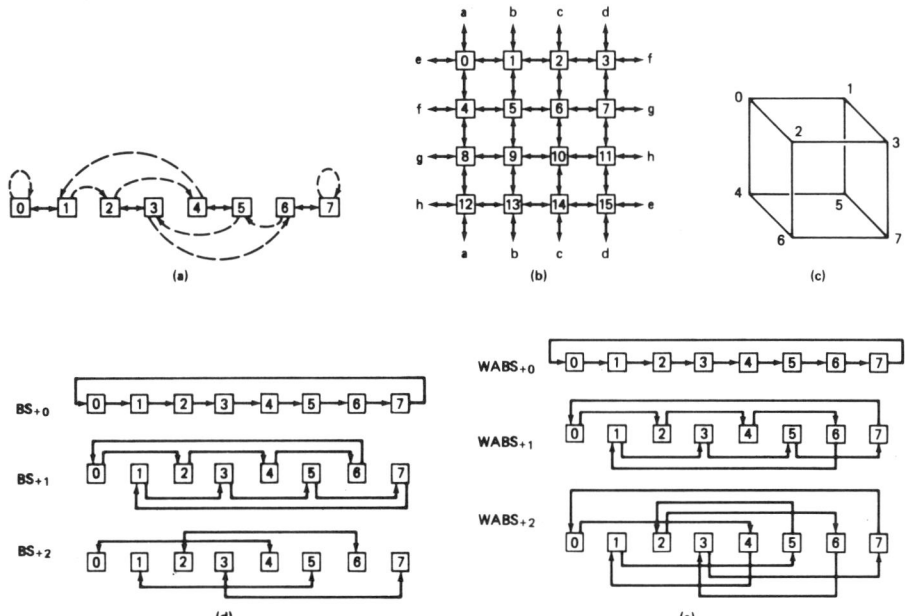

FIG. 19. Interconnection networks for SIMD array processors (Siegel, 1979). (a) Perfect shuffle network for $N = 8$; solid line is *exchange*, dashed line is *shuffle*. (b) ILLIAC network for $N = 16$; vertical lines are R_{+n} and R_{-n} connections, horizontals are R_{+1} and R_{-1}, where $n = \sqrt{16} = 4$. (c) Cube network for $N = 8$; horizontal lines are $cube_0$ connections, diagonals are $cube_1$, and verticals are $cube_2$. (d) Barrel-shifting network for $N = 8$. (e) Wraparound barrel shifting network for $N = 8$.

data must be passed through intermediate PEs by executing a programmed sequence of routing functions. Five interconnection networks are defined below using $i = (p_{m-1} \cdots p_1 p_0)_2$ to denote the binary address of PE_i and $\bar{p}_j$ is the complement of p_j, where $N = 2^m$ is assumed.

The perfect shuffle network consists of a shuffle function and an exchange function as defined below (Stone, 1971):

$$\begin{aligned} \text{shuf}(p_{m-1}p_{m-2} \cdots p_1 p_0) &= p_{m-2} \cdots p_1 p_0 p_{m-1} \\ \text{exch}(p_{m-1} \cdots p_1 p_0) &= p_{m-1} \cdots p_1 \bar{p}_0 \end{aligned} \qquad (6)$$

This network as depicted in Fig. 19a has been the basis of Omega network (Lawrie, 1975) and is included in the networks of Omen (Higbie, 1972).

The Illiac network (Fig. 19b) can be defined by four routing functions:

$$\begin{aligned} R_{+1}(x) &= x + 1 (\text{Mod } N), & R_{+n}(x) &= x + n (\text{Mod } N) \\ R_{-1}(x) &= x - 1 (\text{Mod } N), & R_{-n}(x) &= x - n (\text{Mod } N) \end{aligned} \qquad (7)$$

where $n = \sqrt{N}$ and N is assumed to be a perfect square ($N = 64$ for Illiac IV, the case of $N = 16$ is shown).

The cube network (Fig. 19c) consists of m functions defined by

$$\begin{aligned} \text{cube}_i(p_{m-1} \cdots p_{i+1} p_i p_{i-1} \cdots p_0) \\ = p_{m-1} \cdots p_{i+1} \bar{p}_i p_{i-1} \cdots p_0 \qquad \text{for } 0 \leq i < m \end{aligned} \qquad (8)$$

The STARAN network (Batcher, 1976) and the indirect binary n-cube (Pease, 1977) applied the cube functions, which connects each PE to its m neighbors.

The barrel shifting network (Fig. 19d) consists of $2m$ functions defined by

$$\begin{aligned} BS_{+i}(j) &= j + 2^i (\text{Mod } N), \\ BS_{-i}(j) &= j - 2^i (\text{Mod } N) \end{aligned} \qquad \text{for } 0 \leq i < m \qquad (9)$$

The data manipulator by Feng (1974) is based on BS functions.

The wraparound barrel shifting (WABS) network (Fig. 19e) consists of $2m$ functions defined by

$$\text{WABS}_{\pm i}(p_{m-1} \cdots p_i \cdots p_0) = q_{m-1} \cdots q_i \cdots q_0$$

where

$$q_{i-1} \cdots q_0 q_{m-1} \cdots q_{i+1} q_i = (p_{i-1} \cdots p_0 p_{m-1} \cdots p_{i+1} p_i) \pm 1(\text{Mod } N) \\ \text{for } 0 \leq i < m \qquad (10)$$

where the indices $+i$ and $-i$ correspond to $+1$ and -1 on the right, respectively. WABS functions are similar to BS functions except any "carry" or "borrow" will wrap around through the $(i - 1)$st bit position. For example, $\text{WABS}_{+2}(101) = 010$, whereas $\text{BS}_{+2}(101) = 001$, as shown in the figure. Note that if the PEs of an SIMD machine are fully interconnected, then crossbar networks are required. Crossbar interconnection network has been used in BSP (Burroughs, 1977). Crossbar networks are most flexible but very expensive, especially when N becomes large. Combinations of the above routing functions may result in different network configurations. Cost-effectiveness is the key criterion in designing SIMD interconnection networks (Pradhan and Kodandapani, 1980; Wu and Feng, 1980).

5.2 Burroughs Scientific Processor (BSP)

The BSP extends the array processing capability of Illiac IV to a vectorized FORTRAN machine. With a maximum speed of 50 Mflops, BSP was designed to perform large-scale computations in such fields as numerical weather prediction, nuclear energy, seismic signal processing, structure analysis, and econometric modeling. It is not a stand-alone processor. The BSP serves as a back-end processor attached to a host machine called the system manager, such as the B7800 depicted in Fig. 20. The motivation for attaching BSP to a system manager is to free the BSP from routine management and I/O functions so that it can concentrate on large-scale vector computations.

The system manager provides time-sharing services, data and program file editing, data communication to RJE stations, terminals and networks, compiling and linking of BSP programs, long-term data storage, data-base management, and other general-purpose processing using various high-level languages. Major components in BSP include the Control Processor (CP), Parallel Processors (PPs) and a File Memory (FM) as shown in Fig. 20.

The CP provides the supervisory interface to the system manager in addition to controlling the PPs and the FM. The scalar processor in the CP processes all operating system and user program instructions, which are stored in the task memory. It executes some serial or scalar portions of user programs with a clock rate of 12 MHz and is able to perform up to 3 Mflops. All vector instructions and certain chained scalar instructions are passed to the parallel processor controller, which validates and transforms them into microsequences that control the operation of the 16 Arithmetic Elements (AEs) in the PPs. The bipolar task memory has 256K words with a 160-nsec cycle time. Each word has 48 bits plus eight parity-check bits to provide SECDED capability. The control and maintenance unit is an interface between the system manager and the rest of CP for initiation, communication of supervisory command, and maintenance purposes.

The parallel processors performs vector computations with a basic clock period of 160 nsec. All of the 16 AEs can execute the same instruc-

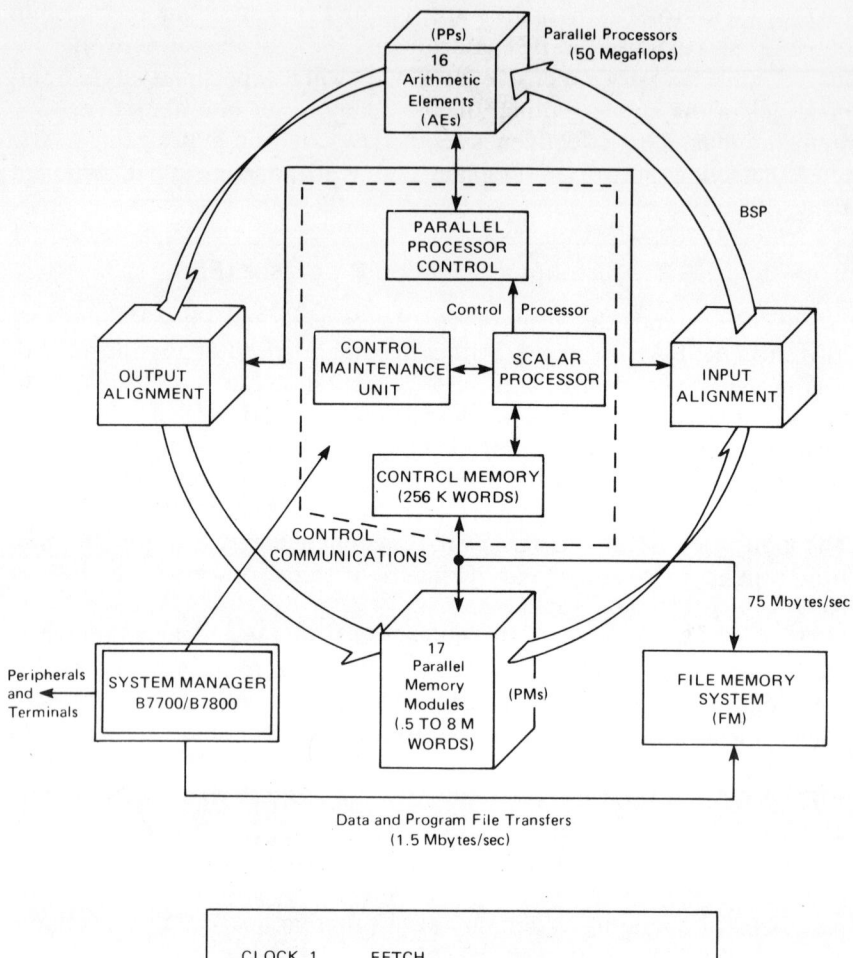

Fig. 20. Functional block diagram of BSP and pipelined array processing (Lawrie and Vora, 1980).

tion, broadcast from the parallel processor controller, over different data sets. Most arithmetic operations can be completed in two clock periods (320 nsec), so that the PPs can execute up to 40 Mflops. Data for the vector operations are stored in the 17 bipolar parallel memory modules (PMs), each of which contains up to 512K words with a cycle time of 160 nsec. The transfer rate of data between the PMs and AEs is 100M words per second. The organization of the 17 PMs provides a conflict-free memory that allows access to vectors of arbitrary length and skip distance which is not a multiple of the prime number 17.

Memory-to-memory vector-valued floating-point operations are pipelined in the PPs of BSP. The organization of the PPs is pipelined with five functional stages. First, 16 operands are fetched from the PMs, routed via the input alignment network into the AEs for processing, and routed via the output alignment network into the PMs for storage. These steps are completely overlapped, as illustrated in Fig. 20. Note that the input alignment and output alignment are physically done by the same alignment network. The division shown here presents only a functional partition of pipeline stages. In addition to the spatial parallelism exhibited by the 16 AEs and the temporal parallelism by the pipelined PPs in locked steps, the vector operations in the PPs can also overlap with the scalar processing in the CP. This results in a powerful and flexible system suitable for processing both long/short vectors and isolated scalars.

The file memory is a high-speed secondary storage built with charge-coupled devices (CCDs). It is loaded with BSP task files from the system manager. These tasks are then queued for execution by the CP. The FM is the only peripheral device under the direct control of the BSP; all other peripheral devices are controlled by the system manager. Scratch files and output files produced during execution of a BSP program are also stored in the FM, before passed to the system manager for output to the user. The CCD memory provides a 12.5M word/sec data transfer rate. This speed exceeds conventional disks and drums by an order of magnitude, and thus greatly alleviates the I/O-bound problem in conventional computer system.

5.3 Linear Vectorization to Parallelism

BSP offers a linear vector approach to parallelism. Methods of achieving such parallelism are described in this section. The basic quantity susceptible to parallelism is the linear vector. A linear vector is a vector whose elements are mapped into the memory of a computer in a linear fashion; i.e., linear vector components are separated by a constant distance **d**. For example, in a FORTRAN columnwise mapping, columns has $\mathbf{d} = 1$, rows have $\mathbf{d} = n$, forward diagonals have $\mathbf{d} = \mathbf{n} + 1$, etc. The manipulation of linear vectors in a BSP utilized both spatial and temporal parallelism.

A unique feature of BSP is its conflict-free memory access. The program may access row, columns, or diagonals of matrices without conflicts in the PMs. The hardware techniques used to ensure conflict-free access are a prime number of PMs, full crossbar alignment networks, and special memory index generation along with crossbar switch tag generation. The BSP memory mapping algorithm is illustrated in Fig. 21.

For simplicity of illustration, let us consider a BSP-like machine with 6 AEs and 7 PMs in which 7 is a prime number. The Tag μ is the memory module number in which the element address associated with the linear address **a** is stored. This Tag is computed by

$$\mu = \mathbf{a}(\text{Mod } M) \tag{11}$$

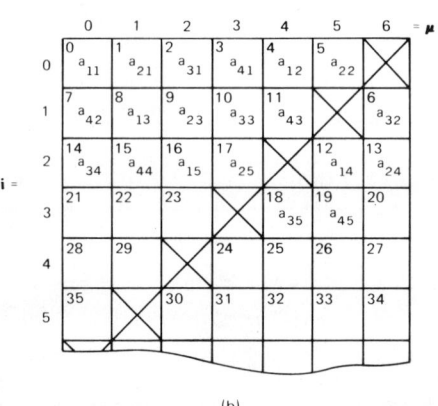

FIG. 21. The BSP memory mapping for linearized vector of matrix elements (Burroughs, 1978): (a) a 4 × 5 matrix; (b) physical mapping of the 4 × 5 matrix; (c) mapping of 4 × 5 matrix if, for example, $M = 7$ and $N = 6$.

VECTOR-PROCESSING COMPUTERS

where M is the number of PM modules. The Index i corresponds to the offset within the assigned module, which can be calculated by

$$i = \lfloor a/N \rfloor \tag{12}$$

where N is the number of AEs in the system. As long as $N \leq M$, the sequence of tag values will connect different PM module to each AE. The particular storage pattern for the system with $N = 6$ AEs and $M = 7$ PMs for the 4×5 matrix is shown in Fig. 21. For example, if row 2 is wanted, then the start address is 1 and the skip distant d is 4. Thus we obtain the following Index and Tag values:

$$\begin{aligned}
\mu &= |1|_7, \quad |5|_7, \quad |9|_7, \quad |13|_7, \quad |17|_7, \\
&= 1, \quad\; 5, \quad\;\; 2, \quad\;\; 6, \quad\;\;\; 3 \\
i &= \lfloor 1/6 \rfloor, \lfloor 5/6 \rfloor, \lfloor 9/6 \rfloor, \lfloor 13/6 \rfloor, \lfloor 17/6 \rfloor \\
&= 0, \quad\;\; 0, \quad\;\; 1, \quad\;\;\; 2, \quad\;\;\; 2
\end{aligned} \tag{13}$$

The unused memory cells are the result of having one more PM than there are AEs. For the real BSP with $N = 16$ and $M = 17$, division by 16 is much simpler and faster than division by 17. Note that conflicts does occur if the addresses are separated by an integer multiple of the number M. This means that skip distances of 17, 34, 51, etc. should be avoided in BSP. The design of BSP offers a significant improvement over its predecessor, Illiac IV. The performance of BSP is yet to be assessed after sufficient processing experiences are accumulated from using the system. However, with its vectorized FORTRAN and parallel structures, BSP will significantly ease the user's efforts and provide much wider applications than those of Illiac IV.

5.4 The Massively Parallel Processor (MPP)

A large-scale SIMD array processor developed at NASA Goddard Space Flight Center for processing satellite imagery is described in this section (Batcher, 1980). The ultra-high-speed image processing computer has been named Massively Parallel Processor (MPP) due to the fact that $128 \times 128 = 16,384$ microprocessors are mesh interconnected to perform bit-serial computations over arbitrary-length operands. The MPP is an SIMD machine with a microprogrammable control unit, which can be used to define a quite flexible instruction set for vector and scalar arithmetic and I/O operations. A minicomputer is used in the system for back-end data base and program management. Multidimensional Access (MDA) memories are used for data manipulation. The MPP system is constructed entirely with solid-state circuits using VLSI CMOS/SOS microprocessor subarray chips and bipolar RAMs.

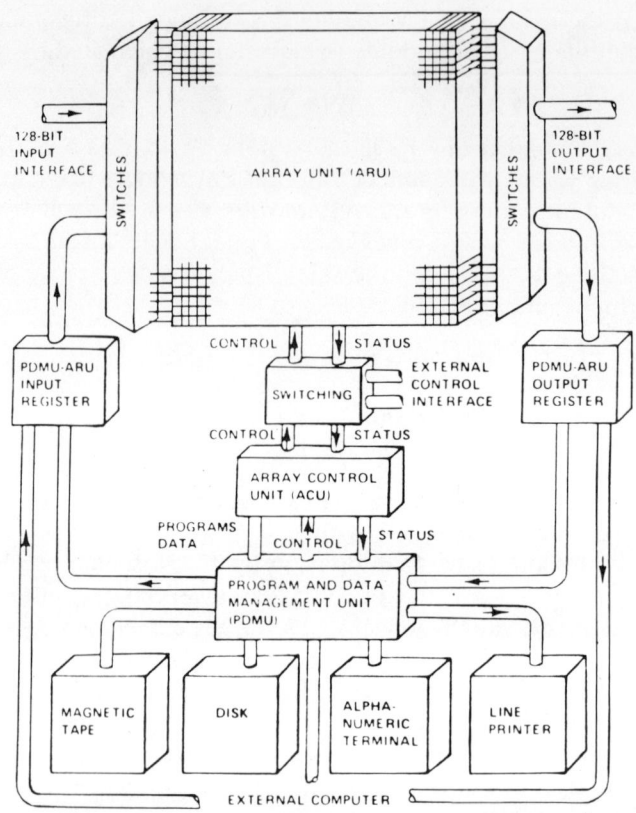

FIG. 22. Block diagram of massively parallel processor (MPP) (Batcher, 1980).

The system architecture of MPP is shown in Fig. 22. The array unit (ARU) operates with SIMD mode on two-dimensional data in a 128 × 128 array of Processing elements (PEs). Each PE is associated with a 1024-bit random-access memory. Parity is included to detect memory faults. Each PE is a bit-slice microprocessor connected to its nearest neighbors. The programmer can connect opposite array edges together or leave them open so the ARU topology can be changed from a plane to a horizontal cylinder, a vertical cylinder, or a torus. This feature reduces routing time significantly in a number of applications.

For improved reliability and maintainability the ARU array has a redundant four-column group of PEs so that the physical structure is 132 columns by 128 rows. Hardware faults are masked out with circuitry to bypass columns and leave a logical structure of 128 × 128. Arithmetic in each PE is performed in a bit-serial manner using a serial-by-bit adder and shift register to recirculate operands through the adder. This increases the speed of multiplication, division and floating-point operations significantly. The fundamental clock rate is 10 MHz for a cycle time of 100 nsec. The ARU is controlled by the array control unit (ACU), which is a microprogrammable control processor. ACU supervises the SIMD operations in the ARU, the scalar arithmetic within ACU, and the shifting of I/O data through the ARU.

The Program and Data Management Unit (PDMU) is a back-end minicomputer. The PDMU manages data flow between the MPP units, loads programs into the ACU, executes system-test and diagnostic routines, and provides program development facilities. It is a PDP-11/34 minicomputer with RXS-11M operating system. It interfaces to the ACU, the ARU (PDMU-ARU input and output registers) and the external computer. The PDMU peripherals include a magnetic tape drive, (nine-track, 800/1600 BPI), two 67-megabyte disks, a line printer and an alphanumeric terminal with CRT display.

The PDMU-ARU I/O registers can reformat the data so that images are transferred in and out of the ARU in the ARU format (serially by bit-plane) and images are transferred to and from the PDMU or external computer in the conventional format (serially by pixel). The registers can store 65,536 bytes built with the Multidimensional Access (MDA) memories (Batcher, 1977). The MDA memory provides data buffering as well as performs data manipulations between the ARU, PDMU, and an external host computer.

The MPP system has more than one operational mode. In the stand-alone mode, all program development, execution, testing and debugging is done within the MPP system and controlled by operator commands on the PDMU alphanumeric terminal. Array unit data can be transferred in and out, through the PDMU disk and tape units or through the 128-bit MPP interfaces. In the on-line mode, the external computer can enter array data, constants, programs and job requests. It will also receive the output data and status information about the system and the program. Data can be transferred between the MPP and the external computer at a 6 megabyte/sec rate. In the high-speed data mode, data is input and output through the 128-bit external interfaces under control of the MPP at rates up to 160 megabytes/sec.

Each PE in the 128 × 128 square communicates with its nearest neighbor; up, down, right, and left—the same routing topology used in Illiac IV. A typical ARU interconnection is shown in Fig. 23. The ability to access data in different directions is important when arrays of data are input and output; it can be used to reorient the arrays between the bit-plane format of the ARU and the pixel format of the outside world. Around the

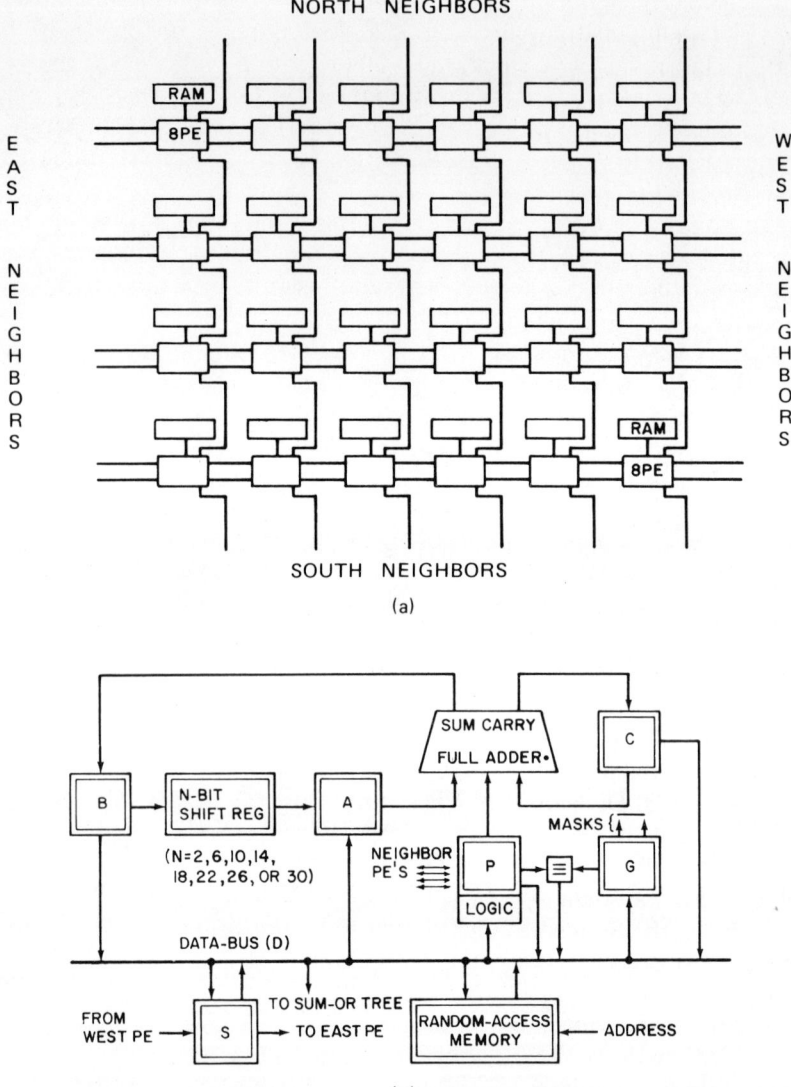

FIG. 23. (a) Typical ARU interconnection of 8-PE VLSI chips (Goodyear, 1979). (b) Functional diagram of each PE in MPP.

edges of the 128 × 128 array of PE's, the edges can be left open (e.g., a row of zeros can be entered along the left edge when routing data to the right) or the opposite edges connected. Cases were found where open edges were preferred and other cases where connected edges were preferred. It was decided to make edge connectivity a programmable function. The top and bottom edges can either be connected or left open. The connectivity between the left and right edges has four states; open (no connection); cylindrical (connect the left PE of each row to the right PE of the same row); open spiral (for $1 \leq n \leq 127$, connect the left PE of row n to the right PE of row $n - 1$); and closed spiral (like the open spiral, but also connect the left PE of row 0 to the right PE of row 127). The spiral modes connect the 16,384 PEs together in one long linear array.

Eight Processing Elements (PEs) in the ARU are built within a VLSI chip in the form of a 2×4 subarray. Each of the 16,896 PE's has six one-bit registers (A, B, C, G, P, and S), a shift register with a programmable length, a random-access memory, data bus (D), a full adder, and some combinatorial logic (Fig. 23). The basic cycle time of the PE is 100 nsec. MPP can perform over 6.5 billion eight-bit integer additions per second. For floating-point operation over 32-bit operands, its addition speed exceeds 430 megaflops.

The P register in each PE is used for logic and routing operations. A logic operation combines the state of the P register and the state of the data bus (D) to form the new state of the P register. All 16 Boolean functions of the two variables, P and D, are implemented. A routing operation shifts the state of the P register into the P register of a neighboring PE. The G register can hold a mask bit that can control the activity of the PE. The full adder, shift register, and registers A, B, and C are used for bit-serial arithmetic operations. Multiplication is a series of addition steps where the partial product is recirculated through the shift register and registers A and B. Division is performed with a nonrestoring division algorithm (Hwang, 1979a).

While the PE's are processing data in the random-access memories, columns of input data are shifted into the left side of the ARU (Fig. 22) and through the S registers (Fig. 23) until a plane of 16,384 bits is loaded. The input plane is then stored in the random-access memories in one 100-nsec cycle by interrupting the processing momentarily in all PEs and moving the S-register values to the memory elements. Planes of data are output by moving them from the memory elements to the S registers and then shifting them out column by column through the right side of the ARU. The shift rate is 10 Mhz; thus, up to 160 megabytes per second can be transferred through the ARU I/O ports. Processing is interrupted for 100 nanoseconds for each bit plane of 16,384 bits transferred.

Like the control units of other parallel processors, the Array Control Unit (ACU) performs scalar arithmetic and controls the PEs. It has three sections that operate in parallel; PE Control, I/O Control, and Main Control. PE Control performs array arithmetic of the application programs.

I/O Control manages the flow of data in and out of the ARU. Main Control performs all scalar arithmetic of the application program. This arrangement allows array arithmetic, scalar arithmetic, and input/output to be overlapped for minimum execution time.

The MPP, to be delivered to NASA in 1982, will use a DEC VAX-11/780 computer as a host. The interface to the host has two links: a high-speed data link and a control link. The high-speed data link connects the PDMU–ARU I/O registers of the MPP to a DR-780 high-speed user interface of the VAX-11/780. Data can be transferred at the rate of the DR-780 (6 megabytes per second). The control link is DEC's standard DECNET link between a PDP-11 and a VAX-11/780. The DECNET hardware and software let VAX users transfer programs and program requests to the MPP. MPP is thus far the largest SIMD machine ever being constructed. Its unique feature of bit-slice processing over operands of arbitrary lengths and the use of back-end data base manager and extra host processor make the system applicable not only to image processing applications but also other array-oriented computations as well.

5.5 Shared-Resource Multiple Array Processors

Array processors with shared resource pool of processing elements can be used for parallel vector processing in Multiple-SIMD (MSIMD) mode. An MSIMD machine is composed of multiple CU's sharing a finite number of PEs through interconnection networks. The organizations of an MSIMD array processor is shown in Fig. 24a. The m CUs and r PEs are interconnected through an $m \times r$ interconnection network, where the number r is usually greater than m by two or three orders of magnitude. The inter-PE communication network provides all the necessary connecting paths for permuting or exchanging data among the PEs. Each CU is equipped with processor, memory and I/O facilities and each PE consists of a processor and its local memory.

Each CU is required to be allocated with a subset of PEs for the execution of a single vector job (an SIMD process). The only way vector jobs can interact with each other is by their independent needs for the same PE resources. Several parallel machines capable of executing multiple vector jobs have been proposed in the past. For example, the original Illiac IV design (Fig. 25a) was for four ($m = 4$) CUs sharing $r = 256$ PEs. The PM^4 system (Fig. 25b) proposed at Purdue University (Briggs et al., 1979) is for mixed MSIMD and MIMD operations. The subset of PE's allocated to each CU may vary in size for different jobs. In the case of the original Illiac IV, the 256 PEs can be allocated to different numbers of active CUs according to the following four possible partitions:

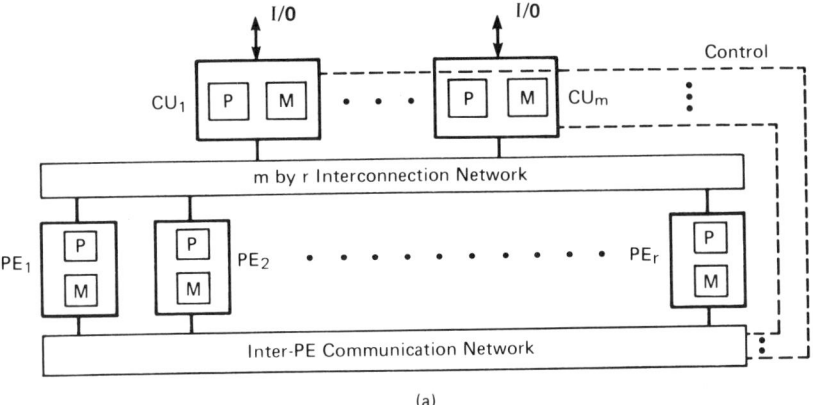

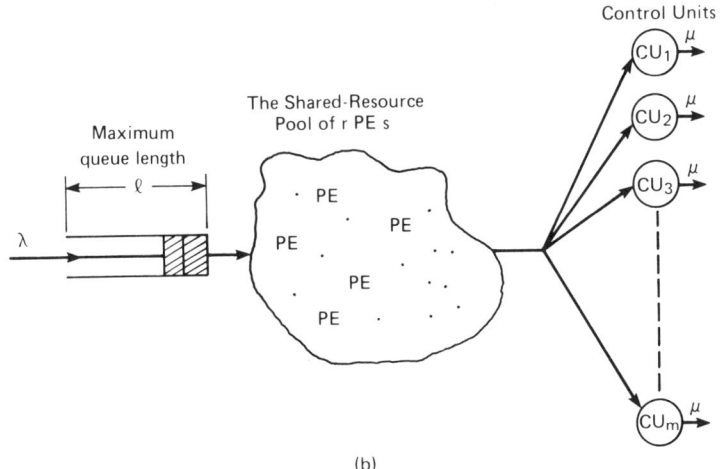

FIG. 24. Multiple-SIMD (MSIMD) computer architecture: (a) MSIMD computer; (b) the queueing model (λ, Poisson arrival rate of input processes; μ, exponential service rate of each control unit). (Hwgan and Ni, 1980.)

64,	64,	64,	64	(4 active CUs)
64,	64,	128		(3 active CUs)
128,	128,			(2 active CUs)
256				(1 active CU)

Note that the four cases correspond to four, three, two, and one instruction streams handled by the same numbers of active CUs. In other words, some of the CUs may be idling due to limited number of PEs in the resource pool.

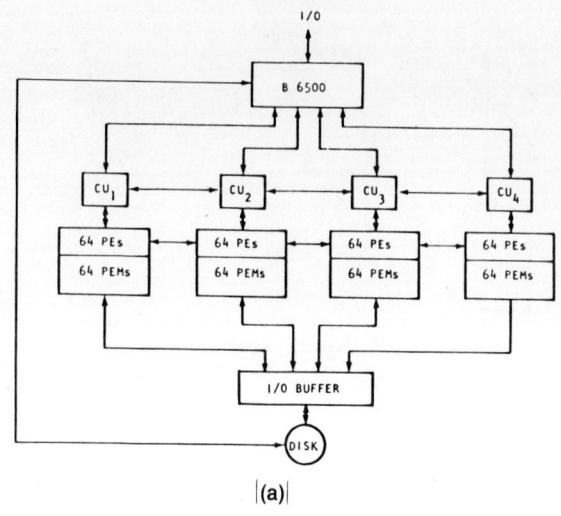

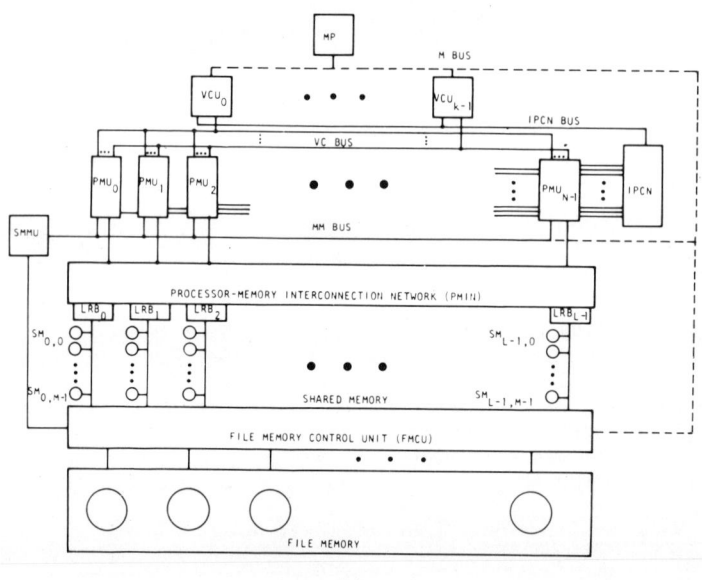

Fig. 25. (a) Original ILLIAC IV design and (b) the Purdue PM[4] system: MP, monitor processor; VCU, vector control unit; PMU, processor memory unit; IPCN, interprocessor communication network; SMMU, shared memory management unit; LRB, line request buffer; SM, shared memory module. (Barnes *et al.*, 1968; Briggs *et al.*, 1979.)

Due to above shortcomings of fixed-block partitions, dynamically partitionable MSIMD machine organization becomes more attractive. The shared PEs are divided into arbitrary partitions as described by the queueing model shown in Fig. 24. The performance of MSIMD computers is measured by the utilization factors of the CUs and PEs, by the average job response time, and by the total system throughput. Briefed below are two analytical methods developed by Hwang and Ni (1979, 1980) to optimize the resources in an MSIMD array processor with respect to any vector workload distribution:

(1) The size of the shared PE resource pool can be optimized with given number of CU's and a known vector job distribution. The criterion is based on choosing the pool size resulting maximal throughput at minimum system cost.

(2) The effective size of the buffer area for holding input vector jobs, as modeled by the waiting queue in Fig. 24b, can be also optimized subject to some constraints of cost effectiveness.

Dynamically reconfigurable array processors with shared PE pool offers great potentials for efficient parallel vector processing. In addition to the Illiac IV and PM^4 systems, the Multiple-Associative Processor (MAP) (Nutt, 1977), the Shared Computing Resource (SCR) (Thomasian and Avizienis, 1975), and the multiple array processing system with switched MIMD streams (Radoy and Lipovski, 1974) all fall into this category. Performance modeling of MSIMD computers using Markov chains can be found in Ni and Hwang (1981).

6. Vector Processor Performance Evaluation

In this section we review some models that have been proposed to evaluate the performance of array and pipeline processors. The system performance is measured in terms of processor utilization and the speedup over serial computers. The efficiency of a parallel processor depends heavily on the inherent parallelism in the programs it executes. Fully exploring the embedded parallelism is the responsibility of both machine designer and computer users. An intelligent vectorizer can be designed to detect possible parallelism in sequential programs. Some optimization techniques in a vectorizing FORTRAN compiler are compared. It seems natural to combine the advantages of both array and pipeline processors in the design of an integrated high-performance vector machines.

6.1 Performance Modeling of Vector Processors

An analytic tool is presented to evaluate the system performance of array and pipeline processors from the viewpoints of system capabilities (e.g., PE size and number of pipeline segments) and of workload distributions. Instruction pipes appear in both types of vector computers. The two classes of computers differ mainly in their execution units. Lang *et al.* (1979) has described a simulation model for predicting the performance of pipelined central processors. The model presents a functional representation of instruction execution sequences. This approach provides a natural mapping of the instruction set onto the hardware architecture. The model has been applied to evaluate CRAY-1, TI-ASC, and STAR-100, using actual trace data from these machines. Bovet and Vanneschi (1976) proposed an analytic method to evaluate the performance of synchronized pipeline processors in the instruction level. The influences of branching and logical dependencies were considered in evaluating the system performance.

A theoretical measure of the system performance of a vector processor is the maximum throughput (W) measured in maximum number of results that can be generated per unit time. Another measure often used is the number of floating-point operations (flops) that can be executed per second. A space–time diagram (Chen, 1971) can be used to describe the behavior of a parallel processor. The processing of a job in a parallel processor occupies the equipment space (e.g., PEs, functional segments) over certain length of time space. The enclosed area in a space–time diagram depicts hardware utilization as a function of time.

We shall compare an array processor with m PEs and a pipeline processor with m functional segments. Generally speaking, data operands in an array processor should be uniformly distributed among the PEs. This effectively creates m separate data streams. Ideally, the system utilization is m times better than a corresponding serial computer. The segments of a pipeline processor operate on distinct data operands. Pipelining increases the bandwidth by a factor approaching m, since it may carry m independent operand elements in the m segments concurrently. The pipeline processor requires more hardware and complex control circuitry than the corresponding serial computer, but it requires less hardware than a comparable array processor.

The following notations are used in presenting the evaluation models:

m Number of PEs in an array processor or the number of segments in a functional pipe
t_a Execution time of a PE to complete a broadcast instruction
t_p Time spent in a pipe from entering the pipe until exit from the pipe
k Number of operations required to finish a specific job
$N(i)$ Length of a vector operand in the ith operation ($1 \leq i \leq k$)

W_a Throughput of an array processor
W_p Throughput of a pipeline processor
$T_a(i)$ Time required to finish the ith operation in an array processor
$T_p(i)$ Time required to finish the ith operation in a pipeline processor
T_a Total time required to finish a job in an array processor
T_p Total time required to finish a job in a pipeline processor
S_a Speedup of an array processor over a corresponding serial processor
S_p Speedup of a pipeline processor over a corresponding serial processor
U_a Utilization of an array processor
U_p Utilization of a pipeline processor

The parameters t_a and t_p are assumed to be independent of the type of operations. The magnitude of t_p is usually greater than t_a because of long pipeline delay. $N(i) = 1$ means a scalar operation; $N(i) > 1$ refers to a vector operation. Figure 26 is an illustration of the space–time diagrams in performing the ith vector operation on an array processor and on a pipeline processor, where $N(i)$ has a value of 10 and m equals 3. In gen-

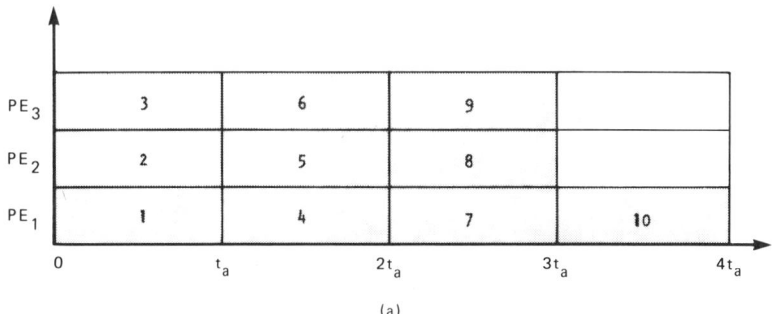

(a)

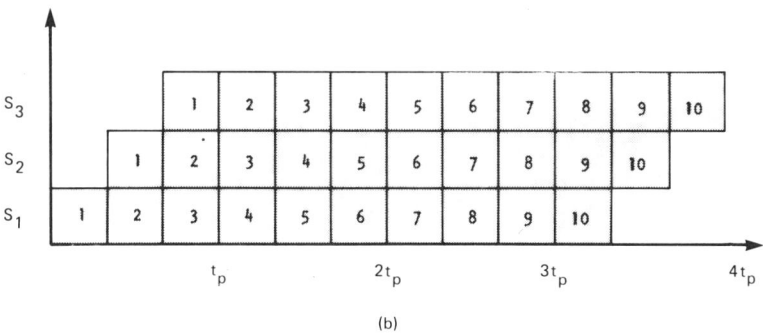

(b)

FIG. 26. Space–time diagrams for: (a) an array processor with 3PEs; (b) a pipeline processor with three segments. (The vector operand has 10 elements.)

eral, in an array processor

$$T_a(i) = \lceil N(i)/m \rceil t_a \tag{14}$$

$$W_a = \frac{N(i)}{T_a(i)} = \frac{N(i)}{\lceil N(i)/m \rceil t_a} \simeq \frac{m}{t_a} \quad \text{as} \quad N(i) \to \infty \tag{15}$$

In a pipeline processor, the average delay in each segment is t_p/m. We can write

$$T_p(i) = (m-1)(t_p/m) + N(i) \cdot (t_p/m) = [N(i) + m - 1](t_p/m) \tag{16}$$

where the first term represents the time required to fill up the pipe. As $N(i)$ increases, $T_p(i)$ approaches $N(i) \cdot t_p/m$. The system throughput W_p approaches m/t_p. If t_a is very close to t_p, array and pipeline processors have the same maximum throughput when $N(i)$ is large. The above derivation is for a single-vector operation with vector length $N(i)$.

Let us now consider a job which can be decomposed into a sequence of k vector operations. The maximum degree of parallelism for each vector operation is represented by the vector length $N(i)$, for $i = 1, 2, \ldots, k$. Suppose that the execution of different types of vector operation takes the same time if they have the same length. The total execution times required to complete a specific job in an array and a pipeline processor can be expressed as

$$T_a = \sum_{i=1}^{k} T_a(i) = t_a \sum_{i=1}^{k} \lceil N(i)/m \rceil \tag{17}$$

$$T_p = \sum_{i=1}^{k} T_p(i) = (t_p/m)\left[(m-1)k + \sum_{i=1}^{k} N(i)\right] \tag{18}$$

The same job if executed on an equivalent-function serial processor needs a time delay equal to the numerators shown in Eqs. (19) and (20). The improvement in processing speed is represented by the following speedup of either processor type over a serial computer that does the same job:

$$S_a = \frac{t_a \sum_{i=1}^{k} N(i)}{T_a} = \frac{\sum_{i=1}^{k} N(i)}{\sum_{i=1}^{k} \lceil N(i)/m \rceil} \tag{19}$$

$$S_p = \frac{t_p \sum_{i=1}^{k} N(i)}{T_p} = \frac{\sum_{i=1}^{k} N(i)}{[(m-1)k/m] + (1/m)\sum_{i=1}^{k} N(i)} \tag{20}$$

VECTOR-PROCESSING COMPUTERS

The efficiency with which a job utilizes the available facilities of a processor is measured by the processor utilization. This may be defined as the total space–time product required by the job, divided by the total available space–time product:

$$U_a = \frac{t_a \sum_{i=1}^{k} N(i)}{m \cdot T_a} = \frac{S_a}{m} \tag{21}$$

$$U_p = \frac{t_p \sum_{i=1}^{k} N(i)}{m \cdot T_p} = \frac{S_p}{m} \tag{22}$$

Clearly, the processor utilization can be interpreted as the ratio of the actual speedup to the maximum possible speedup m. Numerical examples are used to demonstrate the analytic results. Consider a job with the following vector-length distribution:

i	$N(i)$	i	$N(i)$
1	7	6	6
2	3	7	2
3	10	8	5
4	1	9	2
5	4	10	4

where $k = 10$ and t_a, t_p are each assumed to be 1 unit time. Figure 27 is a plot of S_a and U_a (S_p and U_p) against different values of m. The solid line and dashed line correspond to execution on array and pipeline processors, respectively. When m increases beyond the average value of $N(i)$ (i.e., 4.4 in our example), the increase in speedup becomes rather flat while the processor utilization continues to decline. The array processor is shown slightly better than the pipeline processor on both performance measures.

In general, both types of vector processors are in favor of long vectors. The longer the vector fed into a pipeline processor, the less the effect of overhead will be. But for array processors, not only the vector length but also the residue of the vector length will affect the system performance. For example, a vector operation of length 65 to be executed in an array processor with 64 PEs, the residue is $1 = (65 - 64)$. It needs one iteration to complete the residue job. The system performance is degraded, owing to small residues. Figure 28 shows the relation between vector length and the system performance on both array and pipeline processors. Here, we assumed $k = 1$ and $m = 8$. Solid lines and dotted lines represent the performance indices measured on array and pipeline processors, respectively. The maximum speedup, 8, is reached, when $N(i)$ is a multiple of 8

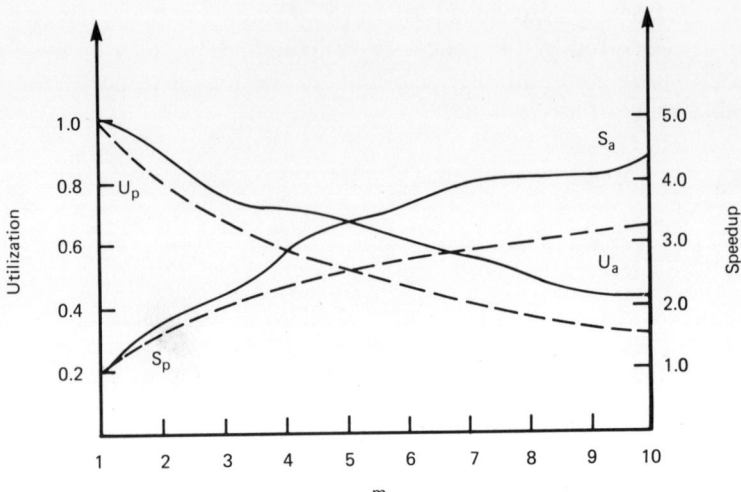

Fig. 27. Processor utilization and speedup for the given vector-length distribution on both array and pipeline processors.

in an array processor. For small residues the speedup drops quickly. But when $N(i)$ approaches infinity, the effect of the residue can be neglected. For a pipeline processor, the speedup increases monotonically until reaching the maximum value of $m = 8$, when $N(i)$ approaches infinity. The processor utilization versus the vector length has the same pattern except with different scale. Both types of processor utilization approach 1 when vector length goes to infinity. The dashed line in Fig. 28 displays the effect due to the partition of vector operands into 16-element groups. The maximum value of the speedup, which equals $8 * 16/(16 + 7) = 5.565$, occurs when the vector length is a multiple of 16.

Obviously, the most important factor that affects a vector processor utilization is the vector length distribution. Too many scalar operations of different types will definitely degrade the system performance. To overcome this drawback, an intelligent vectorizer can help improve the situation. CRAY-1 has a scalar processor that is more than two times faster than the CDC 7600. When the vector length is short, execution by a scalar processor may be faster than that executed in a pipeline processor.

6.2 Optimization of Vector Operations

A vectorizing FORTRAN compiler formulates vectors as computational entities. Scalar operations that can be executed in vector form must be extracted by the vectorizer. A major factor in designing an optimal

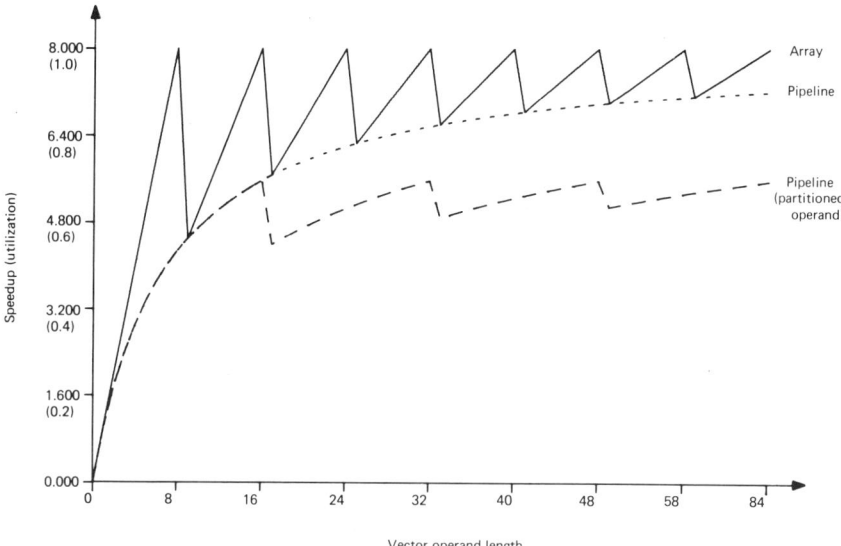

FIG. 28. The speedup (processor utilization) against vector length on array and pipeline processors, where $m = 8$.

vectorizing FORTRAN compiler is the extent to which code generated from a conventional FORTRAN compiler can be used. In other words, we want to extend existing FORTRAN compiler with minimum effort to produce efficient codes for vector processing.

A FORTRAN compiler consists of mainly the following phases. The first is a lexical scan-and-parse phase, which converts the source program to some intermediate code, quadruples, for example. Quadruples usually have fields specifying the operations, up to two source operands, a result operand, and auxiliary information; the auxiliary field is used by the two phases of code optimization and code generation in order to specify which operands are found in registers, which registers are occupied, whether the instruction should be deleted, and so on.

In the second phase for optimization, the compiler accepts quadruples as inputs and produces modified quadruples as outputs. The optimizer will eliminate some redundant subexpressions, those values that have been previously computed. The optimizer may also discover that some variables will never be used again, so that all of its use can be directly replaced by the original expression and its definition can be eliminated. A register allocator attempts to assign heavily used quantities to CPU registers. If it is discovered that a variable is frequently used, it will be probably assigned to a register and recorded as auxiliary information.

In the third phase, the code generator translates the final intermediate code into a machine language program based on the auxiliary information. A code fragment is selected to represent the quadruple in machine code. The code fragment, along with all other fragments and some initializing code, would be written in linkage editor format.

In a vectorizing FORTRAN compiler, the scanner and parser need not be modified. In order to take advantage of the scalar code already in place, we want to handle series of scalar operations as vectors as well. Now, let us consider the optimization techniques which are applicable to the extended intermediate code. Since the optimization techniques are machine dependent, we will consider the CRAY-like structure in which all the vector operations are defined over registers. Eight vector optimization techniques are described below.

6.2.1 Redundant Expression Elimination

After the scan-and-parse phase, some redundant operations in the intermediate code could be eliminated. The number of memory access and the execution time can be reduced. Let us consider the following example:

$$\text{DIMENSION A(100), B(50), C(50)} \tag{23}$$
$$C(1:50) = A(1:99:2) * B(1:50) + A(1:99:2) * C(1:50)$$

A possible set of intermediate code is shown on the left. With elimination of redundant code, the simplified code is generated on the right:

$$
\begin{array}{l}
V1 \leftarrow A(1:99:2) \\
V2 \leftarrow B(1:50) \\
V3 \leftarrow V1 * V2 \\
V4 \leftarrow A(1:99:2) \\
V5 \leftarrow C(1:50) \\
V6 \leftarrow V4 * V5 \\
V7 \leftarrow V3 + V6 \\
C(1:50) \leftarrow V7
\end{array}
\Rightarrow
\begin{array}{l}
V1 \leftarrow A(1:99:2) \\
V2 \leftarrow B(1:50) \\
V1 \leftarrow V1 * V2 \\
V1 \leftarrow 2 * V1 \\
C(1:50) \leftarrow V1
\end{array}
\tag{24}
$$

6.2.2 Constant Folding

In its full generality, constant folding means shifting computations from run time to compile time. Although the opportunities to perform operations on constant arrays is not often, such opportunities will crop up occasionally, particularly as initialized tables. For example, a DO loop for generating the array $A(I) = I$ for $I = 1, 2, \ldots, 100$, can be avoided in the execution phase, because the array A(I) can be generated by a constant vector $(1, 2, 3, \ldots, 100)$, initialized in the compile time.

6.2.3 Code Motion

The innermost loops are often just scalar encodings of vector operations. In such case, the innermost loop can be replaced by some vector operations if there is no data dependence relation or no loop variance. If some of the statements are loop variant, the loop-invariant operations may be moved out of the loop. This is called code motion. Code motion is extremely useful in compilers that include an automatic vectorization phase. Readers may refer to Hwang *et al.* (1980) for detailed examples on code motion.

6.2.4 Pipeline Chaining

In a pipeline processor with multiple pipeline functional units, the system performance can be upgraded by chaining several pipelines. The result from one pipeline may be directly used as an input operand to another pipeline. The time delays due to forwarding intermediate results are thus eliminated. The intermediate results need not be stored back into the memory as exemplified in Section 4.3. An intelligent compiler should have the capability to detect sequence of operations that can be chained together.

6.2.5 Vector Register Allocation

On a machine like CRAY-1 allowing the chaining of vector operations, the importance of register allocation cannot be overlooked. To achieve the maximum computing power, the execution units must be fed with a continuous stream of operands. Retaining vectors in registers between operations is one way to achieve this. However, owing to the limited number of available vector registers in a system, the strategy of vector register allocation emphasizes local allocation rather than global allocation. Sites (1978) has given several good examples of technique to allocate registers.

In general, an optimizing compiler will simulate the instruction timing, and keep assigning intermediate results to new registers until a previously assigned register becomes free. In the absence of a careful timing simulation, the best strategy that a compiler can adopt is the round-robin allocation of registers.

Another solution to the register allocation problem is to generate code for a group of arithmetic expressions (i.e., all those in a basic block that has no branches) using large number of virtual registers, then schedule the resulting code to minimize issue delays and map the virtual registers into a finite number of real registers. This process has the danger of requiring more than the number of available registers, in which case some spilling must be done. Besides, moving instructions around to minimize issue delays may destroy the use of common subexpressions. This poses potential problems worthy of further study.

6.2.6 Reorder the Execution Sequence

In a multifunction pipeline, reconfiguring the pipe for different function requires the overhead of flushing the pipe, establishing new data paths, etc. Instructions of the same type maybe grouped together for pipelined execution as demonstrated by the following example:

$$\left.\begin{array}{l} A1 \leftarrow A2 + A3 \\ A4 \leftarrow A5 * A6 \\ B1 \leftarrow A7 + A8 \\ B2 \leftarrow B3 * B4 \\ B5 \leftarrow C1 + C2 \end{array}\right\} \rightarrow \left.\begin{array}{l} A1 \leftarrow A2 + A3 \\ B1 \leftarrow A7 + A8 \\ B5 \leftarrow C1 + C2 \\ A4 \leftarrow A5 * A6 \\ B2 \leftarrow B3 * B4 \end{array}\right\} \quad (25)$$

The sequence on the left requires four functional reconfigurations, whereas the right sequence requires only one reconfiguration. Thus, significant time saving can be achieved by reordering the execution sequence.

6.2.7 Temporary Storage Management

In the optimization phase of the vector compiler, the generation of too many intermediate vector quantities can quickly lead to a serious problem. For example, to execute the vector instruction $A(1:4000) = A(1:4000) * B(1*4000) + C(1:4000)$ in CRAY-1, may need 63 vector registers (with 64 components each) to temporarily hold all intermediate product terms. CRAY-1 does not have this many vector registers to store all the intermediate results. Therefore, the intermediate results must be temporarily stored in memory. For this reason, the vector compiler must manage its temporary storage carefully. Temporary arrays need to be allocated and deallocated dynamically. Since vector registers may be thought of as temporaries and spillage out of them needs memory, temporary storage management is closely related to the policy of register allocation. The use of a vector loop (Section 4.3) is machine dependent and has been called stripmining (Loveman, 1977). In any case, run-time storage management is an expensive feature to be included in a FORTRAN-based language. There are two techniques to reduce the design cost. First, if the compiler allocates a specific area to fixed-length and variable-length temporaries, the allocation of the fixed-length area can be done at compiling time, eliminating some run-time overhead and permitting access of the temporaries by some generated codes. Second, the number of fixed-length temporaries can be increased by strip mining with a width equal to the length of vector registers in the target machine.

6.2.8 Code Avoidance

A somewhat radical approach to the optimization of vector operations is based on the technique of copy optimization (Schwarts, 1975). The idea is to avoid copying arrays whenever possible. In other words, copy only when forced to do so by the semantics of the language. For examples on code avoidance, readers are advised to read Kennedy (1979) and Hwang et al. (1980).

In summary, a vectorizing compiler should consist of the following capabilities:

(1) lexical analysis and parsing
(2) automatic vectorization
(3) high-level optimization
(4) expansion of access functions (strip mining)
(5) vector register allocation
(6) scalar optimization
(7) scalar register allocation
(8) storage assignment and code generation

7. Conclusions and Future Trends

We have studied the characteristics, implementation schemes, and vector processing capabilities of array and pipeline processors. The merits of these two types of computers are complementary in achieving high system throughput. In other words, a high-performance vector-processing computer may be equipped with multiple processors, each of which assumes pipelined structure. Vector operands are routed to a set of functional units, which operate parallel to generate multiple results per cycle. Unlike the array processor whose PEs operate synchronously, all functional units in a parallel-pipeline computer system operate asynchronously. In other words, each of the functional pipes may execute different vector operations on different data operands. As a result, independent instructions are streamed through different functional pipes with the objective of achieving high system throughput. For parallel execution of vector instructions, a high throughput pipeline computer may be equipped with multiple copies of the following types of pipeline processors:

(1) dynamic pipes
(2) multifunction static pipes
(3) unifunction pipes of different kind
(4) unifunction pipes of the same kind

The trend of having multiple number of pipelines may continue in future generations of vector processors. Special-purpose static pipes may still dominate the design in the near future, because of less control and the declined hardware cost. However, systems requiring reliable and flexible designs may wish to use dynamic pipes in order to enhance fault tolerance capability and resource utilization rate.

Array processor will be equipped with both scalar processor and parallel processing elements as seen in Illiac IV, BSP, etc. The parallel PEs operate synchronously in a lock-step fashion for processing vectors, while the asynchronous scalar processor can operate simultaneously on scalar quantities. The overlapped scalar/vector processing is amenable to all future array processors.

The interconnection network among the PE's or the alignment network between PEs and parallel memories are required to have high bandwidth for both random access or block-oriented packet accesses. Cost-effective designs of such networks range from single-stage recirculating networks to fully connected crossbar switches. The recent development of delta networks (Patel, 1979) opens up a new research front in this direction.

Vectorizing high-level language compilers is desired in all vector processors for vector computations, including language extensions to facilitate the specification and manipulation of vector-valued data. In general, parallel programming languages are sought in both array and pipeline vector processors. The software used in application should be designed to maximize the resource utilization and achieve concurrent computations, independently of vector lengths.

Cellular array of processors operated in pipelined fashion has been proposed by Kung and Leiserson (1978) and extended by Hwang and Cheng (1980, 1981) for large-scale vector or matrix computations. Such pipelined computing structures are especially attractive to be implemented with the merging VLSI technology. The VLSI computing structures may have a great impact on the design of future vector processing computers, if the I/O problem of VLSI chips can be effectively solved. Design changes as the results of large-scale or very large-scale integration (LSI/VLSI) are evident in the latest vector computers. Two good examples are the CYBER-205 and MPP. The CYBER-205 used ECL LSI logic arrays with 168 gates per chip and subnanosecond switching speed. The MPP uses

CMOS/SOS VLSI device, which contains 8-bit-slice microprocessors on a single chip.

The design of conflict-free parallel memories, like the prime memory system (Lawrie and Vora, 1980) used in BSP, is desired in future SIMD array processors. However, the distance skewing in prime number of memory modules may pose difficulty in addressing the memory. This addressing problem is worth further study to ease the programming efforts. The new multiple-read single-write memory by Chang (1980) presents a potential use in array processors. The design of an array processor with multiple CU's and shared PE-resource pool for multiple-SIMD operations presents a viable approach to parallel-vector processing.

Multifunction dynamic pipeline processors and shared-resource MSIMD array processors are two research fronts in designing advanced vector computers. The development and operational experiences accumulated from STAR, ASC, CYBER-205, Illiac-IV, CRAY-1, BSP, AP-120B, and MPP have provided us with an overview assessment of two generations of vector processors in more than 20 years of evolution. In order to ease a user's efforts in fully exploring the parallelism embedded in these vector processors, vectorization techniques for pipeline/array computers are emphasized. The optimization of vector operations and parallel programming languages for vector processors are still wide-open areas that require further research and development.

ACKNOWLEDGMENTS

Research connected with this paper has been supported in part by National Science Foundation Grant No. MCS-78-18906 and in part by Department of Transportation research contract No. R92004. The authors are indebted to Mr. Andy Hughes and his staff members for typing several versions of the manuscript.

REFERENCES

Amdahl Corp. (1975). "Amdahl 470 V/6 Machine Reference Manual." Sunnyvale, California.

Anderson, D. W., Eagle, J. G., Goldschmidt, R. E., and Powers, D. M. (1967). The IBM system/360 model 91: Floating-point execution unit. *IBM J. Res. Dev.* **11**, No. 1, 34–53.

Baer, J. L. (1980). "Computer Systems Architectures." Computer Science Press, Potomac, Maryland.

Banerjee, U., Gajski, D., and Kuck, D. (1980). Array machine control units for loops containing IFs. *Proc. Int. Conf. Parallel Process., 1980* pp. 28–36.

Barnes, G. H., *et al.* (1968). The ILLIAC IV computer. *IEEE Trans. Comput.* **C-17**, No. 8, 746–757.

Baskett, F., and Keller, T. W. (1977). An evaluation of the CRAY-1 computer. *In* "High Speed Computer and Algorithm Organization" (D. J. Kuck, D. H. Lawrie, and A. H. Sameh, eds.), pp. 71–84. Academic Press, New York.

Batcher, K. E. (1974). STARAN parallel processor system hardware. *Proc. Natl. Comput. Conf.* (AFIPS Press), **43**, 405–410.
Batcher, K. E. (1976). The flip network in STARAN. *Proc. Int. Conf. Parallel Process., 1976* pp. 65–71.
Batcher, K. E. (1977). The multi-dimensional access memory in STARAN. *IEEE Trans. Comput.* **C-26**, No. 2, 174–177.
Batcher, K. E. (1980). Design of a massively parallel processor. *IEEE Trans. Comput.* **C-29**, 836–840.
Bernhard, R. (1981). Minis and mainframes: Design changes are spurred by LSI. *IEEE Spectrum*, Jan., pp. 42–44.
Bouknight, W. J., *et al.* (1972). The Illiac IV system. *Proc. IEEE* **60**, No. 4, 369–388.
Bovet, D. P., and Vanneschi, M. (1976). Models and evaluation of pipeline systems. In "Computer Architectures and Networks" (E. Gelenbe and R. Mahl, eds.), pp. 99–111. North-Holland Publ., Amsterdam.
Briggs, F. A. (1978). Performance of memory configurations for parallel-pipelined computers. *Proc. 5th Annu. Symp. Comput. Archit.* pp. 202–209.
Briggs, F. A., and Davidson, E. S. (1977). Organization of semiconductor memories for parallel-pipelined processors. *IEEE Trans. Comput.* **C-26**, No. 2, 162–169.
Briggs, F. A., Fu, K. S., Hwang, K., and Patel, J. H. (1979). "PM^4: A reconfigurable multiprocessor system for pattern recognition and image processing. *Proc. NCC, AFIPS, 1979* pp. 255–265.
Burroughs Co. (1977). "BSP: Implementation of FORTRAN," Doc. 61391, Nov.
Burroughs Co. (1978). "BSP: Overview Perspective, and Architecture," Doc. 61391, Feb.
Chang, S. L. (1980). Multiple-read single-write memory and its applications. *IEEE Trans. Comput.* **C-29**, No. 8, 689–694.
Chen, T. C. (1971). Parallelism, pipelining, and computer efficiency. *Comput. Des.* Jan., pp. 69–74.
Chen, T. C. (1980). Overlap and pipeline processing. In "Introduction to Computer Architecture" (H. S. Stone, ed.), 2nd ed., pp. 427–486. Associates, Inc., Chicago, Illinois.
Cheung, L., and Mowle, F. J. (1974). Suggestions for improvements to a pipelined computer system. *Proc. 12th Annu. Allerton Conf. Circuit Syst. Theory* pp. 670–677.
Control Data Corp. (1973). "Control Data STAR-100 Features Manual," Publ. No. 60425500, Oct. CDC, St. Paul, Minnesota.
Control Data Corp. (1976). "Control Data STAR-100 FORTRAN Language Version 2 Reference Manual," Publ. No. 60386200. CDC, St. Paul, Minnesota.
Control Data Corp. (1980). "Introducing the Control Data CYBER-205: The Supercomputer for the 80's." CDC, St. Paul, Minnesota.
Cooper, R. G. (1977). The distributed pipeline. *IEEE Trans. Comput.* **C-26**, No. 11, 1123–1132.
Cordennier, V. (1975). A two dimension pipelined processor for communication in a parallel system. *Proc. Sagamore Comp. Conf. Parallel Process., 1975* pp. 115–121.
Cray Research, Inc. (1977). "CRAY-1 Computer System Hardware Reference Manual," Publ. No. 2240004. Bloomington, Minnesota.
Cray Research, Inc. (1978). "CRAY-1 Computer System Preliminary CRAY FORTRAN (CFT) Reference Manual," Publ. No. 2240009. Bloomington, Minnesota.
Datawest Corp. (1979). "Real Time Series of Microprogrammable Array Transform Processors," Prod. Bull. Ser. B.
Davidson, E. S. (1971). The design and control of pipelined function generators. *Proc. Int. IEEE Conf. Syst., Networks, Comput., Oaxtepec, Mexico, Jan., 1971*.
Davidson, E. S., Shar, L. E., Thomas, A. T., and Patel, J. H. (1975). Effective control for pipelined computers. *COMPCON Proc. IEEE Computer Soc.*, pp. 181–184.

Dorr, F. W. (1978). The CRAY-1 at Los Alamos, *Datamation* **24**, No. 10, 113–120.
Emer, J. S., and Davidson, E. S. (1978). Control store organization for multiple stream pipelined processors. *Proc. Int. Conf. Parallel Process., 1978* pp. 43–48.
Evansen, A. J., and Troy, J. L. (1973). Introduction to the architecture of a 288—element PEPE. *Proc. Sagamore Conf. Parallel Process., 1973* pp. 162–169.
Feng, T. Y. (1974). Data manipulation functions in parallel processors and their implementations. *IEEE Trans. Comput.* **C-23**, No. 3, 309–318.
Floating Point System, Inc. (1976). "AP-120B Processor Handbook," Publ. No. 7259-02, May. Portland, Oregon.
Flynn, M. J. (1972). Some computer organization and their effectiveness. *IEEE Trans. Comput.* **C-21**, No. 9, 948–960.
Gao, Q. S., and Zhang, X. (1979). Cellular vector computer of vertical and horizontal processing with vertical common memory. *J. Comput.* No. 1, pp. 1–12 (in Chinese).
Gao, Q. S., and Zhang, X. (1980). Another approach to making supercomputer by microprocessors—cellular vector computer of vertical and horizontal processing with virtual common memory. *Proc. Int. Conf. Parallel Process., 1980* pp. 163–164.
Ginsberg, M. (1977). Some numerical effects of a FORTRAN vectorizing compiler on a Texas instruments advanced scientific computer. *In* "High Speed Computer and Algorithm Organization" (D. J. Kuck, D. H. Lawrie, and A. H. Sameh, eds.), pp. 461–462. Academic Press, New York.
Goodyear Aerospace Co. (1979). "Massively Parallel Processor (MPP)," Tech. Rep. GER-16684, July, Akron, Ohio.
Graham, W. R. (1970). The parallel and the pipeline computers. *Datamation* **16**, No. 4, 68–71.
Hallin, T. G., and Flynn, M. J. (1972). Pipelining of arithmetic functions. *IEEE Trans. Comput.* **C-21**, No. 9, 880–886.
Händler, W. (1977). The impact of classification schemes on computer architecture. *Proc. Int. Conf. Parallel Process., 1977* pp. 7–15.
Hayes, J. P. (1978). "Computer Architecture and Organization." McGraw-Hill, New York.
Higbie, L. C. (1972). The OMEN computer: Associative array processor. *Digest of Papers IEEE COMPCON* pp. 287–290.
Higbie, L. C. (1978). Applications of vector processing." *Comput. Des.*, **17**, No. 4, April, 139–145.
Hintz, R. G., and Tate, D. P. (1972). Control data STAR-100 processor design. *Digest of Papers, IEEE COMPCON Proc.* Sept., pp. 1–4.
Hufnagel, S. (1979). Comparison of selected array processor architecture. *Comput. Des.* **18**, No. 3, March, 151–158.
Hwang, K. (1979a). "Computer Arithmetic: Principles, Architecture and Design." Wiley, New York.
Hwang, K. (1979b). Global and modular two's complement array multiplies. *IEEE Trans. Comput.* **C-28**, 300–306.
Hwang, K., and Cheng, Y. H. (1980). VLSI arithmetic arrays and modular networks for solving large-scale linear system of equations. *Proc. Int. Conf. Parallel Process., 1980* pp. 217–227.
Hwang, K., and Ni, L. M. (1979). Performance evaluation and resource optimization of multiple SIMD computer organizations. *Proc. Int. Conf. Parallel Process., 1979* pp. 86–94.
Hwang, K., and Ni, L. M. (1980). Resource optimization of a parallel computer for multiple vector processing. *IEEE Trans. Comput.* **C-29**, 831–836.
Hwang, K., Su, S. P., and Ni, L. M. (1980). "Vector Processing Computer Architectures," TR-EE 80-37. School of E. E., Purdue University, Lafayette, Indiana.

Hwang, K., and Cheng, Y. H. (1981). "Partitioned Algorithms and VLSI Structures for Large-Scale Matrix Computations in Solving Linear Equations," *Proc. 5th Symp. Comput. Arithmetic, IEEE Comput. Soc.*, May 18–19, Ann Arbor, 1981.

Ibbett, R. N. (1972). The MU5 instruction pipeline. *Comput. J.* **15**, No. 1, 42–50.

IBM, Inc. (1977). "IBM 3838 Array Processor Functional Characteristics," Form No. GA 24-3639. Armond, New York.

Irwin, M. J. (1978). A pipelined processing unit for on-line division. *Proc. Symp. Comput. Archit., 5th, 1978* pp. 24–30.

Jin, L. (1980). A new general-purpose distributed multiprocessor structure. *Proc. Int. Conf. Parallel Process., 1980* pp. 153–154.

Johnson, P. M. (1977). "CRAY-1 Computer System." Publ. No. 2240002A. Cray Research, Inc., Bloomington, Minnesota.

Johnson, P. M. (1978). An introduction to vector processing. *Comput. Des.* **17**, No. 2, Feb., 89–97.

Jump, J. R., and Ahuja, S. R. (1978). Effective pipelining of digital systems. *IEEE Trans. Comput.* **C-27**, No. 9, 855–865.

Kartashev, S. I., and Kartashev, S. P. (1980). Problems of designing supersystems with dynamic architectures. *IEEE Trans. Computer*, Dec., pp. 1114–1132.

Kascic, M. J., Jr. (1980). Vector processing, problem or opportunity? *COMPCON Proc.* pp. 270–276.

Kaufman, M. T. (1974). An almost-optimal algorithm for the assembly line scheduling problem. *IEEE Trans. Comput.* **C-23**, No. 11, 1169–1174.

Kennedy, K. (1979). Optimization of vector operations in an extended fortran compiler. *IBM Res. Rep.* **RC-7784**.

Kozdrowicki, E. W., and Theis, D. J. (1980). Second generation of vector supercomputers. *IEEE Comput. Mag.* **13**, No. 11, Nov., pp. 71–83.

Kuck, D. J. (1968). ILLIAC IV software and application programming. *IEEE Trans. Comput.* **C-17**, No. 8, 758–770.

Kuck, D. J. (1977). A survey of parallel machine organization and programming. *Comput. Surv.* **9**, No. 1, March, pp. 29–59.

Kuck, D. J. (1978). "The Structure of Computers and Computations," Vol. 1. Wiley, New York.

Kung, H. T., and Leiserson, C. E. (1978). Systolic arrays (for VLSI). *In* "Spare Matrix Proceedings, (I. S. Duff, *et al.*, eds.), pp. 245–282. Soc. Ind. Appl. Math., Philadelphia, pp. 245–282.

Lang, D. E., Agerwala, T. K., and Chandy, K. M. (1979). A modeling approach and design tool for pipelined central processors. *Proc. 6th Annu. Symp. Comput. Archit. IEEE Computer Soc.*, pp. 122–129.

Larson, A. G. (1973). "Cost-effective processor design with an application to fast Fourier transform computers. Ph.D. Thesis, Stanford University, Stanford, California.

Larson, A. G., and Davidson, E. S. (1973). Cost-effective design of special-purpose processors: A fast Fourier transform case study. *Proc. Allerton Conf., 11th, 1973* pp. 547–557.

Lawrie, D. H. (1975). Access and alignment of data in an array processor. *IEEE Trans. Comput.* **C-24**, No. 12, 1145–1155.

Lawrie, D. H., and Vora, C. (1980). The prime memory system for array access. *Proc. Int. Conf. Parallel Processing, 1980* pp. 81–87.

Lee, R. B.-L. (1980). Empirical results on the speed, efficiency, redundancy and quality of parallel computations. *Proc. Int. Conf. Parallel Process., 1980,* pp. 91–96.

Loveman, D. B. (1977). Program improvement by source-to-source transformation. *J. Assoc. Comput. Mach.* **24**, 1, 121–145.

Majithia, J. C. (1976). Some comments concerning design of pipeline arithmetic arrays. *IEEE Trans. Comput.* **C-25,** No. 11, 1132–1134.
Mayeda, W. (1975). Two Methods for improving throughput of a pipeline. *Proc. Allerton Conf., 13th, 1975* pp. 873–886.
Naga, N. M., and Field, J. A. (1978). A pipelined direct execution high level language machine. *Proc. Int. Conf. Parallel Process. 1978* pp. 49–51.
Nassimi, D., and Sahni, S. H. (1980). Data broadcasting in SIMD computers. *Proc. Int. Conf. Parallel Process., 1980* pp. 325–326.
Nelson, H. L. (1980). Multi-precise arithmetic on a vector processor, or how we found the 27th Mersenne prime. *COMPCON Proc.* pp. 265–269.
Ni, L. M., and Hwang, K. (1981). Performance modeling of shared resource array processor. *IEEE Trans. Software Eng.* **SE-7,** No. 4.
Nutt, G. J. (1977). Memory and bus conflict in an array processor. *IEEE Trans. Comput.* **C-26,** No. 6, 514–521.
Owens, R. M., and Irwin, M. J. (1979). On-line algorithms for the design of pipeline architecture. *Proc. 6th Annu. Symp. Comput. Archit.* pp. 12–19.
Padua, D. A., Kuck, D. J., and Lawrie, D. H. (1980). High-speed multiprocessors and compilation techniques. *IEEE Trans. Comput.* **C-29,** 763–776.
Parasuraman, B. (1976). Pipelined architectures for microprocessor. *COMPCON Proc.* pp. 225–228.
Patel, J. H. (1976a). Improving the throughput of a pipeline by insertion of delays. *Proc. 3rd Annu. Symp. Comput. Archit.* pp. 159–164. IEEE Computer Soc.
Patel, J. H. (1976b). Improving the throughput of pipelines with delays and buffers. Ph.D. Thesis, University of Illinois at Urbana-Champaign.
Patel, J. H. (1978a). Pipelines with internal buffers. *Proc. 5th Annu. Symp. Comput. Archit.* pp. 249–254. IEEE Computer Soc.
Patel, J. H. (1978b). Performance studies of internally buffered pipelines. *Proc. Int. Conf. Parallel Process., 1978* pp. 36–42.
Patel, J. H. (1979). Processor-memory interconnections for multiprocessors. *Proc. 6th Annu. Symp. Comput. Archit.* pp. 168–177. IEEE Computer Soc.
Paul, G. (1978). Large-scale vector/array processors. *IBM Res. Rep.* **RC 7306,** 1–24.
Paul, G., and Wilson, M. W. (1978). An introduction to VECTRAN and its use in scientific applications programming. *IBM Res. Rep.* **RC 7287.**
Pease, M. C. (1977). The indirect binary n-cube microprocessor array. *IEEE Trans. Comput.* **C-25,** 458–473.
Pradhan, D. K., and Kodandapani, K. L. (1980). A uniform representation of single-and multistage interconnection networks used in SIMD machines. *IEEE Trans. Comput.* **C-29,** No. 9, 777–790.
Purcell, C. J. (1974). The control data STAR-100—performance measurements. *Proc. Natl. Comput. Conf.* **43,** pp. 385–387. AFIPS Press.
Radoy, C. H., and Lipovski, G. J. (1974). Switched multiple instruction, multiple data stream processing. *Proc. 2nd Annu. Symp. Comput. Archit.* pp. 183–187.
Ramamoorthy, C. V., and Kim, K. H. (1974). Pipelining—the generalized concept and sequencing strategies. *AFIPS NCC Proc.* pp. 289–297.
Ramamoorthy, C. V., and Li, H. F. (1974). Efficiency in generalized pipeline networks. *AFIPS NCC Proc.* pp. 625–635.
Ramamoorthy, C. V., and Li, H. F. (1975). Sequencing control in multifunctional pipeline systems. *Proc. Sagamore Comp. Conf. Parallel Processing, 1975* pp. 79–89.
Ramamoorthy, C. V., and Li, H. F. (1977). Pipeline architecture. *Comput. Surv.* **9,** No. 1, 61–102.

Remund, R. N., and Taggert, K. A. (1977). To vectorize or to "vectorize": That is the question. *In* "High Speed Computer and Algorithm Organization" (D. J. Kuck, D. H. Lawrie, and A. H. Sameh, eds.), pp. 399–410. Academic Press, New York.

Roesser, R. P. (1978). Two-dimensional microprocessor pipelines for image processing. *IEEE Trans. Comput.* **C-27**, No. 2, 144–156.

Russell, R. M. (1978). The CRAY-1 computer system. *Commun. ACM* **21**, No. 1, 63–72.

Schlankser, M., and Atkins, D. E. (1977). A complexity result on a pipelined processor design problem. *In* "High Speed and Algorithm Organization" (D. J. Kuck, D. H. Lawrie, and A. H. Sameh, eds.), pp. 129–142. Academic Press, New York.

Schwartz, J. T. (1978). Optimization of very high level language. I. Value transmission and its corollaries. *J. Comput. Lang.* **1**, 161–194.

Senzig, D. N., and Smith, R. V. (1965). Computer organization for array processing. *AFIPS FJCC Proc.* Part I, pp. 117–128.

Shar, L. E., and Davidson, E. S. (1974). A multiminiprocessor system implemented through pipelining. *Computer* **7**, No. 2, Feb., pp. 42–51.

Siegel, H. J. (1979). A model of SIMD machines and a comparison of various interconnection networks. *IEEE Trans. Comput.* **C-28**, No. 12, 907–917.

Sintz, R. H. P. H. (1980). Optimal use of a vector processor. *Digest of Papers, IEEE COMPCON, Spring 1980*, pp. 277–281.

Sites, R. L. (1978). An analysis of the CRAY-1 computer. *Proc. 5th Annu. Symp. Comput. Archit.* pp. 101–106.

Smith, B. J. (1978). A pipelined, shared resources MIMD computer. *Proc. Int. Conf. Parallel Process., 1978* pp. 6–8.

Sperry Rand (1971). Array processing. *Sperry Rand Eng.* **2**, No. 4, 2–8.

Stephenson, C. M. (1973). Control of a variable configuration pipelined arithmetic unit. *Proc. Allerton Conf., 11th, 1973* pp. 558–567.

Stevenson, D. K. (1980). Numerical algorithms for parallel computers. *Proc. Natl. Comput. Conf.* **49**, pp. 357–361. AFIPS Press.

Stokes, R. A. (1977). Burroughs scientific processor. *In* "High Speed Computer and Algorithm Organization" (D. J. Kuck, D. H. Lawrie, and A. H. Sameh, eds.), pp. 85–89. Academic Press, New York.

Stone, H. S. (1971). Parallel processing with the perfect shuffle. *IEEE Trans. Comput.* **C-20**, No. 2, 153–161.

Stone, H. S. (1978). Sorting on STAR. *IEEE Trans. Software Eng.* **SE-4**, No. 2, pp. 138–146.

Stone, H. S. (1980). Parallel computers. *In* "Introduction to Computer Architecture" (H.S. Stone, ed.), 2nd ed., pp. 318–374. Science Research Assoc., Inc., Chicago, Illinois.

Texas Instruments, Inc. (1971). "Description of the ASC System," Parts 1–5, Manual Nos. 934662–934666.

Texas Instruments, Inc. (1972). "ASC FORTRAN Reference Manual," Publ. No. 930044. Austin, Texas

Theis, D. J. (1974) Special tutorial: Vector supercomputers. *IEEE Comput. Mag.* **7**, No. 4, April, pp. 52–61.

Thomas, A. T., and Davidson, E. S. (1974). Scheduling of multiconfigurable pipelines. *Proc. Allerton Conf., 12th, 1972* pp. 658–669.

Thomasian, A., and Avizienis, A. (1975). A design study of a shared resource computing system. *Proc. 3rd Annu. Symp. Comput. Archit.* pp. 105–112.

Thornton, J. E. (1970). "Design of a Computer: The Control Data 6600." Scott, Foresman, Glenview, Illinois.

Thurber, K. J. (1976). "Large Scale Computer Architecture—Parallel and Associative Processors." Hayden Book Co., Rochelle Park, New Jersey.

Thurber, K. J. (1979a). Parallel processor architectures. Part I. General purpose system. *Comput. Des.* **18,** No. 1, Jan., pp. 89–97.

Thurber, K. J. (1979b). Parallel processor architectures. Part II. Special purpose systems. *Comput. Des.* **18,** No. 2, Feb. pp. 103–114.

Tomasulo, R. M. (1967). An efficient algorithm for exploiting multiple arithmetic units. *IBM J. Res. Dev.* **11,** No. 1, 25–33.

Vanaken, J., and Zick, G. (1978). The X-pipe: A pipeline for expression trees. *Proc. Int. Conf. Parallel Process., 1978* pp. 238–245.

Watson, W. J. (1972). The TI ASC—a highly modular and flexible super computer architecture. *FJCC Proc.* pp. 221–228. AFIPS Press.

Watson, W. J., and Carr, H. M. (1974). Operational experiences with the TI advanced scientific computer. *Proc. Natl. Comput. Conf.* **43,** pp. 389–397. AFIPS Press.

Wittmayer, W. R. (1978). Array processor provides high throughput rates. *Comput. Des.* **17,** No. 3, March, pp. 93–100.

Wu, C. L., and Feng, T. Y. (1980). On a class of multistage interconnection networks. *IEEE Trans. Comput.* **C-29,** No. 8, 694–702.

An Overview of High-Level Languages

JEAN E. SAMMET

IBM Federal Systems Division
Bethesda, Maryland

1. General Introduction	200
1.1 General Approach and Contents	200
1.2 Definition of High-Level Languages	201
1.3 Importance of Application Areas	203
1.4 Retrospective View of Twenty (+) Years	204
2. Trends and Activities	208
2.1 Introductory Remarks	208
2.2 Statistics and Usage	208
2.3 Publications and Organizations Concerned with High-Level Languages	210
2.4 Programming Language Standardization	212
3. Relationship of High-Level Languages to Software Engineering and Software Methodology	217
3.1 Introductory Remarks	217
3.2 Language Involvement in the Life Cycle Steps	219
3.3 Other Issues Involving High-Level Languages	225
4. Some "Modern" Languages	227
4.1 Introductory Remarks	227
4.2 Specific Languages (ALGOL 68, Pascal, CLU, Euclid, SETL)	228
4.3 Ada	232
5. Research and Advanced Development Language Topics	238
5.1 Introductory Remarks	238
5.2 Data Abstraction	239
5.3 Verification	240
5.4 Reliability	240
5.5 Automatic Programming	242
5.6 Functional Programming	243
5.7 Query Languages	244
5.8 Language Metrics	245
6. Future Trends	246
6.1 Introductory Remarks	246
6.2 Hoped-For Future Trends	246
6.3 Expected Future Trends	251
6.4 Some Future Trends *Not* Expected	253
6.5 Interrelationship of Future Trends	255
7. Summary and Conclusions	255
References	255

1. General Introduction

1.1 General Approach and Contents

A lengthy overview article on high-level languages could be written from many different viewpoints. For example, it could be primarily tutorial, or it could discuss specific languages in detail and with numerous examples, or it could focus on current major developments, etc. Such an article can be aimed at widely differing audiences, e.g., the language specialist who wishes to find out from a single document what other specialists are doing, or the reader who wants to learn how to select the proper language for his or her next application, or the manager who wishes to understand what this subject which occupies so much of everyone's time is all about, etc.

Rather than try to select from the indicated list (even as augmented) of possible audience types, and rather than using one of the indicated viewpoints, I have tried to make this contribution very broad, rather than deep in any particular area. With that approach, it probably will be true that each potential reader will find at least one section of direct interest, and some other section of at most peripheral value. It is also true that language specialists will find much of this material to be technically superficial. I have tried in this article to provide an overview of *all* the issues which I think are worth mentioning in 1980. As a result, the coverage of most sections is superficial, but I have tried to compensate for that by providing enough bibliographic citations to permit the reader to obtain more information on topics of particular interest.

Having indicated above the general philosophy for this article, I want to provide a brief overview of the varying sections, and the reasons for including them.

The remainder of Section 1 provides the basic definitional framework, and emphasizes the importance of application areas with respect to languages. Because this is the twentieth volume of this series and it is often useful to remember our technical roots, there is a very brief history of major language developments.

Section 2 provides practical information on various aspects. In particular, the small amount of available statistical information about language development is given. For those readers desiring to learn more about languages there is a brief description of the major publications and organizations concerned with languages. Finally, the whole matter of language standards is discussed at considerable length because of its importance to practical work in the computing field.

One of the most pervasive aspects of the software field in at least the last half of the 1970s has been the concern with what is known as software engineering or software methodology. The importance of languages in different phases of the life cycle and the relation to software engineering are described in Section 3.

Section 4 provides a flavor of what are considered "modern" languages in 1980. A few have been selected, and a very simple description of their highlights is given. In my judgement, the most important of these modern languages (by quite a wide margin) is Ada, and so a thorough description of the development and background for this is given, along with a brief indication of its technical highlights and new features.

For the person interested in learning what types of current research and advanced development is underway, Section 5 provides an overview of some of the topics that I consider interesting and/or important in the environment of 1980.

Finally, because many readers want to know what might happen in the future, there is a section on future trends. These have been divided into separate sections, to indicate (a) what I *hope* will happen; (b) what I *expect* will happen; and (c) what I do *not* expect to happen. This type of crystal ball is interesting, because it is a game the reader can also play, by forming mental agreements or disagreements with the material presented here.

Finally, a brief summary with a few conclusions is given.

There are obviously many, many different ways to divide up the language field for presentation. Because there are numerous interlocking issues, there is no single "correct way." Furthermore, regardless of how one divides up the material, some topics will always show up in more than one place. It has been pointed out, for example, that in this article the subject of verification appears independently in several sections. That does not seem bad to me, since there are many facets to that topic, as to others such as data abstraction.

In spite of the fact that programming languages—as a specific topic—is not as important an area for research as it was in the 1960s, it nevertheless pervades the entire programming process. This contribution can barely skim the surface of some of the issues involving languages.

All the views stated in this article are the personal opinions of the author and do *not* represent the opinion of my employer, the IBM Corporation.

1.2 Definition of High-Level Languages

In spite of the length of time that "high-level languages" have been around, there is still no really adequate definition of what that term means. For the purposes of this article, I will use the definition that I have used for many years, simply because no one has proposed a better one. The purpose of this definition is to distinguish between those things we intuitively think of as high-level languages (e.g., FORTRAN, COBOL) and those we intuitively know are not high-level languages (e.g., assembly languages). Unfortunately, because of the lack of adequate definitions, the distinction between a high-level language and a very advanced application package is not clear, and this is discussed later.

In my definition, a high-level language is a set of characters and the rules for combining them that have the four characteristics shown below. Comments which enhance or clarify these characteristics but are not considered part of the definition are shown within square brackets.

(1) The language requires no knowledge of machine code by the user in order to actually use the high-level language. [This characteristic makes no attempt to take efficiency into consideration.]

(2) The language is inherently independent of any particular computer, and hence it should be easy to take a program written in a high-level language and run it on many machines. [In much earlier times, this concept was referred to as "machine independence"; we are sophisticated enough now to know that such perfection has not been achieved, but, nevertheless, it is a major characteristic of what we think of as high-level languages. As with the first characteristic, efficiency is ignored in this concept.]

(3) There is usually a one-to-many translation from executable elements in the source code to specific machine instructions. [This measurement is, of course, meant to apply most of the time and not to any particular single instruction or element in the source code. Since it is meant to apply only to those elements in the source code that are inherently executable in themselves, it does not apply to data declarations. Furthermore, microprogrammed implementations of a language are not considered in this characteristic.]

(4) The notation of the high-level language is fairly natural relative to the problem area for which it is intended and it is not in a fixed tabular format. [This is the least concrete of these characteristics, since "natural" is a subjective value judgment. The intent of this characteristic is definitely to rule out fixed-format systems such as report program generators or decision tables. They are also valuable means of communicating with a computer but it is a technical definition and taxonomy that is being discussed here, not relative importance nor value.]

There is a difficulty in applying some of these concepts in borderline cases. For example, there is a class of languages sometimes referred to as

OVERVIEW OF HIGH-LEVEL LANGUAGES 203

"midway" or MOL (Machine-Oriented Languages) that have some higher level constructs in them, but also provide very direct access to the machine code. The earliest and the major prototype for most of these is Wirth's PL/360 (1968). Assembly languages with powerful sets of embedded macros are also difficult to distinguish from some very simple high-level languages.

There are some programming languages which have such simple commands and notation that programs look like parameters for an application package. Conversely, there are application packages that are sufficiently flexible to allow different types of parameters and control statements and the distinction between the application package and a programming language then becomes quite blurred. One can say in general that application packages generally (a) have fixed sets of routines but do not allow new ones; (b) accept only parameters as inputs; and (c) have fixed file and data formats. On the other hand, high-level languages generally (a) allow any routine to be written; (b) have flexible commands; and (c) allow general file and data formats.

Throughout this article, I will use the terms "high-level language" and "programming language" interchangeably; it should be understood that whenever the latter term is used, it means the former in the sense defined in this section.

1.3 Importance of Application Areas

In my view, the most important characteristic of a high-level language is its intended application area. This can be broad or narrow, and one's viewpoint often depends on how much one knows about the application area. For example, in a broad sense one certainly can say that FORTRAN is primarily useful for scientific applications. However, that statement does not make any distinction between numeric calculations and formula manipulation and the latter cannot be done (effectively) in FORTRAN. It turns out that the less one knows about a particular field, the more homogeneous it appears, and hence the casual observer thinks that there is little need for separate languages. For example, if one considers engineering as a broad application area, it might be difficult for a nonengineer to realize that separate languages might be needed for applications as diverse as logical design and civil engineering. Even after one accepts the diversity of those two areas, it is hard to believe that civil engineering itself can be broken down into differing aspects such as structural, survey work, roads, etc. Lest anybody think I am exaggerating, there are, in fact, languages for each of these three areas, plus others, in the civil engineering field. Admittedly, not all are widely used.

Some of the borderline cases (with respect to being a high-level language) also can be considered as in the specialized category, e.g., command languages, text-editing languages.

It should be clear that a language may be designed to be used in a particular application area, but nevertheless may be used in others; that does not change the original intent of the language.

1.4 Retrospective View of Twenty (+) Years

Although this article is certainly not meant to be about history, nevertheless it does appear in the twentieth volume of this publication. For that reason, and given my own predilictions and interest toward history, it seems appropriate to include a short section discussing what has happened during the last 20 years, and to go back even further than that to provide a perspective for where we are now.[1]

1.4.1 1945–1953

The earliest work known which legitimately fits the programming language definition given earlier is the "Plankalkül" by Zuse in Germany (1945). Unfortunately this was not implemented. The next step was Short Code, implemented by John Mauchly and others at Remington Rand Univac (1949–1950) and then the unnamed and unimplemented language developed by Rutishauser in Switzerland (1952). The Speedcoding system for the IBM 701 was developed by John Backus and others at IBM in 1953. In this time frame, Remington Rand produced the A-2 and A-3 systems (based on three-address pseudocodes to indicate mathematical operations) and Boeing Airplane Company developed BACAIC for the 701. All these languages, plus others of that period, attempted to provide scientific computer users with a notation slightly more natural to mathematicians than was the machine code. Some permitted the users to write mathematical expressions in relatively normal format, but most did not. None of them had any significant or lasting effect on language development, and apparently minimal effect (if any) on people's thinking.

In May 1953 J. H. Laning, Jr. and N. Zierler at MIT had a system running on Whirlwind that appears to be the first system in the United States to permit the user to write expressions in a notation resembling normal mathematical format, e.g.,

$$c = 0.0052(a - y)/2ay,$$
$$y = 5y,$$

---

[1] The remainder of Section 1.4 is a prepublication of Section 2 of Sammet (1981b), copyright © International Business Machines Corporation, 1981, reprinted by permission.

An excellent description of most of these early mathematical systems, plus others, appears in Knuth and Trabb Pardo (1977), and some of them are described briefly in Sammet (1969), and even more briefly in Backus (HOPL, 1981).

1.4.2 1954-1960

In 1954, work on FORTRAN started under the leadership of John Backus at IBM, and it was released in late 1956.

Around the same time the preliminary FORTRAN report was issued, a group at Remington Rand Univac under Grace Hopper's direction began the development of a system originally called AT-3 and then renamed MATH-MATIC. (John Backus says that he sent them a copy of his November 1954 preliminary FORTRAN report, but I cannot determine how much influence it had on MATH-MATIC. The documentation of the preliminary FORTRAN specifications precedes any language design documents on MATH-MATIC from Remington Rand Univac.) MATH-MATIC [described by Sammet (1969) and by Knuth and Trabb Pardo (1977)] was similar in spirit to FORTRAN, although different in syntax, and it seems to be unclear which of the two systems was actually *running* first. However, of all the parallel work going on in the mid-1950s, only FORTRAN has survived, and by 1957 there were the first glimmerings of significant practical usage of a high-level language similar to those we know of today.

While the main emphasis prior to 1958 was on the development of languages for scientific applications, the first English-like language for business data processing problems, namely FLOW-MATIC, was planned and implemented on the Univac I under the direction of Dr. Grace Hopper at Remington Rand Univac, and released in 1958. [A description appears in Sammet (1969).]

One other language activity of this early period is worth mentioning, namely APT. Work on that started in 1956 at MIT under the leadership of Douglas T. Ross. It was a language for numerical machine tool control, and hence was the first language for a very specialized application area. [See Ross (HOPL, 1981) for full details on the early development.] APT (albeit modified over time) is still in use in 1980.

By some strange quirk, it appears that the years 1958 and 1959 were among the most prolific for the development of programming languages. The following events in universities and industrial organizations all occurred during those two years:

(1) The development of the IAL (International Algebraic Language), which became known as ALGOL 58, and the publication of its definition in Perlis and Samelson (1958). IAL had a profound effect on the

computing world, because of (a) its follow-on ALGOL 60—which is clearly one of the most important languages ever developed, and (b) the development of three languages based on the IAL specifications, namely NELIAC, MAD, and CLIP (which eventually was the foundation for JOVIAL). All except CLIP became widely used.

(2) The availability in early 1958 of a running version of IPL-V (a list-processing language).

(3) The start of work on the development of LISP, a list-processing language which had the motivation of being useful in artificial intelligence applications.

(4) The first implementation of COMIT, a string-processing language.

(5) The formation in May 1959 of the CODASYL (Conference on Data Systems Languages) Short Range Committee which developed COBOL, and the completion of the COBOL specifications.

(6) The development and availability of language specifications for AIMACO, Commercial Translator and FACT, all of which were for business data-processing problems.

(7) The availability of specifications for JOVIAL.

Of all these languages from 1958–1959 and earlier, those that survive (albeit in modified form) *and* have significant usage in 1980 are ALGOL 60, APT, COBOL, FORTRAN, JOVIAL, and LISP. References and a discussion of *all* the languages named in this section can be found in Sammet (1969). The detailed history of the early development of the six languages just cited are described in Wexelblat (HOPL, 1981).

A large impetus for most of this work was economic—even then programming costs were large, and any steps or tools which could reduce those costs were looked upon favorably. However, the crucial issue often was whether any "slowdown" in run time caused by these systems exceeded the overall savings in people's money or time; generally the answers favored the use of such systems even after allowing for compilation time.

1.4.3 1961–1970[2]

The period 1961–1970 saw some maturation of the programming language field. During this time the battle over the use of high-level languages was clearly won, in the sense that machine coding had become the excep-

---

[2] The material starting "The period of 1961–1970" is taken almost verbatim from Sammet (1972b, p. 607). Copyright 1972, Association for Computing Machinery, Inc., by permission. Descriptions of, and references for all the languages mentioned are in Sammet (1969).

tion rather than the rule. (This comment is based only on the author's opinion and perception because there simply are no data to verify or contradict this statement.) Although the concept of developing systems programs by using high-level languages was fairly well accepted, there was more machine coding of systems programs than of application programs. The use of powerful macrosystems, and "half-way" languages such as PL/360 (see Wirth, 1968) provided some of the advantages of high-level languages but without any attempt to be machine independent.

The major new batch languages of this decade were ALGOL 60, COBOL, and PL/I, of which only the last two were significantly used in the United States. While ALGOL 68 was defined, its implementation was just starting around 1970.

The advent of (interactive) time-sharing in the mid-1960s brought a host of on-line languages, starting with JOSS and later followed by BASIC, both of which became very widely used. Each had many imitators and extenders. APL\360 was made available in the 1960s, and became popular among certain specific groups.

The development of high-level languages for use in formula manipulation was triggered by FORMAC and Formula ALGOL, although only the former was widely used. String processing and pattern matching became popular with the advent of SNOBOL.

The simulation languages GPSS and SIMSCRIPT made simulation more available to most users and also encouraged the development of other simulation languages. A number of other languages for specialized application areas (e.g., civil engineering, equipment checkout) continued to be developed.

Perhaps one of the most important practical developments in this time period, although scorned by many theoreticians, was the development of official standards for FORTRAN and COBOL, and the start of standardization for PL/I.

1.4.4 1971–1980

The period 1971–1980 involved relatively few *significant pure language* developments. Those few include (1) the implementation and initial small usage of ALGOL 68; (2) the implementation and heavy use of Pascal; (3) the massive effort by the Department of Defense to develop a single language—eventually called Ada—for embedded computer systems (and described in Section 4.3); (4) the concept of data abstractions; (5) specific concepts of functional programming by Backus (1978); and (6) experimental languages such as CLU, EUCLID, SETL (all described briefly in Section 4.2). It is too early to tell which—if any—of these concepts or languages will have a fundamental effect on the computer field.

2. Trends and Activities

2.1 Introductory Remarks

Because of the very wide usage of high-level languages, there are a great many myths and rumors which continually pervade the field (and sometimes the literature) about how many languages there are, and what kinds. Section 2.2 attempts to provide some actual numbers based on rosters which I have developed for many years. While the results certainly should not be considered definitive, they are probably as accurate as anything which exists, and certainly were *not* developed to prove any particular point or espouse any specific view.

Considering the importance of programming languages to any daily computer activity, it is not surprising that there are several organizations and publications devoted solely to this topic. These are discussed in Section 2.3, and standardization is discussed in Section 2.4.

2.2 Statistics and Usage

One of the most difficult aspects of high-level languages to get a handle on is anything pertaining to the measurement of a language or its usage. Some of the research issues pertaining to the measurement of high-level languages are discussed in Section 5.8, but the intent in this section is to indicate the small amount of data that is available and how uncertain even that information is.

The first and most fundamental problem is in fact to distinguish between two languages that are fundamentally different, and two languages of which one is a minor deviation of the other. On that very fundamental (and currently poorly defined) issue hinges any count on the actual number of languages that exist. One certainly cannot go by names, since there exist in varying places languages with the names SIMSCRIPT I, I.5, II, II.5, and II.5+. For myself I have made a value judgment that there are two substantively different languages in that sequence, namely SIMSCRIPT I.5® and II.5®, each of the others is simply a minor deviation of one of these. However, another person could legitimately draw a different conclusion. This issue is very significant in attempting to obtain a count of the number of past or present languages.

As some readers are well aware, I have for a number of years published *Roster of Programming Languages,* which provide a listing of each language in use within the United States and some basic information about it (see specifically Sammet, 1972c, 1973, 1974, 1976, 1978). In making these lists, I have restricted inclusion to those languages in actual use within the United States. The reason for this restriction is that there is no adequate way for me to obtain the data on *all* of the programming languages in the world, and my feeling is that grossly inaccurate data are worse than none at all. I make no claims that the statistics from these rosters are accurate; on the other hand, it is at least consistent within my own technical judgments. To be consistent with the philosophy espoused in Section 1.3, I have grouped the languages by the major application area for which each was originally intended, and/or where the current major usage occurs. Thus, the Rosters use the categories of numerical scientific, business data processing, string and list processing, formula manipulation, and multipurpose. The latter is what is often referred to as "general purpose" but I consider that term misleading. If we had any really "general-purpose" languages, then there would be no need for the others. However, it is worth noting that some of the major languages (e.g., BASIC, COBOL, FORTRAN) continually have their scope extended far beyond their original purpose, and thus either consciously or unconsciously tend toward being "multipurpose."

There is also another major category of languages, which I refer to as "languages for specialized application areas" (abbreviated as "specialized application languages"); other people refer to these as "special-purpose languages." A general discussion of this concept is given in Sammet (1972a). Examples of languages in this category are APT (machine tool control), COGO (coordinate geometry), and SIMSCRIPT (discrete simulation). Some people have wondered why formula manipulation is not considered a "specialized" category; the reason is that formula manipulation is really nonnumerical mathematics, and mathematics is used in so many application areas that it is too broad to be considered "specialized."

The following interesting phenomenon was observed by me a number of years ago: each time I prepared one of these Language Rosters, the number of languages for specialized application areas was approximately half the total number of all of the languages that I was able to report. Since I certainly did *not* set out to prove this, and have no motivation to concoct the numbers, it is a phenomenon that is at least as consistent as any of the other data here. It should also be noted that the number of languages in different areas does not change significantly from year to year as can be seen by Table I, which shows the data gleaned from Language Rosters covering the indicated years.

I will be the first to admit that these are not solid data and one should not draw major conclusions from this table; on the other hand, these are the only data of this kind that are available.

The data in Table I should be viewed only for the trends they show, and

TABLE I

OVERALL HIGH-LEVEL LANGUAGE STATISTICS[a]

Application area	1977	1975	1973	1972	1971
Numerical scientific	20	28	32		
Business data processing	4	4	3	Data not	
String and list processing	11	12	14	available	
Formula manipulation	10	11	12		
Multipurpose	34	24	24		
Specialized applications	90	88	86		
Total:	169	167	171	184	165

[a] The data in this table are based on the Language Rosters covering the information available at the end of the years indicated in the column heading; see Sammet (1972c, 1973, 1974, 1976, 1978). The 1977 and 1975 Rosters each cover a two-year period. The first Roster was published in 1968, and there are also Rosters for 1969 and 1970. However, the data collection was even weaker then and so those totals are not shown here. In 1971 and 1972 no delineation of languages by application area was made.

definitely *not* for the validity of the actual numbers therein. For example, the decline in the number of languages for numerical scientific applications is due partly to a recent reclassification of some of those languages (e.g., APL) into the multipurpose category. In my view the tiny number of Business Data Processing languages is due to the preeminence of COBOL.

One of the questions that frequently arises is "which is the most widely used language?" In my own view, this is a poorly framed question, and hence, it is not possible to give an accurate answer. There are a number of parameters which could be used to measure the usage of high-level languages. For example, one might use any one of the following numbers to answer that question (if one could obtain them): installations, individual users, programs, lines of source code, lines of object code, compilers, computers with compilers, documented algorithms. One might also measure the amount of machine time used for: compilation, development, debugging, and production runs. Hence, in the future, any reader who is either asked or told about the "widely used languages" should ask how the speaker knows, and what measurement was used.

2.3 Publications and Organizations Concerned with High-Level Languages

There are many publications and organizations specifically concerned with one or more programming languages. The reader can decide whether

OVERVIEW OF HIGH-LEVEL LANGUAGES

or not this is a good thing, but it is important to be conscious of the various organizations which have a direct involvement with high-level languages; this section attempts to indicate the major ones, but there is no guarantee that something has not been omitted. And no attempt is being made to list those publications or organizations which have at least (but only) a peripheral or partial interest in programming languages. This section goes from the general to specific.

2.3.1 Publications

There are two fully refereed journals that deal almost exclusively with programming languages. One is the *ACM Transactions on Programming Languages and Systems* (TOPLAS) published by ACM (Association for Computing Machinery), and the other is *Computer Languages,* published by Pergamon Press. Each accepts and publishes papers dealing with general aspects of the language field as well as articles on specific languages; both tend to publish novel or research-oriented material. Numerous other journals do publish a number of original papers on programming languages along with papers on other computing topics.

In addition to the journals, there are two types of newsletters: general, and language specific. The only general newsletter is the highly respected *ACM SIGPLAN Notices,* put out by the ACM Special Interest Group on Programming Languages (SIGPLAN). This consists of news, notices, announcements, and a number of informal unrefereed papers. It is used as a means of communication (with short dissemination cycles) among people interested in this subject area. It has also been used to publish the proceedings of a number of conferences sponsored by ACM SIGPLAN, and occasionally even to publish the definition of specific languages (e.g. EUCLID, Preliminary Ada). Thus, although it is not a formal journal, in my view *SIGPLAN Notices* is the single most valuable source of information about current programming language issues.

A number of newsletters for specific languages are put out by informal groups, or organizations (including user groups), or even by individuals. The languages for which these exist are ALGOL (60 and 68), APL, COBOL, FORTRAN, JOVIAL, MUMPS, and Pascal. The purpose of each newsletter is to inform about technical and administrative matters pertaining to the specified language.

2.3.2 Organizations

There are several types of professional organizations concerned with languages. These include groups concerned with general language development, and/or with standardization, and user groups for a particular language. The only truly general group concerned with languages is the ACM Special Interest Group on Programming Languages (SIGPLAN), which had over 10,000 members in 1980. The two main activities of SIGPLAN have traditionally been the holding of technical conferences and the issuance of *SIGPLAN Notices,* which was described above.

There are several independent groups concerned in a major way with language development. The oldest and most significant of these is CODASYL (Conference on Data Systems Languages), which was formed in 1959 and was the organization responsible for the development of COBOL. Its primary concern has continued to be COBOL, but CODASYL has also been interested in other issues involving languages such as data bases and operating system control languages. IFIP (International Federation for Information Processing) was the organization sponsoring the development of ALGOL 68 (under IFIP Working Group 2.1) and has in some way been concerned with ALGOL 60 (under IFIP Working Group 2.1) since 1962. SHARE (an IBM user's group) joined with IBM in 1963 to produce PL/I. In the early 1970s the U.S. Air Force sponsored the development of JOVIAL 73. In the late 1970s, the U.S. Department of Defense [specifically the Defense Advanced Research Projects Agency (DARPA)] sponsored the development of Ada; this is discussed in great detail in Section 4.3. Finally, ANSI (American National Standards Institute) has done development work in those cases where no other organization had created an obvious candidate for standardization.

It should be emphasized that language development and language standardization are different activities. One of the major organizations concerned with programming languages has, of course, been ANSI, which has done almost all of the United States standardization of programming languages except those languages handled solely by the Department of Defense and its military components. The standardization is discussed in Section 2.4. The one language that has been officially standardized outside of ANSI is JOVIAL (J73), which is a U.S. Air Force standard.

2.4 Programming Language Standardization

It is well known that the eyes of many technical people glaze over and their interest disappears when the subject of programming language standardization arises. Unfortunately, these people fail to realize that the standardization process has a more profound economic (and even technical) impact on programming languages than any other single activity. Standardization tends to be lengthy, tedious, frustrating, and fraught with difficulties and perils. Nevertheless, it is an activity that prevents the field from being completely fragmented. Standardization enables users to obtain consistent tools; it also gives software vendors a set of specifications for the development of their products and users a criteria by which to examine these products. Standards simplify training, documentation, portability of programs (and people), and development of compilers and related tools.

The fundamental problem in standardizing a language is timing. Standards are almost always either too early or too late. If they are promulgated too early, before a language has the chance to be widely used, and modified based on experience, then some bad features are sure to be included in the standard due to lack of experience. On the other hand, if no standardization is started until after wide usage, then numerous dialects emerge, and then it is a large battle to reconcile the diverse views; there are technical issues and reputations at stake in this process, and usually large economic investments in particular versions of the language.

Because this article is appearing in the twentieth volume in this series, it is worth devoting some space to a very brief retrospective view of the changing philosophy on language standardization. When the ANSI (American National Standards Institute, with previous names of USASI —United States American Standards Institute, and ASA—American Standards Association) committee on programming language standardization (then called X3.4) was formed in the early 1960s, everybody involved was new to the standardization business. In fact, it is probably fair to say that a programming language was far and away the most complex object for which any ANSI standardization had ever been attempted. In some of the early discussions (in which I participated), there was a lot of consideration as to whether or not there should be a *single* programming language standard. That idea was quickly dispelled as being impractical both technically and politically. However, there was serious consideration given to the concept of having a single language standard for each identifiable area of application—the primary ones being scientific computation and business data processing at that time. Because COBOL was the only potential candidate for standardization in the business data processing area, no selection was needed and hence no problem existed. However, in the scientific computation field, both FORTRAN and ALGOL 60 existed, and each had major contenders claiming that *it* should be the single language standardized. While obviously the standardization of one of these would not cause the other one to disappear *automatically,* it was quickly recognized by the proponents of each that standardization of the other would give it an enormous foothold in the claim on user interest. And since neither side was willing to give up the apparent advantage that would come from its standardization, X3.4 eventually—and somewhat reluctantly—decided to develop standards for both. That led tacitly, and then directly, to the situation that still exists in ANSI, namely that a decision would be made on whether it is appropriate to standardize a *particular language,* regardless of whether or not there are others attempting to deal with the same application area. There is an elaborate mechanism whereby proposals for standardization are brought to the appropriate groups for consideration; it may not be obvious to readers of this article, but it is extremely expensive to standardize a language when one considers the costs for labor, travel, and printing that are incurred in the process. Hence, it is necessary for X3 to be sure that a new language standard would be useful before authorizing the development of a standard.

Within ANSI, there are subunits called sectional committees, each of which is concerned with a particular facet of modern society. For example, C78 deals with Electric Lamps and Z39 is responsible for Library Work, Documentation, and Related Publishing Practices. The committees must be broadly based and have representatives from manufacturers, users, and general interest groups. From our viewpoint, the major committee in 1980 is X3 (Computers and Information Processing).

But, of course, ANSI is not the only group concerned with computer standards. There is the National Bureau of Standards, which develops standards for the Federal Government (and is also a member of X3); there are professional societies that develop their own standards (e.g., ISA—Instrument Society of America); there are standards organizations in other countries; finally there is an International Standards Organization (ISO). The complexity of the interrelationships among these and other groups is overwhelming; there is an interesting booklet by Prigge *et al.* (1978), which discusses these matters, but from here on I will limit myself to a discussion of the ways in which programming languages can be standardized and which ones have actually achieved that status, both within the United States and internationally.

There are three ways a language can actually become an ANSI standard. One is for the X3 committee to form a technical committee to develop a standard (generally based on existing defining documents). After the technical committee does its work, the results are publicly disseminated as a Preliminary Draft Standard and comments are received and considered by the technical committee. When they have considered them, and possibly made changes, then a Draft Proposed Standard is submitted to X3, which then votes on whether to send the language standard to a higher unit in ANSI (specifically the Board of Standards Review) which gives final official approval. Final approval at ANSI requires a "consensus" by X3, not just a bare majority.

The second method of standardization is by the "canvass," in which some organization other than X3 takes responsibility for the creation of

OVERVIEW OF HIGH-LEVEL LANGUAGES

the standard. The other organization circulates the Draft Proposed Standard to a "canvass list" for comment, and then considers the responses for possible changes. After that, the language standard is sent to the same higher unit in ANSI to which X3 submits its material. Part of the approval process includes determining whether the "canvass list" is representative of the industry.

A third method for creating standards is for an external organization to be accredited by ANSI to develop its own method of obtaining consensus. The results are then submitted to ANSI for approval.

The languages APT, BASIC, COBOL, FORTRAN, and PL/I were all processed by the technical committee method. That method is also being used to process APL and Pascal. The language MUMPS was handled by the canvass method, and the plan (in September 1980) is that Ada will also be handled by the canvass method. No languages have been handled through accredited organizations. Table II shows the standard numbers, and the approval dates, for ANSI and ISO. In 1980, technical committees exist for the standardization of APL and Pascal, and also for the topics of data definition language, graphics language, and operating system control language.

It would indeed be desirable from many (although not all) viewpoints to expect that once a language standard was established, it would remain as

TABLE II

LIST OF PROGRAMMING LANGUAGE STANDARDS

Language	ANSI standardization numbers[a]	ISO approved[a]
Ada	Work started	
ALGOL 60	[b]	[b]
APL	Work started	
APT	X3.37–1977	
BASIC	X3.60–1978	ISO 6373–1980
COBOL	X3.23–1968[c]	ISO 1989–1972
	X3.23–1974	ISO 1989–1978
FORTRAN	X3.9–1966[c]	ISO 1539–1972
	X3.9–1978	ISO 1539–1979
Basic FORTRAN	X3.10–1966[c]	ISO 1539–1972
MUMPS	X11.1–1977	
Pascal	Awaiting ISO	DP 7185–?
PL/I	X3.53–1976	ISO 6160–1979
PL/I subset	X3.74–1981?	ISO 6522–1981?

[a] The year the standard was approved is part of the standard number.

[b] Existed as an ISO Standard for some period of time but has been withdrawn completely.

[c] Withdrawn.

such in perpetuity. In practice this situation does not occur. For one thing, ANSI procedures require that a standard be updated every five years (although the updating can just affirm the existing standard). Independent of this procedural requirement, language adherents continually want to improve their language; they know it is the language standard that will generally be implemented and used, and so in order to promulgate improvements in a language, the standard itself must be changed. In addition, language updates must be made to support new hardware facilities (e.g., screen management). Furthermore, as new people join the standardization committees, their own views and judgments of what is appropriate in the language frequently differ from those of their predecessors, and so they push for changes.

[As an example of this, the most radical of all the proposed suggestions that I have ever seen relating to a language standard is the serious proposal in 1980 that the blank character should be made a syntactically significant character in the next FORTRAN standard. This is deemed radical because, from its inception, a major characteristic of FORTRAN has been the lack of significant blanks; I am neither defending the original concept nor opposing it but am merely stating that it has been a fundamental characteristic of the language syntax. The people who wish to change it are doing so (in my opinion) because many of the other changes they would like to see made to FORTRAN are impossible while that language characteristic remains. Should this change be made, every FORTRAN program now existing might be invalidated. The current devotees of FORTRAN are discovering what the developers of PL/I realized in 1963, namely that FORTRAN cannot be modernized in an upward compatible way.]

In a more general framework, one aspect of standardization that in my opinion has caused the most difficulty is the fact that the proponents of a language continually wish to extend its scope so that it becomes more suitable for a larger class of problems. The most notable examples of this have been BASIC and FORTRAN. The former was originally (designed as) a very simple language, but so many things have been added to it in the ongoing standardization process that one would hardly recognize it as being a simple language. The same extension mania applies to FORTRAN, and COBOL has also had significant additions over the years. One can, of course, argue that all of these changes (not just additions) are in the name of progress, and as new capabilities and needs arise, then they should be put into the base language. In my view, these languages will eventually approach in complexity and size those languages which were designed from the very beginning to be large, namely PL/I, ALGOL 68, and Ada. Then we will have to create new *simple* languages. Unfortunately, the smaller languages (e.g., BASIC) will become large in a very *ad hoc* fashion, and as a result just cannot be as effective as a language designed from its inception as an integrated *large* language. The discussion that follows here is an attempt to indicate what is likely to happen in the future for language standards.

For BASIC, a major new standard with language enhancements is expected in a few years. For COBOL, the next standard is again expected within a few years. The next FORTRAN standard is not even targeted any earlier than 1985, and if the time span between the original FORTRAN standard and its first revision (12 years) is any guide, it might be 1990 before there is a third FORTRAN standard. For PL/I, the major issue is the formal approval of a specific subset, and that probably will have been done by the time this article is published. The next PL/I standard is targeted for several years off, but is not likely to involve major changes, although there might be significant functional additions.

A Pascal standard is being developed with major efforts in both the United States and in Great Britain, and that draft standard should be available fairly soon. A committee to develop the first standard for APL was only formed in mid-1980 in the United States, and so its results are probably several years off. In the case of the operating system control language, there is no base document from which to work, and there is serious technical question as to whether this type of development can even be done. It should be noted that both the Pascal and APL standards efforts were initiated in Europe, and proposed draft ISO standards were sent to ANSI; the United States committees have been working on those drafts. Except for ALGOL 60, all other language standards have originated in the United States.

As far as Ada is concerned, because the original language was publicly developed (in ways that are described in Section 4.3), the canvass method should produce an official ANSI standard in 1982.

3. Relationship of High-Level Languages to Software Engineering and Software Methodology[3]

3.1 Introductory Remarks

There is a lot of material in the literature about software engineering and software methodology, and much (if not all) of it seems to have some relationship to high-level languages. Unfortunately the connection has

---

[3] This section is based almost entirely on the author's paper "Language Aspects of Software Engineering" appearing in "Software Engineering" (H. Freeman and P. Lewis, eds.), pp. 181–194, Academic Press, New York, 1980.

never been clearly stated. The purpose of this section is to attempt to clarify the role played by high-level languages in the overall software concerns that are referred to as "software engineering" and "software methodology."

In order to achieve the stated objective for this section, it is necessary for me to provide my own definition of software engineering so that readers will understand the approach and concepts that I am using:

> Software engineering is the set of disciplines, tools, and methodologies (both technical and nontechnical) needed (and/or used) to produce efficient, correct, reliable, ...
> ⟨any adjective denoting good⟩
> software in a manner that is timely, and is cost effective over the entire life cycle of the software.

Using the above definition or similar ones, it is clear that software engineering has two components—management and technical. This section deals with only a subset of the technical aspect, namely that involving languages.

By now there are almost as many definitions of the life cycle of program development as there are people who wish to prepare such definitions. In compliance with fairly commonly accepted lists, I consider the major steps in the life cycle to be: requirements definition, specification definition, design, coding, testing, documentation, verification, and maintenance. (Generally the first two steps involve the problem definition, the next three produce the problem solution, and the last three involve the actual software.) It is *not* the purpose of this article to debate the merits of this particular list (or any other) but rather simply to use this list as the launching point for discussing the relationships among these ideas and various aspects of languages.

The term "languages" as used *in this section* covers a wider spectrum than delineated by the definition of high-level languages in Section 1.2. It is beyond the scope of this section to define that spectrum except by examples or discussions.

Table III lists the steps in the life cycle and the importance of languages currently and extrapolated into the future. The "current status" and "future status" columns indicate whatever type of language is most appropriate to that phase of the life cycle (as discussed in the following sections). The last column specifically refers to the future relevance of what are currently considered the common types of high-level languages to the indicated step in the life cycle. Where an upgrading from the current status to the future status is shown, this means that in my opinion a change will occur; even more importantly there is a need for research and development to cause that change to take place.

TABLE III

IMPORTANCE OF LANGUAGES IN THE SOFTWARE
DEVELOPMENT LIFE CYCLE[a]

Activity	Status		Future relevance of high-level languages
	Current	Future	
Requirements definition	L–M	M	0
Specification definition	L–M	M–H	0
Design	M	H	M
Code	H	H	H
Test	L	L	L
Document	M	M	M
Verify	L–M	H	M
Maintain	L–M	M–H	M

[a] L, low relevance; M, medium relevance; H, high relevance; 0, not relevant.

3.2 Language Involvement in the Life Cycle Steps

3.2.1 Requirements Definition

The matter of stating the requirements for a particular problem to be solved on a computer is more often a matter of psychology, and perhaps clairvoyance, than technology. However, in spite of that somewhat cynical statement, there is considerable research being done to improve the methods of stating requirements. In the simplest form, one would like merely to say to a computer "calculate the payroll" or "calculate the best route to fly from New York to Los Angeles." Of course, in neither one of these examples is the information in quotation marks anywhere near sufficient for even the most science-fiction dreams of computers to provide answers, simply because there is not adequate information even for humans to solve the problem. In the case of the payroll, one needs to provide the data for each employee along with such basic facts as whether the payroll is generated weekly, semimonthly, or monthly, whether people are paid in cash or by check, what reports must be provided to the IRS, etc. In the case of the air route the definition of "best" is certainly ambiguous. It might mean speediest, or smoothest for the passengers, or most economical in fuel expenditure; these details on the requirements must be specified. In an ideal world, once the individual had simply stated a general conceptual requirement, the system should be knowledgeable enough to ask all the right questions. Naturally, we are a long way from that, and even if the correct answers were provided to define the problem clearly, there could still be a large gap until the problem solution were obtained.

Examples of specific languages that provide facilities for stating requirements include PSL/PSA (which is also considered a specification language) described in Teichroew and Hershey (1977), the Requirements Specification Language (RSL) of Davis and Rauscher (1979), AFFIRM by Musser (1979), and the RDL of Heacox (1979).

3.2.2 Specification Definition

There is considerable debate concerning the distinctions between requirements and specifications; some people combine the concepts for the purpose of life-cycle definition. The distinction I would make here is that the specifications are meant to be much more detailed than they would be in a requirements statement, even if the latter did have considerable detail. Thus, for example, in the case of the payroll application one might answer all of the implied questions listed above (as well as others) to provide all the requirements, but the specifications would be more rigorously and rigidly stated with considerably more detail (e.g., delineating day/hour/format of input and output data, maximum number of employees, relation to other personnel data, type of security needed). In some instances, the borderline between requirements and specifications is *not* very clear.

A table of languages and/or systems being used for defining specifications, appears in Biggerstaff (1979). Of the eight listed there, the two which appear to be in wider use than the others are PSL/PSA (mentioned as a requirements language just above) and SPECIAL (Robinson and Roubine, 1977).

A major aspect of a specification language is the potential for (and necessity of) tying in to both design and verification. Specifications indicate *what* is to be done and the design (as discussed in the next section) should indicate *how* it is to be done within the specific constraints imposed on the designer. However, since the design must reflect the specifications, any relationship between those specification and design languages must be carefully understood.

The connection between specifications and verification is even more important. Obviously, to verify a program, one needs a baseline against which to provide and perform this verification. Clearly one can only verify against what was intended. In our current terminology the most likely place at which to measure or indicate what is intended is in the specifications. (It is necessary to assume the specifications are correct or else the verification becomes meaningless.) It would be more desirable to be able to verify the requirements but this may be impossible, and certainly is so difficult as to be beyond comprehension at this time in the state of the art.

Specification languages should have two characteristics that are needed to reflect their major interface with the users. On one hand, the specifications should be natural to the specific application user, and on the other hand, they should be readable by other people (e.g., testers). The reason that these are cited as two different characteristics is because there are potentially two different audiences involved. Clearly if the user is going to look at the specifications to see whether they really meet the needs, then the material must be in a natural notation. On the other hand, many people besides the users will need to work with these specifications, for example, the program designers. Furthermore, as indicated above, those people trying to verify the final program will need to come back to the specifications. And if they are unable to read the specifications, then obviously they will not be able to verify that the program meets them. (Note that being natural and being readable are not the same thing if two different audiences are involved.)

3.2.3 Design

A significant amount of work has been done in the development of what are called "process design" or "program design" or "design" languages. In fact, the initials PDL are generic but also specific for certain languages (e.g., Linger *et al.*, 1979; Caine and Gordon, 1975). In this context PDL as a generic term means some semiformal notation that allows people to indicate the design of a program but without actually doing the coding. Many of the process/program design languages allow and/or encourage stepwise refinement and with verification at each refinement step. They do this by essentially allowing a portion of the program to be written in a formal notation but also allow another portion of it to be written in any language that is natural and convenient to the designer. For example, one can write

>   WHILE
>   socsectax < maxvalue
>   DO
>   deduct socsectax
>   ENDDO

where the words WHILE, DO, and ENDDO are part of the formal notation, and the lower-case words represent an informal process description. Since the use of a design language usually involves an informal notation, the design languages are generally not executable.

There is a significant but unresolved problem of how to interface between the design languages and the executable languages (e.g., FORTRAN). In some cases, the former are just as formal as the latter, or could easily be made so. But the programmer must go through a relatively (but unfortunately not completely) mechanical step of converting the design language to the "normal" high-level language that can be compiled into machine code. This conversion can only be partly automated, and only under certain circumstances.

For reasons similar to those given above it is important that the design languages be natural and readable to some (although not necessarily all) of the end users and programmers.

3.2.4 Coding

In some discussions of the life cycle or the subset involving specific program development, the word "programming" is used rather than "coding." "Programming" usually is meant to encompass at least part (if not all) of the design process. Since part of the basic point of this discussion is to delineate clearly the different steps in the life cycle, I have chosen to use the word "coding" to mean the specific steps of writing down a program that can be put into a computer for eventual execution.

A major aspect of the programming language relationship to software engineering and software methodology involves the term "structured programming"; this is another one of those phases that has almost as many meanings as there are people. In this context I mean that there is only a small set of allowable control structures in the programming language. Normally this set would include (a) statements to be executed sequentially, (b) some type of iteration statement (which might be "WHILE $\cdots$ DO $\cdots$" or "FOR $I = \cdots$ DO $\cdots$") and (c) some decision statement, usually denoted by "IF $\cdots$ THEN $\cdots$ ELSE $\cdots$", all with the general constraint of flow paths allowing only one entry at the beginning and one exit at the end.

In order to obtain the maximum benefits of the "engineering" aspect of "software engineering" the coding should be done in a high-level language such as COBOL, FORTRAN, or PL/I. Using a high-level language generally results in a program which is more readable than assembly language, and which then facilitates debugging and other steps (especially, documentation) in the life cycle. The report by Shaw *et al.*

(1978) compares portions of COBOL, FORTRAN, JOVIAL, and the IRONMAN requirements (which were the basis for Ada) [DOD (1977)] for issues those authors deem significant from a software engineering viewpoint.

One possible approach to coding is to devise high-level languages that are natural to the problem area of the user, although they are quite different from the more common high level languages. The former are what I have referred to in earlier sections as "languages for specialized application areas" or "specialized application languages." The most common examples are COGO (COordinate GeOmetry) for civil engineers, and APT (Automatically Programmed Tool) for numerically controlled machine tools. The advantages of these languages are that it is possible to enhance readability for people in each relevant field and to facilitate ease of learning because of the close connection between the language notation itself and the field of application.

3.2.5 Testing

Testing is not closely related to programming languages, although obviously testing is extremely important in the life cycle. But aside from including in a specific language certain features that make the testing easier, and aside from the development of languages to help write programs to generate test cases, there is not much connection. This does not mean that testing is unimportant; on the contrary, there is a lot of consideration being given to this subject (see, e.g., Goodenough, 1979) but most of the issues are not particularly related to languages. For example, the question of how fully testing can and should be done is not a language issue.

It is worth noting for the reader who may be unfamiliar with this general subject that testing and validation/verification are not the same. Definition of these terms and a delineation of the differences are beyond the scope of this paper. The interested reader should contrast the concepts in the paper on verification by London (1979) and on testing by Goodenough (1979), both in the same volume. Some further remarks about verification appear in this article in Sections 3.2.7, 5.3, and 6.2.3.

3.2.6 Documentation

It is clear, on one hand, that each of the steps above need documentation, in the sense of describing and/or explaining both the formalism and the intent of the material that is written down. On the other hand, if what is written down is readable by those working on that phase of the job, then it is self-documenting (i.e., does not need a separate explanation) to that same extent. Furthermore, if it were possible to have a complete sequence of automatic translations from requirements statements to specification statements to design statements and then into the program, then we would not need documentation except for the computer operators.

3.2.7 Verification

This is a very controversial subject, and I do not want to get involved in the discussion of how or when programs can be verified and to what level, nor whether or not such verification is important. My concern here is only with indicating the relationship to programming languages. As mentioned earlier, if the specifications are clearly written and can be automatically (or at least semiautomatically) translated down into executable code, then verification becomes very much easier. However, this seems to be beyond the current state of the art. We, therefore, have two types of approaches. One is to include in existing programming languages certain additional statements or features to make them more easily verifiable. The other, which is certainly a topic of great research these days, is to develop specific (new) languages that are designed with easy verifiability in mind. [EUCLID, described in Lampson *et al.* (1977) is a language designed with that objective.] The flaw in the concept of a verifiable *programming language* is that one really must ultimately verify the executable code against the specifications. Thus, if a specification says to produce 10 copies of a report, then the language should make it easy to verify that the code written (and executed) will in fact produce 10 copies.

3.2.8 Maintenance

The word "maintenance" covers several aspects of program development, namely correction of bugs, correction of design deficiencies, and enhancement. In each case, the relationship of programming languages to the indicated aspect of the maintenance task depends entirely on the material discussed above, that is, the language elements in earlier steps of the life cycle. On the other hand, it is worth noting that some of the modern language concepts (e.g., data abstraction, modularization) make maintenance of programs written in such languages easier.

3.3 Other Issues Involving High-Level Languages

3.3.1 Reliability

There is naturally great concern about developing languages that make it easy to produce reliable programs. Special languages and language features have been developed which the designers claim provide more reliability [see, for example, the languages described in ACM SIGPLAN (1977)]. There is unfortunately no data (or at least none that I can discern) pertaining to this matter, and the issue seems to involve matters of personal judgment more than anything else. Thus, some special features which can be required in a language, and which allegedly lead to more reliability, are based on the personal judgment that a particular style or feature will lead to more reliable programs. Thus, for example, there are people who argue that more reliable programs will be produced if the language requires that all data be declared and no defaults are allowed, or people who insist on strong typing and allow absolutely no implicit conversion as a means of producing more reliable programs. While I tend to agree with many of these viewpoints, I also recognize the validity of a counterargument that says that when you make the programmer write *more* and when you force him to do things which *could* be done implicitly by the compiler, then you have *not* improved reliability. (The requirement that the programmer write down the assumptions in a form which can be checked by a compiler is, in my view, a double-edged sword.)

While many of these issues are still (in my opinion) matters of individual professional judgment, fortunately there has been some work in attempting to provide valid experimental data on which language features seem to cause higher (or lower) programmer error rates. See for example, Gannon (1977) and the references in that paper, as well as numerous related papers in the proceedings containing Gannon and Horning (1975).

3.3.2 Portability

Inherent in any concept of software engineering is the potential need for portability, that is, the ability to move a running program from one computer or operating system to another, or to get the same results using different language processors for the same language. The reason that this is a fundamental concept is that installations change their needs and requirements, and hence their computing environments, but still want to run existing programs without changing them. The economics of selling (and buying) software also make portability an important goal.

Now the major concern of most people is, of course, portability between different computers, where in this context it is assumed that we are talking about machines of different architectures or different order codes. (I am specifically *not* referring to a family of upward compatible machines because that generally is—or should be—no problem.) The desire to move programs across machines has existed since an early time in the computer field. However, what seems to be much less well known—although it is in fact more important—is the problem of portability across operating systems and compilers. This point deserves amplification, for the simple reason that compilers are changed more often than operating systems, and operating systems are changed (or at least modified) more often than machines. In some instances an installation wants more than one compiler per language, each with different objectives (e.g., checkout versus efficient object code). (Updates to operating systems can hamper portability as well, but that problem is not germane to this discussion unless there are commensurate difficulties with the compiler.)

Most vendors who produce a compiler try to produce a better one than their previous version or than their competitor's. But this often plays havoc with a program. Part of the reason is that many of our languages do not have rigorous definitions, and even for those that do, there is no assurance that the compiler actually complies with the definition. Even though there are many formal techniques for defining the syntax and semantics of programming languages (see, e.g., the survey of Marcotty and Ledgard, 1976) few (if any) compiler writers are able to use formal language definitions in a way that guarantees compiler compliance with them. Put still another way, the problem of verifying a compiler is the same conceptually as verifying any program. One needs to see whether the compiler meets its specifications—in this case, the language definition. I do not believe that there has been any substantial case of compiler verification. There have been small or experimental instances of such work, but those are inadequate for a production environment. For all these reasons a "new" compiler may cause previously correct programs to become invalid.

Another area of lack of portability to a new compiler occurs when a compiler that implements a standard language also adds and provides additional features so that the user rapidly becomes accustomed to this unexpected luxury, which is not present in the standard language. A new compiler may not provide those same luxuries, or, more commonly, may provide a different set of luxuries, thus rendering the original programs unusable. Finally, many compilers depend on a specific operating system for object time facilities, and the programmer discovers this and uses that information in his program; this naturally reduces portability. Furthermore, the changes in an operating system may be subtle and hence difficult to detect.

In order to achieve portability across computers, there should be little or no machine-dependent features and elements in the program and/or language. This is far easier to say than to accomplish. While there are certain obvious issues (e.g., word length, which affects the accuracy of any numerical computation), and even moderately obvious ones (e.g., collating sequence, which affects the way in which tests of nonnumeric inequality are carried out), there are more subtle issues (e.g., whether zero is treated as positive or negative or unsigned).

As with so many other things in the computer field, one can achieve portability if one is willing to pay a price in efficiency. One example, and an extreme case, would occur if a language had a command which allowed one to read a magnetic tape in reverse order. If the programmer writes a program with that command and then moves the program to another machine that does not have that hardware capability, it can, of course, be simulated by rewinding a tape and reading forward one less record than before. It is certainly unlikely, and probably inconceivable, that such inefficiency would be tolerated.

4. Some "Modern" Languages

4.1 Introductory Remarks

This section provides a very brief introduction to some of the languages that are often referred to as "modern." That word applies either because of the time when they were developed, or their attempts to support verifiability, or their emphasis on data abstractions, or other reasons. Only a very brief introduction to any of these languages is given, except for a lengthy discussion in Section 4.3 of Ada. Significant emphasis is given to Ada in this paper because of the author's belief that it will eventually have a profound effect on the computer field.

The languages are introduced in roughly chronological order of their development, although this is not a rigorous application of the time scales involved.

4.2 Specific Languages (ALGOL 68, Pascal, CLU, Euclid, SETL)

There are two languages omitted from this section which deserve some mention, namely SIMULA 67 described in Dahl and Nygaard (1967) and Alphard (see Shaw *et al.*, 1977). SIMULA 67 has been omitted from any further discussion because it really is too old to be considered "modern." However, its introduction of the "class" concept is the forerunner of much of the modern work done on data abstractions. In fact, the developers of both Alphard and CLU acknowledge their debt to the SIMULA 67 concepts.

While numerous papers on Alphard have been published, the language has not been implemented, and I do not wish to discuss unimplemented languages. Other modern languages which are in use but are not described here are Mesa described by Geschke *et al.* (1977) and Modula described by Wirth (1977).

4.2.1 ALGOL 68

Not too many years after the introduction of ALGOL 60, a number of people turned their attention to ways in which it could be enlarged or extended. This article is not the place to go into that history. Suffice it to say that around 1968, a language called ALGOL 68 was developed by Van Wijngaarden and others in Europe. It is definitely *not* an upward extension of ALGOL 60, and in my own view can and should be considered the last of the "older large" languages. The other language of equivalent size and power is PL/I, which was developed around 1964 and introduced many new ideas. Because ALGOL 68 is less well known and also introduced some interesting ideas it is worth discussing here.

One of the key ideas in ALGOL 68 is that of orthogonality. This means that there are a small number of basic constructions and rules for combining them in a regular and systematic way. ALGOL 68 is a block-structured language and is also extensible. It has a rich collection of data types (called modes), and facilities to allow programmers to define their own new data types.

ALGOL 68 is an expression language, which means that every construction in the language yields a value and in principle can appear on the righthand side of an assignment statement. Arrays and structures are included, and there is a means of generalizing the concept of subscripting to yield cross sections of the original array.

ALGOL 68 provides two storage management facilities: local and heap. Local is the normal block directed facility usually implemented by a last-in first-out stack. Heap is a single homogenous section of

OVERVIEW OF HIGH-LEVEL LANGUAGES 229

memory from which storage can be acquired by heap generators. When a block is entered, local storage is allocated and then is released when the block is exited. However, heap objects allocated during execution of a block do not vanish when the block is exited.

The term "coercion" is the ALGOL 68 term for automatic mode conversion. Unlike PL/I, there are very few automatic conversions allowed. Unlike ALGOL 60, ALGOL 68 contains a number of input/output procedures. There are some language provisions for parallel processing.

An excellent introduction to ALGOL 68 is given by Tanenbaum (1976).

ALGOL 68 has been implemented by a few different groups and runs on several computers.

4.2.2 Pascal

Of all the languages developed since PL/I and currently in use, Pascal appears to be the most important. It was initially developed by Niklaus Wirth in 1968 and the first compiler became operational in 1970. The definitive document is Jensen and Wirth (1978). It is one of the only two languages in wide use which can truly be said to have been developed initially by a single person, the other being Kenneth Iverson's APL.

Pascal is a block-structured language, and its major innovative features involves data typing. Pascal introduced into a general language the concept of an ennumerated type wherein specific finite values of a particular variable are defined and subranges may be declared. For example, the user can write

> *type* day = (mon, tues, wed, thurs, fri, sat, sun);

and

> *type* weekday = mon..fri;

Homogeous arrays and structures of nonhomogeneous elements called records are permitted. Records may contain variants, which simply means variables with different structures although the variables are said to be of the same type.

Quoting from Wirth's original report in Jensen and Wirth (1978, p. 133):

> The development of the language *Pascal* is based on two principal aims. The first is to make available a language suitable to teach programming as a systematic discipline based on certain fundamental concepts clearly and naturally reflected by the language. The second is to develop implementations of this language which are both reliable and efficient on presently available computers.

It appears that Pascal is becoming increasingly taught in universities, although by 1980 it is apparently not in major use in environments with large numbers of programmers writing production programs. Pascal has been implemented on most large, medium, and minicomputers, and the compilers are usually written in Pascal. It is also being implemented on a number of micro computers and some of the "personal" computers. A common "P code" is used as the intermediate language from which the target code for various computers is generated. Pascal is certainly serving as a springboard for new languages (e.g., Ada) just as ALGOL 60 served as the springboard for Pascal and other languages.

In my own view, although Pascal introduced some new ways of dealing with data types, its primary contribution has been the way in which known language features were combined (or omitted) to produce a coherent, elegant useful language. And for those readers who are still interested in the GOTO controversy, Pascal *does* contain a GOTO statement!

Additions were made to create a language called Concurrent Pascal by Brinch Hanson (1977) which is useful for doing concurrent programming. Wirth also used Pascal as a base to develop another language, Modula (Wirth, 1977), which is meant to be particularly suitable for multiprogramming and real-time programming.

4.2.3 CLU

Quoting from the paper by Liskov *et al.* (1977, p. 565), "CLU has been designed to support a methodology ... in which programs are developed by means of problem decomposition based on the recognition of abstractions." From the summary of that paper (p. 564):

> CLU is a new programming language designed to support the use of abstractions in program construction. Work in programming methodology has led to the realization that three kinds of abstractions—procedural, control, and especially data abstractions—are useful in the programming process. Of these, only the procedural abstraction is supported well by conventional languages, through the procedure or subroutine. CLU provides, in addition to procedures, novel linguistic mechanisms that support the use of data and control abstractions.

A CLU program consists of a group of modules. Three kinds of modules are provided: procedures for procedural abstraction, iterators for control abstraction, and clusters for data abstraction.

A procedure takes zero or more arguments and produces zero or more results. An iterator is called by a *for* statement, which contains a body of statements to be executed once for each item. A cluster implements a data type, which is a set of objects together with a set of operations. The operations may be either procedures or iterators. The objects of a type can be created and manipulated only via the operations of that type; hence, object representation information is completely encapsulated by the cluster. Procedures, iterators, and clusters can all be parameterized, allowing the definition of a class of related abstractions by means of a single module. For example, a single cluster can define sets of arbitrary element type.

The basic elements of CLU semantics are objects and variables. Objects are the data entries manipulated by programs; variables are simply names used to refer to objects. An object can be referred to by any number of objects including itself. Thus, recursive and shared data structures are possible without explicit reference types.

CLU has been implemented at MIT and runs on the DEC System 20.

4.2.4 Euclid

One of the interesting experiments in language design involves the definition of Euclid, which was done by B. W. Lampson, J. J. Horning, R. L. London, J. G. Mitchell, and G. L. Popek. They were in different locations, working for different organizations, and used the ARPANET for much of their group communication! The primary public defining document for the language is Lampson *et al.* (1977).

The basic objective of Euclid was to create a new programming language to be used for writing systems programs which are to be verified. Euclid is fundamentally a modification or rewrite of Pascal to provide for verifiability; in fact, the Euclid report (Lampson, *et al.*, 1977) was written as a heavily edited version of the revised Pascal report. By their own admission, they also used ideas and features from numerous other languages, including some of those described in this article.

A brief summary of some of the differences (as identified on pages 2 and 3 of the defining document just cited) is as follows:

The program must list all identifiers imported into and out of modules.

Two identifiers in the same scope can never refer to the same or overlapping variables.

The program can control allocation of storage for dynamic variables explicitly.

A new kind of record, called a module, can contain routine and type components, and thus provides a facility for modularization.

Features of the underlying machine can be accessed, and the type-checking can be overridden in a controlled way. Except for these explicit loopholes, Euclid is designed to be typesafe.

Assertions can be supplied at convenient points.

Some Pascal features have been deleted—in particular, input/output, reals, multidimensional arrays, labels and gotos, and functions and procedures as parameters.

Euclid has been implemented at the University of Toronto and runs on the PDP-11.

4.2.5 SETL

SETL is a language developed at the Courant Institute at New York University and is described in several published papers (e.g., Dewar *et al.*, 1979). Its main thrust is, and hence its basic semantic constructs are, mathematical sets. Primitive operations in SETL include set membership, union, intersection, power set construction, etc. Both unordered sets and sequences are allowed as aggregate data types. SETL also provides Boolean expressions, and the universal and existential quantifiers of the first-order predicate calculus.

Unlike many of the other current experimental languages, SETL is *not* strongly typed. In fact, one of the SETL objectives is to allow an algorithm to be stated in a manner which is independent of specific data structuring. SETL programs have very few declarations in them.

One of the key characteristics of SETL, and one that to some extent justifies its claim to being a "very high-level language" (which is a completely undefined term—but see the discussion of nonprocedural languages in Section 6.2.4 in this article), pertains to writing algorithms at a high level of abstraction, and then refining them for efficiency. The key point is that even the high-level version can actually be executed and answers produced. An example of this is given in Dewar and Schonberg (1979). Thus, SETL can be used as a example of the concept of "top-down programming," except that early stages can be executed. At lower levels additional information about the data structures can be supplied.

SETL has been implemented at New York University and runs on the CDC 6600, the PDP-10, the VAX 11/780, and the IBM System/370.

4.3 Ada

4.3.1 Introductory Remarks

Many readers of this article may have heard some or all of the following terms over the past several years: DOD-1, STRAWMAN, TINMAN, IRONMAN, STEELMAN, Ada, and the colors Blue, Green, Red, Yellow. The terms relate to a language effort that has been underway within the Department of Defense (DOD) since 1975. Because of

OVERVIEW OF HIGH-LEVEL LANGUAGES

its importance to the entire computing field (and not just DOD), this section describes in considerable detail the background and a little of the technology of that effort.

In 1975, a number of people within DOD began to feel that there were too many high-level languages being used. As part of its attempt to minimize the number of languages in use within the Department of Defense, they issued two directives in 1976. The first, numbered 5000.29 said (in part), "DOD approved high-order programming languages will be used to develop Defense systems software unless it is demonstrated that none of the approved HOLS are cost effective or technically practical over the system life cycle. ... Each DOD approved HOL will be assigned to a designated control agent." As of September 1980, the approved languages and their control agents were:

Language	Control agent
FORTRAN, COBOL	Assistant Secretary of Defense (Controller) with NBS
TACPOL	Army
CMS2	Navy
SPL/1	Navy
JOVIAL J3	Air Force
JOVIAL J73	Air Force

The undesirability of such a proliferation of languages, along with the continuing and expected expense of upgrading and supporting them, made it desirable that steps be taken to see if something more cost effective could be done. Thus, a High-Order Language Working Group (HOLWG) was chartered by DOD to (a) formulate requirements for a common DOD high-order language, (b) compare those requirements with existing languages, and (c) recommend adoption or implementation of the necessary common language. The initial Chairman of the HOLWG was Lt. Col. William Whitaker, of the Defense Advanced Research Projects Agency (DARPA); after he was rotated to another job he was replaced by Dr. David Fisher (Office of the Under Secretary of Defense for Research and Engineering, OUSDRE). The technical work has primarily been monitored by Mr. William Carlson (DARPA), who succeeded Fisher as the HOLWG Chairman.

An investigation of applications in the three military services led to the conclusion that a single, common high-level language could conceivably serve all of the services. (That was not at all obvious when they started.) The working name for the language, up until late 1978, was DOD-1, at which time it was officially named Ada, in honor of Ada Augusta Lovelace, who was allegedly the "first" programmer and assisted Charles Babbage in the mid 1800s. The types of applications considered were for embedded computer systems, that is, software that is integral to large systems such as tactical weapons, communications, or avionics.

4.3.2 Language Requirements Documents and Language Design Contracts

Rather than starting immediately (as so often happens) to design a language to meet vague requirements, a preliminary document, named STRAWMAN, was created; it described detailed requirements for a language that was to meet goals such as software cost reduction, transportability, ease of maintenance, high reliability, readability, and sufficiently efficient object code.

These STRAWMAN requirements were circulated to the military departments, other government agencies, the academic community, and industrial organizations. Comments were solicited from all of those groups and many of the responses were made public by placing them on the Advanced Research Projects Agency Network (ARPANET), DOD's nationwide computer system. Based on comments received about the STRAWMAN requirements, two subsequent requirement documents named WOODENMAN and TINMAN [DOD (1976)] were developed, the latter in January 1976. During 1976, over 20 high-level languages were formally evaluated against the TINMAN requirements to see if any was sufficiently close to meeting the requirements to be chosen as the language (perhaps with minor modifications).

Not too surprisingly, no language was deemed close enough to permit it to be used as the base with only minor changes. However, it was recognized that PL/I, ALGOL 68, and Pascal were powerful enough languages that any of them could be used as a base for the development of a new language.

Another set of requirements called IRONMAN was issued by DOD (1977), and in July of that year four language design contracts were awarded. The four vendors selected were deemed to be in a competition to provide preliminary (called Phase 1) language designs. The designs were submitted to DARPA in February 1978. They were color coded to permit objective evaluation, which took place during the following month; the language designs were commented upon in a very public fashion by anyone who cared to take the time to read through the voluminous material. Again, this included individuals and groups from the academic, military, and industrial communities in this country, as well as from Europe. In April 1978, Phase 2 language design contracts were awarded to Intermetrics (Red) and Cii Honeywell-Bull (Green).

4.3.3 Language Technical Base

All four of the contractors selected for Phase 1 based their language design proposals on Pascal, although this was definitely *not* a requirement. Hence, the final language is based on Pascal, but there seems to be some misunderstanding as to what it means to say that the final version of Ada is "based on Pascal." Many people think this means that Ada is a superset of Pascal. This is absolutely false; "based on" really refers to the use of ideas and concepts from Pascal, as well as to the strategy of making no unnecessary syntactic changes to Pascal. (Naturally everyone has a different idea of what is unnecessary.) This is analogous to the origins of PL/I, which can be described as based on FORTRAN, or based on ALGOL; in reality it has ideas from both those languages as well as from COBOL and other languages, but in no sense can PL/I be considered simply an extension of any of its "base" languages.

4.3.4 Language Requirements Examples and Broad Categories

Since so much has been said about the sequence of requirements documents, and they represent the only major attempt to define such information prior to any language design, two examples from DOD (1978) are useful just to give the flavor of them. The first one (p. 9) deals with integer and fixed point numbers, the second (p. 14) with sequential control:

> Integer and fixed point numbers shall be treated as exact numeric values. There shall be no implicit truncation or rounding in integer and fixed point computations.

> There shall be a control mechanism for sequencing statements. The language shall not impose arbitrary restrictions on programming style, such as the choice between statement terminators and statement separators, unless the restriction makes programming errors less likely.

Readers who are familiar with high-level language specifications can clearly see that these are requirements rather than detailed specifications. The final version of the requirements—called STEELMAN—was issued in June 1978 (DOD, 1978) and was used by the two final language design teams. The full sequence of requirements documents was prepared by Dr. David Fisher, who was then at the Institute for Defense Analysis (IDA).

The broad headings for the requirements topics are as follows: General Design Criteria; General Syntax; Types (including numeric, enumeration, and composite types, sets, and encapsulated definitions); Expressions, Constants, Variables, and Scopes; Classical Control Structures; Functions and Procedures; Input/Output, Formatting, and Configuration Control; Parallel Processing; Exception Handling; Representation and Other Translation Time Facilities; Translation and Library Facilities; Support for the Language.

4.3.5 Environmental Requirements

In parallel with some of the later language requirements development, work was performed as early as 1978 to produce requirements for the program development *environment* in which the language is to exist after it is designed and implemented. Such issues as who will decide on changes and clarifications to the language, how compilers will be validated, what type of training aids will be available, need for application libraries, editors, etc. are all considered part of the environment. Again, the material is a list of requirements rather than the specific implementation plan. The current version of the technical aspects of the environment was issued in February 1980 with the name STONEMAN (DOD, 1980a).

4.3.6 Test and Evaluation Phase

By now, the computing community has had enough collective experience with languages to know that one should not really thrust a new language full blown onto the user community and just say, "Use it." After the selection of the final language, "Green," from Cii Honeywell-Bull in April 1979, DOD held a Test and Evaluation phase of the language from approximately May to December 1979, and once again comments from all parts of the computing community were solicited. The Test and Evaluation Phase consisted primarily of desk programming of existing applications to see whether Ada really is suitable for these applications, and also to suggest improvements based on programming some concrete examples. Over 45 organizations participated, and about 90 programs (some of which were quite large) were written by December 1979.

4.3.7 Language Design and Redesign

By prior arrangement, when the language design developed by Cii Honeywell Bull (in France), under the leadership of Mr. Jean Ichbiah was se-

OVERVIEW OF HIGH-LEVEL LANGUAGES

lected by the HOLWG in May 1979, the language definition and a rationale were immediately published in two parts as the June 1979 issue of *ACM SIGPLAN Notices*. This assured wide dissemination of the information, since SIGPLAN itself had over 9000 members at that time, and DOD had another distribution list of hundreds (and perhaps thousands). Public comments were again solicited, both as commentaries on the language and as part of the Test and Evaluation phase discussed above. A small group of about ten people known as the "Distinguished Reviewer" panel was established in July 1979 to examine these multitudinous comments and provide suggested evaluations of them to the Honeywell language design team. In July 1980, Ichbiah and his colleagues produced the *final* language design (DOD, 1980b) which was subsequently sent out for public comment as part of the canvass for ANSI standardization process.

4.3.8 Major Language Characteristics

Because of the power and complexity of the language, it is not possible to convey in a few pages anything significant about the details of the language. Rather than do it an injustice, I will limit myself to pointing out what I consider some of the highlights. The official manual is DOD (1980b).

There is a powerful set of data typing mechanisms, allowing the user to specify data types of various kinds, and then to refine these into subranges, subtypes, and derived types. Careful attention has been given to fixed-point data because of the needs of the applications for which Ada is intended. Rules for naming and expression creation are not unusual, except for noting that Ada is a strongly typed language, i.e., it is not legal to combine data of different types, and the compiler is supposed to catch such errors. The statements are fairly standard, and there is a provision for both procedures and functions. Operators can be overloaded (i.e., assigned more than one meaning in different parts of the program).

One of the most innovative features of Ada is the concept of "package," which is a further advance and abstraction of the well-known concept of procedures. Packages are executable, but their details (containing information about data and processes which they use) are hidden from the user, who merely invokes the package. Packages also provide descriptions of common data and thus can serve a role similar to the JOVIAL COMPOOL or the COBOL Data Division. Packages can also serve as data abstractions.

Subprograms and packages can be generic, which means that they are templates of program units and can have parameterized types. As a simple example, a generic program unit could have scalars, vectors, or matrices as specific instantiations of the input data type.

There is a tasking facility to permit parallel processing, and there are various provisions for handling real time applications (including the existence of a CLOCK data type). Powerful interrupts and exception handling facilities are provided. Separate compilation of individual procedures is permitted. For input/output there are some very primitive operations, but more powerful I/O is meant to be handled by creating packages. Machine efficiency can be enhanced (with a corresponding loss of portability) by using "representation" declarations which specify how data is to be represented internally.

4.3.9 Prognosis

Since some readers may wonder, I will state my own opinion that Ada is more powerful and more complex than was needed to meet the IRONMAN requirements. It is certainly the pinnacle of what is currently known about large powerful language design in the mid-to-late 1970s, and it will keep students, language designers, other computer scientists, and of course the application-oriented users busy for many years understanding its full nuances. Not until the first production compilers are available (in the 1982–1983 time frame) will people have an opportunity to understand the full ramifications of using this language. But I do think that it is worthwhile, and it was created in exactly the right way—with much public comment but final decisions in the hands of a small group and its team leader.

5. Research and Advanced Development Language Topics

5.1 Introductory Remarks

There are a number of areas that are under investigation in the programming language community today. Some have been around for a long time (e.g., automatic programming), whereas others are only now beginning to be examined (language metrics). Within the space constraints of this article, it is only possible to give a superficial indication of some of the technical issues. This section certainly does *not* include *all* research areas; for example, data flow languages, the relation of languages to machine design, and work on requirements/specification languages are not discussed. (The latter was mentioned briefly in Section 3.2.) The topics that *are* discussed are data abstraction, verification, reliability, automatic programming, functional languages, query languages, and language metrics.

5.2 Data Abstraction

The term "data abstraction" has come very much into vogue in the last half of the 1970s as a significant area of language research. The concept of "abstraction" has been around for a long time in the language feature commonly referred to as "procedure," "subroutine," or "function." In this instance, the user calls for the execution of a portion of code which is to accomplish a specific purpose, but the user neither knows nor cares how it is being executed and accomplished. A trival example is the elementary mathematical functions to calculate square root, or sine. More complex procedures might involve a Sort, or even a major portion of a program. In the early days, this gave rise to the statement that one person's program was merely another person's subroutine.

The key concept of abstraction is that the user writing one portion of a program has access to work being done in another, but need not know how that work is being done, and even more importantly, has no control over it. In "data abstraction," not only is the format of the data layout unknown to the using programmer, but only the operations allowable on the data are known to the programmer. Quoting specifically from Liskov et al. (1977, p. 565),

... the following requirements that must be satisfied by a language supporting data abstractions:

(1) A linguistic construct is needed that permits a data abstraction to be implemented as a unit. The implementation involves selecting a representation for the data objects and defining an algorithm for each operation in terms of that representation.

(2) The language must limit access to the representation to just the operations. This limitation is necessary to insure that the operations completely characterize the behavior of the objects.

The simplest and most common illustration of the data abstraction is that of a "stack," which allows the normal operations of PUSH and POP, and the less common (but still necessary) operations of creating it, testing for empty, etc. Unlike a single procedure, the key element is a data type and the operations associated specifically and only with that data type. This contrasts with the procedure in which a certain number of parameters are provided as input, and the output parameters represent the answer. It also contrasts with the COBOL data, which is accessible to every program.

An introduction to the concept of data abstraction is given by Shankar (1980). A description of language issues and abstraction is in Shaw (1980).

5.3 Verification

Program verification has been flourishing as a research area since the early 1970s. Some indication of growth of the field is exhibited by the fact that when I published my book (Sammet, 1969), there were no references to any papers on verification even though the book itself contained over 800 references. At that time, there were very few papers being written on that subject; while I have no statistics today, it is certainly true that there is a great deal of work being done, and most of it involves programming languages, either directly or indirectly. Quoting one of the major workers in this field (London, 1979, p. 302), "The task of program verification is to show or prove that computer programs are consistent with detailed specifications of what the program does."

A key point is the use of the phrase "consistent with detailed specifications" because the technology for today and the foreseeable future enables us only to deal with a comparison of the program against its specifications; the latter may or may not be a sound representation of what is desired.

The issue of verification boils down to a language issue in the sense that the specifications must be represented in some form of a language, and it is a program (normally written in a high-level language) which is to be verified. One basic concept/method is that of using assertions, an idea introduced by Floyd (1967). In this approach, the programmer inserts in his program, in appropriate places, assertions about variables. The proof involves verifying that each assertion is always true, including those placed in loops.

By the early 1980s, a number of relatively small programs had been verified using various techniques, but with proofs which were enormously longer than the programs. A discussion of the state of the art and with many references to other more detailed material appears in London (1979). See Sections 6.2.3 and 6.3.4 of this paper for a discussion of the expected (non) practicality of this work.

From a purely language point of view, attempts are being made to define languages which are particularly suitable for verification. The most well known of these is Euclid, which was described in Section 4.2.4.

5.4 Reliability

The concern of technical people with the relationship of reliable software to languages is exemplified by the ACM Conference on Language Design for Reliable Software (ACM, 1977). In the past, concerns about

OVERVIEW OF HIGH-LEVEL LANGUAGES 241

the quality of programs were primarily on efficiency and/or portability. However, as more of the world becomes dependent on computer programs (e.g., air traffic control, national defense, complete financial records), the issue of reliability has become a very important goal. In my own view, it is likely in the future to surpass efficiency as the prime criterion for success of a program. Fortunately, or unfortunately, depending on one's background, hardware seems to have become more and more reliable and software has become—if not less reliable—certainly not much more so than it was a long time ago.

In my view, which I think is not shared by many of my colleagues, the question of which features in a language lead to reliable software is as much a matter of personal opinion as most other aspects of the computer field. There is not yet a clear delineation of what is meant by "features that help or cause reliable software to be written." About the only concept on which there appears to be universal agreement is that "strong typing" is an important feature to help programmers create reliable software. By strong typing, we mean facilities in a language by which each variable is declared to be a particular type or form, and different data types may not be combined without the user calling for the execution of specific conversion routines; the compiler is supposed to catch any violations. Interestingly enough, even an ancient language like FORTRAN had strong data typing in at least one respect, namely that the original language specs did not allow an integer to be added to a floating-point number. In the later languages, the extreme manifestation of weak typing was PL/I in which one could combine almost any two data types and be assured of an answer; the rules spelling out the results of such combination took many pages in the PL/I manuals. Although newer languages such as Pascal (and Ada) have strong data typing, there is by no means universal agreement that strong typing will produce more reliable programs. Some people believe that the facility to combine unlike data types is an advantage, because the programmers can write shorter programs and reliability should be enhanced if the program is shorter.

It is worth noting that virtually all of the papers at the aforementioned ACM conference discussed specific languages and why the developers thought they were more reliable. There was little or no discussion, and certainly no decision on what reliable software meant or how the languages were going to solve the problem. A selected subset of those papers appears in the August 1977 *Communications of the ACM*.

If the reader feels that this section provides no clear indication of how languages help people create reliable software, that is because in my view, there is no agreed upon approach. Nevertheless, people keep trying!

5.5 Automatic Programming

In the early days of computers (ca. 1950s) the phrase "automatic programming" merely meant the use of any tool or technique which was easier for the programmer to use than coding in octal, binary, or with absolute machine addresses. It rapidly became a synonym for "high-level languages" and then was dropped as a term in favor of "automatic coding," which more accurately reflected the "coding" help coming from the high-level languages and their translators. (Nevertheless, the phrases were often used interchangeably.) We have now come full circle, because the current use of the term "automatic programming" tends to have two manifestations—one refers (again) to the case of "very high level" or "nonprocedural languages" (discussed in Section 6.2.4), and the other to attempts to specify "what" is to be done rather than "how."

It is important to note that in considering the broad spectrum of programming, there are other aspects to automate besides just the languages. For example, operating systems and data-base management systems are, or help in, automating the production of answers to a particular problem. Concepts of "programmer's workbench" or "programmer's assistant" or "high-level programming systems" (see, e.g., Winograd, 1979) provide environments to ease the programmer's work and hence go far beyond pure language work.

From a pure language viewpoint, "automatic programming" in 1980 tends to mean the use of languages which are somehow "higher level" than the common ones such as COBOL, FORTRAN, and Pascal. Since we do not have a measure of "higher level," the conclusions on when languages are more nonprocedural (or even "very high level") is intuitive. Although SETL (see Section 4.2.5) is often given as an example of a VHLL, this is not because of any clear-cut criteria. (See further discussion of this issue in Sections 6.2.4 and 6.3.3.)

Since the objective is to allow the user to specify more of "what" is to be done, rather than "how" it is to be done, automatic programming is often deemed to be in the domain of artificial intelligence. From there it is an easy step into considering the "knowledge-based" systems such as MYCIN and DENDRAL.

MYCIN provides advice to the user about diagnosing and treating medical problems involving blood infections. DENDRAL provides analysis of mass spectrograph data. Both have received actual practical use!

Experimental work has been done in developing numerous systems, but the stumbling block in each case has been efficiency. Even with the increased speed of computers, the time taken to run an unoptimized program written in one of these languages would be prohibitive. And the methods for optimizing these "what to do" languages have not yet been solidified.

A detailed discussion of many of these points, and an indication of specific projects in this area is given by Hammer and Ruth (1979) and Prywes (1977). Another approach is in Winograd (1979).

5.6 Functional Programming

A broad survey article such as this one would be remiss if it did not mention the research work done over the past several years by one of the key people in our field, John Backus. In his ACM Turing Award paper of 1978, he explicated at considerable length the basic conceptual defects in programming languages as we have known them; they are based on a machine characteristic which he calls the "von Neumann bottleneck." This refers to the hardware characteristic that enables (but also requires) that a single word be transmitted between the CPU and the memory. He points out that programming languages as they currently exist involve (a) variables which imitate the hardware memory, (b) control statements to match the test and jump instructions, and (c) assignment statements to correspond to the fetching, storing, and arithmetic of the computer. As Backus puts it, "The assignment statement is the von Neumann bottleneck of programming languages and keeps us thinking in word-at-a-time terms in much the same way the computer's bottleneck does" (Backus, 1978, p. 616).

Backus describes a class of simple applicative programming systems he calls "functional programming (FP) systems, in which 'programs' are simply functions without variables" (Backus, 1978, p. 619). Using that as a base, he then defines Formal Systems for Functional Programming (FFP Systems), which he states (p. 631) "are similar to, but simpler than, the Reduction (Red) languages of an earlier paper" (Backus, 1973).

The basic concept of an FFP system is that it is built on a set of atoms which are then used to create *objects* and *expressions*. An *application* is the particular form of expression $(x:y)$, where x and y are themselves expressions. There are other facilities, such as *metacomposition, fetch,* and *store* (the latter two applying to particular objects called *cells*).

Another concept introduced by Backus is an Applicative State Transition System (AST System), which he views as an alternative to the von Neumann system modeled by our "normal" languages such as ALGOL. An AST system is made up of an applicative subsystem (such as an FFP system), and its definitions, and a set of transition rules to describe how inputs are transformed into outputs.

While parts of what Backus describes will remind some people of characteristics of both LISP and APL, he has in reality created a new set of concepts for programming languages. Previous developers of some functional programming concepts (e.g., Landin, 1964; Burge, 1975) have not been able to change our basic style of languages. Whether Backus' ideas can ever be made practical remains to be seen.

5.7 Query Languages

With the increased importance of data bases and database management systems, there has been increased need for what are informally called "query languages." As with so many other aspects of programming languages, this complex subject is dependent upon the viewpoint from which one sees the field. For example, the database administrator (i.e., the person responsible for the data base itself) must have language facilities for creating and updating the database. Second, there is the viewpoint of the person interested in describing the way that the data is actually laid out; this leads to concern with a Data Description Language (DDL), and the hope of those involved that this may help transportability if the data base must be moved to other equipment. Finally, there is the user, who wishes to obtain information from the database without knowing (or caring) about its internals.

The largest amount of work in this area has been done by those who are concerned with the user interface to the database. The two major types of user languages are "standalone" and "attached to a host language." In the first case, the user needs to know only the specific query language; in the latter case, the query facilities are "added" to a host language such as PL/I or COBOL.

For standalone languages, there is, of course, a significant concern with the amount of "naturalness" which such languages should have. Thus, the query "List the suppliers that supply all the parts used by Dept. 50" must be phrased or formatted in the specific way required by the particular system being used. Ideally this could be used as input directly. Other issues concerning the language involve "two-dimensional" languages versus "key-word" or "fixed-format" languages. Also at issue is the amount of interactiveness which the user has, because in a pure batch environment the user must be much more careful about the formulation of his query.

A good discussion of the human factors aspect of query languages is given by Shneiderman (1978). The best survey of query languages that I have seen is the report by Lehmann and Blaser (1979).

5.8 Language Metrics

I do not know of any active research program pertaining to language metrics. Nevertheless, because I think that this is an area which should be studied, it is worth mentioning. As a member of a panel sponsored by the U.S. Office of Naval Research (ONR) and chaired by Professor Alan Perlis, I conducted a brief study into the problem of language metrics. Some of the issues uncovered are indicated here; for further details, see Sammet (1980b).

First, it is essential to realize that language metrics and program metrics are quite different. The latter is indeed a significant research topic, as shown by perusing the entire book resulting from this panel (i.e., Perlis *et al.* 1981). To make the difference clear, note that programs can be measured for such characteristics as program length, number of variables used, time taken to prepare the program, running time of the object program, length of the object code, error rate after completion, etc. (Some of these characteristics, such as running time of the object program, are also dependent upon the compiler as well as the environment in which the program is developed and executed.)

Metrics for high-level languages are entirely different. Examples of such metrics include:

(1) Elements related to the language design, such as numbers of key words or numbers of production rules in the grammar.

(2) Applicability of a language to a specific application area. How could we measure the fact that COGO and GPSS are more suitable for civil engineering and discrete simulation than conversely? (If there was a specific way to measure such applicability, many problems of language selection would disappear.)

(3) Deviations of one language from another. For example, how do we tell when one language is merely a minor dialect of another, and when it really should be perceived as a new language?

(4) Functionality of language components. For example, a CALL clearly provides more useful function to the programmer writing the code than a GOTO, but how does one measure the difference? (A solution to this problem would help provide a solution to the problem of measuring programmer productivity.)

There are various other language metrics, associated research problems, and references. These are discussed in more detail in Sammet (1980b).

6. Future Trends

6.1 Introductory Remarks

Anybody who discusses future trends takes his or her life (or at least their professional reputation) into their own hands. There is enormous vulnerability to finger pointing if the predictions do not come true. However, in attempting to give an overview of any topic at a given point in time, it is only fair to the reader, and appropriate posterity to provide some indication of what the author believes will occur in the future.

When predicting the future, there is a significant distinction between those trends or activities that one thinks *will* happen as contrasted with those that one *hopes* will happen, and there is still a third category of those items that one feels *will not* happen. Obviously there is an infinite class of the latter, but a later section indicates some areas in which some people *might* expect significant accomplishments in the future, although I do not feel that they will occur.

6.2 Hoped-For Future Trends

6.2.1 Natural Language

For many years I have preached the virtues of allowing people to communicate with a computer in their own natural language (which is simply meant to be the language native to the group that is using it, e.g., English, French, German, and which also contains scientific notation wherever it is appropriate). One of the primary advantages of this concept is to make it easier for any person to communicate with a computer to get his or her task done. People might argue that with the enormous increase in computer teaching at even the elementary school level, and certainly high school, that this facility is unnecessary because almost everybody will eventually grow up learning how to program a computer. Well, I personally feel that merely being exposed to a course in BASIC, or whatever simple language is taught ten or twenty years from now, will not turn each person into a professional programmer, nor should it. Furthermore, even if there is no shortage of skilled programmers, there probably will be a shortage of calendar time, and an individual who is able to indicate very specifically and directly to the computer what task needs to be done will be able to save a great deal of time and will be more productive in the required

OVERVIEW OF HIGH-LEVEL LANGUAGES 247

daily activities. With the continually decreasing costs of hardware, this is probably economically feasible.

One of the common mistakes in considering this concept of communicating with the computer in a natural language is a failure to distinguish between what is inherently a query and something which really requires taking significant action of the kind that is normally embodied in a program. An example of a query is the following:

LIST THE DEPARTURE TIMES OF ALL THE TRAINS FROM PODUNK TO OSHKOSH WHICH ARRIVE AFTER 6:00 P.M. BUT BEFORE 8:00 P.M. AND WHICH HAVE DINING CARS.

That type of query can be handled in many database management systems today, and does not require sophisticated linguistic analysis. But contrast this with the following (which is taken verbatim from an early FORTRAN manual and used as the problem definition from which a program was to be written):

A DECK OF CARDS IS GIVEN TO BE READ IN FORMAT (I3, F10.2), ONE CARD FOR EACH PERSON IN A CERTAIN VILLAGE. THE NUMBER IN THE FIRST FIELD IS THE PERSON'S AGE. THE NUMBER IN THE SECOND IS HIS INCOME FOR 1960. FOLLOWING THIS DECK IS A CARD WITH -1 IN THE FIRST FIELD; THIS INFORMATION WILL BE USED TO TEST FOR THE END OF DECK.

FIND THE AVERAGE SALARY OF THE PEOPLE IN EACH FIVE YEAR AGE GROUP I.E., 0-4, 5-9, 10-14, ... , 95-99. PRINT OUT THE LOWER AGE LIMIT FOR EACH GROUP I.E., 0, 5, 10, ... , 95, THE AVERAGE SALARY FOR THAT GROUP, AND THE NUMBER OF PEOPLE IN EACH GROUP. PRECAUTIONS SHOULD BE TAKEN TO AVOID DIVISION BY 0 IN CASE THERE ARE NO PEOPLE IN AN AGE GROUP.

The latter clearly requires careful linguistic analysis of the description in order to cause it to be executed.

It is important to emphasize that even when using natural language it is essential to be able to state clearly and completely all the details required to solve the problem. It may be necessary to carry out a "dialogue" with the computer just as one does with another human if the "reader" does not understand the specifications.

6.2.2 Specialized Application Languages with an Automatic Method to Define and Implement Them

If the tools for allowing users to communicate with the computer in their natural language are not available, then the next best thing is to allow people to communicate by the use of specialized application languages (as discussed in earlier sections). Since these are formal languages, they are not "natural" in the sense of the preceding section, but they are more natural than a general language like PL/I. Preferably each group of users should be able to have a special artificial language that is particularly relevant to their needs. Thus, the terminology of banking is different from that of insurance, and one of the major characteristics of any specialized application language is to allow the use of the jargon for the particular field. Considering the very large number of this class of languages that have been developed over time (see the numbers in Section 2.2) it is clear that this is a very popular way of communicating with a computer because so many people and/or groups have developed such languages. However, in almost every case, they have been forced to use the conventional syntactic methods for defining a language, and then implement it by writing a compiler or an interpreter, or in a few cases a preprocessor. I hope that we could develop tools and techniques wherein it would be possible for users to describe the type of vocabulary and the type of operations that are relevant to their application area, and provide some indication of the style of language that they like (e.g., free form, English oriented, simple notation); then there should be a computer program which would first generate a syntactic definition of the language and, once that was shown to be satisfactory, would then automatically produce the translator. Unfortunately, this has been a research topic since the early 1960s, and the problem does not seem to be any closer to solution than it was then.

Another approach to providing some facilities to a user in a specialized application area is via "menu" systems. These generally display options on a screen from which the user chooses his next action(s). Although this is useful in some instances, it has the same disadvantages as the application packages mentioned in Section 1.2.

6.2.3 Program Verification

Certainly, one of the greatest difficulties in the software field is the inability to determine whether or not a particular program really is correct. (In fact, we even have difficulty defining rigorously what is meant by "correct," but let us assume a very rough working definition of saying a correct program always produces the correct answer for valid input data and always rejects invalid input data.)

There are actually two levels of verification required. The first is to find a way to rigorously determine the intent of the original problem, i.e., one has to look at the requirements and/or specifications and determine whether or not the program—if it is assumed to be correct—really satisfies the specifications and/or requirements. Then the second level of proof obviously involves the program itself with respect to what the programmer states as the intent of the program. The hope here is to make this a practical reality and not merely an intellectual exercise. There has been a lot of the latter, and it is very interesting and often very good; however, the desirable objective is for a practical system, and not merely one that can be used on small problems.

In a very interesting paper by DeMillo *et al.* (1979) it is argued that program verification can *never* become practical because the proof of a significant program would be almost impossible to develop in a reasonable time period. The authors assert that the very nature of program development—which involves changes to the specifications and the program—would prevent the creation of a proof for the current version of the program since the new proof cannot necessarily build on the old. The view of these authors is depressing—but probably correct. Comments on this article, including both support and objections appear in the November 1979 *Communications of the ACM*.

6.2.4 More Nonprocedural (Equals Less Procedural) Languages

The basic concept involved here is to allow the user to specify more of "what" is to be done and much less of "how" it is to be done. Ideally, the user should be able to simply indicate the requirements of the problem and allow some system to generate (first) the program and (then) the answers to the stipulated problems. The techniques that are involved in this type of work come under the heading of automatic programming, specification languages, problem defining languages, very high level languages, and more nonprocedural languages. Since nonprocedural language is a relative term that changes as the state of the art changes (see the basic discussion of this concept in Leavenworth and Sammet, 1974), it is an area in which we could perhaps make small steps of progress as time goes on. In other words, the solution to this particular trend is evolutionary, rather than being described with a discrete YES or NO. What is needed is to increase the level of nonproceduralness.

6.2.5 More Theoretical Approaches

Programming in general, and programming languages in particular, need to be established on a more abstract and theoretical foundation. While a great deal of work toward this end has been going on for many years, much remains to be done. It is within this framework that I think we need to make programming more of a science and less of an art and even less of an engineering discipline. Some people contend that programming is—and should be—an engineering discipline. They suggest that the proper use of theoretical developments will improve the quality of the engineering discipline. My own view continues to be that programming (and software development generally) is a science which we have not yet succeeded in crystallizing.

Regardless of whether you view programming as a science or as an engineering discipline, there is a strong need for more theoretical developments. Furthermore, there is no conflict with the hoped for trend of using natural language, because that concept involves the method of communication between the person and the computer, whereas the theory is needed to provide a framework for the acceptance and proper handling of such conversations.

6.2.6 Influence on the Query Part of Database Systems

Every database management system in existence today has associated with it a "language" of some kind even though it may not be called a "language" or it may not appear to be one. Nevertheless, human beings are communicating with the database system in some manner and it is this front end which needs far more attention from a language. In essence, we need "query languages" that are more rigorously defined, more flexible, and more natural for the user.

6.2.7 Increased Use of High-Level Languages For Systems and Real-Time Programming

The old cliche, that the shoemaker's children are often the ones to go without shoes certainly applies to systems programmers who have done much of their work in assembly language or at best macro- or midway languages. The basic problem has been that systems programmers, and real-time systems applications and the "embedded computer system" applications so prevalent in the Department of Defense all have a very legitimate efficiency requirement. Generally, the requirements relate to both time and storage space. The latter may be solved more easily with better hardware technology, but the former remains an unsolvable obstacle. If two planes are flying and an air traffic control system is to deal with them, then obviously we want to make sure that the necessary calculations will be finished in adequate time. What is needed here are languages and compilers (and hardware processors) which can produce the maximum efficiency needed for the application.

OVERVIEW OF HIGH-LEVEL LANGUAGES 251

6.3 Expected Future Trends

This section deals with those trends that I think will occur. Some of these items are related to hoped for trends and others are quite independent.

6.3.1 Continued Heavy Use of Current Major Languages

I believe there will be continued heavy use of those major languages which currently seem to receive very heavy use—namely FORTRAN, COBOL, and BASIC. I expect that the adherents of each will continue to add features to them so that eventually these three will be very similar in functional capability but will remain significantly different in syntax. BASIC will become even more popular because of its current large user base and its increased use in the personal computers. Pascal will become more widely used, and may eventually replace BASIC on the micro- and personal computers. (It is impossible for me to even guess whether BASIC or Pascal will be more widely used.) APL will continue to be popular, but probably will not develop a lot of new users.

Other current languages which will continue to receive the heaviest use in their application area are LISP (list processing), SNOBOL (string processing), and REDUCE and MACSYMA (formula manipulation).

6.3.2 Continued Proliferation of New Languages

I believe there will continue to be an uncontrollable proliferation of new languages. I believe that the statistics shown in Section 2.2 will continue to be borne out, and that as languages die each year, other new ones will come into existence. If we could be sure that the new ones were going to really contribute something significant to the state of the art, this would be a desirable state of affairs. Unfortunately, for every significant language like Pascal that we get, there are probably 20 others that are created to either satisfy the developer's ego or to provide a Ph.D. thesis topic.

I think there will be a continued increase in the number of languages for specialized application areas; to be consistent with my earlier hopes, I do *not* find that objectionable, provided that there really are *new* languages for *new* application areas.

6.3.3 Increase in Nonprocedurality

I believe there will be some increase in nonprocedurality. Thus, languages will be developed which allow the user to provide fewer details.

The best examples are likely to occur in the database area, but that is only one application area, albeit one with wide usage. In the general cases, the improvement will be small unless there is some major breakthrough which I cannot forsee.

6.3.4 Verification Will Not Become Practical

While there will continue to be new and better work on program verification, I do not think it will ever become practical. I personally regret this, because I feel this would be a major constructive step in the software field, analogous to the hardware breakthroughs of the transistor and the integrated circuit. I believe that the program verification situation is analogous to that which occurred with the Vienna Definition Language (VDL) described by Lucas and Walk (1969), where it was clear to most knowledgeable language and compiler people that the VDL was an excellent way to define a language rigorously and get compilers written consistently. Unfortunately, VDL turned out to be impractical in terms of writing production compilers within specified schedules and budgets.

6.3.5 Increased Use of Theory

I do see an increased use of theory. In fact, that is probably the brightest light on the horizon. As more and more people are trained in computer science, there is simply more brain power available to use this type of methodology. One example where good theoretical training would help is in tracing through the full software life cycle and defining rigorously how information can flow, and is transformed, from requirements through maintenance. Another example is in the automatic generation of efficient compilers from formal specifications for large languages; although work on this problem has been underway since the early 1960s, it is still not a solved problem. Even the simpler cases discussed in Section 6.2.2 have not been solved. Finally, the implications of data abstractions are just beginning to be understood, and this may have unpredictable results.

6.3.6 Better Query Languages

I believe there will be a greater influence on the query languages from high-level language experts, but it will be a long time before significant results are obtained. (See Section 6.2.6 for a description of "better query languages.")

OVERVIEW OF HIGH-LEVEL LANGUAGES

6.3.7 *More Use of High-Level Languages in Systems Programming*

I really do believe that high-level languages will be used much more widely for even the critical systems in real-time programming. The increasing cost over the life cycle of a complex application such as an operating system or a weapons system, or an oil refinery system will mandate that almost all of the program will be written in a high-level language. What will happen in many cases, I believe, is that the entire program will be written in a high-level language and then certain absolutely critical portions will be recoded in assembly language to save every nanosecond of time. I think that another motivating factor in this direction will be work on program verification, since people will want to try to prove the correctness of (at least portions of) these programs and their criticality is obvious.

6.4 Some Future Trends *Not* Expected

6.4.1 *No Extensible Languages*

Extensible languages seem to have died as a major research topic. I do not think that it will be resurrected, although in some language work, people are paying attention to methods, and including specific features within a language, to permit certain types of simple extensibility. For example, in ALGOL 68 new operators can be defined, and Ada allows new meanings to be given to existing operators. Some people claim that data abstractions (and even subroutines) are a form of extensibility, but I do not agree. I use the term "extensibility" to mean the ability to add new syntax (and related new semantics) to an existing language based on constructs already in the language. In many ways, I regret this lack of development because I think the basic concept of an extensible language is an excellent one, and it certainly is a tool that could be used to generate the myriad of application oriented languages of the type discussed above. Unfortunately, I believe that the claims of what could and would be done in extensible languages were so outrageous in the late 1960s and early 1970s (relative to what was actually being accomplished) that this just put a permanent (or at least a very long) damper on this research area.

6.4.2 *No Special Languages for Distributed Systems*

I do not think there will be any specialized languages for distributed systems or networks. There may be a few additional features added to operating systems, but most of the problems pertaining to languages on a network also pertain to languages used separately from a network.

6.4.3 No New Single Major Conceptual Step

I do not see any new single major conceptual steps becoming of practical usage. Regardless of the merits of any new concepts (e.g., the functional programming of Backus, 1978) or any other ideas, the economy of program development is so far along now that it would take more than just a great intellectual breakthrough to cause us to shift. Another way to phrase my view is to say that I think future changes will come from technical evolution, not revolution.

6.4.4 Ada Will Not Replace Many Non-DOD Languages

I do not think that Ada will replace the other major programming languages outside of the Department of Defense (DOD) community. I do think that it will be used in many ways outside of DOD, but for the same reason that any language has trouble replacing a previous one, there are too many adherents to existing languages to permit the languages to be eliminated.

TABLE IV

INTERRELATIONSHIP OF FUTURE LANGUAGE TRENDS

Trend	Hoped for	Expected	Not expected
Natural language	×		×
Specialized application languages with automated method of definition and implementation	×	?	?
Practical methods for program verification	×		×
Less procedural (= more nonprocedural) languages	×	×	
Theoretical approach	×	×	
Better Query languages for DBMS	×	×	
Increased use of high-level languages for systems and real-time programming	×	×	
Continued heavy use of current major languages		×	
Continued uncontrollable proliferation		×	
Extensible languages	(×)		×
Special languages for networks			×
Improvements in job control languages	(×)		×
New major conceptual steps	(×)		×
Ada replacing non-DOD languages			×

6.5 Interrelationship of Future Trends

From the textual format of the previous sections, it is difficult to see the interrelationships of the items in various categories. Table IV shows this succinctly.

7. Summary and Conclusions

This article has provided an overview of a number of facets of high-level languages, starting with some definitions and a brief history of the past twenty years. There was then a discussion of the milieu in which language work is going on and is reported. Because of the importance of the current ideas in software engineering and software methodology, a large section was devoted to showing the involvement of languages. A tiny introduction to five "modern" languages was given, followed by a lengthy description of the background of the newest (albeit not the most modern) language of all, namely Ada. A brief overview of some of the current research and advanced development topics was given, which then led into a section on future trends—those hoped for and those expected (which are definitely not the same).

As I look both backwards and forwards in the general field of high-level languages, the only conclusion I can reach is not a very earth shattering one—namely that the only way to make maximum use of the computer power which the engineers keep producing is to have an easy means of communicating with the computer. Because machine efficiency will be less of an issue in most future applications, the ease of this communication will become the pervasive factor. Work on languages will continue to be one of the cores of research and development in the computer field.

ACKNOWLEDGMENTS

I would like to thank the following people, each of whom looked at one of the drafts of this entire paper and provided me with very useful comments: Burt Leavenworth, Jan Lee, Michael Marcotty, Robert Rosin, Richard Wexelblat, and Marshall Yovits. Any deficiencies in the paper are clearly my fault and definitely not theirs.

REFERENCES

ACM* *ACM Transactions on Programming Languages and Systems* (TOPLAS) ACM, New York.

* Association for Computing Machinery, Inc.

ACM (1977). *Proceedings of the ACM Conference on Language Design for Reliable Software, ACM SIGPLAN Notices,* Vol. 12, No. 3, March. ACM, New York.

ACM (1979a). *Preliminary Ada Reference Manual, Part A, ACM SIGPLAN Notices,* Vol. 14, No. 6, June. ACM, New York.

ACM (1979b). *Preliminary Ada Reference Manual, Part B, ACM SIGPLAN Notices,* Vol. 14, No. 6, June. ACM, New York.

Backus, J. (1973). Programming language semantics and closed applicative languages. *Conf. Record ACM Symp. Principles Programming Languages, 1973,* pp. 71–86. ACM, New York.

Backus, J. (1978). Can programming be liberated from the von Neumann style? A functional style and its algebra of programs. *Commun. ACM* **21,** No. 8 (Aug.), 613–641.

Backus, J. (1981). The history of FORTRAN I, II, and III. *In* "History of Programming Languages" (R. L. Wexelblat, ed.), pp. 25–45. Academic Press, New York.

Biggerstaff, T. J. (1979). The unified design specification system (UDS^2). *Proc. IEEE Comput. Soc. Conf. Specifications Reliable Software,* 1979, IEEE Cat. No. 79 CH1401-9C, pp. 104–118. IEEE, New York.

Burge, W. H. (1975) "Recursive Programming Techniques." Addison-Wesley, Reading, Massachusetts.

Caine, S. H., and Gordon, E. K. (1975). PDL—A tool for software design. *Proc. AFIPS NCC* **44,** pp. 271–276.

Computer Languages. Pergammon, Oxford.

Dahl, O. J., and Nygaard, K. (1967). "SIMULA 67 Common Base Definition," Norwegian Computing Center, No. S-2, Oslo, Norway.

Davis, A. M., and Rauscher, T. G. (1979). Formal techniques and automatic processing to ensure correctness in requirements specifications. *Proc. IEEE Comput. Soc. Conf. Specifications Reliable Software,* 1979, IEEE Cat. No. 79 CH1401-9C, pp. 15–35. IEEE, New York.

DeMillo, R. A., Lipton, R. J., and Perlis, A. J. (1979). Social processes and proofs of theorems and programs. *Commun. ACM* **22,** No. 5 (May), 271–280.

Department of Defense,* High-Order Language Working Group (1976). "Department of Defense Requirements for High-Order Computer Programming Languages—TINMAN," June. DOD, Washington, D.C.

Department of Defense, High-Order Language Working Group (1977). "Department of Defense Requirements for High-Order Computer Programming Languages—IRONMAN," January. DOD, Washington, D.C.

Department of Defense, High-Order Language Working Group (1978). "Department of Defense Requirements for High-Order Computer Programming Languages—STEELMAN," June. DOD, Washington, D.C.

Department of Defense, (1980a). "Requirements for Ada Programming Support Environments—STONEMAN," February. DOD, Washington, D.C.

Department of Defense (1980b). "Reference Manual for the Ada Programming Language," July. Defense Advanced Research Projects Agency, DOD, Washington, D.C.

Dewar, R., and Schonberg, E. (1979). The elements of SETL style. *Proc. Ann. Conf., Assoc. Comput. Mach., 1979,* pp. 24–32.

Dewar, R. B. K., Grand, A., Liu, S-C., and Schwartz, J. T. (1979). Program by refinement, as exemplified by the SETL representation. *ACM Trans. Program. Lang. Syst.* **1,** No. 1 (July), 27–49. ACM, New York.

Floyd, R. W. (1967). Assigning meanings to programs. *In* "Proceedings of a Symposium in

---

* Department of Defense references are cited as DOD in the text.

Applied Mathematics (J. T. Schwartz, ed.), Vol. 19, pp. 19–32. American Math. Soc., Providence, Rhode Island.

Gannon, J. D. (1977). An experimental evaluation of data type conventions. *Commun. ACM* **20**, No. 8 (Aug.), 584–595.

Gannon, J. D., and Horning, J. J. (1975). The impact of language design on the production of reliable software. *Proc. Int. Conf. Reliable Software, ACM SIGPLAN Notices*, Vol. 10, No. 6 (June), pp. 10–22. ACM, New York.

Geschke, C. M., Morris, J. H. Jr., and Satterwaite, E. H. (1977). Early experience with Mesa. *Commun. ACM* **20**, No. 8 (Aug.), 540–553.

Goodenough, J. (1979). A survey of program testing issues. *In* "Research Directions in Software Technology" (P. Wegner, ed.), pp. 316–340. MIT Press, Cambridge, Massachusetts.

Hammer, M., and Ruth, G. (1979). Automating the software development process. *In* "Research Directions in Software Technology" (P. Wegner, ed.), pp. 767–790.

Hanson, P. Brinch (1977). "The Architecture of Concurrent Programs." Prentice-Hall, Englewood Cliffs, New Jersey.

Heacox, H. C. (1979). "RDL: A Language for Software Development." *ACM SIGPLAN Notices*, Vol. 14, No. 12 (Dec.), pp. 71–79. ACM, New York.

HOPL (1981). "A History of Programming Languages" (R. L. Wexelblat, ed.). Academic Press, New York.

Jensen, K., and Wirth, N. (1978). "Pascal User Manual and Report," 2nd ed. Springer-Verlag, Berlin and New York.

Knuth, D., and Trabb Pardo, L. (1977). Early development of programming languages. *In* "Encyclopedia of Computer Science and Technology" (J. Belzer, A. G. Holzman, and A. Kent, eds.), Vol. 7, pp. 419–493. Marcel Dekker, New York. *Also in* "A History of Computing in the Twentieth Century" (N. Metropolis, J. Howlett, and G.-C. Rota, eds.), pp. 197–274. Academic Press, New York, 1980.

Lampson, B. W., Horning, J. J., London, R. L., Mitchell, J. G., and Popek, G. L. (1977). "Report on the Programming Language Euclid." *ACM SIGPLAN Notices*, Vol. **12**, No. 2 (Feb.). ACM, New York.

Landin, P. J. (1964). The mechanical evaluation of expressions. *Comput. J.* **6**, No. 4, 308–320.

Leavenworth, B. M., and Sammet, J. E. (1974). An overview of nonprocedural languages. *Proc. Symp. Very High-Level Languages, ACM SIGPLAN Notices*, Vol. 9, No. 4 (April), pp. 1–12, ACM, New York.

Lehmann, H., and Blaser, A. (1979). "Query Languages in Data Base Systems," TR79.07.004, July. IBM Heidelberg Sci. Center, Heidelberg, Germany.

Linger, R. C., Mills, H. D., and Witt, B. I. (1979). "Structured Programming: Theory and Practice," Addison-Wesley, Reading, Massachusetts.

Liskov, B., Snyder, A., Atkinson, R. and Schaffert, C. (1977). Abstraction mechanisms in CLU. *Commun. ACM* **20**, No. 8 (Aug.), 564–576.

London, R. L. (1979). Program verification. *In* "Research Directions in Software Technology" (P. Wegner, ed.), pp. 302–315. MIT Press, Cambridge, Massachusetts.

Lucas, P., and Walk, K. (1969). On the formal description of PL/I. *Ann. Rev. Autom. Program.* **6**, No. 3, 105–182.

Marcotty, M., and Ledgard, H. F. (1976) A sampler of formal definitions. *ACM Comput. Surv.* **8**, No. 2 (June), 191–276. ACM, New York.

Musser, D. R. (1979). Abstract data type specification in the Affirm system. *Proc. IEEE Comput. Soc. Conf. Specifications Reliable Software*, 1979, pp. 47–57, IEEE Cat. No. 79 CH1401-9C. IEEE, New York.

Perlis, A. J., and Samelson, K. (for the committee) (1958). Preliminary report—International algebraic language. *Commun. ACM,* **1,** No. 12 (Dec.), 8–22.

Perlis, A. J., Sayward, F., and Shaw, M. (eds.) (1981). "Software Metrics: An Analysis and Evaluation." MIT Press, Cambridge, Massachusetts.

Prigge, R. D., Hill, M. F., and Walkowicz, J. L. (1978). "The World of EDP Standards." Sperry-Univac, GS-4248.

Prywes, N. S. (1977). Automatic generation of computer programs. *Adv. Comput.* **16,** 57–125.

Robinson, L., and Roubine, O. (1977) *"SPECIAL—A SPECIFICATION AND ASSERTION LANGUAGE."* Tech. Rep. CSL-46, Jan. Stanford Res. Inst., Menlo Park, California.

Ross, D. (1981). Origins of the APT language for automatically programmed tools. *In* "History of Programming Languages" (R. L. Wexelblat, ed.), pp. 279–338. Academic Press, New York.

Sammet, J. E. (1969). "Programming Languages: History and Fundamentals." Prentice-Hall, Englewood Cliffs, New Jersey.

Sammet, J. E. (1972a). An overview of programming languages for specialized application areas. *Proc. AFIPS SJCC* **40,** 299–311.

Sammet, J. E. (1972b). Programming Languages: History and Future. *Commun. ACM* **15,** No. 7 (July), 601–610.

Sammet, J. E. (1972c). Roster of programming languages, 1971. *Comput. Autom.* **20,** (June 30), 6–12.

Sammet, J. E. (1973). Roster of programming languages, 1972. *Comput. Autom.* **21,** No. 6B (Aug. 30), 1–11.

Sammet, J. E. (1974). Roster of programming languages for 1973. *Comput. Rev.* **15,** No. 4 (Apr.), 147–160.

Sammet, J. E. (1976). Roster of programming languages for 1974–75. *Commun. ACM* **19,** No. 12 (Dec.), 655–669.

Sammet, J. E. (1978). Roster of programming languages for 1976–77. *ACM SIGPLAN Notices* **13,** No. 11 (Nov.), 56–85. ACM, New York.

Sammet, J. E. (1980). Language aspects of software engineering. *In* "Software Engineering" (H. Freeman and P. M. Lewis, II, eds.), pp. 181–194. Academic Press, New York.

Sammet, J. E. (1981a). High-Level language metrics. *In* "Software Metrics: An Analysis and Evaluation" (A. Perlis, F. Sayward, and M. Shaw, eds.) pp. 131–142. MIT Press, Cambridge, Massachusetts.

Sammet, J. E. (1981b). History of IBM's technical contributions to high-level programming languages. *IBM J. Res. Dev.* **25,** No. 5 (Sept.).

Shankar, K. S. (1980). Data structures, types, and abstractions. *Computer* **13,** No. 4 (Apr.), 67–77.

Shaw, M. (1980). The impact of abstraction concerns on modern programming languages. *Proc. IEEE* **68,** No. 9 (Sept.), 1119–1130.

Shaw, M., Wulf, W. A., and London, R. L. (1977). Abstraction and verification in Alphard: Defining and specifying iteration and generators. *Commun. ACM* **20,** No. 8 (Aug.), pp. 553–564.

Shaw, M., Almes, G. T., Newcomer, J. M., Reid, B. K., and Wulf, W. A. (1978). "A Comparison of Programming Languages for Software Engineering," CMU-CS-78-119, April. Dept. of Computer Science, Carnegie-Mellon University, Pittsburgh, Pennsylvania.

Shneiderman, B. (1978). Improving the human factors aspect of database interactions. *Trans. Database Syst.* **3,** No. 4 (Dec.), 417–439.

Tanenbaum, A. S. (1976). A tutorial on ALGOL 68. *Comput. Surv.* **8,** No. 2 (June), 155–190.

Teichroew, D., and Hershey, E. A. (1977). PSL/PSA: A computer-aided technique for structured documentation and analysis of information processing systems. *IEEE Trans. Software Eng.* **SE-3**, No. 1 (Jan.), 41–48.

Wexelblat, R. L. (ed.) (1981). "History of Programming Languages." Academic Press, New York.

Winograd, T. (1979). Beyond programming languages. *Commun. ACM* **22**, No. 7 (July), 391–401.

Wirth, N. (1968). PL360, A programming language for the 360 computers. *J. Assoc. Comput. Mach.* **15**, No. 1 (Jan.), 37–74.

Wirth, N. (1977). Modula: A language for modular multiprogramming. *Software Pract. Exp.* **7**, No. 1 (Jan.–Feb.), 3–35.

Author Index

Numbers in parentheses are reference numbers and indicate that an author's work is referred to although his name is not cited in the text. Numbers in italics indicate the pages on which the complete references are given.

A

Ackoff, R., 10, *29*
Adams, C., 17, *29*
Agerwala, T. K., 180, *194*
Ahuja, S. R., *194*
Almes, G. T., 222, 223, 228, *258*
Altaber, J., 85(66), *114*
Alter, S., 21, *29*
Alty, J. L., 85(70), *114*
Anderson, D. R., 85(40), *113*
Anderson, D. W., 117, *191*
Anderson, G. A., *81*
Anderson, R. J., 84(9), *112*
Anshen, M., 9, 10, *29*
Ansoff, H., 9, *29*
Anthony, R., 17, *29*
Aramis, E., 85(34, 35), 102(34), *113*
Argyris, C., 21, *29*
Aron, J., 12, 13, *29*
Ashenhurst, R. L., 25, *29*, 85(44), *113*
Astrahan, M., 7, *29*
Aswen, D., 7, *29*
Atkins, D. E., *195*
Atkinson, R., 230, 239, *257*
Atwater, T. V., Jr., 16, *32*
Avizienis, A., 179, *196*

B

Bach, G., 10, *29*
Backus, J., 205, 207, 243, 254, *256*
Baer, J. L., 118, *191*
Baker, N., 21, *35*
Ball, J. E., 85(64), *114*
Banerjee, U., *191*
Barber, D. L. A., 42, *82*
Bariff, M., 22, *29*
Barnard, C., 6, *29*
Barnes, G. H., 118, 178, *191*
Baskett, F., *191*

Batcher, K. E., 118, 122, 166, 171, 172, 173, *192*
Bedford, N. M., 16, *29*
Beer, S., 6, *29*
Beged-Dov, S., 9, *29*
Bell, W., 7, *29*
Benbasat, I., 22, *29*, *35*
Bender, M. A., 62, *81*
Berg, H. K., 65, *82*
Berkeley, E., 10, *30*
Bernard, D., 16, *30*
Bernhard, R., *192*
Biba, K. J., 85(37), 90(37), *113*
Biggerstaff, T. J., 220, *256*
Binder, R., 85(55), *114*
Blaser, A., 244, *257*
Blum, A., 11, *30*
Blumenthal, S., 14, *30*
Boebert, W. E., 65, *82*
Boggs, D. R., 49, *82*, 85(53), *114*
Bostwick, C. L., 16, *30*
Bouknight, W. J., 118, *192*
Bovet, D. P., 180, *192*
Bowles, S. W., 85(49), *113*
Briggs, F. A., 176, 178, *192*
Bright, J., 6, *30*
Brinch Hansen, P., 73, *82*, 230, *257*
Brooks, F., Jr., 22, *35*
Buckingham, W., 3, *30*
Bullis, K., 81, *82*
Burch, J., 13, *30*
Burck, G., 10, *30*
Burge, W. H., 244, *256*
Burlingame, J., 9, *30*
Burnett, D. J., 85(26), *113*

C

Caine, S. H., 221, *256*
Canning, R., 7, 9, 14, 25, *30*

AUTHOR INDEX

Carlin, F., 7, *30*
Carlson, E. D., 16, 28, *30*
Carpenter, R. J., 85(56), *114*
Carr, H. M., *197*
Chandy, K. M., 180, *194*
Chang, S. L., 191, *192*
Chapin, N., 7, *30*
Chen, T. C., 117, 180, *192*
Cheng, Y. H., 187, 189, 190, *193*
Chervany, N., 18, 21, 22, *30, 31, 35*
Cheung, L., *192*
Chlamtac, I., 43, *82*
Christenson, G. S., 107(76), *114*
Christman, R. D., 85(65), *114*
Churchill, N., 17, *30*
Clark, D. D., 84, 105(7), *112*
Cleland, D., 14, *30*
Coleman, R., 13, *30*
Collins, J., 7, *30*
Cooper, R. G., *192*
Cordennier, V., *192*
Cornette, W., 14, *31*
Cotton, I. W., 83(2), 84(8), 105(8), *112*
Couger, J. D., 10, 14, 21, 26, 27, *30, 31*
Cunningham, R. J., 65, *82*

D

Dahl, O. J., 228, *256*
Daniel, R., 10, *31*
Danzinger, J., 17, *31*
Davidson, E. S., 132, 133, 134, 135, 140, *192, 193, 194, 196*
Davies, D. W., 42, *82*
Davis, A. M., 220, *256*
Davis, G., 5, 13, 14, 16, *31, 33*
Dean, N., 11, *36*
Dearden, J., 10, 11, 15, 25, *31*
DeMillo, R. A., *256*
Demski, J. S., 16, *32*
Dewar, R., 232, *256*
Dewar, R. B. K., 232, *256*
Dickey, E., 11, *31*
Dickson, G. W., 5, 12, 16, 18, 20, 21, 22, *30, 31, 35, 37*
Diebold, J., 6, 9, 10, *31*
Dijkstra, E. W., 62, *82*
Dock, V., 12, 14, *31*
Dorr, F. W., *192*

Drucker, P., 9, *31*
DuPont, H., 7, *31*
Dyer, A., 11, *31*

E

Eagle, J. G., 117, *191*
Ebdon, J., 7, *31*
Eller, W. R., 106(75), *114*
Elliot, J., 9, *31*
Emer, J. S., *193*
Emery, J. C., 15, 16, 17, *30, 31, 32*
Estrin, T., 18, *34*
Evans, M., 11, *32*
Evansen, A. J., 118, *193*
Everest, G., 14, *31*

F

Farber, D. J., 85(31), *113*
Farmen, W. D., 102(74), *114*
Farmer, W. D., 49, *82*
Feltham, G. A., 16, *32*
Feng, T. Y., 166, 167, *193, 197*
Ference, T., 17, *32*
Ferguson, R., 22, *32*
Field, J. A., *194*
Finke, W., 7, *32*
Fiock, L., Jr., 10, *32*
Firth, M., 22, *32*
Fletcher, J. G., 85(68), *114*
Floyd, R. W., 240, *256*
Flynn, M. J., *193*
Forrester, J., 8, *32*
Franck, A., 83(3), 85(62), *112, 114*
Franta, W. R., 43, 65, *81, 82*
Fraser, A. G., 84(10), 85(15, 22), *112*
Freeman, H. A., 83(1), 84(6), 85, 105(6), *111, 112*
Fu, K. S., 176, 178, *192*

G

Gajski, D., *191*
Gallagher, C. A., 16, *32*
Gallagher, J., 10, *32*
Gannon, J. D., 225, *257*

Gao, Q. S., 118, *193*
Garrity, J., 10, 11, *32*
Gerhardstein, L. H., 85(38), *113*
Gerrity, T., Jr., 28, *32*
Geschke, C. M., 228, *257*
Gibson, C., 15, *32*
Gille, F., 7, *32*
Ginsberg, M., *193*
Ginzberg, M., 21, *32*
Goldschmidt, R. E., 117, *191*
Goodenough, J., 223, *257*
Gordon, E. K., 221, *256*
Gordon, R. L., 85(17, 57), *112, 114*
Gorry, A., 18, *32*
Grace, B., 28, *30*
Gradnitski, G., 13, *30*
Graham, W. R., *193*
Grand, A., 232, *256*
Greenlaw, P., 10, *35*
Gregory, R. H., 16, *32*
Guest, L., 7, *32*
Guthrie, A., 17, *32*

H

Händler, W., 130, *193*
Hague, L., 11, *32*
Hallin, T. G., *193*
Hamilton, S., *33*
Hammer, M., 243, *257*
Hardin, E., 11, *32*
Hartman, H., 12, *32*
Hartman, W., 15, *32*
Hayes, J. P., 118, *193*
Heacox, H. C., 220, *257*
Head, R., 15, 17, *32*
Heames, T., 13, *33*
Heimen, O., 21, *35*
Hershey, E. A., 220, *258*
Hertz, D., 9, *32*
Hertzberg, R. Y., 85(48), *113*
Higbie, L. C., 116, 166, *193*
Hill, M. F., 214, *258*
Hinton, O. R., 85(13), *112*
Hintz, R. G., *193*
Hoare, C. A. R., 71, *82*
Hockman, J., 9, *33*
Hoos, I., 9, *33*
Hootman, J. T., 16, *33*

Hopkins, G. T., 85(59), *114*
Hopper, A., 85(23), *112*
Horning, J. J., 224, 225, 231, *257*
Huen, W., 85(39), *113*
Hufnagel, S., *193*
Hupp, J. A., 102(72), *114*
Huysmans, J. H., 22, *33*
Hwang, K., 118, 175, 176, 177, 178, 179, 187, 189, 190, *192, 193, 195*

I

Ibbett, R. N., *193*
Innes, D. R., 85(70), *114*
Irwin, M. J., *194, 195*
Ives, B., 19, *33*

J

Jenkins, A., 18, *33*
Jensen, E. D., 63, *81, 82,* 85(32), *113*
Jensen, K., 229, *257*
Jin, L., *194*
Johnson, J., 7, *33*
Johnson, P. M., 116, 147, 150, *194*
Johnson, R., 10, *33*
Jones, D., 22, *32*
Joslin, E., 14, *33*
Jump, J. R., *194*

K

Kanter, J., 13, *33*
Kartashev, S. I., *194*
Kartashev, S. P., *194*
Kascic, M. J., Jr., *194*
Kast, F., 10, *33*
Kaufman, F., 11, *33*
Kaufman, M. T., *194*
Keen, P., 21, 27, *33*
Keller, T. W., *191*
Kelly, J., 13, *33*
Kempster, J., 17, *30*
Kennedy, K., 189, *194*
Kennevan, W., 5, *33*
Kim, K. H., *195*
King, J. L., 21, *33*

King, W., 14, *30*
Kircher, P., 7, 14, *33*
Kleijnen, J. P. C., 16, *33*
Knapp, R., 14, *31*
Knox, C., 7, *33*
Knuth, D., 205, *257*
Knutson, H., 15, *33*
Kodandapani, K. L., 167, *195*
Kozar, K., 18, *30*
Kozdrowicki, E. W., 124, 156, 160, *194*
Kozmetsky, G., 7, 14, *33*
Kraemer, K. L., 21, *33*
Kramer, J., 65, *82*
Krause, L., 13, *33*
Kriebel, C. H., 12, 13, 16, *33*
Kuck, D., *191*
Kuck, D. J., 118, 122, *194, 195*
Kuhns, R. C., 85(41), *113*
Kung, H. T., 190, *194*

L

Lach, E., 11, *33*
Lamport, L., 78, *82*
Lampson, B. W., 94(71), 97(71), *114*, 224, 231, *257*
Landin, P. J., 244, *257*
Lang, D. E., 180, *194*
Langefors, B., 14, *34*
Larson, A. G., *194*
Lawrie, D. H., 122, 168, 191, *194, 195*
Leavenworth, B. M., *257*
Leavitt, H., 4, 7, *34*
Ledgard, H. F., 226, *257*
Lee, C. C., 85(46), *113*
Lee, R. B.-L., *194*
Lehmann, H., 244, *257*
Leiserson, C. E., 190, *194*
LeLann, G., 41, *82*
Levin, R., 64, 73, *82*, 85(28), *113*
Li, H. F., 117, 124, 131, *195*
Lidinsky, W. P., 85(52), *114*
Lin, K., 85(25), *112*
Linger, R. C., 221, *257*
Lipovski, G. J., 179, *195*
Lipton, R. J., *256*
Liskov, B., 74, 82, 230, 239, *257*
Liu, M. T., 85(33, 36), *113*
Liu, S-C., 232, *256*

London, R. L., 223, 224, 231, 240, *257, 258*
Loveman, D. B., 188, *194*
Lucas, H., Jr., 13, 18, 21, *34*
Lucas, P., 252, *257*
Luchsinger, V., 14, *31*
Lusk, E., 22, *29*

M

McColley, J., 21, *35*
McDonough, A., 10, *34*
McFarlan, F., 10, 15, *31, 34*
McKenney, J., 11, *34*
McLean, E., 15, *34*
Majithia, J. C., 85(47), *113, 194*
Malcomb, D., 8, 9, *34*
Mann, F., 11, *34*
Mann, W. F., 85(50), *113*
Manning, E. G., 85(20), *112*
Mao, T. W., 74, *82*
March, J., 6, *34*
Marcotty, M., 226, *257*
Martin, J., 14, *34*
Mason, R., 18, *34*
Matlin, G. L., 16, *34*
Matthes, H., 15, *32*
Mayeda, W., *194*
Maynard, A., 7, *34*
Mehra, S. K., 85(47), *113*
Metcalfe, R. M., 49, *82*, 85,(18, 53), 90(18), *112, 114*
Mills, D. L., 85(42), 90(42), *113*
Mills, H. D., 221, *257*
Mitchell, J. G., 224, 231, *257*
Mitroff, I., 18, *34*
Mock, T., 18, 22, *34*
Morris, J. H. Jr., 228, *257*
Mowle, F. J., *192*
Munro, M., 26, *34*
Murdick, R., 2, 13, *34*
Musser, D. R., 220, *257*

N

Naga, N. M., *194*
Nassimi, D., *195*
Nelson, D. L., 85(57), *114*
Nelson, H. L., *195*

AUTHOR INDEX

Neuschel, R., 11, *35*
Newcomer, J. M., 222, 223, 228, *258*
Newell, A., 6, 8, *35, 36*
Newell, E. E., 49, *82*, 102(74), *114*
Ni, L. M., 118, 177, 179, *193, 195*
Nolan, R., 15, 19, *31, 32, 33, 34, 35*
Nolan, R. L., 16, *30*
Norton, D., 15, *34*
Nutt, G. J., 179, *195*
Nygaard, K., 228, *256*

O

Olson, M., 21, *35*
Onsi, M., 16, *29*
Oppermann, E. B., 21, *31*
Optner, S., 14, *35*
Orden, A., 8, *35*
Orlicky, J., 14, *35*
Owens, R. M., *195*

P

Padua, D. A., *195*
Parasuraman, B., *195*
Patel, J. H., 133, 140, 141, 176, 178, 190, *192, 195*
Patton, P. C., 83(3), *112*
Paul, G., 117, 124, *195*
Pease, M. C., 166, *195*
Peebles, R. W., 85(20), *112*
Perlis, A. J., 205, *256, 257, 258*
Pierce, J. R., *82*, 102(73), *114*
Pogran, K. T., 85(14, 63), *112, 114*
Pohm, A. V., 85(45, 46), *113*
Popek, G. L., 224, 231, *257*
Popescu-Zeletin, R., 85(19), *112*
Post, D. L., 62, *82*
Pounds, W., 12, *35*
Powers, D. M., 117, *191*
Powers, R., 20, *35*
Pradhan, D. K., 167, *195*
Price, W. L., 42, *82*
Prigge, R. D., 214, *258*
Prince, T., 10, *35*
Proeme, A., 15, *32*
Prokop, J., 22, *35*

Prywes, N. S., 243, *258*
Purcell, C. J., *195*

Q

Quatse, J. T., 85(29), *113*

R

Radford, K., 13, *35*
Radnor, M., 21, *35*
Radoy, C. H., 179, *195*
Ramamoorthy, C. V., 117, 124, 131, *195*
Rauscher, T. G., 220, *256*
Rawson, E. G., 85(18), 90(18), *112*
Reed, D. P., 85(14), *112*
Reid, B. K., 222, 223, 228, *258*
Remund, R. N., *195*
Richards, M., 10, *35*
Riley, M., 13, *30*
Robinson, L., 220, *258*
Roesser, R. P., *195*
Rosen, S., 85(43), *113*
Rosenzweig, J., 10, 11, *33, 35*
Ross, D., 205, *258*
Ross, J., 13, *34*
Roubine, O., 220, *258*
Rowe, A., 8, 9, *34*
Rubenstein, A., 21, *35*
Rubey, R. J., 63, *82*
Russell, R. M., *195*
Ruth, G., 243, *257*

S

Sahni, S. H., *195*
Sakai, T., 85(51), *113*
Saltzer, J. H., 85(63), *114*
Salveson, M., 7, 9, *35*
Samelson, K., 205, *257*
Sammet, J. E., 204, 205, 206, 208, 209, 210, 240, *257, 258*
Sanders, D., 3, 13, 14, *35*
Satterwaite, E. H., 228, *257*
Sayani, H., 14, *36*

Sayward, F., *258*
Schaffert, C., 230, 239, *257*
Schiebe, L. H., 107(77), *114*
Schlankser, M., *195*
Schlosser, R., 11, *35*
Schonberg, E., 232 *256*
Schroeder, R. G., 17, 22, 29, *35*
Schwartz, J. T., *196,* 232, *256*
Schwartz, M., 14, 15, *35, 36*
Scott, R. H., 16, *30*
Scott Morton, M., 27, 28, *33, 36*
Scott Morton, S., 18, *32*
Senewseib, N., 11, *31*
Senn, J., 13, 22, *31, 36*
Senzig, D. N., *196*
Sethi, H. R., 85(26), *113*
Shankar, K. S., 239, *258*
Shannon, C. E., 15, *36*
Shar, L. E., *192, 196*
Sharpe, W., 16, *36*
Shaw, J., 6, *35*
Shaw, M., 222, 223, 228, 239, *258*
Sherman, R. H., 85(54), 90(54), *114*
Shneiderman, B., 244, *258*
Shoch, J., 102(72), *114*
Shoch, J. F., 84(11), 105(11), *112*
Shoquist, M. C., 85(41), *113*
Shultz, G., 8, *35, 37*
Siegel, H. J., 165, *196*
Simmons, J. K., 21, *31*
Simon, H., 6, 8, *34, 35, 36*
Sintz, R. H. P. H., *196*
Sites, R. L., 187, *196*
Smith, B. J., *196*
Smith, R. V., *196*
Smith, S. M., 85(69), 90(69), *114*
Snyder, A., 230, 239, *257*
Soden, J., 15, *34*
Springer, J. F., 85(27), *113*
Statland, N., 16, *36*
Steele, J. M., 85(43), *113*
Stephenson, C. M., *196*
Stevenson, D. K., *196*
Stigler, G. J., 16, *36*
Stokes, R. A., 116, *196*
Stoller, D., 8, *36*
Stone, H. S., 166, *196*
Strater, F., 13, *30*
Su, S. P., *193*
Sutton, J., 28, *30*
Swan, R. J., 84(12), 85(12), *112*

Sweda, R., 15, *36*
Szurkowski, E., 85(61), 90(61), *114*

T

Taggert, K. A., *195*
Tamaru, K., 85(58), *114*
Tanenbaum, A. S., 229, *258*
Tate, D. P., *193*
Taylor, J., 11, *36*
Taylor, R., 22, *29*
Teichroew, D., 220, *258*
Terbough, G., 6, *31*
Theis, D. J., 124, 156, 160, *194, 196*
Thomas, A. T., 135, *192, 196*
Thomasian, A., 179, *196*
Thompson, H., 9, 28, *36*
Thornton, J. E., 117, *196*
Thorton, J. E., 85(60), *114*
Thurber, K. J., 83(1), 84(6), 85, 105(6), *111, 112, 118, 196*
Tiechroew, D., 14, *36*
Tokoro, M., 85(58), *114*
Tomasulo, R. M., *196*
Trabb Pardo, L., 205, *257*
Troy, J. L., 118, *193*

U

Uretsky, M., 17, *30, 32*

V

Vanaken, J., *196*
Van Horn, R., 8, 13, 20, *33, 36*
Vanneschi, M., 180, *192*
Vasarhelyi, M., 18, *34*
Vazsonyi, A., 7, 14, *36*
Vitalari, N., 3, *36*
Vonderohe, R. H., 85(44), *113*
Vora, C., 168, 191, *194*

W

Walden, D. C., 73, *82*
Waldman, H., 3, *36*

Walk, K., 252, *257*
Walkowicz, J. L., 214, *258*
Watson, W. J., *196, 197*
Weaver, W., 15, *36*
Weinwurm, G., 9, *36*
Wendler, C., 12, *37*
Wetherbe, J. C., 14, 16, 19, *35, 37*
Whisler, T., 4, 7, 8, 21, *34, 35, 37*
Whittemore, B., 16, *37*
Wiener, N., 6, 14, *37*
Willard, D. G., 85(16), *112*
Williams, L., 11, *34*
Wilson, M. W., 124, *195*
Winograd, T., 242, 243, *259*
Wirth, N., 203, 207, 228, 229, 230, *257, 259*
Witt, B. I., 221, *257*
Wittie, L. D., 85(24), 105(24), *112*
Wittmayer, W. R., *197*
Wolf, J. J., 85(36), *113*
Wood, D. C., 85(21), *112*

Wu, C. L., 167, *197*
Wulf, W. A., 85(28), *113,* 222, 223, 228, *258*

Y

Yajima, S., 85(67), *114*
Yeh, J. W., 85(37), 90(37), *113*
Yeh, R. T., 74, *82*
Yourdon, E., 14, 15, *37*
Yovits, M. C., 16, *37*

Z

Zani, W., 15, *37*
Zawacki, R. A., 21, *31*
Zhang, X., 118, *193*
Zick, G., *196*

Subject Index

A

Access path, defined, 89
ACM Conference on Language Design for Reliable Software, 240-241
  see also Association for Computing Machinery
ACM SIGPLAN Notices, 211-212, 237
ACM Transactions in Programming Languages and Systems, 211
ACU, see Array control unit
Ada language, 207, 232-238
  non-DOD languages and, 254
  "package" concept in, 237
Administrative Behavior (Simon), 6
AFFIRM, 220
AIDS, see American Institute for Decision Sciences
ALGOL 58, 205
ALGOL 60, 206-207, 211-212
ALGOL 68, 211-212, 228-229, 243, 253
ALU, see Arithmetic/logic unit
American Institute for Decision Sciences, 25
American National Standards Institute, 212-217, 237
American Standards Association, 213
Analog/digital conversion, in local computer networks, 89
Andalternate windows, in HXDP system, 70
ANSI, see American National Standards Institute
AN/USQ-67, 90, 97-98
AP-120B Floating-Point Systems, 118, 136, 160-164
AP-120B processor, block diagram of, 161-162
APL/360, 207, 211, 217, 229
Applicative State Transition System, 243
APT language, 209, 215
Arithmetic/logic circuit level, in pipeline processors, 130
Arithmetic/logic unit, in HXDP system, 58
Arithmetic pipeline, operational configuration for, 140
ARPANET (Advanced Research Projects Agency Network), 91, 231

Array control unit, of MPP processor, 175
Array processors, see also Vector processors
  BSP-like, 121
  future trends in, 189-191
  as pipeline processor, 180-182
  recent advances in, 164-179
  SIMD computers as, 118
  vectorization in pipeline type, 124-126
  vector length in, 183-184
  vector processing in, 120-122
Array unit interconnection, of 8-PE VLSI chips, 174
ASC central processor, functional block diagram of, 154, see also TI-ASC computer
ASC system, see also TI-ASC system
  arithmetic pipeline in, 156
  as first-generation vector supercomputer, 155
  main memory of, 154
ASM, see Association for Systems Management
Association for Computing Machinery, 23, 25, 146, 211
Association for Systems Management, 23
AST system, see Applicative State Transition System
Automatic programming, programming languages for, 242-243

B

BACAIC, 204
BASIC, 207, 209, 216-217, 251
Binary exponential back-off scheme, 94
BIU, see Bus interface unit
Boeing Airplane Company, 204
Boolean objects, in HXDP system, 65
Branching, in instruction pipeline, 137
BSP-like array processors, 121
BSP, see Burroughs Scientific Processor
Burroughs Parallel Element Processing Ensemble, 118
Burroughs Scientific Processor, 116
  block diagram of, 168

SUBJECT INDEX

linear vector approach to parallelism in, 169–171
memory mapping in, 170
pipelined array processing and, 168
processing capability of, 167
Bus allocation, vector-driven proportional access in, 55
Business Data Processing languages, 210
Bus interface unit
in distributed computer systems, 51
identifications for, 56
local message addressing in, 57
in message transfer protocol, 57–58

C

California, University of, 25
Cambridge ring, 104
Carnegie School, 27
CDC, see Control Data Corporation
Cellular vector computer, 118
Central processing unit, in vector/array processing computers, 116–117
CIU, see Communication interface unit
CLIP, 206
CLU, 207, 230–231
COBOL, 206, 209–212, 222–223, 251
CODASYL, 206, 212
Coding, of programming language, 222
COGO, 209
Collision-free task scheduling, in pipeline processors, 131–135
Colorado, University of, 25
COMIT, 206
Communication, in distributed computer systems, 76–80
Communication interface units, 51, 53
Communications of the ACM, The, 23
Communication subnetwork, 89
Computer Age, The (Burck), 10
Computer centers, of future, 110
Computer Languages, 211
Computer Revolution, The (Berkeley), 10
Computer systems, real-time distributed, see Real-time distributed computer systems
Computing
communication and, 76–80
expenditures for, 1–2

Connection topologies, of distributed computer system, 47–50
Contention channels, 92–94
Control Data Corporation, 3, 107
Control Data STring ARray, 116, *see also* STAR-100 computer
Control unit, in vector/array processing computers, 117
Courant Institute, 232
CPU, *see* Central processing unit
CRAY-1 computer, 138 *see also* CRAY-1 system; Vector processors
address functional pipes in, 145
front-end host computer and, 141
I/O section and, 142
maintenance control unit in, 141
memory section in, 141
multiple functional pipes in, 145–146
P register in, 144
scalar mode in, 150
as second-generation vector processor, 155
vector functional units in, 145
V registers in, 144
CRAY-1 system, 116–117, 124, 129, 135
architecture of, 141–145
block diagram of, 143
pipeline chaining and vector loops in, 146–150
temporary storage management in, 188–189
vector register allocation in, 187
CVCVHP, *see* Cellular vector computer
CYBER-205 computer, 116–117, 129, 141
system architecture of, 157

D

DARPA, *see* Defense Advanced Research Projects Agency
Data-base management systems, query part of, 250
Data links, in local networks, 89
Datamation, 7, 23
Data-processing budgets, size of, 1970–78, 1
Data Processing Management Association, 23
Data-routing register, 120
Datawest Array Transform Processor, 118
DDLCN, 90

SUBJECT INDEX 271

Decentralized control, in real-time systems, 63–64
Decisions Support Systems, 27
Decision systems, MIS and, 5
DECNET concept, 106
Decomposition criteria, real-time control environment and, 44
Defense Advanced Research Projects Agency, 212, 233
Defense Department, U.S., 232–238, 254
Demodulation interface, in HXDP system, 59
Dialog manager, in local computer network, 89
Digital real-time control systems, 43–45
Direct memory access, in HXDP system, 59
Display message, in HXDP system, 57–58
Distributed computer systems
 advantages of, 88
 attractiveness of, 80
 bus interface unit in, 51, 56–58
 characteristics of, 41
 connection topologies in, 47–50
 defined, 40
 error control in, 53
 function allocation in, 52–53
 functional overview of, 51–52
 general structure alternatives in, 46–50
 hardware for, 45–61
 interconnection topologies in, 47–48
 problems associated with implementing of, 42–43
 promises of, 41–42
 real-time environment of, 43–45
 ring topologies in, 49–50
 schematic of, 46
 specialized languages for, 253–254
 system expendability and, 48
 system reliability in, 47–48
 system topology and, 48–49
Distributed processing, 40–43, *see also* Distributed computer systems
Distributed real-time systems, software for, 62–79, *see also* Distributed computer systems
DLCN loops, strategy for, 102–104
DMA, *see* Direct memory access
DOD, *see* Defense Department, U.S.
DPMA, *see* Data Processing Management Association

DSS, *see* Decision Support Systems
Dynamic pipeline, with shared resources, 139, *see also* Pipeline

E

EDP Analyzer, 25
EFT systems, *see* Electronic fund transfer systems
Electronic data processing, "seven deadly dangers" of, 10
Electronic fund transfer systems, 109
Ethernet concept, 90–97
EUCLID, 207, 211, 231–232
Executive kernel, in HXDP system, 66, 70, 74–76
Executive status information, in HCDP system, 74

F

FACT, 206
Fault isolation, in real-time systems, 63
Feedback control system, real-time control computer and, 44
FFP systems, *see* Formal Systems for Functional Programming
First Conference on Information Systems (1980), 25
Floating-point addition, in STAR-100 computer, 152
Floating-Point SIMD array processors, 116
Floating-Point Systems AP-120B, 118, 136, 160–164
 block diagrams of, 161–162
Floating-point vector dot product, 139–140
FLOW-MATIC, 205
FORMAC, 207
Formal Systems for Functional Programming, 243
Formula ALGOL, 207, *see also* ALGOL
FORTRAN, 128, 206, 209, 211, 213, 216–217, 222–223, 241, 251
 early work in, 205
 in scientific applications, 203
FORTRAN computer, vectorizing, 179
FORTRAN vectorization, 128–129, 179
FP, *see* Functional programming systems
Functional modularity, objective of, 63
Functional programming systems, 242–244
Functions of the Executive (Barnard), 6

SUBJECT INDEX

G

Goodyear Aerospace MPP, 118
Goodyear Aerospace STARAN, 118
GPSS, 207

H

Harvard Business Review, 7
High-level languages, 199–255, *see also* Programming languages
  application areas for, 203–204
  defined, 201–203
  expected future trends in, 251–253
  "modern," 227–238
  portability in, 225–227
  publications and organizations concerned with, 210–212
  reliability of, 225
  requirements definition in, 219–220
  retrospective view of, 204–207
  software engineering and methodology in relation to, 217–227
  standardization of, 212–217
  in systems programming, 253
  for systems and real-time programming, 250
  trends and activities in, 208–217
  trends not expected in, 253–255
High-Order Language Working Group, 233, 237
Honeywell Experimental Distributed Process system, 45–81, *see also* Distributed computer systems
  addressing in, 54
  arithmetic/logic unit in, 58
  blocking in, 71
  Boolean objects in, 65
  bus allocation in, 55–56
  bus details in, 60
  bus interface unit in, 51, 54, 58–59
  communication primitives in, 67–68
  decentralized control in, 75–76
  demodulation interface in, 59
  error checking in, 56
  executive status information in, 74
  executive kernel and, 66, 70, 74–75
  fault isolation in, 75
  fundamental modularity in, 75
  general communication subnet structure options in, 51–53
  hardware architecture for, 50–51
  hardware design details for, 53–61
  hardware mechanisms in, 56–57
  hardware structure for, 58–60
  independent verifiability in, 76
  input controller in, 58
  interconnection specifications in, 73–74
  kernel function and implementation in, 66–75
  message addressing in, 67
  message buffers in, 71
  message flow control in, 54–55
  message transfer protocol in, 57
  message transmission efficiency in, 77
  policies utilized in, 54
  process blocking in, 66
  queue management in, 54
  rationale in, 70–74
  separate signal interface in, 71–72
  software architecture for, 64–65
  software design in, 75–77
  software message handling in, 66–79
  status monitoring in, 56
  time-slot vectors in, 57
  undeliverable messages in, 69–70
  vector-driven proportional access in, 55, 60–61
  virtual architectures in, 65
  virtual processing elements in, 64
  VPE/VA construction in, 78
HXDP system, *see* Honeywell Experimental Distributed Process system
HYPERcache, 106
  defined, 101
HYPERchannel®, 86, 90–91, 99–102, 106
  schematics of, 99–100

I

IAL, 205
IBM-1401 computer, 3
IBM Research Laboratory, 28
IC, *see* Input controller
Illiac-IV-like array processors, 122
Illiac-IV processor, 118
  BSP and, 167
  as first-generation vector supercomputer, 155
  original design of, 178
Information and Management, 24

SUBJECT INDEX 273

Information processing, history of, 3
Information systems, see also Management information systems
   applications and techniques of, 10-11
   behavioral aspects of, 11
   caveats on, 10
   definitions and forecasts for, 9-10
   takeoff and maturity of, 12-17
   total systems and, 11-12
Information technology
   defined, 4
   management and, 7
   MIS and, 5-6
Infosystems, 23
Input controller, in HXDP system, 58
Institute for Defense Analysis, 235
Institute of Management Science, 23
Instruction pipelining, see also Pipeline; Pipeline processor
   branching in, 137
   at instruction execution level, 131
Interconnection network, of SIMD computers, 165-167
Interconnection topologies, of distributed computer system, 47-48
International Algebraic Language, 205
International Business Machines Corporation, 204
Interrupe controller, in HXDP system, 59
I/O channel, 32-bit parallel, 98
IPL/V, 206
IRONMAN, 232, 234, 238
ITC, see Interrupt controller

J

JOVIAL, 206, 211
JOVIAL, J73, 212, 233
JOVIAL COMPOOL, 237

K

Kernel function and implementation, in HXDP system, 66-75

L

Language
   high-level, see High-level language
   natural, 246-248
   programming, see Programming languages
   research and advanced development, 238-245
LCN, see Local computer network
Life-cycle steps, language involvement in, 219-220
LIPS, 206
LNI, see Network Systems LNI
Local computer networks
   application-embedded hardware and, 106
   architecture and strategies for, 83-111
   chips and chip sets in, 107
   components and modules in, 107
   contention channels of, 92
   decentralized vs. centralized computation in, 88-89
   defined, 83
   Ethernet and, 91-97
   examples of, 89-90
   functions of, 89
   future computer centers and offices for, 109-111
   hardware availability of, 105-109
   subsystem building blocks and, 106-107
   system summaries in, 90-105
   technology trends and, 87-88
   terminology and nomenclature in, 87
   turnkey systems in, 106
Long vectors, 122, 183

M

Machine Accounting and Data Processing, 7
MAD, 206
Management and the Corporation (Anshen and Bach), 10
Management Information and Control Systems Symposium, 8
Management information decision systems, 4
Management information systems
   conceptual development of, 12-17
   criticism of, 28
   Davis-Ives-Hamilton research classification taxonomy in, 20
   Decision Support Systems and, 27
   defined, 4-5
   educational progams in, 25-27

evolution and status of, 1–29
experimental studies in, 22–23
future of, 27–29
history of, 3
journals in, 23–24
Minnesota Experiments and, 22
Nolan-Wetherbe research classification taxonomy in, 19
organizational studies in, 20–21
popular textbooks on, 13
research in, 17–23
research classification taxonomies in, 19–20
research frameworks and methodological issues in, 18–22
support mechanisms in, 23–25
systems implementation and, 21
systems planning, analysis, design, and development in, 14–15
takeoff and maturity of, 12–17
Management information systems activity, managing of, 15
Management Information Systems Quarterly, 23–24
Management Science, 11, 23
Massachusetts Institute of Technology, 25, 204–205
Massively parallel processor, 116, 171–176
 array control unit of, 175–176
 block diagram of, 172
MASSTOR Corp. shared VSS®, 101, 106
MATH-MATIC, 205
MBU, *see* Memory buffer unit
Memory buffer unit
 in ASC central processor, 154–155
 in HXDP system, 71, 135
Message-based systems
 addressing in, 65–66
 general design options in, 65–66
Message handling, in HXDP software, 66–79
Message transfer protocol, in HXDP system, 57–58
Metacomposition, in functional programming, 243
Minicomputer, real-time environment of, 44
Minnesota, University of, 19, 22, 25
Minnesota Experiments, 22
MIS, *see* Management information systems
MIS Interrupt, 26

Money, 26
MPP, *see* Massively parallel processor
MSIMD, *see* Multiple-SIMD mode
Multidimensional access memories, in MPP, 171
Multifunction pipeline, reconfiguring pipe for different functions in, 188
Multifunction pipeline processors
 future research in, 191
 shared-resource, 176–179
Multiple-SIMD mode, 176
Multiplexing, in local networks, 89
MUMPS, 211

N

Natural language, programming language and, 246–248
NCR Corporation, 3
n-bit shift register, 132
NELIAC, 206
Network-like systems, 85
Network Systems Corporation, 86, 99, 102, 106–107
Network Systems LNI, 108
Newell loops, 102–103
New York University, 25, 232
Nonprocedural languages, 249

O

OCTOPUS, 90
Oralternate groups or window, in HXDP system, 70
Output controller, in HXDP system, 59

P

Parallel Element Processing Ensemble, 118
Parallelism, linear vector approach to, 169–171
PARC (Palo Alto Research Center–Xerox), 91
PASCAL, 217, 229–230
PEM, *see* Processing element memory
PEM_i local memory, 120–122
Pennsylvania, University of, 25
PEPE (Parallel Element Processing Ensemble), 118
Pierce loop, 102
PIO, *see* Programmed input/output

SUBJECT INDEX

Pipeline
  arithmetic, 140
  branching of, 137
  dynamic, 139-141
  multifunctional, 133
  reservation table of, 131-132
  throughput of, 133
  unifunction, 131-132
Pipeline/array processors, vectorization in, 124-129
Pipeline chaining
  in CRAY-1 system, 146-150
  in pipeline processors, 187
Pipelined array processing, in BSP, 168
Pipeline designs, in STAR, ASC, and CYBER-205 processors, 150-160
Pipelined vector processing, 122-124
Pipeline processors, *see also* Vector processors
  arithmetic pipelining in, 130-131
  vs. array processors, 180-182
  branch-type instructions in, 137-138
  classification of, 130
  collision-free task scheduling in, 131-135
  congestion and branch controls in, 135-138
  design considerations in, 129-141
  future trends in, 189-191
  long vectors in, 122, 183
  pipeline chaining in, 187
  processing speeds of segments in, 135
  static vs. dynamic pipelines and, 131
  two-function, 134
Pipelining
  arithmetic, 130
  instruction vs. processor type, 131
  static vs. dynamic pipelines in, 131
Plankalkul, 204
PL/I language, 207, 212, 215-217, 228-229, 244
Prime Computer Corp., 106
Process blocking, in HXDP software architecture, 66
Processing elements
  in ARU of MMP processor, 174-175
  in vector-processing computers, 117
Programmed input/output, in HXDP system, 60
Programming languages
  for automatic programming, 242-243
  coding in, 222-223
  data abstraction and, 239
  documentation and, 223-224
  environmental requirements of, 236
  heavy use of major languages in, 251
  language design and redesign in, 236-237
  language metrics and, 245
  language requirements in, 235-236
  maintenance of program development and, 224
  major language characteristics in, 237-238
  "modern," 227-238
  natural language and, 246-248
  new-language proliferation in, 251
  nonprocedural languages and, 249-252
  "package" concept in, 237
  program verification and, 240, 248-249
  query languages and, 244, 250, 252
  reduction languages and, 243-244
  reliability of, 240-241
  for research and advanced development, 238-245
  test evaluation phase of, 236
  testing and, 223
  verification and, 224, 240, 248-249, 252
Programming Language Standards, list of, 215
Program verification, 240, 249-249, 252
PSL/PSA language, 220
PUP protocol hierarchy, 94-95
Purdue PM system, 178

Q

Query languages, 244, 250, 252

R

Ready-only memory, 139
Real-time computer systems, experimental design in, 45, *see also* Distributed computer systems
Real-time control computer, 44
Real-time control environment, decomposition criteria and, 44
Real-time control systems, 43-45
Real-time distributed computer systems, 39-81, *see also* Distributed computer systems

SUBJECT INDEX

Real-time environment, 43-45
Real-time software, 62-78
  decentralized control and partitioned system state in, 63-64
  fault isolation in, 63
  functional modularity in, 63
  independent verifiability and context independence in, 64
  nonfunctional objectives in, 62
Reduction languages, 243-244
Remington Rand Univac, 204-205
Requirements Specification Language, 220
RINGNET, 90, 106
ROM, see Ready-only memory
Roster of Programming Languages, 208

S

SAGE system, 8
SDS, see System Development Corporation
SETL, 207, 232
SHARE, 212
Shared VSS®, 100-101, 106
Shift register, unifunction pipeline and, 132
SHINPADS, 90
Short Code, 204
SIGPLAN, 211
SIGPLAN Notices, 211-212, 237
SIMD array processors
  architectural configurations in, 121
  array unit of, 172
SIMD computers
  array processors as, 118
  interconnection modeling of, 165-167
SIMSCRIPT, 207
SIMSCRIPT I, 208
SIMSCRIPT I.5(R), 208
SIMULA 67, 228
Single Instruction and Multiple Data streams, 118, see also SIMD computers
SMIS Award Paper Contest, 16, see also Society for Management Information Systems
SNA concept, 106
SNOBOL, 207
Society for Management Information Systems, 17, 25
Software development
  for HXDP system, 66-79

language involvement in, 219-224
life cycle of, 219
Software engineering, high-level languages and, 217-227
SPECIAL language, 220
Speedcoding system, 204
STAR-100 computer, 140, 146, see also Vector processors
  as first-generation vector supercomputer, 155
  FLP adder in, 152
STAR-100 system, 116-117, 124, 129, 135, 138
  arithmetic pipes in, 153
  pipeline designs in, 150-160
  system architecture of, 151
STARAN, 118
STEELMAN, 232, 234-235
STRAWMAN, 232, 234
System Development Corporation, 8
Systems, Objectives, Solutions, 24
System topology, in distributed computer systems, 48-49

T

TACPOL, 233
Task scheduling, collision-free, 131-135
Texas Instruments, Inc., 116
Thurber-Freeman LCN taxonomy, 85
TI-ASC computer (Texas Instruments Advanced Scientific Computer), 116, 124, 129, see also Vector processors
TI-ASC system, 136, 139
Time-slot vectors, in HXDP system, 57
TINMAN, 232, 234
Token passing, defined, 103
Toronto, University of, 232
Total systems approach, 11
Turnkey systems, in local computer networks, 106

U

Undeliverable messages, in HXDP system, 69-70
Unifunction pipeline, characterization of, 132
UNIVAC array processor, 118
UNIVAC I, first electronic computer, 3

SUBJECT INDEX

V

VDPA, see Vector-driven proportional access
Vector/array computations, 116–117
 vector statements in, 126–127
 vector identifiers in, 126
Vector-driven proportional access, in HXDP bus management, 55, 57, 60–61
Vector dot product, pipeline configuration for, 139–140
Vectorizing FORTRAN compiler, 179
 vector formulation by, 184–185
Vector-length distribution, in array and pipeline processors, 183–184
Vector mask, 138
Vector operations
 characteristics of, 119–120
 optimization of, 184–189
 in vector/array computers, 127
Vector loops, in CRAY-1 system, 146–150
Vector processing, in array processors, 120–121
Vector processors (vector-processing computers), see also Array processors; Pipeline processors
 architecture of, 115–191
 code avoidance in, 189
 code motion in, 187
 constant folding in, 186
 future trends in, 189–191
 long vectors in, 183
 performance evaluation in, 179–189
 performance modeling in, 180–184
 pipeline chaining in, 187
 pipeline processors and, 130–131
 reconfiguring pipe for different functions in, 188
 redundant expression elimination in, 186
 temporary storage management in, 188–189
Vector register allocation, in vector processors, 187–188
Vector register file, 124
Vector supercomputers
 architectural features of, 158–159
 first-generation, 155
VECTRAN, 124
View message, in HXDP system, 68
Virtual processing elements
 extended functionality and, 70
 in HXDP system, 64–65, 72–73
 "manager" vs. "service" types in, 78
 queue type, 78–79
VPEs, see Virtual processing elements
VRF, see Vector register file
VSS®, shared, 100–101, 106
VSUM vector instruction, 124

W

Windows, in real-time software, 65

X

Xerox Corporation, 90
Xerox Palo Alto Research Center, 91

Z

Z-NET®, 106

Contents of Previous Volumes

Volume 1

General-Purpose Programming for Business Applications
 CALVIN C. GOTLIEB
Numerical Weather Prediction
 NORMAN A. PHILLIPS
The Present Status of Automatic Translation of Languages
 YEHOSHUA BAR-HILLEL
Programming Computers to Play Games
 ARTHUR L. SAMUEL
Machine Recognition of Spoken Words
 RICHARD FATEHCHAND
Binary Arithmetic
 GEORGE W. REITWIESNER

Volume 2

A Survey of Numerical Methods for Parabolic Differential Equations
 JIM DOUGLAS, JR.
Advances in Orthonormalizing Computation
 PHILIP J. DAVIS AND PHILIP RABINOWITZ
Microelectronics Using Electron-Beam-Activated Machining Techniques
 KENNETH R. SHOULDERS
Recent Developments in Linear Programming
 SAUL I. GLASS
The Theory of Automata, a Survey
 ROBERT MCNAUGHTON

Volume 3

The Computation of Satellite Orbit Trajectories
 SAMUEL D. CONTE
Multiprogramming
 E. F. CODD
Recent Developments of Nonlinear Programming
 PHILIP WOLFE
Alternating Direction Implicit Methods
 GARRET BIRKHOFF, RICHARD S. VARGA, AND DAVID YOUNG
Combined Analog-Digital Techniques in Simulation
 HAROLD F. SKRAMSTAD
Information Technology and the Law
 REED C. LAWLOR

Volume 4

The Formulation of Data Processing Problems for Computers
 WILLIAM C. MCGEE

All-Magnetic Circuit Techniques
  DAVID R. BENNION AND HEWITT D. CRANE
Computer Education
  HOWARD E. TOMPKINS
Digital Fluid Logic Elements
  H. H. GLAETTLI
Multiple Computer Systems
  WILLIAM A. CURTIN

Volume 5

The Role of Computers in Electron Night Broadcasting
  JACK MOSHMAN
Some Results of Research on Automatic Programming in Eastern Europe
  WLADYSLAW TURKSI
A Discussion of Artificial Intelligence and Self-Organization
  GORDON PASK
Automatic Optical Design
  ORESTES N. STAVROUDIS
Computing Problems and Methods in X-Ray Crystallography
  CHARLES L. COULTER
Digital Computers in Nuclear Reactor Design
  ELIZABETH CUTHILL
An Introduction to Procedure-Oriented Languages
  HARRY D. HUSKEY

Volume 6

Information Retrieval
  CLAUDE E. WALSTON
Speculations Concerning the First Ultraintelligent Machine
  IRVING JOHN GOOD
Digital Training Devices
  CHARLES R. WICKMAN
Number Systems and Arithmetic
  HARVEY L. GARDER
Considerations on Man versus Machine for Space Probing
  P. L. BARGELLINI
Data Collection and Reduction for Nuclear Particle Trace Detectors
  HERBERT GELERNTER

Volume 7

Highly Parallel Information Processing Systems
  JOHN C. MURTHA
Programming Language Processors
  RUTH M. DAVIS
The Man-Machine Combination for Computer-Assisted Copy Editing
  WAYNE A. DANIELSON
Computer-Aided Typesetting
  WILLIAM R. BOZMAN

Programming Languages for Computational Linguistics
    ARNOLD C. SATTERTHWAIT
Computer Driven Displays and Their Use in Man/Machine Interaction
    ANDRIES VAN DAM

Volume 8

Time-Shared Computer Systems
    THOMAS N. PYKE, JR.
Formula Manipulation by Computer
    JEAN E. SAMMET
Standards for Computers and Information Processing
    T. B. STEEL, JR.
Syntactic Analysis of Natural Language
    NAOMI SAGER
Programming Languages and Computers: A Unified Metatheory
    R. NARASIMHAN
Incremental Computation
    LIONELLO A. LOMBARDI

Volume 9

What Next in Computer Technology
    W. J. POPPELBAUM
Advances in Simulation
    JOHN MCLEOD
Symbol Manipulation Languages
    PAUL W. ABRAHAMS
Legal Information Retrieval
    AVIEZRI S. FRAENKEL
Large Scale Integration—an Appraisal
    L. M. SPANDORFER
Aerospace Computers
    A. S. BUCHMAN
The Distributed Processor Organization
    L. J. KOCZELA

Volume 10

Humanism, Technology, and Language
    CHARLES DECARLO
Three Computer Cultures: Computer Technology, Computer Mathematics, and Computer Science
    PETER WEGNER
Mathematics in 1984—The Impact of Computers
    BRYAN THWAITES
Computing from the Communication Point of View
    E. E. DAVID, JR.
Computer-Man Communication: Using Computer Graphics in the Instructional Process
    FREDERICK P. BROOKS, JR.

Computers and Publishing: Writing, Editing, and Printing
  ANDRIES VAN DAM AND DAVID E. RICE
A Unified Approach to Pattern Analysis
  ULF GRENANDER
Use of Computers in Biomedical Pattern Recognition
  ROBERT S. LEDLEY
Numerical Methods of Stress Analysis
  WILLIAM PRAGER
Spline Approximation and Computer-Aided Design
  J. H. AHLBERG
Logic per Track Devices
  D. L. SLOTNICK

Volume 11

Automatic Translation of Languages Since 1960: A Linguist's View
  HARRY H. JOSSELSON
Classification, Relevance, and Information Retrieval
  D. M. JACKSON
Approaches to the Machine Recognition of Conversational Speech
  KLAUS W. OTTEN
Man-Machine Interaction Using Speech
  DAVID R. HILL
Balanced Magnetic Circuits for Logic and Memory Devices
  R. B. KIEBURTZ AND E. E. NEWHALL
Command and Control: Technology and Social Impact
  ANTHONY DEBONS

Volume 12

Information Security in a Multi-User Computer Environment
  JAMES P. ANDERSON
Managers, Deterministic Models, and Computers
  G. M. FERRERO DIROCCAFERRERA
Uses of the Computer in Music Composition and Research
  HARRY B. LINCOLN
File Organization Techniques
  DAVID C. ROBERTS
Systems Programming Languages
  R. D. BERGERON, J. D. GANNON, D. P. SHECHTER, F. W. TOMPA, AND A. VAN DAM
Parametric and Nonparametric Recognition by Computer: An Application to Leukocyte Image Processing
  JUDITH M. S. PREWITT

Volume 13

Programmed Control of Asynchronous Program Interrupts
  RICHARD L. WEXELBLAT
Poetry Generation and Analysis
  JAMES JOYCE

Mapping and Computers
    PATRICIA FULTON
Practical Natural Language Processing: The REL System as Prototype
    FREDERICK B. THOMPSON AND BOZENA HENISZ THOMPSON
Artificial Intelligence—The Past Decade
    B. CHANDRASEKARAN

Volume 14

On the Structure of Feasible Computations
    J. HARTMANIS AND J. SIMON
A Look at Programming and Programming Systems
    T. E. CHEATHAM, JR., AND JUDY A. TOWNELY
Parsing of General Context-Free Languages
    SUSAN L. GRAHAM AND MICHAEL A. HARRISON
Statistical Processors
    W. J. POPPELBAUM
Information Secure Systems
    DAVID K. HSIAO AND RICHARD I. BAUM

Volume 15

Approaches to Automatic Programming
    ALAN W. BIERMANN
The Algorithm Selection Problem
    JOHN R. RICE
Parallel Processing of Ordinary Programs
    DAVID J. KUCK
The Computational Study of Language Acquisition
    LARRY H. REEKER
The Wide World of Computer-Based Education
    DONALD BITZER

Volume 16

3-D Computer Animation
    CHARLES A. CSURI
Automatic Generation of Computer Programs
    NOAH S. PRYWES
Perspectives in Clinical Computing
    KEVIN C. O'KANE AND EDWARD A. HALUSKA
The Design and Development of Resource-Sharing Services in Computer Communications Networks: A Survey
    SANDRA A. MAMRAK
Privacy Protection in Information Systems
    REIN TURN

Volume 17

Semantics and Quantification in Natural Language Question Answering
  W. A. WOODS
Natural Language Information Formatting: The Automatic Conversion of Texts to a Structured Data Base
  NAOMI SAGER
Distributed Loop Computer Networks
  MING T. LIU
Magnetic Bubble Memory and Logic
  TIEN CHI CHEN AND HSU CHANG
Computers and the Public's Right of Access to Government Information
  ALAN F. WESTIN

Volume 18

Image Processing and Recognition
  AZRIEL ROSENFELD
Recent Progress in Computer Chess
  MONROE M. NEWBORN
Advances in Software Science
  M. H. HALSTEAD
Current Trends in Computer-Assisted Instruction
  PATRICK SUPPES
Software in the Soviet Union: Progress and Problems
  S. E. GOODMAN

Volume 19

Data Base Computers
  DAVID K. HSIAO
The Structure of Parallel Algorithms
  H. T. KUNG
Clustering Methodologies in Exploratory Data Analysis
  RICHARD DUBES AND A. K. JAIN
Numerical Software: Science or Alchemy?
  C. W. GEAR
Computing as Social Action: The Social Dynamics of Computing in Complex Organizations
  ROB KLING AND WALT SCACCHI

RAYMOND H. FOGLER LIBRARY
DATE DUE